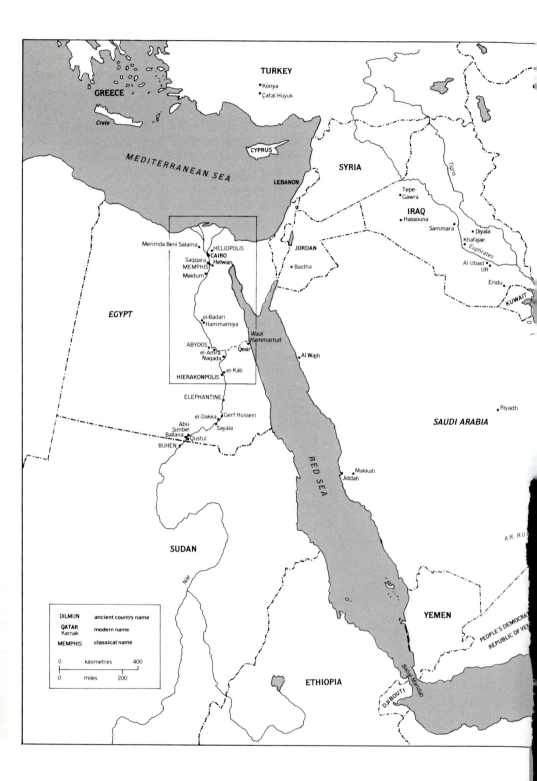

TURKEY
• Konya
• Çatal Huyuk

GREECE

Crete

CYPRUS

MEDITERRANEAN SEA

LEBANON

SYRIA

Tigris

IRAQ
Tepe-
Gawra
• Hassouna
Sammara •Diyala
Khafajae
Euphrates
Al-Ubaid•
UR
Eridu•

KUWAIT

JORDAN

• Baidha

Merimda Beni Salama•
HELIOPOLIS
CAIRO
Saqqara• •Helwan
MEMPHIS•
Maidum•

EGYPT

el-Badari•
•Hammamiya

Wadi
Hammamat
ABYDOS
el-Amra• •Qesir
Naqada•
•el-Kab
HIERAKONPOLIS

• Al Wajh

SAUDI ARABIA

• Riyadh

ELEPHANTINE
•el-Dakka •Gerf Hussein
Abu
Simbel
Ballana•
•Qustul
BUHEN•

Sayala

RED SEA

•Makkah
Jiddah•

SUDAN

Nile

AR RU

DILMUN   ancient country name
QATAR   modern name
Karnak
MEMPHIS   classical name

0   kilometres   400

0   miles   200

ETHIOPIA

YEMEN

PEOPLE'S DEMOCRA

REPUBLIC OF YEM

Bab el Mandeb

DJIBOUTI

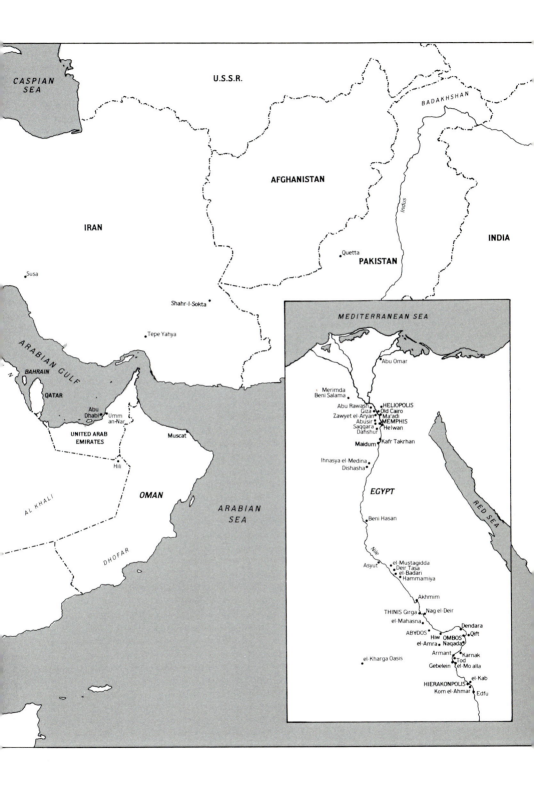

CASPIAN
SEA

U.S.S.R.

BADAKHSHAN

AFGHANISTAN

Indus

IRAN

INDIA

Quetta

PAKISTAN

Susa

Shahr-I-Sokta

Tepe Yahya

ARABIAN GULF

BAHRAIN

QATAR

Abu Dhabi

Umm an-Nar

UNITED ARAB EMIRATES

Muscat

Hili

AL KHALI

OMAN

ARABIAN SEA

DHOFAR

MEDITERRANEAN SEA

Abu Omar

Merimda Beni Salama

Abu Rawash

HELIOPOLIS

Giza

Old Cairo

Zawyet el-Aryan

Ma'adi

Abusir

MEMPHIS

Saqqara

Helwan

Dahshur

Kafr Takrhan

Maidum

Ihnasya el-Medina

Dishasha

EGYPT

Beni Hasan

RED SEA

Nile

el-Mustagidda

Asyut

Deir Tasa

el-Badari

Hammamiya

Akhmim

THINIS Girga

Nag el-Deir

el-Mahasna

Dendara

ABYDOS

Qift

Hiw

OMBOS

el-Amra

Naqada

Armant

Karnak

Tod

Gebelein

el-Mo alla

el-Kharga Oasis

el-Kab

HIERAKONPOLIS

Kom el-Ahmar

Edfu

Egypt's Making

Formative influences in the political and social organization and art of Egypt, the nature of Egypt's contact with lands bordering the Arabian Gulf (especially 'the island at the edge of the world') and the earliest identifiable developments of the historic Egyptian personality.

EGYPT'S MAKING

The Origins of Ancient Egypt
5000–2000 BC

MICHAEL RICE

LONDON and NEW YORK

For
G.A.M., who sailed on the Nile with me,
A.-C.B., who lives in Egypt, and
A.L.M., who saw it written

First published 1990

Paperback edition first published in 1991
by Routledge
11 New Fetter Lane, London EC4P 4EE

Simultaneously published in the USA and Canada
by Routledge
a division of Routledge, Chapman and Hall, Inc.
29 West 35th Street, New York, NY 10001

© 1990, 1991 Michael Rice

Printed in Great Britain by
Butler & Tanner Ltd, Frome and London

British Library Cataloguing in Publication Data

Rice, Michael
  Egypt's making: the origins of ancient Egypt, 5000–2000 BC.
  1. Egypt, history, to BC 2052
  I. Title
  932

Library of Congress Cataloging in Publication Data

Rice, Michael
  Egypt's making: the origins of ancient Egypt 5000–2000 BC.
  Michael Rice.
      p.   cm.
  Includes bibliographical references and index.
    1. Egypt—Civilization—To 332 BC.   I. Title.
  [DT61.R493   1991]
  932—dc20   91–8197

  ISBN 0-415-06454-6

Contents

Illustrations

Colour plates (*between pp 278–279*)

Preface

I began writing this book as a sort of celebration of most ancient Egypt, of the origins of a culture which seems to me to be without precedent or equal. I have no idea why so many people from my native island in the North Atlantic, which is after all pretty remote from the Nile Valley, should feel so profound an attraction to Egypt; but they do and I am one of them. From the first moment I set foot in Egypt, more than twenty-five years ago, I have experienced a sense of belonging which is most peculiar: as far as I am concerned it defies explanation. Certainly I do not look for explanations which depend upon a previous incarnation (very dubious) or the occult (idiotic). But the fact remains. . . .

When finally I came to Egypt I was fortunate. The elements of chance in my professional life brought me to Egypt at a low point in the country's long sequence of history; the optimistic upsurge which had seized the people of Egypt after the revolution of 1952 and the débâcle of the Anglo–French–Israeli collusion of 1956 (one of the most ill-omened events in the politics of the postwar period) had burned itself out. Egypt was then stuck in that dismal morass of half-baked socialism which was the ruination of so many Third World countries in the 1950s and 1960s. A series of diplomatic and military misadventures further isolated the country. Few visitors went there; the great temples and the other sites surviving from the most majestic civilization yet to be assembled on the face of the earth were empty and desolate. But for the very few it was a time of privilege, to be able to wander uninterrupted amongst these splendid monuments, savouring them and finding them ready to reveal themselves to those who were able to give them time – the most precious of commodities in contemplating the past – in generous measure. It was rather like finding oneself transferred to Egypt in the early nineteenth century, when European travellers were few, though without the discomfort.

Of all Egypt's localities the one which to me is the most seductive and the most enduring in its interest is Saqqara, the site of the great burials from the time of the archaic kings and of the unique pyramid complex of the Third Dynasty king, Djoser Neterikhet. I spent long tranquil hours there alone or with a few companions: it is one of the most magical places on earth. As I wandered through the ruined buildings of Djoser's monument or saw the excavations, conducted by Brian Emery for the Egypt Exploration Society, of the First and Second Dynasty tombs, or 'read' the records of life in the Fifth Dynasty tombs of Ti and Mereruka, I became more and more attracted by these early periods, before the end of the Old Kingdom, when the spirit of ancient Egypt was at its most vital, its most vibrant. From that time onwards my interest came to focus on these earlier periods of Egyptian history, with a commensurate delight in the artefacts produced by Egyptian craftsmen in prehistoric times and in the early formative centuries. These were perhaps the first in the history of the world to be conscious of their craft and to take a proper, professional pride in it.

I have always been interested in origins of things, ideas, or institutions. I am especially interested by the development of our species in the post-Neolithic period, after the tremendous change from living in hunting bands to the beginnings of settled community life. Hence the origin of the city concerns me profoundly, as do the insecurities or aspirations which led men to live within a city's walls.

It may be paradoxical, therefore, that I have chosen to write about Egypt in the fourth and third millennia, when the city became established as a historical phenomenon in the burgeoning societies of the Near East. The paradox lies in the fact that the Egyptians, unlike a number of their neighbours and contemporaries, were not great city builders. But they were the inventors of the most advanced and highly developed pristine society that we know, whose beginnings we may observe and attempt to understand. Their failure to build cities on any scale is indeed part of that story.

I am fascinated by the elegance and assurance of early Egypt, by the sumptuous character of the society which grew out of its simple beginnings, by the sophistication and complexity of the institutions which so swiftly were established within it, and by its innocence. The earliest Egyptians were god-ruled but not god-obsessed; they were, in this regard, as in so many others, fortunate.

I too was fortunate in these years to find many friends in Egypt. I was received with equal cordiality in the high, imperial rooms of the British

Embassy and in the houses of small officials in little towns. In one such, on a summer night, I heard the watch calling the hours, a lantern carried on his shoulder. It was like the end of the second act of *Die Meistersinger*, but without the tumult.

I travelled up and down the Nile, the first of rivers. Once, I had arranged to meet a boat below the middle Egyptian town of Minia, to sail upstream to the rock tombs of Beni Hasan. I arrived in the little town just before dawn; I was escorted along the river banks just as the sun returned, a god as much as ever he was, through villages to whose inhabitants I must have been as strange a phenomenon as a Martian. We reached the point where a rowing boat was waiting to take me from the west to the east bank, where I would meet the river boat on which I would travel to Beni Hasan. The boatman greeted us; he was a giant, nearly seven feet tall, with flaming red hair, not altogether a common sight in Egypt. His boat was moored a yard or so from the bank; he picked me up, carried me in his arms as he waded in the water and deposited me, with great gentleness, in the boat. He did not speak as we crossed the river, nor when I thanked him and said goodbye; he would take nothing from me, but smiled with a curious tenderness and something like complicity. I think he may have been a mute; I suspect that he had been on that stretch of the river for a very long time.

For many years I had a friend who was amongst the most promising Egyptologists of his generation. Together we explored the reaches of the river from Cairo to Aswan. He was deeply sceptical of many of the most cherished Egyptian artefacts in European and, particularly, in American museums. In his eyes not even the pyramids could presume to automatic acceptance of their authenticity; his most frequently used adjective was 'dubious'. Sadly, he is dead but I have recalled him often when writing this book; from the Duat where I am sure he will have found justification, I think I hear the echo of that word . . . 'dubious'. I doubt that he would have agreed with much of what I have written.

I am not at all sure what Egyptologists as a group will make of it. I am, I hope, properly diffident about trampling over the ground carefully cultivated by professionals in this or in any other field. They are no doubt accustomed to all manner of strange people advancing stranger theories about a discipline which they have worked hard to rid of its more luscious and bizarre accretions. I have tried to respect the findings of contemporary Egyptological scholarship and not to stray too far into the wilder growths of speculation or interpretation. Clearly, I have felt able to raise issues and to discuss possibilities which perhaps few professional Egyptologists would consider appropriate, since current professional thinking leans towards the austere in scholarship and away from the speculative. But what I have written is rooted in an essentially humanistic ground and does not, I hope, disregard the historical proprieties. However, I must acknowledge that it is idiosyncratic in that it pursues issues which interest me especially and that it does not adhere to a very rigid chronological sequence; rather it follows where my particular interest leads. Egyptology has become, like many aspects of archaeology, intensely specialized; it is no doubt the most scholarly of all archaeological disciplines, with the best part of two centuries of scholarship behind it. Few professional Egyptologists nowadays are inclined to take a synoptic view; fewer still to venture into areas outside their own specification. They are the angels in this instance.

To the members of another professional group I feel that I must also make some reparation. These are the Jungian psychologists who may well feel that I am imperfectly grounded in their discipline, yet have not hesitated to invoke Jung and my understanding of his ideas in an attempt to throw light upon the development of Egyptian society in its earliest manifestations. Again, if I have offended I can only ask for pardon; my admiration for Jung is boundless and I believe that in his system and in the directions he indicated for the analysis of myth, the collective unconscious, and the character of social groupings, lie the best prospect of understanding the nature of the human psyche in its societal context. I have no doubt, however, that the principles which Jung articulated so generously can be applied to the emergence of a society like Egypt's, with great profit for those who would seek to understand the processes which were at work.

Practitioners of other vocations may, on the other hand, be quite pleased with me and with what I have done. One is a profession to which I belong myself, though nowadays somewhat vicariously: I think I may be said to have pushed back the origins of state propaganda to a very satisfactory antiquity, though perhaps few people will thank me for having done so; heraldry and the designing of all manner of containers equally can be shown to have an ancestry of a very respectable extent. In planning and decision-making in Archaic Egypt, in the interplay of management decision and specialist advice, the processes involved must have been little different from those which now pertain, with the professionals' exasperation with the whimsicality (or worse) of the client no doubt as powerful a factor then as it is today.

I said that this book began as a celebration of most ancient Egypt; it has not entirely ended as that. For many years I have been deeply interested in and concerned with the archaeology of the Arabian Gulf and of the Arabian peninsula. In this connection I have come increasingly to wonder at the possibility of contact between the peoples of these two nearby but very different cultures. As a consequence I have found myself being drawn further and further into a consideration of where these two may have met, in time as well as in location. I have found far more to engage my interest than ever I thought when I began; I believe that the question of where, when, and how the Egyptians, the Gulf people, and the Mesopotamians met is one of great importance that will now repay study in the light of what the Arabian peninsula is beginning to reveal.

Though I have sustained a particular affection compounded with a more or less limitless admiration for ancient Egypt through most of my life, for the past twenty years or so I have been involved professionally in the development of museums in the Arabian peninsula and the Arabian Gulf. This indeed has been the reason for my interest in the archaeology of the region. It is a branch of the archaeology of the ancient Near East which has been singularly overlooked until the most recent times. The neglect of so large an area of the ancient world is remarkable and is no longer to be justified by dismissing it as peripheral or as culturally and historically as arid as admittedly is much of its land surface. Already the past decade has produced a wealth of material which demonstrates, on the one hand, the complexity of the various historic cultures which flourished in different parts of Arabia in pre-Islamic times and, on the other, the richness of the Arabian Gulf cultures of the third and second millennia which maintained wide-ranging trading contacts, often over immense distances, based especially on the search for copper and fine stone.

An involvement with the archaeology of the Arabian Gulf is in itself no qualification for pontificating about the origins of Pharaonic Egypt. However, as I have said, I have inevitably found myself becoming aware of the many elements of similarity between Egypt in the late Predynastic age and the cultures of Sumer in what is today southern Iraq and Elam, in south-western Iran; the latter is particularly relevant. These similarities have long been known and have frequently been reviewed, but I have been impressed, too, by the curious incidence of similarities in form and content of the art of most ancient Egypt and of some of the cultures which flourished in the Gulf in the late third and early second millennia. The hiatus in time, of something approaching a thousand years in some cases, is perplexing.

It seemed to me that it might be rewarding to look again at what is known as the origins of the Egyptian state from the perspective of the eastern extremity of the Arabian peninsula and from the mysterious rectangular sheet of largely shallow water which comprises the Arabian Gulf. On that almost inland sea and on its shores so much of the early history of 'man the dweller in cities' was acted out, so many of the myths which have later influenced the civilized world were given form and substance, and so much of the apparatus of the sort of society which we have come to regard as the normal lot of city-dwelling man was first developed. To look back from the Gulf towards Egypt at the time when both societies were young has proved, indeed, a remarkable vantage point.

Some further consideration of the problems relating to chronology must be given, if only because the various comparisons between Egypt, Mesopotamia, the Gulf, and western Persia which will be made throughout this text depend for their relevance upon their being contemporary, or at least approximately so. Throughout this book I have, in referring to dates, employed what might be termed the 'conventional chronology'. This assumes that the First Dynasty of Egyptian Kings began in the thirty-second century BC, probably c. 3180 BC, though many scholars today who accept the conventional framework of Egyptian chronology regard this date as too early, preferring to place the beginning of the First Dynasty at around 2900 BC. It was preceded by some 2,000 years of the Predynastic period and succeeded by approximately one thousand years of the Archaic period and the Old Kingdom. This generally accepted Egyptological chronology places the collapse of the Old Kingdom following the reign of King Pepi II, at around 2180 BC.

A settled chronology for Egypt is central to the chronological structure of the early historical period in the whole of the ancient Near East. This is why it has always been considered as of such importance; without a secure chronology for Egypt, the history of the early Aegean, the Levant, even of the Mesopotamian cultures, begins to come apart.

The accepted chronology of Egypt is derived from an amalgam of otherwise quite disparate sources. The Egyptians, unhelpfully, had several calendars by which they regulated their years. They were acute observers of the heavenly bodies and were competent, if rather limited, mathematicians. The Egyptian year notionally began with the first appearance of the Dog Star, Sirius, known to the Greeks as Sothis, and to the Egyptians as Sopdu. Its rising was considered by the Egyptians as marking the first day of the first month of the Inundation, the first of the three seasons into which their year was divided.

It is the Greek name for the star which has stuck and the calendar which is inaugurated by the appearance of Sirius is in consequence known as the Sothic calendar. The problem with the Sothic year is that it does not correspond exactly with the solar year, but is shorter than it by approximately six hours. This results in the two years, the Sothic and the solar, gradually slipping apart; the same situation would pertain in the western or Gregorian calendar without the intercalation of a leap year in every four.

The Egyptian year was originally 360 days in duration. It was, at some remote time in the past, extended to 365 by the introduction of five extra days but still the six hours' gap remained. As the years went by and became centuries, the calendar became seriously out of alignment, with all the seasons falling at the wrong time of the year, as it were.

The Egyptians were perfectly aware of the deficiency of this calendar and quite happily introduced two others which were more accurate. But they kept records of the Sothic cycle, which takes the formidable term of 1,460 years to return to its beginning.

Censorius states that the Sothic and the civil New Year coincided in AD 139. With the known factor of 1,460 as the length of the Sothic cycle it is possible to calculate backwards in time to set the beginning of earlier cycles in 1317 BC and 2773 BC. Two inscriptions from the New Kingdom and one from the Middle Kingdom give reasonably firm dates for Sothic risings, though not the beginning of the cycle.

The Egyptian bureaucracy, from the earliest times, kept records of the annual inundation of the Nile, associating them with the reigns of the Kings. Of such records the inscribed tablet, of which various fragments survive and which is known as the Palermo Stone, is the most important. By a combination of the extension of the Sothic cycles backwards in time and their alignment with the names of the Kings and the length of their reigns in the Palermo Stone and other inscriptions, a rough chronological structure begins to emerge.

In addition to the Palermo Stone, king lists from Abydos, Turin, and Saqqara have provided information about the names of the Kings and some of the important or striking events of their reigns. Such lists, and possibly others now lost, were doubtless available to Manetho, the High Priest of Heliopolis in the reign of Ptolemy II Philadelphus, who reigned from 285 BC to 246 BC. He wrote a history of Egypt, parts of which have survived only in extracts quoted by other authors; these are fragmentary and often corrupt.

Manetho's history was devised in three parts. The first dealt with the time of the gods, the second with those mysterious figures 'the spirits of the dead, the demigods', who were said to have succeeded the gods in the rule of Egypt; the third relates the histories of the mortal Kings. It is thus this part which provides the basis for all the records of the Kings, published first by followers of Manetho in late antiquity and which still informs all subsequent histories of Egypt.

Clearly Manetho had access to valuable records of the Kingship, now lost. He it was who first imposed the idea of the 'Dynasties', linking groups of Kings by familial ties or by their origins in a particular district or town of Egypt. Manetho lists thirty dynasties in all, the first, as we have seen beginning with the Unification. Dynasty follows dynasty, neatly but unhistorically; we know that a number of dynasties listed by Manetho as following one upon another were in fact coterminous, or overlapping. In some cases he lists lines of Kings for which there is little or no historical evidence.

Manetho gives, in many cases, estimates for the reign of individual Kings and totals for the duration of the dynasties; the two figures do not always tally. It is the attempt to relate Manetho's computations to known historical sequences which has caused many Egyptologists some very difficult and perplexing arithmetical problems.

The crucial date is, of course, the beginning of the First Dynasty. The estimates for this critical event have become later, over the past century or so, in the most remarkable fashion. The range of dates extends from Petrie's estimate of 5546 BC, a figure which no one would support today, through 3500 BC by Hall, 3400 BC by Breasted, down to the more generally accepted range of 3200–3100 BC, promoted by Sewell, Drioton and Vandier, Frankfort, and Hayes, amongst others. Scharff and Moortgat would put the date as late as 2850 BC, nearly *three thousand* years later than Petrie.

Computing the extent of the Predynastic period is even more fraught. To some extent, at least, Petrie's sequence dating, in itself a helpful device but one of no absolute chronological value, has made the situation more complex. He assumed that one style in pottery making or design followed *from* another; he assumed, too, that an extended timescale would be required to move from the origins of a form to its elaborated or degenerated successors. In fact, of course, it is impossible to quantify such a sequence, in the sense of applying a timescale to the process. The design of a pot may go through a series of transformations very rapidly; similarly a type like the black-topped vases, originally associated with the Badarians and hence the senior of all Egyptian pottery types, may persist over the centuries, even over millennia.

The fact is that there is really no reliable archaeological evidence to support the accepted dating of the Predynastic periods. There is only one stratified Predynastic site, and that a very small one, which yields Badarian, Naqada I, and Naqada II levels together; current work at the site of Hierakonpolis, of which much will be said later in this text, may elucidate the sequence further. Most cautious writers on the Predynastic periods are careful to issue a caveat and to observe on what fragile and often antique evidence the generally accepted ideas about the predynastic are based. They are right to do so.

Another disconcerting factor is that though most of the material evidence for the Predynastic is drawn from excavated or plundered graves, the quantity of graves concerned is really very small when given the apparent spans of time involved and the extent of the settlements. The argument is usually advanced that Predynastic cemeteries, like Predynastic settlements, were generally sited on the edge of the cultivation and hence have been long since buried beneath the accretions of centuries of occupation and agriculture. There may well be some truth in this but it is disconcerting none the less that a great early dynastic site like the one at Helwan, to the south of Cairo, can yield some 10,000 graves of officials and the like whilst there are no comparable burials known from the immediate predecessors of the Helwanites in anything like the same quantity.

At Hierakonpolis, one of the most important early sites, the present estimate is that the late Predynastic population was around 5,000. The evidence for this assertion is also slight. The absence of extensive cemeteries makes the estimation of such communities at best speculative. Nor are there any extensive settlements on which estimates might be based or checked.

It is generally assumed on the basis of the very extensive repertory of pottery and later stone vessel shapes that the Predynastic period in Egypt lasted for some 2,000 years – from *c.* 5000 BC to *c.* 3000 BC. Once again, there is no archaeological or historical corroboration for the attribution of such a timescale; it could be 500 years as easily as 2,000. The problem is compounded by the fact that Egyptian chronology is the control by which the chronologies of the ancient Near East as a whole are formulated. When, for example, a historian observes that Naqada II in Egypt corresponds with the late Uruk in Mesopotamian chronology he really means no more than that it has been agreed that the late Uruk period in Mesopotamia corresponds with Naqada II in Egypt. There are, as yet, simply no absolute standards by which real dates in these early times can be established.

Nor is the evidence of carbon 14 dating altogether conclusive. In any batch of dates obtained from organic materials drawn from the same sources or archaeological horizon there will often be fairly violent discrepancies between the range of one date and another. The archaeologist's tendency when faced with a number of inconsistencies in the materials for which he is trying to secure a date is, perhaps understandably, to dismiss those which do not conform to recognized time-frames as 'aberrant' and to see them as affected by external factors, like changes in the radiation to which they have been exposed, or in some other way infected. Carbon 14 sequences may be useful in determining relative sequences of objects but they are at best of dubious value in computing absolute dates.

There are some disconcerting gaps in the evidence as it stands at present, which may not be evident from the confidence with which some assertions relating to datings are made. These discrepancies tend to be given added support by the discovery of a flourishing mercantile culture in the Arabian Gulf islands and the surrounding coastlands contemporary with the later Old Kingdom, and Akkadian and neo-Sumerian Mesopotamia; this will no doubt focus attention again on the question of chronology. When it was first excavated, the foundation of the great temple complex at Barbar, Bahrain, was dated to the early part of the third millennium. This attribution has now been revised and it is proposed that the first temple was probably built there around the twenty-fourth century BC, not long before the likely end of the Old Kingdom in Egypt. However, as will be seen from the narrative below, there are a number of factors in the context of the Gulf's archaeology – elements of design, artefacts, and architecture – which would either be more acceptable were they attributable to a period earlier in the millennium than appears to be the case or if their parallels in Egypt could be dated to the end of the third millennium rather than to its beginning.

There are two small editorial observations that I would make. I have confined notes in the text to a limited number of parentheses, giving references mainly (though not exclusively) from Arabian or Western Asiatic archaeology; these may not be familiar to Egyptologists, who will, otherwise, be fully conversant with the references which draw upon their discipline. Some Egyptological references I have, however, inserted where I felt that it was appropriate to do so.

The other observation relates to the photographs and illustrations. I have tried, wherever possible, to use illustrations which may not be so familiar to readers of books on Egyptology. The inheritance from Egypt is so exceptionally generous that it seemed to me worth rummaging through some of what might appear to be the more neglected storerooms of that inheritance. To the specialist there will be no revelations, but to those whose concern with Egypt is not professional I hope that some at least of these objects will bring surprise and delight, as much as they have done to me.

One last point: Egyptologists will detect an echo in the title which I have given to this book. *Egypt's Making* deliberately recalls one of the last books published in his long lifetime by Sir Flinders Petrie, who virtually invented Egyptology. In 1939, too, I discovered Egypt through the BBC broadcast of the sounding of the war trumpets of Tutankhamun from the Cairo Museum. As I write this, it is fifty years to the day that the

Second World War began in September 1939. So formidable a cluster of anniversaries, great and small, is pleasing, and through the plagiarism of his title I am able to pay some respect to the man who, perhaps more than any other, tried to penetrate the origins of the essential character of the Egyptian state.

At the end of the day, I have had only one aim in writing this book other, obviously, than that of satisfying myself by writing it. It is that I too may direct attention to this magical land, to the less familiar periods of its history, and, in particular, to the origins of its historic institutions. Ancient Egypt is at its most compelling in the wonders which it reveals and the directness with which its people – craftsmen as well as Kings – can speak to us today. If we listen, we may learn, before it is entirely too late.

Michael Rice

Acknowledgements

I have been greatly assisted, in preparing this book, by the readiness of museums all over the world to allow me to reproduce works from their collections. To them I am profoundly grateful. I have tried, wherever it has been possible, to use less familiar images; in this I have been greatly helped by several photographers specializing in Egyptological studies, particularly my friends Roger Wood and John Ross. I have also been helped by various institutions, notably the Egypt Exploration Society, who have allowed me to reproduce illustrations from their publications.

I have been stimulated and frequently bewildered by my old friend Michael Sanders's views on ancient chronology which, if I have not been able to follow them in their entirety, have made me look again at the whole matter of Egyptian chronology with a sceptical and puzzled eye.

1

The land of Egypt

There was a time when, in one small strip of the world's land surface, man achieved an almost total equilibrium with his environment and created a society as near perfect as he has so far been able even to dream about. This was the Golden Age. Sadly enough for the race of men it ended all too soon, rather more than 4,000 years ago, by the chronology customarily adopted today.

It was not a mythical time; no centaurs galloped equivocally across these lands, nor did fabulous beasts arch their necks, except in the art which the people created so finely and so remarkably. We may still walk where the people walked and, when the light is right and when we look with eyes not too clouded and baffled by the impressions of the present day, we may even see their world in something of the way in which they saw it.

The land, of course, is Egypt; it could be nowhere else. The time in which this fusion of the marvellous and the real occurred was a magical millennium, a thousand years or so of superb achievement, of an unexampled advancement of the human spirit, spanning the closing centuries of the fourth millennium before the present era, and continuing through most of the third millennium. In terms of historical time as it would be expressed today, this represents the period from around 3200 BC to 2200 BC. There has been no other time quite like it in all human history.

It is difficult enough, and indeed probably presumptuous to boot, to attempt to penetrate the perceptions of a people so remote in time from ourselves and to speculate about the nature of a culture which is so far removed in all vital aspects from our own as that which determined the beliefs and customs of the inhabitants of the Nile Valley, 5,000 years and more ago. The times involved represent what historians categorize as the Predynastic and Archaic periods and the Old Kingdom, the time of

Egypt's first and finest greatness. It is as distant an epoch as may be found in the study of preliterate and literate societies. None the less we can recognize that the people of that thousand years produced a way of life so powerful and enduring that it lasted, in outward form at least, for more than 3,000 years, even surviving several extended interruptions. It continues to this day to exercise a unique fascination and to induce in its observers either a sense of almost fearful wonder, or an exuberant borrowing of forms and motifs, often in the most bizarre and inappropriate contexts. The recollection of Ancient Egypt (or, more accurately, what often stands for Ancient Egypt) has, in a quite extraordinary way, managed to infiltrate itself into so many aspects of the modern world. But often the forms which later ages have taken to be Egyptian are in fact only the debased simulacra, infected by centuries of foreign influence, of the real forms which can only properly be traced in the dawn and springtime of Egyptian civilization. It will be the purpose of this present study to analyse some of these characteristics and to try and identify their original forms.

Furthermore, amongst other themes that will be explored is the possibility that some of the concepts which have been developed in the past century to explain aspects of the human personality and the identification of the individual in the practice of psychiatry and analytical psychology can, with appropriate reservations, be applied to an understanding of the factors which determined the emergence of the historic Egyptian personality in its earliest manifestations. Thus the idea of the archetypes, developed in particular by Carl Jung (see Chapter 6), seems particularly apt when applied to some of the mighty images which stream out of Egypt in the earliest periods of its existence as a state. It seems equally likely that the extraordinary appeal which Egypt has exercised on the modern world (the world, that is, since the late eighteenth century when ancient Egypt first began really to penetrate European consciousness) is a consequence of this marshalling and unleashing of the archetypes. Egypt has been an almost inexhaustible source of images and forms which have excited and inspired artists and craftsmen as no other society of comparable antiquity. But then, it must be remembered that with the exception of the Egyptians' contemporaries and near neighbours, the Sumerians of southern Iraq, there is no other developed society of comparable antiquity known to us. The unique inheritance which the world draws from most ancient Egypt consists not only of the pyramids and superlative works of art, surviving in extraordinary quantity from the earliest periods onwards, but also of the identification and then the releasing of the archetypes into the consciousness of men, the consequence of the genius of Egyptian artists and designers who first gave the archetypes their form.

Whenever the people of other lands observed Egypt and speculated about the nature of her culture and society, in all ages they seem to have harboured the suspicion that Egypt was in touch (or certainly at some time had been in touch) with powers beyond the confines of the world they knew to be around them and of which they were part. Understandably the Egyptians did nothing to diminish the aura of mystery and the numinous quality with which their land seemed to be suffused, as much as it was suffused with the light of the sun which, paradoxically for a land so occult in its reputation, lit the river banks and surrounding desert with a brilliant radiance. They were not disposed to admit, even to themselves, that the wonders of Egypt and the proximity of her gods were alike the consequence of man's invention. That that invention itself was so superlative that it seemed superhuman does not diminish the essential humanity of the Egyptian achievement, nor, for that matter, does it significantly augment it, for in most ancient Egypt the sense of the human and the divine come very close together, as aspects of the same integral experience.

It is amongst Egypt's most notable characteristics that in all essentials its nature was determined in the earliest days of its existence and that those essentials continued to dominate Egyptian history for her entire lifetime. Egyptian culture very swiftly reached peaks of elegance and sophistication and Egyptian art of technical perfection, which have perhaps never again been equalled. Once the Kingship appeared, Egyptian state institutions rapidly achieved a maturity and effectiveness which allowed the state to endure in the same essential form over the succeeding three millennia.

These achievements, in virtually every department of the state and of life, resounded down the centuries; they were in large part the work of a succession of extraordinary men, the earliest Kings of the united land of Egypt, and their immediate colleagues and supporters. Between 3200 BC and 2700 BC they seeded Egypt deep in the fertile soil of the Valley; for another 500 years what they planted flourished wonderfully. Though the early Kings are shadowy figures, the shadows which they cast on history are very great.

The early Egyptians had a genius, never remotely approached by any other ancient society, for devising symbols which instantly encapsulate complex and diverse concepts. The Egyptians indeed are the supreme symbolists; every aspect of their society – art, religion, and the life which revolved around the King – reflects this strange and very individual quality. Kingship was the ultimate Egyptian institution: the King represents the absolute focus of all early Egyptian history. His Kingship was personified, in what is surely one of the most inspired images in the entire course of symbolism, as a golden hawk soaring limitlessly high above the world, a creature of the sun, infinitely remote, one whose natural habitat is the empyrean, in the exalted firmament where his home, other than in the fortunate land of Egypt, lay beyond the Imperishable Stars. Not even the majestic lion or the raging, dominant bull, though they were both creatures associated with the Kingship in early times, quite achieved the breathtaking vision of the falcon of gold as the ultimate icon in which the concept of the Kingship was so perfectly enshrined.

The Egyptians recognized that if a man, with all the too unmistakable evidences of humanity, was to be exalted above all other men and to be given total and absolute rulership over them, his simple mortality must be thrust down and his mortal nature replaced by something altogether more sublime. Thus came the audacious idea of recognizing the holder of the Kingship as himself divine, his divinity confirmed by his assumption of the crowns and regalia which were the marks of the ruler of the Two Kingdoms. It is a neat equation, even if, like the serpent which eats its own tail, the argument strikes the dispassionate observer as notably circular.

The course of Egyptian history produced thirty dynasties of Kings. We are concerned here with the period which preceded the unification of Egypt, generally called the Predynastic period, and with only the first six groups of historic Kings; of these the first two, grouped conventionally under the term 'the Archaic period' are the most immediately important, as well as the most tantalizing and obscure. The later dynasties all produced remarkable men but it is the Archaic Kings who really were the begetters of Egyptian civilization, even in its most luxuriant flowering; it was their immediate successors, the Kings of the Old Kingdom, who drew the benefit of their extraordinary enterprise.

Even so, the earliest Kings whose names are recorded as the First Dynasty, were not the first Kings in Egypt. The origins of the Egyptian Kingship, though it is without doubt the most ancient in the world, are lost in the obscurities of the later centuries of the prehistoric period, in the latter part of the fourth millennium BC. It is only with the coming of writing that it is possible to put names to the Kings with any sort of assurance. It is remarkable, though, that one of the greatest documents of the time of the actual unification (or perhaps re-unification) of Egypt into the world's first unitary state probably reveals the name of the founder of the First Dynasty, perhaps the Unifier himself. But before his time there are hints of prehistoric chieftains, even of Kings who ruled part or all of the land which was to become Egypt. These names are matters of conjecture; the material remains associated with their rulerships are sparse and fragmentary. We can only glimpse them occasionally through the prehistoric, preliterate

4

miasma; none the less, they were the forerunners of the Kings of historic times. Their titles, elements of their regalia, customs associated with their roles as the links between the visible and the unseen worlds, were abstracted and adapted by the later Kings for their own use and for the augmentation of their own majesty. The various crowns, the crook, the flail, the bull or monkey tail, the lion's and leopard's pelts, all were once the properties of lesser princes which came to add to the splendour of the universal King who ultimately triumphed over all of them, soaring above them high into a firmament of majestic and untrammelled splendour, sovereign and alone.

To the historians of the late nineteenth and early twentieth centuries, it seemed possible to detect darker echoes, too, from this remote and distant time. It has frequently been asserted that the ancient and terrible African practice of the ritual sacrifice of the ageing King once held sway in prehistoric Egypt. At some predetermined time or when his physical powers began to fade (a phenomenon probably revealed first by the inhabitants of the royal harem), the King, it was suggested, was put to death, thus effecting the sacrifice of the god whose blood, let into the earth, ensured the prosperity of his people and his house. There is in fact not one whit of evidence to support the idea that the King in Egypt was ever sacrificed. It was a notion which greatly appealed to an earlier generation of anthropologists and historians who believed that virtually all 'primitive' monarchies underwent the process in the course of their evolution.

In Egypt however, Kingship was never really primitive and the existence of a festival of rejuvenation, the *Heb-Sed* jubilee, a fact well attested, is not in itself evidence that it was a later substitute for an earlier ritual of the killing of the King. As will be seen, the sovereign's servants and his favourites were certainly sacrificed to go with him when his natural term on earth was completed.

Whilst the King, in the earliest times, was not merely a god but quintessentially *the* God (Neter Nefer, the Good God) he was, none the less, not the only god. Egypt has several colleges of gods; they fall broadly into three groups: the first is probably the earliest and is characterized by fetishes, the second represents the gods of human form, the third an entire menagerie of animal divinities. The last are what most people will think of as exemplifying the gods of Egypt, a procession of dogs, cats, rams, baboons, ibises, crocodiles, bulls, lionesses, geese, even beetles, vultures, shrews, the ichneumon, and many more. The zoomorphic gods of Egypt, generally a benign company who might well be found in Comus' train, also reflect the infinite delight which Egyptians, from the earliest times, took in the creatures which shared the Valley and the deserts with them. The powers of observation of Egyptian artists and craftsmen were phenomenal, never more so than when they were portraying animals, in the chase, at play, or simply engaged in their own faunal pursuits. This delight in nature is evident as soon as the Egyptians began to make what we might recognize as works of art, stone and wood carvings, pottery finely painted, in later times, metalwork beautifully wrought, or, supremely, the glorious reliefs and paintings of the Old Kingdom which are, in their totality, a joyous hymn to life and the spirit of existence. Even the concept 'to be joyful' was expressed as a hieroglyph by the representation of a cow turning around to succour its calf, (𓃜) a scene that was also memorably recorded on the walls of several Old Kingdom tombs. The Egyptians brought the same zest and the same delight in animal forms when they came to that other most Egyptian of pastimes, the making of gods.

The invention of richly complex and often overlapping families of gods was one powerful manifestation of the Egyptian creative urge. Its origins are lost in remote prehistory, in the early settlements of the Valley. In later times, the Third to the Sixth Dynasties marked the high point of the Egyptians' creative explosion: at the same time a subtle change came over the gods of Egypt. Not only did the craftsmen then produce works of an ineffable beauty but they made objects with a truly wonderful technique and an applied and disciplined skill hardly ever equalled anywhere in the world in later centuries. Indeed the Egyptian craftsmen of the earliest periods deserve to be recognized as amongst the supreme master craftsmen of all history. Not for nothing was the High Priest of Ptah, the paramount creative god of Memphis, called the Master of the Master Craftsmen.

In all of these activities, indeed in the entire round of their existence, the Egyptians had but one motivation: it was so evident and fundamental that it never required statement or articulation. They were obsessed in a positive, indeed in a glorious sense, with life. Their genius was directed towards the celebration of life and its prolongation to eternity. The entire power of the state and those who lived in it, from the divine king to the humblest peasant, was focused on this single purpose, to sustain the life of Egypt. In this exalted enterprise art was required to fulfil a particular responsibility.

At no time was this wholesale identification between what might be called the corporate life of the Egyptian state and its harnessing to the objective of the prolongation of life so significant as during its beginnings. It was, indeed, as if the whole genius of the nascent state was directed towards resolving the dilemma of man's transient existence. It is this objective and the extraordinary quality of the works of art and of architecture which were created to advance it that distinguish the first thousand years of Egyptian history and which mark that time out from the long sequence of centuries which succeeded it. What made this period so very exceptional was the purely innovative quality of early Egyptian achievement, as much in art as in state institutions, probably in ritual also, when virtually everything that is identified with what is customarily called 'Pharaonic civilization' throughout its history was invented. In its first flowering it was pristine and in all essentials untouched by conflicting or confusing external influences: it is the pure spirit of the Nile cultures which is then to be seen, not the debased mélange of influences, imposed on the Egyptian matrix, which it became in later periods.

Similar considerations applied to the evolution of the Egyptians' beliefs and intellectual concepts as to the development of the forms of their material culture and of their architecture. The role of Kingship, the nature of the gods, the relationship between the gods and their chosen people, the application of architectural forms, and the flowering of Egyptian art and craftsmanship are all to be seen at their purest and most immediate in the first millennium or so of Egypt's national existence.

After that the unique genius of Egypt begins, though at first almost imperceptibly, to recede, eventually to fail. Although in terms of material wealth and political power Egypt was to reach heights never dreamed of (and probably never sought) in the early period, under the great Kings of the Middle Kingdom and the dominant Emperors of the New Kingdom she had lost her soul. The rituals of her temples became increasingly mechanical and repetitive, the empty recital of liturgies which fewer and fewer of their adherents actually understood. Her art became similarly debased, with hitherto unplumbed depths of meretricious display and vulgarity being reached in the later periods when the sunny humanity and superb restraint of the old designers were lost in a surrender to an increasingly frenetic pursuit of glitter and sheer size: Rameses II, for example, was a megalomaniac of very little taste, whilst poor Tutankhamun was trundled into his tomb accompanied by a great deal of deplorable rubbish, though also with some pieces of enduring merit.

It is to be regretted that so much of the modern world's appreciation of Egyptian art and culture has been formed by the consideration of these later forms. Of course, there are splendid objects from all phases of Egyptian civilization; the craftsmen of Egypt were at all times masters and their genius cannot ever be wholly suppressed. But there is no real comparison between the works created in the third millennium (and some of the late fourth) and those of later centuries. If the essential spirit of Egypt is to be sought in her art, it must be looked for in the earlier times, before the flooding in of alien influences which seem to have burst on Egypt in the

7

last 200 years of the third millennium. After that time, after the seemingly interminable reign of Pepi II, to take a convenient historical point, things were never quite the same again.

In its first flowering, the perfection which Egyptian society achieved can best be apprehended by a parallel consideration of the only other societies which can be compared with it in antiquity and, though very differently, in achievement. These are the contemporary, indeed even slightly older cultures, which arose away to the east of Egypt, one in the Valley of the Tigris and Euphrates and particularly in the southern extremity of that region, in Mesopotamia, 'the land between the Rivers'. This rich and complex culture was known to history as Sumer, and its peer, somewhat to the east and south of Sumer, was in Elam, the region of Iran which has been called Susiana and Khuzistan. These lands, together with the eastern seaboard of the Arabian peninsula, shared the Arabian Gulf as a common highway.

The Sumerians were in many ways the peers of the Egyptians; in some, however, the Mesopotamians could be said to be in advance of their Egyptian contemporaries. It was the Sumerians (so far as we know) who invented writing, the wheel, sailing boats, international trade, banking, and the first profoundly influential corpus of epic literature. They inaugurated the practice of living in cities, of building monumental religious and state architecture, of creating civil and religious hierarchies and administrations. Their contribution to the modern world is immense, to the extent that without them the world would in no wise be what it is today. Less is known of the Elamites, though elements of their culture seem to be derived from Sumer: what is clear however is that they were as intensely visual a people, in terms of the art which they created, as were the Egyptians.

Though the Sumerians were a creative, lively, disputatious people who enjoyed life and the business of living, they had, by comparison with the Egyptians, no sense of special election, no sense of being the favoured children of the gods. When they considered their place in the world they took, generally, a fairly despondent view of it. Their gods were hostile and frequently malignant: at best they might remain indifferent to the affairs of men. Man had, in the Sumerian view, only been created by the higher gods to avoid trouble with the lesser gods, who resented having to carry out disagreeable and laborious tasks while the great gods enjoyed themselves. In consequence a still lesser creature was created, to provide the gods with labourers and perpetually to praise them, a curious psychological need which Near Eastern divinities have always manifested. For such humble reasons was the Sumerian made and there was very little in prospect for him; all that he could hope for, at the best, was to get on with the business of living.

Across the wastes of the Arabian deserts, which lay between Egypt and Sumer, only one god was really well-disposed to man: Enki, the Lord of the Abyss, the god of the sweet waters under the earth. Enki is a complex and well-realized phenomenon. He is particularly identified with the earliest days of the Sumerian people; some authorities would see him (Rice, 1985), indeed, as their original divinity, the most senior of all gods. Enki's name originally meant 'Lord of Earth'; he is the principal figure in the cycle of myths concerned with the Sumerians' concept of their origins and the origins of the arts of civilization. At the centre of these myths lies the mystical and mysterious land of Dilmun, the prototype of the terrestrial paradise. Indeed, perhaps suprisingly, it is the Sumerian legend of the Paradise Land (ibid.) and not the Egyptian which has underlain the myths of Eden and all the other terrestrial paradise lands. Their myths are the first to describe that place of primeval innocence and joy, which has informed the beliefs of religions such as Judaism, Christianity, and Islam, which to a substantial extent are the inheritors of the Sumerian mythologues and of their successors, the Akkadians and Babylonians. The Egyptians did not look back to times past as ideal, for their existence, the perpetual 'now' of the Valley, could not be bettered. They believed that eternity would be represented by the glories of the land of Egypt, written large and sustained for ever. However, it will appear that they may have preserved the memory of a far distant land to the east, an island which they identified with the Rising Sun, as the Land of Light and the place of the origins of their world order.

The men of the earliest societies of Egypt and, to a somewhat lesser degree, of Sumer, were, unknowingly, participating in an extraordinary experiment. They were the first to live in highly organized, highly structured societies, which were hierarchic and, in the case of Egypt, profoundly autocratic. These societies were far removed from the relatively simple communities which descended from the Stone Age. The societies of Egypt and Sumer were the first in which a developed and pervasive culture, extending over a considerable area and persisting through time, became the decisive mechanism of an extended community, its essential motor force. Other societies had experienced random aspects of the growth of institutions or the harnessing of technique comparable with the experience of the society which was to be created beside the Nile or, in different degree, in the cities of Sumer: at Çatal Hüyük, for example, or at Jericho, where early attempts at formulating a sophisticated *civilization* (in the sense that the word implies a relationship with an urban system) were abandoned.

The even more extraordinary and almost unbelievably early experiment in the domestication of plants and animals carried out in Nubia, far to the south of what was to become Egypt, substantially before 10,000 BC, likewise came eventually to nothing (Wendorf and Schild, 1980).

The experience of men living in Egypt at the end of the fourth millennium and for much of the third was of an essentially pristine society, one of the very few occasions in the history of humankind when that term could be used with confidence. It must be repeated that *pristine* does not imply *primitive*: quite the opposite, in Egypt's case. The Egyptians' world really was new: after the millennia-long dream-time of the Stone Age Egyptian man woke to a splendid dawn. From the evidence of his art he saw himself, in the early centuries, as part of a universal order, part of the totality of nature, presided over, with divine condescension, by the immanent god himself. From this perfection of order came that assurance, a calm acceptance of oneness with the divine and with the works of the divine, which is the peculiar mark of Egyptian society at this time. In later times, from the Fourth Dynasty onwards, portraits of individuals show them, tranquil and poised, with their eyes fixed on some distant vision; sometimes the expression is so rapt as to be almost ecstatic. They lack the often apprehensive, anxiety-laden posture of the Sumerians when they portrayed themselves standing humbly in the presence of their gods.

The sense of assurance and security which the god-ordained and directed nature of Egyptian society induced was the product of Egypt's physical topography. By the will of gods she was protected on all sides from incursion, largely also from contamination, by less fortunate or more envious peoples. After the late Predynastic flow of influences from the east which, it will be seen, stimulated rather than confused him, the Egyptian was able, more readily perhaps than any other civilized man, to cultivate in peaceful certainty his responses to the world around him. Although a member of one of the most resourceful, creative, and richly developed societies known to man he was not dependent on a vast library of received impressions flowing into him from outside himself. Such pressures as there were came from a wholly Egyptian environment and were in no way alien to him. Nothing that happened outside the Valley affected him; this could, of course, be said of many peoples in many different times and places but all those who lived after the first half of the third millennium were, willy-nilly, influenced by the aspirations, inventions, or ambitions of others. For the Egyptian in the early centuries, this was simply not so; he lived alone within his own world, with his own kind. He could, as it were, listen to the sound of the world turning and, listening, learn from the sound of its motion. No other influence pervaded the supremely tranquil environment in which he was so securely lodged.

The Egyptians valued order above most other qualities. Order and truth were one and their preservation was the highest good. The King, it was said, ruled in truth; to sustain the truth and order of the universe was the highest good to which even a King of Egypt might aspire.

To know what is true, to be able to define and order the world so that it conforms with its own essential nature, requires an absolute assurance on the part of whoever may set out upon such a task. The certainty that they were not as other men, that their land was different from all other lands and that they alone had certain and untrammelled access to the highest order of divinity was deeply engrained in the Egyptian consciousness, from the very earliest days. Partly this was the consequence, no doubt, of being ruled by an immanent divinity, of knowing that God was a near neighbour, perpetually guiding the universe of which Egypt was, quite clearly, the centre. The Egyptians had a sense of being peculiarly fortunate, singled out by a high and benevolent destiny. They did not proclaim their sense of selection with the strident assertiveness of the much later Hebrews nor with the rather icy arrogance of the Chinese (who simply doubted the actual humanity of the rest of mankind despite all appearance to the contrary), and certainly not with the often implacable cruelty of the Christians. The Egyptians, with a tranquil assurance which can sometimes be exasperating, merely *knew* that they were the favoured children of the gods. They did not need to proselytize – that would have been futile – nor to demand recognition for their distinctiveness, for that would have been irrelevant. They suspected that they alone were truly 'men' though they were also pleased to call themselves 'the cattle of god'; they did not attempt to categorize other peoples but they were confident that Libyans, Asiatics, and probably other Africans were essentially beings of lesser status. They felt some sadness for lands and peoples less fortunate than themselves, but nothing could dent the certainty of their fortune or the security which it induced.

Nothing, that is, until after a thousand years the Golden Age which was early Egypt collapsed in anarchy and dreadful confusion. But this time was distant and mercifully unknown to the creators of the Egyptian state. They could see, for the evidence was all about them, how favoured was their land. But, in a land which was to become a byword for antiquity and the unchanging harmony of life, man was a comparative latecomer. Before man came the Valley was the preserve of a rich and diverse fauna which flourished throughout the millennia, until the climate began significantly to change, probably in the fourth millennium BC.

11

It seems somehow fitting that one of the earliest, if not indeed the very earliest, of the putative common primate ancestors should have chosen to evolve on the primeval Nile terraces. This was the resoundingly named *Aegyptopithecus Zeuxis* (plate 1), who, by the evidence of the reconstruction of his fossil remains, was a spiky and distinctly elegant proto-ape who lived in what was to become Egypt, almost 30 million years ago. Aegyptopithecus is a creature of singular appearance and also, possibly, of considerable importance in the development of the humanoid line. This line is tendentious and obscure. We do not know for sure where the creatures originated which evolved first into apes and then, in all probability, into the various bipedal primates which culminated (if culminated is the right word) in *Homo sapiens* around 35,000 (or, as some would have it now, nearly 100,000) years ago. No more distant ancestor for hominids than Aegyptopithecus can yet be postulated; though the idea is still highly speculative, he has a very fair chance of being the father of both apes and men. The common line diverged many millions of years ago and apes and what were to become men continued on their separate, though cousinly ways. Aegyptopithecus, whose fossils have been found among the rich deposits of the Fayum region in central Egypt, himself disappeared long ago from the catalogue of living fauna.

Whilst Aegyptopithecus was going about his pithecine activities, Egypt's most important physical feature was carving its bed relentlessly from the limestone platform which formed the Valley floor. The Nile indeed had been pouring through the Valley for millions of years before even this distant time, cutting the Valley deeper and deeper as it flowed, its colossal power dominating the landscape then as it still does today.

Egypt's landscape is determined, even in the desert areas, by the presence of the river. Distantly it may be seen glinting suddenly as the sun strikes it through a gap in the hills: close to, it surges or flows imperceptibly, depending on the course through which it runs. No one stretch of the river is quite the same as another: at one moment it may be bound by high limestone rocks, at the next it will open out until it seems as though the traveller is sailing on some boundless lake. At one point, the desert, menacing and implacable, will run down to the river's edge; then, the river turns and the land is fertile, full of small villages and the shouts of children. No representation of Eden is so telling as the banks of the Nile in the richly cultivated areas where the grass, cropped by patient donkeys, runs right to the water's edge.

A prodigality of adjectives, of scale, quantity, and splendour, has been expended recklessly on descriptions of the Nile. All are vain: the Nile is, simply, itself, unique. It is, of course, very much more than a river; the

Egyptians knew it to be the prototype of all streams. As it races or meanders, depending upon its mood and the nature of the landscape through which it flows, it draws into itself all the elements of nature: earth, air, and sky. It is one of the earthly manifestations of the sun in splendour, capturing the sun's rays so that they are spun out across the Two Lands of which it is the one unifying and eternal connection. The Nile is the real King of Egypt, is Egypt.

The Nile is the first and greatest of all rivers. To the Egyptians, indeed, it was, simply, The River; all other rivers were counterfeit, pretenders never wholly to be trusted. Some rivers of which they had knowledge were to the Egyptian mind demonstrably perverse; of these the Euphrates in neighbouring Sumer was the most reprehensible for it flowed from north to south whereas the Nile had made it evident for all to see that a proper river should only flow from south to north. The Euphrates was thus flowing upside down, wholly frivolous and irresponsible riverine behaviour indeed. This fact, of course, merely went to confirm the Egyptian view of foreigners and everything to do with them.

That Herodotus' remark about the Nile has become a cliché employed by every writer who comments on the Egyptian landscape does not diminish its essential truth: 'the Nile is the gift of Osiris, but Egypt is the gift of the Nile'. The Nile is the most paradoxical of rivers for it flows imperturbably through a great desert, its waters rich with life rushing through a landscape that is mostly barren and scoured, typical desert terrain.

Egypt is changeless in beauty and in the ways of its people; it is like no other land. Nowhere does the contrast between rich cultivation and the parched aridity of the desert strike more forcefully. The river, when it returned at the time of the inundation to renew the land, was until very recent times, greeted joyfully as a beloved god, come back to assuage the pain of his people and to bring comfort and prosperity to them. To this day the river is a living creature for the country people and it gives life to the eternal quality of the land so that there is continuity between 'now' and 'then'; desert and sky, the land and the river, birds, animals, and men are brought into a perfect synthesis and express, as nowhere else on earth, the unity and perfection of all life and all creation. The miracle of birth, the cycle of the seasons, the fusion of earth and sky are accomplished in Egypt as they seem hardly to be anywhere else on earth. The gods always seem very close, even today.

The inundation was always magical to the Egyptians, a testimony to the covenant between them and the gods and a guarantee of the gods' concern for the people of the land of Egypt. In the time of Akhenaton, the

Eighteenth-Dynasty reformer, a hymn praised God for the flood and expressed the pious and complacent thought that God had, with singular compassion, placed a Nile in the sky to provide the flood for those who could not enjoy the benefit of the rich deposits which the real Nile's flood left on the banks and marshlands which bounded it.

This was the particular miracle which the Nile delivered every year, unless the whim of the gods or the failure of observances by men interrupted it. The river rose in the summer, the water spread across the banks and fields, filling the canals and allowing the farmers to distribute it even to distant cultivable areas. The earth was black and fertile: blackness was so much a part of the image of Egypt that it was called *Kemi*, the black land. Then, with what seemed extraordinary swiftness, the land was green, giving with abundance and sustaining a large, contented, and well-fed population. All was undoubtedly for the best in the best of all possible lands.

To say that the Nile is Egypt is no more than to express a simple, self-evident truth. The Nile bears Egypt in its flood and over the millennia has laid down and then made fertile by its inundation the black earth from which Egypt is made. To the eye of Horus, floating in the sky high above the land of which he was the divine patron, protector, and, in a sense, the embodiment, Egypt is a slender strip of cultivation, two narrow banks divided by the river. It seems very little ground on which to seed the most splendid manifestation of social creativity yet achieved.

The Nile pours through the Valley which it has made for itself, on its journey from the remote Ethiopian highlands, far beyond the southern confines of Egypt, to the broad, reed-infested waters of the Delta, where it debouches into the Mediterranean, through its several mouths. In length the river journeys some 4,000 miles; this was the torrent which was required to bring to birth the most august civilization that the world has yet witnessed.

So profoundly ingrained in the Egyptian consciousness was the presence of the Nile that it even determined elements in the Egyptian vocabulary. Thus 'north' signified 'to go down stream' whereas 'south' meant 'to go up stream'. 'Right' and 'left' were equated with 'east' and 'west', the orientation being determined by standing on the river's bank and facing in the direction of its flow. 'South' also meant 'face' whereas 'north' seems to have been identified with the back of the head. Everything was oriented to the river and to its flow northwards to the sea.

For the whole extent of human history, until the present day, and for far into the period before man came both to harness and to glorify the Valley, the melting of the snows in the Ethiopian highlands precipitated the Nile's paradoxical inundation, for the flood reached Egypt during the harshest, most deadly months of summer. This fact alone, the mysterious rising of the river's waters when everywhere and everything around its banks was desiccated and in a state of profound exhaustion (like Osiris the Dead God before his revival) gave an uncanny, supranatural quality to the river and the life which it demonstrated, so clearly independent of and, in a sense peculiarly mysterious, superior to the life of the land around it.

At the time of the inundation, when the water flooded back over the land, drawn to areas distant from the river by canals and the immemorial watering system of the *shaduf*, the comfortingly repetitive creaking of this extraordinarily ancient device was always one of the sounds most evocative of the Egyptian countryside. The water was rich in life and revived the dead land; soon the land would everywhere be green.

The Nile is a huge, perpetually moving road, the supreme conveyor of historic experience: it is also a stupendous theatre. Not only was the longest of all recorded histories played out along its banks, with actors and settings of colossal proportions, it was ever capable of remarkable *coups de theatre*, of wonderful effects of light and drama: such effects it can still produce, with the splendid prodigality of an Edwardian actor-manager.

The climatology of deserts and their origin and growth are coming increasingly to be understood. That there have been frequent relatively short-term fluctuations in precipitation and humidity in regions which are now wholly desert is clear, though these should not encourage a picture of lush, verdant landscapes teeming with animals where now there are only rock- or sand-strewn wastes. Even a very small variation in precipitation or mean temperature can permit a significantly larger faunal or human population to become rooted in a particular region. The establishment of a larger community with the introduction of animal species which may cause further depredation or, conversely, the planting of trees and crops which can, for a time at least, arrest it, are factors which promote or control the spread of deserts. However, there is little doubt that where human communities flourish the greatest agent for their spread is man himself, though he is assisted enthusiastically by the goat, one of the earliest of his domesticates.

Ten thousand years or so ago, when settlement began, very marked and remarkable phenomena began to appear in the Near East. To the east of Egypt, across the intervening northern reaches of the Arabian deserts, in the valley watered by the twin rivers of Mesopotamia, men were putting down roots (literally as well as metaphorically) by starting and maintaining small settlements which were to become the first farming villages. They domesticated cereals and crops and animals in addition to the dog, who

15

had for long been the loyal companion of the hunting bands to which these little settlements were the successors. They invented pottery, made toys for their children, and built houses for themselves and modest temples for their gods, whose images they also manufactured hopefully.

In the Nile Valley a somewhat different process was in train. There, though the Neolithic period in the western Sahara was marked by a relatively 'wet' phase, allowing, for example, for the quite extensive afforestation of parts of the Mediterranean coastal regions, there was a gradual drift towards the Valley by the hunters and gatherers who made up the bulk of the population which roamed the savannah-like lands which bore on it. Gradually this movement became more marked, till more and more of the bands settled on the Valley floor or in the wadis around it, as well as on the spurs and terraces which edged it.

This process was, in fact, an ancient one. As the river gradually cut its way deeper and deeper down so the descent of man and his ancestors (in a quite literal sense) may be traced, for at the top is located the earliest evidence of hominid occupation whilst on the Valley floor the most recent inhabitants have left their traces.

It is probable that the Valley floor could not really have supported a substantial human population until about 10,000 years ago. When, for the first time, prospective settlers found their way there, and in so doing at last arrested their journey towards the east, they found a veritable wonderland waiting for them, a superb garden designed by the gods, so it must have seemed, for their most favoured children. Along the river banks vegetation grew lushly, concealing the ready game. The river and its lagoons were abundant with fish whilst on the plains, in the wider parts of the Valley, lion, giraffe, even elephant lived out their lives with lesser beasts in a splendid and harmonious ecology, a symphony of nature to which man alone was eventually to provide the coda.

In historical times Egypt achieved a well-balanced economy, based largely on the management of its natural resources. Agriculture, hunting, fishing, and the raising of breed herds all contributed to the prosperity of the lands. All in fact that man had to do was to harness the resources which lay before him. Typically, however, he overexploited the gifts which the gods had given him; but that was later. In the beginning abundance and a relatively temperate climate combined to produce a situation of unrivalled potential in which to lay down the foundations of a unique human experiment.

The climate in the Nile Valley was marginally more benign in Predynastic times than it was during the early historic periods. It is clear that in the fourth millennium the seasonal rains which activated the wadis, the other-

16

wise dried-up watercourses in the deserts of southern Upper Egypt and lower Nubia, were more considerable than they were in the later third millennium. There is actually some documentary evidence, in the form of the records of the Nile flood levels inscribed on the Palermo Stone, one of the most important third millennium records of the history of the early Kings extant. This large inscription chronicles the principal events of the reigns of the Kings of the earliest dynasties, albeit in a fragmentary and often obscure character. The records, however, show that the levels of the floods decreased during the First Dynasty: the mean level of the flood during the early years of the dynasty was greater by nearly a metre than during the Second to Fifth Dynasties.

Far away, across the breadth of the intervening deserts leading to the shores of the Arabian Gulf, the expanse of relatively shallow water which divides Arabia from Iran, there is also evidence of a significant volatility of climate at this time and during the centuries leading to it. The levels of the Gulf have oscillated fairly violently over the past 17,000 years; for example, the island of Bahrain, now lying in a bay some twenty miles from the Saudi Arabian mainland, was only separated from Arabia about 9,000 years ago. More recently still, between 6,000 and 5,000 years ago, one of the few sites in Bahrain which has yielded pottery of the Ubaid people (the predecessors and presumed ancestors of the Sumerians) was a small, offshore atoll, then lying about a mile away from the principal Bahrain island of which it is now a part. Whilst obviously quite different factors and influences would be at work to affect radical changes in the sea levels in the Gulf and in the annual flood of the River Nile, the coincidence in time of the marked variations which have been described indicate the extent of climatic change in relatively recent times in two parts of the world which otherwise would seem to share many climatic characteristics.

The fact that the Nile generally followed a higher course than it does today or than it did during dynastic times probably means that many late Predynastic settlements, including perhaps some comparable with major centres like Hierakonpolis and Naqada (two cities which will be seen to be of great importance in the late Predynastic period) now lie buried beneath the silt laid down by the inundation. That these may well be the richest of the Predynastic centres, since they lie on the main highway of Egyptian civilization, is something of a melancholy paradox.

The Egyptian, living in the Valley even in times long after his first entry to it, when he had hunted to extinction or driven away the beasts which were once its undisturbed lords, never lost that sense of wonder at the magnificence surrounding him which he must have sensed when first he looked down on the Valley. This sense of wonder accounted for at least two of the most distinctive characteristics of the Egyptian psyche in later, historic times: the belief that the gods had specially favoured Egypt by providing the Valley with an abundance of nature's resources, and a sense of oneness with the animals with which they shared it. This identity with animals is manifested in the personification of even the greatest gods in the form of animals and the reverence which was paid to them, as well as in the ability, amounting frequently to genius, to delineate and to portray animals and their lives with absolute accuracy of observation. This is done, moreover, with no hint of patronage, but rather with abundant delight (plates 2 and 3).

Hunting by man, combined with the probably imperceptible but none the less telling desiccation which occurred at the beginning of the historic period in Egypt, led to the reduction, ultimately to the elimination, of whole species from the upper reaches of the Valley. Between the end of the First Dynasty and the beginning of the Fourth (a period of little more than 500 years) elephant, rhinoceros, giraffe, and the gerenuk gazelle disappeared from the lands north of Aswan. During this time, too, they disappear from the pictorial records in tombs of the chase, which reveal with commendable accuracy the environment and ecology of Egypt at the beginning of her history. Some animals survived, however, despite the odds laid against them by man and climate. Various antelope maintained their herd levels surprisingly well; amongst these was the oryx which, although its numbers declined from its relative density in Predynastic times, clung on in the coastal desert lands. This pattern was repeated in Arabia; but then, the oryx is a survival from the Pliopleistocene and as such it has presumably learned much about adaptation. It was, incidentally, an important animal amongst the clan totems of Egypt for it was the creature identified with the region around Beni Hasan; it was also one of the creatures sacred to the god Set, of whom more will be written.

Aegyptopithecus Zeuxis, that ancient Egyptian proto-ape, chose well when, the first in the hierarchy of primate ancestors, he found the Valley and became its earliest hominid inhabitant. The Egyptians saluted the baboon, an ape of a later sort than Aegyptopithecus, as the wisest of creatures, the embodiment of Thoth, the god of wisdom, of writing and of the moon: once again, it was a symbol well-chosen.

Egyptology is now almost 200 years old. It is the oldest of all branches of scientific archaeology; it has greatly affected the character of archaeology as an academic discipline and as a practice which exercises a dramatic appeal to all sorts and conditions of men. But the search for the origins of Egypt and of the unique political system which it developed started not as one might imagine at the beginning of the study of its past, but relatively late. Though enormous advances had been made in all respects in the uncovering of the ancient world during the nineteenth century, and though Egypt was the focus of both learned and romantic interest, virtually nothing was known of the earliest dynasties until late in the century. The names of the Kings who made up the founding dynasties were known, often in a wildly corrupt form, from Manetho's lists but no material evidence of their existence had been found. Then the French began a series of excavations at Abydos, which throughout Egyptian history was one of the most sacred of her religious centres.

The excavations, if such they could be called when conducted in the closing years of the last century, were a disaster. Directed by Amélineau they were concerned simply with the acquisition of objects for museums and collectors; they were unscientific and, to put it no more forcefully, unscrupulous. There were accusations that objects were destroyed if they appeared to duplicate others, to increase the value of those which remained. The sites themselves were pillaged and no thought was given to the excavations' proper recording or to the protection of the sites involved.

The main site that Amélineau excavated comprised a group of large structures, one of which he confidently pronounced to be the tomb of Osiris, the god to whom Abydos was sacred; he produced a skull which he announced was that of the god himself. He departed from Abydos, leaving the site in ruins and the reputation of French Egyptology, which, by the devoted work of French scholars since the days when Napoleon first opened Egypt to the world deserved to be of the very highest standing, gravely diminished.

By a fortunate chance a young Englishman, William Flinders Petrie, applied to re-excavate the site. He was granted permission and began on a career which was to span the next fifty years and more, during which time he would virtually lay down the outlines of the entire history of Pharaonic Egypt.

He cleared the pits left so disastrously by Amélineau and, by the expenditure of immense patience and labour, pieced together what he presented as virtually the entire chronology of the Kings of the First Dynasty, to the extent that his views still dominate much Egyptological thought to this day. To make so extraordinary a discovery was typical of Petrie. He went on to find similar structures as that which the French abandoned, all dated to the first two dynasties, which evidently represented the burial places (some have said the cenotaphs) of the men and women who had created Egypt, though they may not always have been the tombs of Kings. Later, from the mid-1930s to the 1950s, Petrie was followed by another British archaeologist, W. B. Emery, who excavated a whole series of similar structures on the escarpment at Saqqara. These too were burial monuments of the time of the early Kings; they are amongst the most remarkable buildings to be preserved from high antiquity and their excavator thought *they* were the places of royal burial and, hence, that the tombs at Abydos were not. This issue, an important one in understanding the politics of the First Dynasty (so far as it is possible to do so) will be considered further.

Saqqara had been recognized as early as 1912 as a site of great importance when it was dug first by Quibell, then by Frith. The French, working on the site since the 1930s, have achieved the reconstruction of one of the greatest monuments of human genius, the Step Pyramid complex of King Djoser. Both Petrie's and Emery's excavations of the archaic Royal Tombs have been splendidly published. In particular Emery's volumes are notable for the exceptionally fine drawings and reconstructions with which he, a draughtsman by training and one of a very high order, enriched his reports.

Petrie was responsible for laying down many of the foundations which underlie Egyptology to this day. Recognizing the difficulty (in his day, the virtual impossibility) of establishing an absolute chronology for preliterate, prehistoric periods, he devised the 'sequence dating' of Predynastic pottery. Though now largely superseded, this system was for a long time a valuable technique by which, by tracing the development (sometimes a theoretical one) of one type of pottery from another and hence establishing a sequence of styles, Petrie believed he was able to give a general structure to the prehistoric past which had not previously been attempted.

He established the three (he would have said four) principal southern Predynastic cultures known, from the locations in which they were first recognized, as the Badarian, Amratian, and Gerzean civilizations; the last two are nowadays usually identified as Naqada I and Naqada II. Publications of the tombs of the early Kings and their supporters and of the prehistoric periods alerted the scholarly world to a whole new dimension of history. He also brought out, in the immense stream of publications for which he was responsible, books on the slate or schist palettes which are so significant a category of late Predynastic artefact, as well as works on scarabs, tools, and many which described excavated sites with important Predynastic and archaic components. His two great volumes *Royal Tombs of the First Dynasty* are superbly edited and produced. No work conducted in Egypt subsequently, with the exception of Emery's, has had any influence comparable to that of Petrie in determining scholarly attitudes to the early centuries of Egypt's history.

Other workers in the field did, however, add to the catalogue of reports

DATE

BOF #

4/22/93

_____

UNSUITABLE
FOR BINDING

We regret this volume cannot be
bound as requested. We are
returning it for the reason
checked below:

_____TYPE of binding not indicated

_____HEAVY enameled pages

_____OVER 2-1/2″ thick

_____LESS than 1/8″ thick

_____OVER 12″ high or wide

_____BRITTLE pages

_____NARROW margins

_____MISSING pages

_____TITLE/AUTHOR information needed

_____PAGES torn when received

_____COVER not suitable for type of
        binding requested

_____INSIDE of the cover contains
        important information

dealing with these formative centuries and the sites from which the evidence was drawn. Amongst these one of the most important was Hierakonpolis, once the ancient capital of the dynasty of Falcon princes who set out to unify the Two Lands; however, the publication of the excavations carried out in 1897–8 was less extensive than scholars would have wished, though laudable attempts have recently been made to disinter the material still concealed in the notes and drawings of the site's early excavation (Adams, 1974, 1988).

Lack of thorough publication indeed was the trouble with so many Predynastic and Archaic sites, excepting from the latter category Abydos and Saqqara. From this generalization, too, exception must be made of Petrie's work as a whole; partly because of the power of his analyses of the material which he reviewed (like many early archaeologists he seems to have had the power to sweep aside any criticism of his views which were often expressed in the most dogmatic and trenchant terms), and partly because of the prodigality of the burials of royal personalities, from whose tombs an immense number of artefacts was recovered. His studies on Predynastic Egypt and many of his conclusions still dominate Egyptological thinking about the period. However, very few Predynastic sites have ever been excavated by modern methods, nor have any townships dating from the Archaic periods been adequately researched. Everything that appears in the history books, even those relating specifically to Egypt, dilate upon the earliest periods with every appearance of certainty yet, in terms of modern archaeological method, with very little to go on. Much of the evidence still confidently advanced is the best part of a century old. It is a remarkable fact that the only *stratified* Predynastic site recorded which contains material from the several prehistoric periods is a tiny one at El Hammamiya.

In the century since Petrie started working, or the half century since Emery commenced his excavations at Saqqara, some significant work has of course been undertaken but, by comparison with the attention given to other later periods of Egyptian history, it has been relatively slight. Reisner, the distinguished American Egyptologist, carried out his magisterial review of the development of the Egyptian tomb from Predynastic times to the time of the pyramids, the period with which this book is principally concerned. Similarly Lauer, the French Egyptologist who has been working at the site for many years, has done spectacular work in restoring the Djoser Complex at Saqqara and in so doing revealed its incomparable quality. But the fact remains that this, the most crucial part of Egyptian history, is dependent on researches whose origins are almost lost in the mists of the archaeological beginnings. The superb quality of the artefacts in ivory, stone, pottery, and wood, in many ways the most remarkable to survive from Egypt in any period, and the nobility of the small amount of architecture to survive from the earliest periods, surely makes the need to know more about the people and the society which produced them irresistible.

The nature of Egyptian society in this period, though it is so remote in time from our own, is none the less deeply relevant in the same way as the society developing in the east, in Sumer, is relevant. For the first time men, in both locations, were undertaking large-scale projects in what is effectively social engineering. At the same time, and most particularly in Egypt, they were inventing a series of symbols, forms, and institutions which, because they endured so remarkably well, are still pertinent and potent today. The line which connects our world with theirs is direct and unbroken; they are a profoundly important element in our cultural ancestry. To understand them a little is to add greatly to an understanding of ourselves.

1 *Aegyptopithecus Zeuxis* is a fossil proto-ape, fruit eating and arboreal, from the Oligocene period, approximately thirty million years before the present. It is a true hominid and may well be the most distant ancestor of both apes and men yet to be identified. Remains of the creature come from a site in the Fayum.

2 This baboon nursing its young seems to anticipate the figure of Isis nursing the infant Horus three thousand years later (limestone: height 10cm) from the main deposit at Hierakonpolis. (University College Museum, London, UC15000)

3 The immemorial ability of the people of the Nile Valley to record the fauna around them is brilliantly demonstrated in this line of animals, engraved on a rockface in southern Egypt. The animals depicted were all driven from the Valley north of Aswan by late Old Kingdom times, the consequence of the depletion of stocks by hunting. (Winkler: *Rock Drawings of Southern Upper Egypt*, Vol. I, pl. xx, i)

2

The roots of the Egyptian state

Egyptian society did *not* spring fully ordered and organized instantly into being. The point must still be made, for both the appearance and the reality are so extraordinary: in a matter of a few short centuries the Egyptian Kingdom was devised and formulated, to endure in all its essential characteristics for 3,000 years, the longest lasting of all advanced human societies. Egypt's social sophistication was profound at a time when all the world, except for Sumer, was locked in a benighted barbarism which had been unchanged for thousands of years, since, indeed, Palaeolithic times; if Egyptian society did not in fact emerge fully developed, a casual observer might be forgiven for thinking that it did, so far removed was it from any sort of human experience up to that time.

But Egypt's emergence as a true nation state (she is the very first example in history of that dubious political entity) is well charted. Her roots lay deep in the earth of the Valley on which her splendid temples, palaces, and tombs were to be built; but she was also profoundly African, not by any means wholly impervious to alien influence in the earliest times, though the character and extent of that influence is much debated still.

But, first, the time of which we speak: with the procession of the dynasties Egyptian history is divided, broadly, into two parts, the Predynastic and dynastic periods, and thereafter into a diversity of subdivisions of often bewildering complexity and number. At this point, however, we are concerned with that period which is termed the 'Predynastic', that is to say, the time from somewhat before 5000 BC, when distinct communities can first be seen emerging on the banks of the Nile in the centuries before the unification, which is conventionally dated as taking place during the thirty-second century before the present era. The Predynastic period, therefore, deals with the time to *c.* 3200 BC, from its beginning in the sixth millennium. This period thus spans something less than 3,000 years, not a very long time in which to lay the foundations of so substantial a creation as the Egyptian state.

Just as Egyptian history is divided, arbitrarily but with considerable convenience, into these two broad divisions, so there were always two Egypts. The King was Lord of the *Two Lands*; everything about Egypt was expressed as a duality. Though Egypt was unified in the course of the first centuries of royal rule she always maintained the notion of two Kingdoms, Upper and Lower Egypt, south and north, which the King alone sustained in perpetual equilibrium and whose balance or pivot, the point at which the two Kingdoms were said to meet, was somewhere near Memphis, just south of Cairo, the modern capital city.

It is quite remarkable how this quality of the two Egypts is evident throughout the long march of Egyptian history. It is not merely a poetic concept, not simply the elegant encapsulation of two topographical and historical diversities bound together in a common political destiny. The difference between them is never reconciled; like the concepts of 'left' and 'right' they are eternally opposed, whilst eternally joined. Only the King is common to each and, as common King and, more important still, divine master of each, he brings them into union. The distinction between Upper and Lower Egypt, of south and north, is sustained always and is as apparent in the very earliest times as it is in the later.

The southern Kingdom, Upper Egypt, was clearly conceived as the dominant of the two regions. It was from the south that the most enduring influences in Egyptian society came and without doubt most of its greatest leaders were southerners too. Throughout her long history Egypt constantly needed to return to the south to refresh herself and to restore her institutions, even perhaps her soul, when the weight of years or of external pressures laid too heavily upon her.

Whilst there is abundant evidence for the presence of Predynastic Kingdoms in the south, there is in fact no real archaeological evidence at all to suggest that a Kingdom existed in the north in Predynastic times. Admittedly, there has not been the same amount of excavation of Predynastic sites in northern Egypt as there has been in the south, little indeed though that has been. The fact that much of the Delta is incapable of being excavated, because of the rise in the water table, has not helped matters either. In the historic period a northern entity in the united Egyptian state was postulated, perhaps as an acknowledgement of the need to dualize all the state's institutions, one of the enduring characteristics of the ancient Egyptian mind and one that is probably African in its origin.

In any case, whatever rudimentary political structures existed in the

Valley during the fourth millennium were most likely concentrated in the south. This fact may have been of crucial importance when a family of southern princes appears to have determined on the unification of the Valley.

Long before this point, however, many of the indigenous elements which were evident in Egypt in historical times were already of immense antiquity. Some of them may be traced back to the end of the Stone Age in Egypt, to the profoundly important traditions laid down in late Neolithic times.

The Stone Age is extensively represented in Egypt; indeed, into Pharaonic times the Egyptians were making well-shaped stone tools, in addition to more expensive copper and, later, bronze products. Several of the early stone industries of the land which was to become Egypt show connections with the widely diffused industries of the Old Stone Age (Achulean and Chellian, for example) and also the finer *facies* of the Neolithic period, like those associated with south-western European hunting and gathering groups and known from sites in Arabia and north Africa. There is evidence of a number of well-defined toolmaking groups living in what is now the high desert, deep into Palaeolithic times. Little enough is known of the ways and organization of the hunting bands into which these people, like those who had lived for untold centuries before them, were grouped. It may be guessed that the game in the savannah lands which marched with the Valley provided rich *battues* for the hunters. The gradual desiccation of the region in the sixth and fifth millennia would have brought the experience of hardship to the hunters, perhaps even of deprivation, which would have made the security and abundance of the Valley when they first came upon it seem the more god-given still. It is repeatedly suggested that the division of Egypt in historic times into the administrative divisions or districts which the Greeks called *nomes* (the term has remained in historiographical use today and thus echoes anachronistically in all directions), each graphically identified with a clan totem or fetish, usually, though not invariably, an animal, was a survival of the clan divisions of the late Stone Age hunters, living under their chosen clan symbol; if it is so, the tradition was an enduring one. Even the King himself may once have been 'the Falcon', the eponym of the Falcon Clan, which bore the image of the royal bird as its standard. But we cannot be sure that the clan distinctions actually reach back to the Stone Age; they may be the product of the settled period approaching, around 5000 BC when more and more of the people came to live in more or less permanent groups, to organize themselves, domesticate animals, cultivate their land, and perhaps to feel the need for gods to whom they might address themselves and which they acknowledged as divine representatives of their own tribal or clan identities.

Around 5000 BC the earliest Egyptian villages appear. The communities which they formed were small, no more at best than a few hundred people living together in flimsy huts, close enough to the river to share in its benefits but generally settling themselves on little hillocks or raised ground, to avoid the flood when it came.

Of the three principal Predynastic cultures identified in Upper Egypt (four, if the disputed Tasian culture is included as the earliest; most authorities would regard it as but a variation of the first, the Badarian), each was to leave some mark on the historical period. The first is that identified with the site of the village of El Badari, on the east bank of the Nile, further to the north than its two successors, the earlier named for the site at El Amra (Naqada I).

The Badarian people were farmers and knew of the cultivation of crops and the management of herds; it is not clear whence their civilization came nor from where they themselves originated. They were fisher folk and evidently kept an access to the Red Sea open, as shells from its shores were used for their personal ornament. More particularly, they seem to have had contact to some quite substantial degree with western Asia, for the sheep and goats they bred appear to be of a south-western Asiatic strain. However, it is now apparent that selective herding of animals had been conducted in Egypt from very early times, from long before the first settlements were established in the Valley. To what extent the people who lived, for example, in the eastern Sahara (the western Egyptian desert) were in any way ancestral to the Pharaonic Egyptians is not clear. However, they did maintain herds and the animals were often of strains which survived into Pharaonic times.

The probability is that, on the basis of the evidence now to be recovered from the desert sites, which includes the harvesting and grinding of wild grains and cereals at a very early date, the most ancient inhabitants of Egypt domesticated animals of native Egyptian strains early on. When, however, they encountered the western Asiatic breeds, which were hardier and better suited to life in the Valley, they began to adopt them as their own.

Like the Sumerians, who wore woollen kilts or skirts made of sheepskin, the Badarians dressed in animal skins and this suggests that they may have come from a cooler climate where such clothing would not have been so inappropriate as it must have been for a people living in climatic conditions such as those which persisted in Egypt.

The Badarians are responsible for the first suggestion of Egypt's contact with lands to the east of the Nile Valley, at virtually the earliest period possible. Though they were living, in all probability, barely above subsistence level, they did have the leisure and the ability to develop crafts and skills from which the mighty Egyptian culture of the dynastic future was to stem. Already they seem to have developed a degree of trade with other peoples, including perhaps the importation of wood from the Syrian coast. They had established religious cults, a somewhat higher proportion of female figurines amongst their grave goods suggesting a faith more mother-oriented than that which prevailed in Egypt in later times, when male gods tend to predominate. The figures are often very graceful, both men and women represented as dancers, their hands raised above their heads, a gesture which may also be in imitation of cattle horns (plates 4a and 4b). It will be seen that one of the most significant connections of Predynastic Egypt is with the cattle people of the Valley and it may be that these little figurines are its first manifestation. However, though the female figurines are notable, the Badarians also produced impressive representations of cloaked and bearded males, in ivory and clay (plate 28). They also manufactured a very striking range of combs in ivory; the shape of these is distinctly African and is like the combs used even today by Africans and those of African descent.

The Badarians were remarkably skilled for a people who must be presumed to have moved from something like a simple hunter-gatherer society to a settled state. They carved in bone and, in all probability, in wood; their carvings have a notable power. But the most notable of all their products is their pottery.

Badarian pottery is highly distinctive (plate 5). The style was retained by potters over many generations, even after the Badarian culture had been subsumed into that of its successors. The most frequently encountered Badarian pots are fired to a bright red or brown finish, often with the tops of the vessels burned black, the result it is believed of the pot being inverted in the ashes of the kiln. The fabric of the pots is remarkable; more remarkable still, the earliest of them are often the finest in the quality of their fabrication. The walls of early Badarian vessels are fired to a hardness which approaches that of metal and they are often eggshell-thin. It is not known how the Badarians acquired the knowledge of the techniques of firing their kilns to the high temperatures required to produce such wares, or how they controlled their firing. Even in their earliest products, Egyptian craftsmen showed skills of a quite exceptional and very perplexing quality.

It is remarkable that across the intervening Arabian deserts the contemporaries of the Badarians in Egypt, the early Ubaid potters of southern Iraq, also made pottery with the same characteristic of exceptionally fine quality. This phenomenon, so unlikely in any event and doubly so with two apparently quite disparate peoples living relatively far from each other, is one of the most puzzling of the early, more or less simultaneous, developments of Egypt and of Sumer. A similar observation, marking a decline from the earlier to the later, may also be made of the exceptionally beautiful wares from Hassouna and Sammara in northern Iraq. They are the earliest of all Near Eastern pottery forms and the quality of the earliest is superlative.

The Badarians appear to have lived in tents or in shelters made of skins. Their domestic economy, in addition to the evidence of animal domestication, must have been quite advanced as they made bread, traces of which have been found in their burials. The Badarian is essentially a southern culture; however, it is preceded in the north by peoples identified with two important sites in Lower Egypt. Of these the early inhabitants of the Fayum, the area of the great lake always to be celebrated throughout Egyptian history as perhaps the richest source of game for the hunt, left no traces of structures behind them. They may have been seasonal visitors to the area, like the people far away to the east in Arabia and the Gulf who camped on shore and lakeside sites and left behind them the fragmentary evidence of pottery of the type produced by the 'pre-Sumerian' Ubaid people in southern Mesopotamia.

A large and well-developed northern site has been identified at Merimda, dating from the fifth millennium. The site is approximately 180,000 square metres in extent, and thus represents a major settlement. Some evidence of trade with Palestine, with the people of the Sinai peninsula, and even perhaps with more distant eastern peoples, has been detected here. Among the goods found is a particular type of weapon, the pear-shaped mace which later played an important part in Egyptian history. This type of mace seems to have originated in Mesopotamia and Susa (in south-western Persia) and to have replaced the disc-shaped mace which is more typically Egyptian.

At Ma'adi (today a suburb of Cairo) another major northern Predynastic settlement has been identified. It seems to have owed its origins to an early manifestation of the trade in copper, the source of which was probably located on the Sinai peninsula. Considerable quantities of copper ore have been found at Ma'adi. One of the singularities of the Ma'adi cemeteries of this period, which are very extensive, is the burial of dogs and gazelles, in their own graves. At El Omari, near Ma'adi, one grave revealed a skeleton holding a staff, perhaps the primitive regalia of a chieftain.

From early Badarian times the people of the Nile Valley were seized with a startling and hitherto unexampled creative energy. The quality of Badarian pottery was phenomenal and, in many of its characteristics was hardly ever to be bettered by later productions. In the Naqada periods new influences stimulated new forms and fresh media.

Draughtsmanship, ever one of the glories of Egyptian art (though still relatively unappreciated for its high quality) began, at first tentatively, in the drawings of boats, animals, and rudimentary landscapes which decorated the pottery. Textiles, too, were decorated and one example survives which shows the remarkable standards which the Egyptians achieved, even here: it depicts a fisherman casting his nets in the Nile and is a vivid naturalistic work. A loom is shown on a Naqada I dish, demonstrating that technique and everyday equipment were already respected.

Towards the middle of the fourth millennium the Badarian culture in the south gave way to the first of those identified with Naqada, once more generally called the Amratian. Naqada was the location of one of the most important centres of population traditionally associated with the followers of the god Set, who was particularly identified with the indigenous people of the south. The Amratians were almost certainly the direct descendants of the earlier people and their culture really represents a more advanced phase of the Badarian. They quickly developed a relatively high material culture, based on the greatly increased potential that they realized through the improved domestication of animals. Gradually during this period the old reliance on hunting diminished and the prosperity which came from improved farming techniques led to a substantial increase in population. At this period the goat appears first to have been domesticated. Emmer wheat was grown and the dog became a familiar part of the Amratian household. A pottery dish of the period shows a man holding on leashes hounds of the classic type of hunting dog, the prick-eared slender hound, which was to appear in representations of the chase and as a domestic pet throughout Egyptian history. The Naqada I people built reed boats and began the historic river traffic that was to be the means, for as long as Egypt remained a nation, of ensuring the country's unity and political control. They ornamented their pottery with designs of animals and brought the ancient craft of stone-flaking to a high degree of skill; ivory, presumably traded up from the south, from the obscure regions of dark Africa, was employed, as with the Badarians, for making combs, but now also for knife-hilts and vases, while gold took its place amongst the precious substances with which the craftsman began to familiarize himself. Copper too was used for the first time, hammered cold and shaped into pins and harpoon heads.

Naqada I pottery is, like the products of the Badarian potters, very distinctive; one of the most common forms is produced by a red fabric scored with designs and then filled with a white decorative finish (plate 6).

A wide variety of designs was thus produced, showing animals and the hunt, fishermen, boats, and scenes of what appears to be ritual dancing, with the dancers again holding their arms above their heads.

The pottery is well made, its forms often seeming to imitate other materials. Basket shapes obviously reproduce woven products; of the others, a wide-mouthed vessel like an inverted bell is particularly memorable. Naqada I pottery is diverse and varied; already the Egyptian craftsman is delighting in the exploitation of form and the special relationship which, throughout Egyptian history but particularly in the earliest periods, persisted between the craftsman and the materials which he used. To an extent which is unparalleled in other early cultures the Egyptian craftsman appears always to be wrestling, vigorously and joyfully, with the materials he employs, testing them and seeking to establish how far he can assert his mastery over them. This extraordinary identity of the craftsman with his materials, which was to be one of the marks of the Egyptian artist ever afterwards, appears for the first time in the Naqada I period.

Naqada I pottery reveals some evidence of western Asiatic influence at work on what had already become basic Egyptian forms. Painted vases which have been compared (Baumgartel, 1960) with those recovered from this Egyptian horizon are known in Iran, at Bandar-Bushire and at Old Hormuz. There are similarities with some of the designs developed in south-western Asia, probably in Susa, but some authorities would see them only as general design concepts typical of societies at this stage of development (plate 7). The Iranian cultures of this period may themselves be derived partly from Mesopotamia where the late Ubaid, with which Naqada I is approximately contemporary, marked the end of the sequence which proceeds the appearance of the people who can definitely be identified as the Sumerians. Unlike the Badarians, who buried their dead away from their settlements, the Naqada I people kept their dead close by, suggesting that there was at least some cultural differences between the two groups, or else the acceptance by the later group of some practices unknown to their predecessors.

There seems to be a concentration of important Naqada I sites along the river between Abydos and Naqada, the region from which the most creative forces in Egypt seemed always to spring. Naqada itself was a centre of the people who honoured the great and enigmatic god Set as their supreme deity; their capital was called Nubet, literally 'the town of gold'. Like its counterpart Hierakonpolis, 'the city of the Falcon', identified with Horus, and called Nekhen in antiquity, it was a flourishing settlement in Amratian times.

The Naqada I people seem to have had some curious practices for which there was no evidence of continuation in dynastic times. It has been suggested that they were headhunters, from the number of severed skulls found in their graves; however, this could as likely be the evidence of the dismembering or disarticulation of skeletons practised by various early communities. Certainly there is no evidence of cannibalism in Egypt, other than in literary contexts. The character of life in Egypt at this time must have been tribal and communal; from various representations it seems their warriors wore feathers in their hair, rather like their contemporaries in Susa (plate 8). Other than the bow and arrow and the spear, the Naqada I people's most typical weapon was the disc-shaped mace which was eventually superseded by the pear-shaped mace of south-western Asian origins.

The Egyptians hated the darkness and the cold: the sun was a generous and beloved divinity. In the same mood, gaiety and the love of life are always close to the surface of even the humblest Egyptian art. Animals were a source of delight to the people and many early works convey the sense of wonder and happiness which their observation and that of all the natural world induced. The domesticated species, of course, figure largely in the work of Predynastic artists but even the great beasts, lion and hippopotamus for example, could be treated with friendly licence (plate 9). The hippopotamus was a creature to be feared by the river folk and in later times it often personified the malign forces of the underworld. But in Predynastic times a potter could produce a wide-necked vessel around the rim of which marches solemnly a procession of little hippopotami, moulded expertly. But one of them, evidently bored with the regularity of their progress, turns aside, to peer hopefully over the edge of the bowl, a touch of humour which, because it changes the rhythm of the work as a whole, but gives a point to it, is near to genius. To break the regularity of a line of animals by giving one a particular individuality became a favoured device of artists throughout the Old Kingdom.

The hippopotamus never ceased to amuse the Egyptians, as well as to frighten them. They were fascinated by its massive shape and its anthropomorphic character, with the expression of its massive features and crafty little eyes the very caricature of humanity.

One of the finest pieces of carving (plate 10), in alabaster, of the period probably just around the time of the unification or perhaps a short while before it, is of a hippo, massive and four-square but with a curiously cheerful, even complacent, expression on its face. It is of a monumental quality which anticipates later, larger works.

The latest of the southern Predynastic cultures now succeeds the Amratian, in the form of the second Naqada horizon. In fact, the Naqada II or Gerzean phase presents a natural succession from its immediate predecessor, with the important difference that it was responsive to a much more powerful and, it would appear, more sustained alien influence than either of those which it followed. The Naqada II period is one marked by dynamic changes in Egypt, when these foreign influences seem especially to have heightened the native Egyptian genius and to have produced a galvanic series of new advances in the Valley's society. At much the same time, the appearance in southern Iraq of the Sumerians in their role of city-builders initiated the long course of Mesopotamian history by changing the established character of the earlier, modest villages and little settlements into social and political structures considerably more formidable in scale.

The Gerzean or Naqada II phase of Egyptian later prehistory is one which was crucial for the formation of the Pharaonic or dynastic state. Whilst the foreign influences referred to are discernible now more than ever, the essential, peculiarly Egyptian character of the society was emerging very powerfully. The settlements which were apparent in the Naqada I phase now grow considerably, in the case of Naqada itself and Hierakonpolis, which became to all intents and purposes cities. An engaging model of a town wall from this period shows two little watchmen peering apprehensively over the top of it, on the look-out, presumably, for marauders. One of the problems of living in cities was early on found to be their capacity for exciting the envy and the predatory instincts of peoples living outside their walls.

All forms of manufactured goods proliferate: stone vessel carving becomes an industry which was to be one of the glories of Egyptian art for the next half millennium. Pottery takes on a form quite different from that which characterized the first Naqada period; made in an attractive pale brown to pinkish fabric it is decorated with a brilliant repertory of drawings and designs applied in paint before firing. Some of these are abstract, others repeat the repertory of ships, animals, and hunting introduced in Naqada I. The earliest Naqada II pottery (plate 11) seems to be influenced by foreign forms: vessels supplied with filter spouts and triangular lug handles look like imitations of wares produced by the Ubaid potters of Mesopotamia. By this time, c. 3400 BC, Ubaid pottery production had spread widely from its home in southern Mesopotamia; it has been assumed that the Ubaid-style wares (but not Ubaid pottery itself) that inspired the Egyptian potters reached Upper Egypt by land routes through Palestine. However, a trans-Arabian route is equally feasible; a westward route across the northern deserts, from the head of the Gulf westwards, has long existed.

The Naqada II people seem to have been profoundly impressed by boats; whether this implies that they were originally from a region where water transport was even more important than it was in Egypt, is not certain. But an extraordinary number of their productions, painted on pottery and carved in or on slate and schist, represented boats (plates 12a and 12b). Clearly these are often sacred vessels and as such were the ancestors of the sacred barques in which Egyptian divinities, like their Sumerian counterparts, were accustomed to travel. The representations of boats from this period often contain enigmatic passengers, often in threes and frequently represented with feathers in their hair; many are presented with extraordinary elegance and a highly developed sense of form, showing figures leaping almost balletically. They are, demonstrably, works of art of high accomplishment.

The Naqada II preoccupation with boats, which probably included seagoing craft as suggested by the representations on the rock walls of the Wadi Hammamat, the route which links the Nile Valley with the Red Sea, indicates at least the possibility of the Valley people having maintained quite farreaching trade routes and relations with foreigners far distant from them. At this time, too, considerable specialization in the work of the craftsmen becomes apparent, when contact with south-west Asia appears to be most active.

Many of the representations of sailing vessels show high-prowed boats which appear to be much more typical of Mesopotamia and south-western Iran than of Egypt (plates 13a, 13b, and 13c). Whether or not Asiatic influences reached Egypt by land routes there is little reason to doubt that sea routes were an important factor in the contact between the Valley and the distant eastern lands. The reason for this, it has been suggested, may have been the search for gold (Trigger *et al.* 1983).

Precious metals now begin to be used with some frequency in Upper Egypt. Gold and silver were both accessible to the Valley people though the silver that they used particularly was in fact a 'white gold', a natural amalgam of the two metals found in its native state. The prodigality with which gold in particular is used at this time indicates a marked upturn in the taste of the Egyptian clients who commissioned the vessels and artefacts on which it was used and in their ability to recompense the artists and craftsmen who produced them, as well as being able to maintain the mining expeditions necessary to obtain the ore. Mining became one of the principal industries of Egypt in Naqada II times, with expeditions to Nubia for stone (also a source of gold) and to the turquoise mines of Sinai.

The extent of Egypt's foreign trade network at the time is also demonstrated by the frequency with which lapis lazuli beads and other objects are found in Naqada II graves and in those of the early reigns of the succeeding First Dynasty. Lapis of the quality used both in Sumer and in Egypt comes principally from one source in Badakhshan on the borders of

Afghanistan and Pakistan (more recently a possible source near Quetta has been identified, which would have been marginally easier of access, though it would still represent a formidable journey overland). From Badakhshan it was probably transported by land across Iran, through the important exchange centres of Tepe Yahya and Shahr-I-Sokta, and on to the Susian coast or to the cities of Sumer in southern Iraq. From these points it could have been carried further westward either by land, though this must have been a burdensome routeing before the domestication of the camel (which did not take place, probably, until the end of the second millennium, 2,000 years after this period), or by sea. On balance the sea route seems the more likely; the possibility however must not be overlooked that in the fourth millennium and during the period of somewhat more benign climatic conditions than those which prevailed later, the oases of eastern, central, and western Arabia could have permitted a route across the centre of the Arabian peninsula with the sea traffic being reserved for the crossing of the Red Sea. It is possible too that goods were carried up and down the Gulf to the island of Bahrain, from remote times a focus of mercantile exchange, and the trading centres established on the Arabian shore, near the great Hasa oasis in eastern Arabia. From there it is not inconceivable that trains may have set out westwards moving from water source to water source, through the oases and via the desert wells. In the case of the lapis trade, this becomes particularly important in the context of Hierakonpolis and, possibly, for giving a *terminus post quem*, for Mesopotamian influences reaching Egypt.

Whether there was *direct* contact between the Egyptians of the late Predynastic period and the people of south-western Asia of the late Ubaid, Uruk, and Jemdet Nasr periods is not clear. What is still more obscure is the reason that prompted the contact between them, whether it was direct or indirect. A solution which envisages the south-western Asian people (it is hardly right perhaps to call them either Sumerians or Elamites) becoming aware of the Nile Valley as a source of gold is attractive. After all, the Valley was rich in gold, but how the easterners might have acquired the knowledge of it is another matter; the Sumerians did however sustain long exchange routes and themselves travelled at least as far south as Oman, in search of copper. In Oman there are occasional hints of links with early Egypt: these include the introduction in about 3000 BC of sorghum, the cultivation of which originated in the southern Nile Valley, and striking similarities in design elements in rock carvings in Oman and Egypt.

The theory of the Mesopotamians' search for gold having brought them into contact with the Valley people also proposes an influx of specialists and craftsmen into Egypt drawn there by the reports of the riches of the little independent 'courts' which, it is clear, were established in various of the Predynastic centres of population such as Hierakonpolis and Naqada. The names of the little rulers who actually preceded the Kings of Egypt, rather than those of the 'demi-gods' of the national myth, have been found recorded on the rocks of southern Upper Egypt; unfortunately they are largely indecipherable (cf plate 14). It is, however, part of the concept of the search for gold that they controlled the trade and the access to its services. It would have been to their courts that the gold-hungry easterners made their way.

In considering the possibility of contacts between the people of the Nile Valley and the Mesopotamians there is an important distinction to be made between the impact of this post-Neolithic phase, with which we are dealing, on the peoples of the two regions. In Sumer the whole pattern of the society underwent a radical and permanent change as the city came to predominate as the characteristic Sumerian social institution; in Egypt the shift from the Badarian and Naqada I cultures and the impact of the foreign influences, whilst they produced real effects and marked changes, were more important in inspiring a rapid development of the unique Egyptian personality which was to establish itself over the next few hundred years.

This autochthonous personality remained as the essential form of the society for as long as that society lasted. Considered in another way, the Naqada II phase is an intermission (though an intensely creative one) between the late Neolithic stages of the Valley society's development and the coming of the great dynasts who were to unite the Two Lands and thus create the historic Egypt. None the less, it seems inescapable that influences from the east at this time did act as significant stimulus to the course of Egyptian development. The Egyptians, in historic times, were always deeply resentful of any incursions by easterners into their land. They resisted them vigorously, though with varied success. However, in those early years the influence from the east seems to have been more acceptable; at least it does not appear to have been resisted and, in so far as it touched off some of the most important elements in Egypt's development, seems to have been of quite a different quality from the barbarous onslaughts of the largely savage tribes, whom the Egyptians in later times identified as the 'sand dwellers', originating in the north and east.

The apparently common factors which manifest themselves in Egypt and Sumer around this time are too many not to warrant some speculation about the possibility of their common, or at least their related, origin. A comparative examination of the two peoples is appropriate by reason of their close geographical proximity and the fact that they emerged at roughly the same time in their historic form.

The protohistoric peoples of Egypt and Sumer were immensely in advance of the rest of the world at the time when both societies emerged into the historical record. No other people was to approach their level of development for more than a thousand years, and then only tentatively and almost certainly, at least in part, derivatively. Even the most senior civilizations, Iran (except for the south-west) India-Pakistan, and China, which lay outside the immediate confines of that part of the Fertile Crescent which Egypt and Sumer represent, were still in a state of the most primitive social and cultural development, although Iran and parts of the sub-continent had early on shown the promise of achieving a level of development comparable with that of Sumer or Egypt. But they did not do so, or so at least it seems in the light of the available evidence.

A glance at a map will show that Egypt and Sumer are not really far distant from each other, though they are separated by formidable desert barriers which stretch eastwards from the Nile to the western borders of Sumer, with the Red Sea dividing most of Egypt from Arabia. By early historic times there was a caravan route running north-eastwards out of Egypt, skirting Sinai and climbing up the coastline of the eastern Mediterranean, where it linked with other routes from the Sumerian cities which ran across western Iraq into Jordan and Syria. Even in historic times this route was hazardous, the caravans being preyed on equally by ferocious nomads and the guardians of the cities which straddled the routes; then, if those dangers were surmounted, they survived only at the mercy of the desert, which, though it may have been marginally less dreadful than it is today, would have produced problems of the logistics of survival of immense difficulty for such early travellers. As there is no evidence for the domestication of the camel until long after this time, to speak even of 'caravans' in the earliest period is really anachronistic; if pack animals were employed at all they were probably the fractious and argumentative ass and the onegar. The land routes could hardly have been the most efficient or the most generally used until long after the period with which we are concerned.

Yet contact was established very early on between the Predynastic Egyptians and the Mesopotamians, seemingly in sufficient depth for the later people to have left unmistakable material evidence of their influence on Egypt. The evidence, scanty and often unrelated though it is, makes it clear that the influences at work ran from Sumer or Elam to Egypt and not, apparently, in the opposite direction. It seems likely that the contacts began early in the fourth millennium, even possibly in the fifth, and continued

37

until the two civilizations reached the point where each assumed its distinctive historical character at the end of the fourth millennium and the beginning of the third.

In later historic times there was little enough similarity between the peoples of Mesopotamia and those of the Nile Valley, their contacts, which were slight enough, being limited to trade and, much later still, to the exchange of voluminous diplomatic correspondence. However, the extent of unmistakable Mesopotamian/Sumerian influence in late Pre- and proto-dynastic Egypt is that it is by no means impossible that buried under the later accretions and sophistications of Egyptian myth and custom may be some western Asiatic originals, or at least some such influences, if they could be detected with certainty.

Both the Sumerians and the Egyptians believed that life originated in the primeval waters, a remarkable example of myth anticipating science. The birth of Enki, the benign god of the sweet waters in Sumer, was an important event to the 'black-headed folk', as the Sumerians engagingly called themselves. In Egypt, in the Pyramid Texts inscribed on the walls of the royal tombs of the late Old Kingdom, which contain many mythic elements and incidents from the time before history, the King, who was always identified with the greatest of the gods, is said to have been born 'in Nenu (the primeval waters) before the heaven existed'. Another text observes 'the King judges in the Great Flood between the two who are at strife'. The reference may be to the conflict of Horus and Set, the two gods identified with the Predynastic populations of Egypt, for there was no mythical Great Flood in Egypt as there was in Sumer, other than the beneficent surge of the Nile's waters which was waited for so anxiously each year.

That the two societies, Egypt and Sumer, developed along parallel but wholly disparate lines is a matter of history and would be explained by the entirely different environment which was to be found in Mesopotamia and in Egypt. For centuries Egypt was insulated from any pressure of other peoples which the Egyptians themselves could not easily contain; the majestic flow of the god-congested Nile, once its power was harnessed, provided the means for a standard of living which confirmed the Egyptians in their view that they were the favoured children of the gods, living in an ideal world. They had no need to look back wistfully to a near-mythical paradise as the Sumerians did, struggling with their two turbulent rivers and an otherwise barren and unpredictable flood plain. They did, however, retain some dimly realized myths of origins which may contain memories of a common experience for some component of the Nile people, with the peoples of western Asia.

Of all ancient technical achievements, after the discovery of the methods of crop cultivation and herd management, unquestionably the most important was the recognition that the inundations of the great rivers could be harnessed and the land around them made fertile by the controlled distribution of water. So significant was the contribution that irrigation made to the economy of early Sumer (also perhaps of Egypt) that it has been suggested that the whole of its political structure grew out of the need to organize the people to build earthworks, maintain them, and police them to ensure that all citizens acted responsibly, so that the land of one man was not deprived of water by the malice or culpable incompetence of another; however, it has also been suggested that irrigation on a large scale became possible because of centralized control systems existing in the society, rather than those controls themselves being a primary factor in the society's development. In either event the peoples of both Sumer and Egypt rapidly developed the ability to manage their two very different river systems; they both displayed a high degree of hydrological engineering skill, though the problems they encountered each required different solutions. That the control of the rivers' flood was a major preoccupation of the state in Egypt as well as in Sumer is evident from the Archaic representations of the earliest Kings engaged in the ritual cutting of canals.

According to their own traditions, the Egyptians were from the earliest times so expert in the practice of irrigation that Menes-Narmer himself, displaying a positively heroic enthusiasm for hydraulic engineering, is said to have diverted the course of the Nile to found his capital city at Memphis, near the borders of Upper and Lower Egypt. Certainly in historic times major river works were constantly undertaken by the central as well as by the provincial administrations of Egypt.

Clearly, the discovery of many of the techniques of this branch of engineering by a river people could have been as the result of a process of accident, observation, and experiment. But the fact that both the Egyptians and the Sumerians developed irrigation programmes so early and thus made possible the extraordinary advances of their societies, more or less simultaneously, makes the possibility of yet another area of contact and exchange of ideas between them seem more likely than chance or the uncertainties of diffusion.

It is thus particularly at this point, as the Naqada II horizon appears in the latter part of the fourth millennium, that men who were either Sumerians or who knew Sumer well entered the Nile Valley and contributed uniquely to the foundation of the most wholly monolithic political society known until perhaps the present day. In this characteristic, incidentally, Egypt was very different from Sumer, for the political structure which developed in the valley of the Twin Rivers was characterized by a multitude of little city states, constantly struggling for a short-lived hegemony, one above the rest. Never, whilst Sumerian culture flourished, was a lasting empire established over the little cities. It was only when 'Semitic' influences began to predominate at the end of the third millennium, coming in from the deserts which surrounded Sumer, that one interest was able to assert itself over all the others, typified by the creation of the empire of Sargon the Great. It will, of course, be recognized that 'Semitic' in this context, if it is to have any meaning at all, conveys only a linguistic distinction.

Among the material wealth of the Egyptians in this late Predynastic period, copper is now found in markedly greater amounts than before; it is also of much more sophisticated manufacture than had previously been known. Toilet sets, which were thought to be of Mesopotamian provenance, are found and the most ancient metal axe so far known in Egypt, whose alloy suggests that it is made from Asiatic copper, has been recovered from a site of this period (Baumgartel, 1970a).

The discovery of the use of metal was one of man's more helpful early technological advances. It appears first to have been accomplished, both in Egypt and Sumer, in this period between the end of the Neolithic and the emergence of the societies in their historic form: as a result, this period used to be known as the 'Chalcolithic', a term now largely abandoned despite its usefulness in denoting a society in which both metal and stone artefacts are made. It is difficult to exaggerate the importance of the discovery of copper to the development of either society, but this is especially true of Egypt. The Pyramids, though they are hundreds of years later than this period, could not have been erected without the copper tools which shaped the great stone blocks from which they are built. The marvellous vases and statuary of the earliest dynasties were also fashioned with copper bits and drills.

There would appear to be three options only for the route by which western Asiatic influences may have penetrated the Nile Valley at this time: by land across the Arabian peninsula, by a northern route across the Jordanian–Syrian deserts and then down through Palestine, or by sea. There is little doubt that the second route was used; the question at issue is whether either of the other two was and whether it was the means by which southern Mesopotamian and Elamite influences specifically entered Egypt.

About 130 miles south of the extreme tip of the Sinai peninsula, on the western shore of the Red Sea, lies the Egyptian port of Qesir. It is backed by the harsh, often snow-capped Red Sea mountains, the home of eagles, ibex, and gazelle, which yield only a bare existence to their nomadic inhabitants. The mountains are cut with *wadis*, ancient dried-up water courses, the paths of rivers which have long since ceased to flow but which still, when the early summer comes, rush with water from the snow-laden heights. It is a strange and, even for Egypt, a paradoxical region, in a land crackling with paradox.

One of the largest of these dead river beds is the Wadi Hammamat which runs through the mountains due west of Qesir. Throughout Egypt's history the wadi was a great trading route with the caravans moving to and from the sea coast and the Nile Valley cities, strung out along the river which here makes an enormous bend and runs, first eastwards and then turns back westwards, ultimately to resume its flow to the Mediterranean.

The Romans and their Byzantine successors exploited this region considerably for its rich deposits of porphyry, the superb red and purple stone which produced so many splendid columns in these later empires. From its use in the royal birth chambers of Byzantium, the expression 'to be born in the purple' arose. The mountains are rich in many prized stones including schist, which from the earliest times was used for making the cosmetic palettes which were a feature of early Egyptian ways of life and death. Gold is also found here, that metal which the Egyptians used with such abundance and delight.

Though pottery-making was always one of the subtlest of Egyptian crafts, stone was the medium with which the craftsman felt most assured and in which his genius in the early centuries was best demonstrated (plate 15). Egypt is rich in stone of all colours and compositions, ranging from soft, almost plastic stones like the chlorites, to the hardest diorites and granites. All of these were used in Predynastic times but the really finest stone vessels appear in the First Dynasty: they are perhaps the outstanding products of Egyptian craftsmanship; for technical skill and sheer mastery of form their work in stone is unparalleled. Before this point was reached, however, there was a long tradition of working in stone, which had its roots in Upper Egypt.

For the artist the immutable character of the Egyptian countryside and the security of Egyptian society were profoundly important. He was quite capable of experiment and innovation and he, or his masters, would calmly discard whatever they decided did not fit into the canon of Egyptian taste and convention. The order of the universe was demonstrated by the unchanging shape of a vase or of a copper weapon, once it had been accepted into that canon. The arts were practised, so far as we know, by families which, generation after generation, could perfect their techniques to a degree incomprehensible to modern man. We should not wonder at the superlative quality of the workmanship of, say, an Egyptian potter or stone-vase cutter for the product by which we judge his skill today is the consequence of many decades, sometimes perhaps even of centuries, of inherited skills and practice.

From the earliest times the Egyptian artist demonstrated a characteristic which was wholly his, though it is shared by some other African craftsmen, even those working today. This was the ability to produce works with the immediacy and impact of a sketch, in plastic materials, or even in those less tractable. A little figure lying in the bottom of a boat, who conveys a poignant sense of isolation, even of desolation, is one of these (plate 16); so is a small crouched figure, its head resting on its knees (plate 17). Some Old Kingdom reliefs, though they are carved in stone, have this same quality of instant achievement, which is, in its own way, mildly uncanny.

Related to these works with the capacity for instant communication is another Predynastic figurine, in this case a small bearded, gnome-like creature, its arms drawn back in the manner of some of the representations of captives (plate 44). The figure comes, like so many other remarkable things, from Hierakonpolis and is fabricated in ivory. It has a disturbing suggestion of disintegration about it.

The qualities and skills which the Egyptians themselves admired in their craftsmen and artists are set out in a funerary inscription which, though it comes from a much later period, is probably as appropriate to the early practitioner of the arts as to his successors. The craftsman himself speaks: 'The Chief Craftsman, Painter and Sculptor: I know how to express the movement of a figure, the carriage of a woman, the pose of a single instant, the cowering of an isolated captive or how one eye looks at another.' Here the emphasis is on technique, on what may be learned, by skills which may be acquired by practice. The artist is confident of his abilities, working in the most secure and enduring of traditions.

From Old Kingdom times, when the owners of the great tombs took pleasure in surrounding themselves with scenes which recalled the crafts and skills of the workers on their estates, we know of the techniques which were adopted in the making of stone vessels. A pair of swinging weights, the management of which must have demanded considerable skill, provided the power source for the cutting of stone vessels. All vases made in this way show signs of drilling, unless the regular rings left by the drills have been pared away. What is difficult to understand however, is how, for instance, the craftsmen were able to exert regular pressure *under* the shoulders of a narrow-mouthed bowl or how they were able to cut away, with perfect regularity, the interior of a bowl made from a friable substance such as schist. The point has been made before that the walls of many Egyptian vessels are so fine and so regular that no deviation from a perfect circle can be detected in their shape, nor is any variation in the often exceptional thinness of the vessel's walls to be found (plate 19).

Egyptian stone vessels of the early periods come in an immense variety of shapes and sizes, ranging from tiny cosmetic jars to great pots for the preservation of oil, wine, or grain. The best are exquisitely proportioned and some of the most sumptuous, presumably those destined for royal use or for presentation to the King or the gods, are decorated with gold; this custom is particularly associated with the late Predynastic period and the First Dynasty (colour plate XII), though King Khasekhemui in the Second Dynasty also had vessels mounted with gold fittings. The taste involved in selecting the embellishment of these vessels may be thought to have become a trifle precious, however, in the Second Dynasty. The gold ornamentation imitates, it is thought, the cloth that might have been placed over the vessel's mouth and the strings that tied it on.

Sometimes the early masons and workers in stone display an exuberance quite un-Egyptian in the marrying of one stone with another, often with effects which are not altogether fortunate. An example of this practice is a stone cup or goblet from Queen Her-Neith's Saqqara tomb. Its body is made from a dark and elegant schist, mounted on a foot made of a particularly vibrant pink stone. The form of the goblet was to survive until later in the dynasty although such later examples seem generally to have been made sometimes in copper, but when stone is used, schist for example, or a fine brecciated limestone, the form looks altogether happier (cf. plate 20a).

The Egyptian craftsman was as much at home in working with living rock faces as he was with stone. The rock art of the ancient Near East is certainly the most extensive and probably the most informative documentary source surviving of the life of the people of the hunting bands in their transition from the ancient to a more settled way of life, eventually even to a style of urban living. Rock drawings reveal much about hunting, ritual, the dance, costume, and, in general terms, the way of life of the people who produced them and the fauna with which they shared their lives.

The heartland of the ancient world's rock-carving industry is the Arabian peninsula. Virtually no suitable rock surface in western, southern, and south-eastern Arabia is left unexploited; in the north the art is not so prolific but it is still present in large quantities. In eastern Arabia, with very few exceptions, it is non-existent. In Egypt the densest distribution of rock drawings is in the south, reaching down into Nubia. The great eastern desert wadi system, centred on the Wadi Hammamat and its tributaries, is exceptionally richly furnished with elaborate and often highly skilful representations of men, animals, boats, and formal inscriptions from at least

43

the early third millennium (perhaps earlier still) down to Roman and later times. It is in the Wadi Hammamat region that the drawings which supposedly mark the progress of shipborne travellers from Elam or Sumer are to be found.

Drawings (of course they are more strictly-speaking engravings) are generally incised or pecked onto the relatively smooth and often friable surface of the rocks which border the desert tracks, or on the shaded overhangs of outcrops which have always provided shelter during the fiercest heat of the day. Low hills are sometimes favoured; often a remote chasm or defile will be selected as the site of an outpouring of creative endeavour, in such cases giving the area the character of a sanctuary or sacred place.

The work ranges from the simple doodlings of untalented individuals, through erotic representations of occasionally quite inventive versatility, to productions of a high, almost startling artistic quality. The quite exceptional quantity of drawings in Arabia in particular, executed over many millennia, suggests a significant population of artists dedicated to the exercise of their art; they are not to be dismissed as merely the products of desert ennui, a filling in of the empty hours of a drowsy, sun-drenched afternoon.

A particularly important concentration of rock art is to be found in western Arabia. It is very widespread; it is also, some of it, extremely early, with the representations of large, standing warriors, for example, having been dated to the fourth millennium BC.

The Sultanate of Oman, in the extreme south-east of the peninsula, also has a very rich repertory of rock art. Some of this is engraved high up on towering wadi cliffs; some of the representations show connections with the art of Sumer and, possibly, with Elam in the third millennium. Omani rock drawings are produced with exceptional vigour; a repeated theme is that of a great feline (perhaps a reference to the times when mountain lion was relatively common in these parts) devouring a small, defenceless man. It is a scene which is also to be found in early Egypt, sometimes in a different medium, as it is in Arabia, where one of the chlorite carvings from the island of Tarut, which will be further considered, seems to show the same theme.

Many of the themes found repeatedly in the work of Egyptian rock artists are present in that of other of their contemporaries in Oman, south-western, and western Arabia and even in Iran, though in the last case such correspondences tend to be found in glyptic art and in the decoration of pottery rather than in rock drawings. These common themes include the warrior with a feathered headdress, the buckler with handles projecting from its ends, the lyre, the bucranium (very widespread, in all forms), and a dagger with a lunate pommel, which is also found in Egypt during the First Dynasty.

The Wadi Hammamat forms a natural corridor through the eastern desert which linked the river and the sea, with little more than a hundred miles between them. It is significant that all the principal archaeological evidence which indicates contact with Mesopotamia and western Asia is found in the Predynastic and Archaic sites which are concentrated along this stretch of the Nile. From Hierakonpolis, the capital of the Falcon's domains, in the south, to El Badari in the north, is a distance of only about 130 miles. On many artefacts of the late Predynastic period boats of an apparently Mesopotamian type with notably high prows and sterns have been recognized. Clearly the boat was an important and even perhaps a sacred object to the people who inscribed so many representations of it on the walls of the wadi. If, as seems likely, some travellers at least made the long haul from the Arabian Gulf, far away to the east, to Egypt they may well have thought the fact worth recording, the more so if the boat itself was invested with some sort of sacred character. Several of the representations show a large black ship with a huge sail, which seems to have been especially significant to those who recorded it (plate 21).

It thus seems possible that this sea contact existed between two peoples from a very early period; it seems most likely that the route was east–west, following the course of the sun. From the headlands in the north, where the lagoons, canals, and rivers of what is now southern Iraq made movement by boat the natural means of transport for the early settlers in southern Mesopotamia, the Sumerians set out in search of trade. Hugging the western (Arabian) coast they would have landed at the several islands which were the most important components of the economy of the ancient Arabian Gulf. From these islands, Failaka, Bahrain, Tarut, and, further south, Umm an-Nar, they would have been able to take on water and provisions; the prevailing winds would have sped them on their journey. Then for six months of the year the voyage westwards from the mouth of the Gulf, beyond the Straits of Hormuz, would have been facilitated by currents which would have driven sailing craft rapidly along the south Arabian coast.

It is important, in the context of possible contacts with Egypt by the Sumerians and Elamites, to remember that the Gulf culture, even in its earliest manifestation, was a mercantile, seagoing culture, its people avid for trade. It is entirely possible that their enthusiasm for profit took them all the way across (or around) Arabia to the Valley. It may be argued that so substantial a voyage, around the Arabian peninsula, in extent amounting to some 4,000 nautical miles, would have been far beyond the capacity or the confidence of early seamen. However, man has not changed so much since the end of the Neolithic period that the people of that time would not have found it as impossible to resist the challenge of pushing on beyond each day's horizon as their successors would today. It is very clear, in any case, that from well back into the fourth millennium – perhaps in earlier times still – the peoples of Mesopotamia and Iran maintained extensive and farreaching networks of trade, based on barter and exchange.

The enthusiasm for boats was held by Sumerians and Egyptians alike, not only because they were the most convenient means of transport in their river-based societies, but because they were invested with a mystical significance which transcended their purely functional role. This view both peoples shared, a sharing which is something of a coincidence.

The presence of a boat model in a grave at Eridu, dating from early Sumerian times (in fact, late Ubaid, contemporary with Naqada I) is the first evidence for the invention of sailing boats capable of being launched on the waters of the Arabian Gulf, as well as on Sumer's rivers and lagoons. It is probable that the invention of sailing craft occurred on Sumerian waters; the oldest model of a boat known is from a grave in Uruk. The Egyptians were also buried with boats, which range in size from the small pottery examples found in Predynastic graves to gigantic rivercraft, the evidence of which has been found, for example, in the burial complexes of the Archaic Kings as well as in the pyramids of Khnum-Khufu (Cheops) in the Fourth Dynasty, and Senwosret in the Twelfth. The oldest Egyptian representation of a boat, however, is probably very much earlier, from Naqada I times.

Boats were buried with the Kings of the First Dynasty. A special grave, beside the royal tomb, was prepared for the boat. In later Old Kingdom Egypt the dead King is promised a place of honour in the barge of Re, where he may assist in the Sun God's daily voyage across the heavens. In Mesopotamia, too, sailing seems to have been one of the pastimes of the divinities. The Sumerian gods used boats to visit each other, sailing along the canals which linked the cities (plate 22). Thus Enki visited Inanna, sailing in his boat *The Ibex of the Absu* along the canals; in this progress he is echoed by the great Egyptian god Ptah who visited the goddess Hathor by boat. Enki and Ptah share a number of characteristics, apart from their mutual enthusiasm for sailing.

Ships of the type portrayed on the Wadi Hammamat walls, on countless pots, and other objects, are to be found in many early Mesopotamian and Elamite or Susian media. They are represented widely for example on late fourth/early third millennium cylinder seals found in large numbers on western Asiatic sites, and whose use persisted throughout most of the third millennium. They are represented, too, on the round stamp seals of the Gulf, which are dated to the end of the third millennium and the beginning of the second.

The extraordinary number of representations of boats, in drawings, engravings on rocks, in two- and three-dimensional models, would suggest a positive armada of ships or else a remarkable degree of marine activity. There can be little doubt that boats and their occupants also had a ritual significance, though what that significance might have been is obscure. Many of the most compelling representations show three figures in boats; this constant repetition of the boat with three occupants is too frequent not to be especially significant (plates 23a and 23b). A sizeable vessel with a striped awning amidships is shown with its three occupants distributed one in the stern and two sitting in the powerfully curved prow. A black basalt amulet shows three schematically depicted passengers, seated side by side, in a vessel which has animal heads fore and aft.

In the Egyptian Museum, Cairo, is a decorated knife hilt which shows three figures once again, with an ideogram representing water denoting that they, too, are on board ship. The three hold hands (another common device) and one holds up a sort of stylized weapon or fan. A group of textile fragments, possibly from a shroud, depict a scene painted with exceptional vigour of a high-prowed ship being driven through the waters by its oarsmen.

The theme of 'three standing figures' is one of considerable power in Archaic times (plate 103). It achieves three-dimensional form in three curious figures, made in a dense and heavy fired clay, which look like nothing so much as embryos. One is male, aggressively so, one female; the third is sexually indeterminate. The male figure has been dated by the thermoluminescence process to 3200 BC and the group, which is echoed by a single figure in the Kestner Museum in Hanover and another in the Metropolitan Museum in New York, has been described as 'evidence of a hitherto unknown predynastic subculture' (Munro, 1972). The repetition of the group of three figures in Predynastic Egypt, in Sumer of the same period, in early Elam, and from later times in the Gulf, is one of the more intriguing phenomena in ancient iconography, and the recurrence of motifs which endure in their significance and associations is remarkable.

This phenomenon of the three figures in association, either as a family – father, mother, son – or a trinity or triad, is immensely ancient. Jung recognized 'the Divine Triad' as one of the most ancient of the archetypes; in Egypt it is particularly to be found in the late Predynastic period and in the First Dynasty. It did not, however, rival the dual figure which, for quite different reasons, is among the most persistent of Egyptian forms, first appearing vigorously in the early periods, and then throughout Egypt's lifetime.

An example of the triad, which seems to recall much earlier Egyptian originals (which may, of course, themselves be drawn from western Asiatic precedents), is a stamp seal from Failaka which shows three figures standing in a boat with the smallest (to the right) apparently leaping out of it, grasping some sort of object (plate 104). This figure seems to be nude, whilst the other, larger standing figures, one of which holds a bow, appear to be wearing long robes. However, this seal cannot be dated later than the early second millennium, whereas the Egyptian example, with which it has notable similarities, is taken to be at least a thousand years older.

Human figures were not the only ones to be shown in boats. It will be recalled that the strains of goats and sheep which were domesticated by the earliest settlers in the Nile Valley are thought to be of western Asiatic origin. The implications of this suggestion are formidable: that a people with sufficient knowledge of the principles of selection and breeding to import particular strains of animals from a foreign region into the Valley were already present in Egypt or had access to the new societies establishing themselves there. It may not be without significance that on some Pre-dynastic pots goats and sheep are shown standing in boats (plate 24), as though this was a deliberate attempt to preserve the memory of their journey, from wherever they came, to the Valley. Again, it is possible that these representations may have some cultic or ritual significance.

The domestication of sheep and goats in Naqada II society is well attested. The strain of sheep generally to be found in Egypt at this time is a screw-horned, hairy variety which had largely died out by Middle Kingdom times (plates 26a and 26b). The strain is also known in early Mesopotamia and it seems likely that it was introduced from there to Egypt. The goats which had been domesticated at least since Naqada I times are, on the evidence of their horns, similar to strains which were to be found in contemporary Palestine.

In social and political customs the same theme of similarity and difference will be found in the societies developed by these two contemporary peoples. There is a profound difference between the Egyptian and the Sumerian concepts of the Kingship, for example; one is divine, the other the delegate of the divine, for early Sumerian kings or 'great men' as they were more modestly called, were always, theoretically at least, stewards of a divine master. Each Sumerian city, its temples, fields, even the people themselves, were the property of the god to whom the city belonged.

The divine Kingship, that most typically Egyptian of all philosophical and political concepts, is properly identified with the rulers of the First

Dynasty and here, undoubtedly, African influences played a part in creating the concept of the god incarnate in the earthly ruler. It is to Africa that one must look for the most abiding characteristics of the Egyptian Kingship, which made it the unique institution that it was to become.

There is little similarity, equally, between the way the Egyptians and the Sumerians visualized and personified their gods. Sumerian divinities were essentially human in appearance, and their attributes and their behaviour were merely the characteristics of humankind written large. The Egyptian gods were a great deal more complex and variegated.

It is perplexing that so sophisticated a people as the Egyptians should have chosen to personify some of their greatest gods by what may seem to be some rather unlikely animal forms: the great Amon represented as a goose is a case in point. The symbolism is lost on us but to the Egyptians the divine knew no limitations of immanence.

It appears that the earliest divinities were abstractions, represented by objects which had acquired the character of special sanctity. The most ancient sign for 'god', *ntr* is abstract; it is thought that it represents 'a staff bound with cloth' (plate 27). It is a fetish, an object which, for whatever reason, is perceived to have acquired a particular and numinous character. Fetishes of this sort were evidently adopted as the totems or standards of some of the early clans into which the Predynastic people seem to have divided themselves. The standards can be seen being borne before the earliest Kings on the schist palettes and ceremonial maceheads of the late Predynastic period.

After the emergence of the fetishes, the next phase of Egyptian god-making turned to invest certain animal forms with the prerogatives of divinity. The slate palettes which are amongst the earliest graphic representations to survive provide much of the evidence of this practice: scorpions, lions, bulls, the ubiquitous falcon, the ibex, gazelle, hounds are all shown as personifications of the gods, assisting the King in putting down his enemies or in conducting the rituals of the state. Men needed the power of animals; even the early Kings, in the later Predynastic period and the First Dynasty, called themselves by animal names: Scorpion, Catfish, Fighting Hawk, Serpent are four of the best known. An early palette, now in the collection of the Manchester Museum, shows a man wearing an ostrich mask, evidently hunting the birds which are shown in line at the head of the palette. The artist has contrived, with remarkable skill, to suggest considerable menace in the representation of the birds whose heads actually look like masks themselves.

The last category of divine beings was that which revealed the gods in human form. Many of these are known from the First Dynasty; Re, Ptah,

Atum, Isis, Neith, and, much later, Osiris, are shown as human, albeit with divine attributes.

In later times, though the custom may reach back to the earliest days, the gods took shapes in which human figures were shown surmounted by animal heads, thus neatly conflating two of the categories of divinity. The priests and other officiants in the temple ceremonies wore masks under which they impersonated the gods attendant upon the King.

The anthropomorphic gods were represented as the predecessors of the King on the throne of Egypt. These were Ptah, Re, Shu, Geb, Osiris, Set, and Horus. Then came Thoth and Maat; these concluded the divine dynasties, the reigns of whose Kings were of astronomical length. After the gods came the demi-gods, the 'Spirits of the Dead' (as they were somewhat mysteriously called) who were the 'Followers of Horus'. These seem to have been the chiefs or Kings who were the immediate predecessors of the First Dynasty. The dynasties of historic time then began and the number of gods proliferated as those who were identified with particular districts gradually assumed more and more significance. Thus Min, represented as an ithyphallic, one-armed man, was the patron of that region of the Wadi Hammamat through which Mesopotamian influences supposedly entered Egypt, and there is some evidence that his worship was associated with a fish cult, though this was not sustained. In most of Egypt, by later times, the fish had become as abhorrent to the dynastic Egyptians as had the pig. However, there were important fish cults in Egypt and in Sumer in very early times, notably at Eridu where they were associated with that city's patron, the god Enki. There is evidence of fish cults in the First Dynasty in Egypt and the fish, particularly the Nile perch, was frequently represented in the art of the period. Many palettes were carved in the form of fish; they are also carved on stone and made in pottery. In later times fish were barely ever represented but a significant number of fish models were found in the tomb at Abydos which is thought to be the burial place of Narmer traditionally identified as the unifier of the Two Kingdoms.

Egyptian legend always retained what was represented as a conflict between south and north, Upper and Lower Egypt, before the union. In later times, this became codified into a cycle of myth in which what may have been the battles in the Valley are echoed by a series of clashes in a celestial dimension between Horus, later the house god of the Kings, and Set, the god of Ombos, a cult centre near the Nile outlet of the Wadi Hammamat. In Ptolemaic and Roman times, more than 3,000 years after the time of the unification, the dispute between the gods was still raging but by this time Set had become the personification of evil and his worship sometimes involved the deliberate invocation of the powers of darkness.

This was not so in the earliest times, when Set was a storm divinity and for southern Egypt at least one of the most powerful of the gods, perhaps the greatest of all. He was, incidentally, the patron divinity of the house to which Rameses the Great belonged, whose father, Seti I, was named for the god. Evidently the rulers of the Nineteenth Dynasty did not associate Set with evil and the powers of darkness.

The conflict between the gods was represented as the mirror image of the struggle for the rule of Egypt. In the earliest form of the legends, the elaborate series of spells and incantations carved on the interior walls of the pyramids of some of the Sixth Dynasty Kings which from internal evidence are known to descend from a much earlier tradition, Egypt is divided, north and south, into 'the portion of Horus' and 'the portion of Set'. Later, Horus was represented as having conquered Set, becoming supreme over both lands. There is something of a paradox here as historically it seems to have been the south that conquered the north or, at least, that the southern system of government prevailed over both parts of the Kingdom. But the high and evidently ancient prestige of the falcon cult at Hierakonpolis ('Hawk City') must be borne in mind; there was thus another, still older Horus and elements of the legends and cults of both gods became conflated into the later historic *persona* which Horus assumed. It has repeatedly been suggested that before the unification, which came about on the initiative of southern princes, the north had overcome the south. There is however no evidence for this and indeed it is very doubtful; the paradox of the elder and the younger Horus remains.

It has been proposed, from the days of the earliest chroniclers of Egypt, that Horus, the young falcon god, was in fact an alien and that he originated in Arabia. This alien nature of the falcon is suggested in the Edfu inscriptions which are thought to descend from very ancient originals. It has also been suggested that his name means 'the distant one', recalling perhaps his origins far away from the Valley. It is not unlikely that the falcon, for long one of the most valuable assistants of the Arabians in hunting and the chase, was worshipped by them, though there is not the slightest evidence of such a cult at present. Moreover, virtually nothing is as yet known of the religious cults of Arabia in Neolithic and post-Neolithic times; the uncovering of Arabia's distant past is only now beginning and is likely to cast light on all manner of hitherto obscure issues.

One of the odd discrepancies about the cult of Horus is that the Egyptians do not seem to have employed the hawk as a hunting bird. This is its role *par excellence* in Arabia and it is surprising that neither Horus nor any of the other hawk and falcon gods of Egypt is ever represented as a hunter. It seems unlikely that they had any particular reservation about so representing him: after all the hound, which is particularly identified with the god Set, is often shown as the companion of man at the chase.

It may be, of course, that in the late fourth millennium, when it may be assumed that Horus came into Egypt (if indeed he did) the practice of hunting with hawks was not yet prevalent in Arabia. It is not clear when this custom originated; it probably required a greater degree of social organization and the presence of princes in Arabia before it was generally adopted or developed by the people of the desert.

The 'Hunters' palette', a Predynastic artefact of great importance, has recently been recognized as containing many elements which identify the hunters depicted as west Arabians. Clothing, hairstyles, and weapons are virtually identical with those shown on rock carvings in western Arabia (see Chapter 5). It is not impossible that Horus was the totem of these people.

Other of the great gods were sometimes thought of by the Egyptians themselves as originating outside Egypt. Some were Libyan; several came from Syria and the north, particularly in the later periods. Diodorus reports a tradition, admittedly a very late one, that Osiris and Isis, the immortal brother and sister of later Egyptian myth, were Arabian in origin.

The equivocal nature of Set, the aboriginal and wholly Egyptian god of the southern people, was signalled by the story of the murder of his brother, Osiris, who was eventually to become one of the most powerful of all the gods. But Osiris did not properly emerge into significance until the latter part of the Old Kingdom period. Then he was identified with an Upper Egyptian god of the dead, Khentiamentiu, and with Wepwawet, a god of graveyards, in whose name must surely be heard the lonely barking of a dog in the desert night. Khentiamentiu had an ancient temple at Abydos, whilst Wepwawet was called the 'opener of the ways'; he was the Egyptian *psychopompos*. He was one of the protagonists of the early dynasts in his role of 'guide of the gods': he was portrayed, like Khentiamentiu, as a dog *couchant*. In later times, he became synthesized with the better known Anubis (Anpu, in Egyptian), the dog god who guided the dead to judgement in Osiris' deathly kingdom of the Duat, and who, with ears pricked, for 3,000 years guarded the mummy of Tutankhamun in his forgotten, gold-heaped tomb in the Valley of the Kings in Thebes.

It is a nice speculation, incidentally, whether Anubis and the pack of other canine gods actually was either a jackal or a wolf, as is almost invariably asserted. On many tomb reliefs, on ostraca, painted pottery, and other relics of the Egyptians' endless passion for depicting the world around them, from the very earliest times onwards there appears a handsome, slender hunting dog, with prick-ears, a long muzzle, and a tail which curls round over its back (see p. 235). Often it is shown sitting beneath its owner's chair, alert and watchful or at the chase; sometimes, like its master, it is named. This elegant hound has, it may be suggested, a claim not only to be recognized as the superb Anubis but also as the more equivocal animal of Set. The Anubis dog was in all probability a cross between the gentle eyed wandering desert dogs and the small Egyptian jackals. The Egyptians represented the jackal quite distinctively, emphasizing its thick bushy tail and rounded ears.

The animal by which Set was personified is one of the most enigmatic in the entire catalogue of the gods of Egypt. Various authorities have seen in it a mythical animal, a composite creature, an okapi, a wolf, a jackal, an ant-eater, an ass, or a dog (see also Appendix). It appears on the archaic 'Standards' which were the badges of the ancient tribal confederations and the districts into which Egypt was divided (see Appendix, plates A3a and A3b).

The culmination of the Set animal's career, particularly in the royal iconography, was when it was incorporated into the badge of King Peribsen of the Second Dynasty and stood, crowned with the crown of Upper Egypt, having replaced the otherwise triumphant falcon. Then, a little later, both Set and Horus appear together, reconciled on the badge of the last King of the Second Dynasty, Khasekhemui.

Set himself is an enigmatic figure, a divinity who represents the chaotic and anarchic principles in nature but who also stood for the projection of the people of the south, the personification of the strain from which the initiatives for the union of Egypt proceeded. Set is one of the profound archetypal figures, who haunts all societies, in all times. He is ambivalent and unpredictable; his actions are often masked, obscure, and misleading. He is the Trickster, the figure who teaches men that they must never depend upon appearances but must look for the reality behind appearance. He is the storm, which brings relief in desert lands: but he is also the desert. He is the swift hound, the faithful companion of the chase but also a malevolent, ambiguous creature compounded of mythical as well as real elements. He is a figure of infinite complexity, who changes his shape at will, glimpsed for a moment and then gone.

Osiris, another of the great gods and a somewhat late arrival in the pantheon, is invariably shown in human form, sorrowful of face (which is often painted green) and wrapped in the cerements of a mummy. He was the most beloved of all the gods and was thought of as kingly and just divinity, merciful and comforting, who would reward the justified after death. The legend of his dismemberment by Set is often cited as evidence of his original role as a fertility king who was sacrificed and the various parts of his body ploughed into the ground to ensure its fruitfulness. It is often suggested that this disconcerting African custom was once the fate of Kings of Egypt in Predynastic times but the legends of Osiris' dismemberment, given his late appearance in Egypt, can hardly be taken as evidence of this practice in Egypt, in the absence of any more substantial testimony.

Some authorities have proposed that Osiris originated in western Asia and entered Egypt from the same Red Sea entry as those who brought the Mesopotamian and Elamite influences into Egypt, as suggested by the evidence of the high-prowed ships, until he reached his eventual cult centre, at Abydos in southern middle Egypt. Abydos was one of the most sacred areas in the Two Lands and is the burial place of the earliest of the Kings. If the theory of his western Asiatic origins is at all feasible then Osiris might be identified with that god who was eventually best known as Dummuzi (or, in the Semitic form, Tammuz), the Sumerian divinity who brought the arts of husbandry and agriculture to the black-headed folk and then was killed and descended to the underworld. The parallels between the two gods include Isis searching for her husband Osiris after his murder, like the goddess Innana who descended to the Sumerian underworld seeking the dead Dummuzi. It has also been suggested that Osiris is to be identified with another western Asiatic divinity, Asar, and that his worship is yet more evidence of western Asiatic penetration into Egypt. However, chronology would appear to be against this suggestion, for Osiris' comparatively late arrival into Egypt is long after the stream of western Asiatic influences seems to have dried up.

But it is not perhaps utterly fanciful to suggest that Osiris, swathed in his mummy cloths, came shuffling up the Wadi Hammamat in the wake of his original believers. There is a striking resemblance, which, if it is nothing else, is remarkably suggestive, between representations of Osiris and a number of male pottery figures from Eridu, the city sacred to the Sumerian water divinity, Enki. The Eridu figures come from late Ubaid times; an example is of a menacing, reptilian creature, matched by an equally sinister female figure, holding a child, like some travesty Madonna. The male is high-crowned, holding a sceptre, and with his arms crossed on his breast: in the most familiar representation of Osiris he is always depicted wearing the white crown of the Archaic Upper Egyptian Kings, with the Crook and the Flail crossed on *his* breast, regalia which he inherited from a much earlier, northern god. Indeed, the Eridu figure is indistinguishable in silhouette from the Egyptian god (plate 29).

Occasionally the Egyptians produced figurines with reptilian features. One of these, of Naqada I date, combines a menacing, beaked head (or, perhaps, a mask) and raised hands, like the dancers who dominate so much of the art of the period.

Horus was Osiris' son, incarnate eternally in the living King just as the dead King was identified with Osiris; one of the oldest royal titles names the King 'the Horus'. Horus fought with Set to avenge his father's death, to rule over Egypt in his place, and to carry on his work of bringing the benefits of civilization to the people. A late myth survives which purports to descend from Archaic times; it relates how Horus drove back foreign invaders whence they came, beyond the Red Sea into Asia.

There is a parallel in Sumerian lands to the Egyptian legend of the spirits attendant upon a divine innovator in the form of the Babylonian Oannes' legend, written down by the priest Berossus writing in Babylon in the third century BC, at much the same time that his Egyptian colleague Manetho was writing his history. He relates that a strange creature, half man, half fish, came swimming up the Arabian Gulf, attended by other monsters, and taught the arts of civilization to the people who were to be the Sumerians. The monsters who attended him were the *apkallu*.

In Sumerian legend Enki had his beginnings in the ocean in which he was born; it has been suggested that his cult originated in the Arabian Gulf in the island of Bahrain, which in ancient times was called Dilmun. Whilst the coincidence would certainly not warrant too elaborate a hypothesis being built upon it, the Egyptians, too, had a version of their creation myths in which the self-begotten Atum, the elder god of the theology evolved by the sun priests of Heliopolis, emerges from the waters of chaos on the 'primeval island'. It may be thought surprising, incidentally, that a river people like the Egyptians should have thought of an island playing so important a part in creation, though the customary explanation, that they were thinking of the hillocks which first appear when the waters of the Nile's inundation begin to withdraw, is plausible. The concept of the magical island was a powerful one for the Egyptians; the primeval island was also often thought of as a mountain or hill rising out of the waters. The pyramid was also a development of a similar concept and symbolized both the mountain of creation and the sunlight, streaming down from heaven. The idea behind the Mesopotamian ziggurat is similar in that it, too, is the sacred mountain, but there is otherwise no apparent connection between them although the stepped pyramids, like the great one built for King Djoser at Saqqara, inevitably recall something of the Sumerians' towering terraced structures. The ziggurat, however, did not really develop its full significance in Sumer until long after the age of the pyramids in Egypt; although temples on platforms were known in the fourth millennium, the earliest stepped structure dates from late in the third. None the less, the concept of the Holy Mountain as the place of origins was present in Sumerian religious belief from early times.

The Egyptians preserved the idea of the 'divine emerging island' in a number of their most sacred sites in addition to Atum's island at Heliopolis. Memphis is one such, whilst Thebes, the capital of Egypt in later times was known as 'the island emerging in Nun [the waters of chaos] which first came into being when all other places were still in obscurity'; Hermonthis and Hermopolis were also identified with 'the divine emerging primeval island'. The architecture of the temples involved a similarity of practice to that of the Sumerians who raised their shrines high above the city on terraced structures, for the Egyptian architects designed their temple floors gradually to rise higher and higher, although almost imperceptibly, until the holiest sanctuary was reached.

Enki, Atum, and Osiris each have the characteristics of a very early order of gods, those associated with water. In Enki's case a multitude of poems and hymns of praise to him celebrate his watery proclivities, his concern for the proper distribution of water, the management of canals, and his enthusiasm for fish. Atum, too, rising from out of the ocean of chaos, is water-born. To peoples living, as the Sumerians and Egyptians both did, in lands which depended upon their water supplies to a higher degree than most, the element very early on became the focus of mystical significance, reverence, and ritual. Gods who brought water to the land were both worshipped and to be loved. In another parallel, both Atum in Egypt and An in Sumer, having begun the process of creation, withdrew to the higher, remote heavens, leaving the management of the universe to surrogates.

The greatest of the Egyptian creator gods was Ptah of Memphis, who bears many of the qualities of the amiable Enki of Eridu in Sumer. Ptah was, like Enki, the 'Lord of Earth'; it was said of him 'all gods, all men, cattle, creeping things, everything that lives is Ptah'. He was hailed as Lord of Destiny, Lord of Truth, Master of Fate. He was amongst the most enduring and the most sympathetic of all the gods; in the Memphite theology, developed by Ptah's priests, it was even suggested that *all* Egypt's gods were actually manifestations of Ptah. He is invariably represented in human form, though mummified. He is always shown wearing a tight-fitting cap, a form of headgear quite unique amongst Egyptian divinities. The meaning of his name is unknown: 'Opener', 'Sculptor', and 'Engraver' have been suggested, the latter two being quite appropriate for so great an artificer god.

Ptah was also identified with an immensely ancient divinity associated with the very beginnings of the world, named Tanen. Sometimes Ptah *was*

Tanen; as Ta-Tanen he was identified as the land of Egypt, 'the land named in the great name of Ta-Tanen'. In this context, Egypt is 'the Risen Land', the land that initiated the world's creation. Ptah-Ta-Tanen is 'the Lord of Years'.

In the tendentious area of ancient philosophy another interesting similarity may be detected between Egypt and Sumer, if only, as with the others, mistily. Both groups of gods, Sumerian and Egyptian, bequeathed to their peoples a set of precepts and a concept of order underlying the universal creation. The Sumerians believed that Inanna brought from her father, in this case represented as Enlil, the Lord of the Gods, the fundamental requirements of human life and civilization, immutable manifestations of the divine will which were at the root of Sumerian society. These divinely inspired concepts were called *me* and include the Kingship and the divine, truth, law, rejoicing, the crafts, and a host of others. To the Sumerian these meant civilization, the difference between man's state and the brute creation. They accepted them as the means by which the gods governed their people.

The key to the Egyptian world was represented by the concept *ma'at*, a term which is elusive and which, like the Sumerian *me* resists precise translation. *Ma'at* is order, balance, the harmony of the universe, a disciplined weighing of many elements in a coherent whole; *Ma'at* is also truth, for truth and order, in cosmic or universal terms, must be identical. *Ma'at* is represented in the hieroglyphic dictionary by the most charming of all glyphs, a delicate, adolescent girl, naked but for a single feather in her hair. Again, as in the majestic image of the golden falcon identifying the divine, ever-living King, the representation of truth by this exquisite child is an inspiration of total and poetic genius. One of the most beautiful of the Egyptian myths has the Creator initiating the whole process of creation by lifting *Ma'at* to his lips, and kissing her. From that tender and graceful act the entire cycle of existence unfolds and the universe is born. Even the gods and the King himself were subject to *Ma'at*, just as Wotan in Norse myth cannot gainsay Fate. It has been suggested that the observation of the stars, in which the ancients were skilled, gave rise to the idea of *Ma'at*, the perfect embodiment of order represented by the perpetual round of the never-setting circumpolar stars which exercised a profoundly important role in the early royal cults, at the beginning of dynastic times, before the assertion of the supremacy of the sun.

The influence of Sumer upon Egypt is to be found also in the field of art, and Asiatic influences can be detected in the minor arts in Egypt, at the time of the unification, or immediately before it. These may suggest the actual presence of craftsmen from the east or at least a substantial degree of penetration by their ideas, more than might be expected as consequence, for example, of the exchange of goods or their acquisition through the medium of a third party. Amongst these influences are the appearance of strange saurian creatures with heavy bodies and long necks on which are carried feline heads (plates 30a, 30b, and 30c). These are depicted on some of the decorated palettes produced in Egypt and on cylinder seals from Mesopotamia and Elam at the end of the fourth millennium. On the handles of combs and knives from Egypt lines of animals are represented which also are echoed in western Asiatic art, particularly in seal-making. The seals themselves were reproduced in Egypt and here it is possible to speculate that their makers were Egyptians since the designs are clearly based on Mesopotamian originals, though misunderstood or misinterpreted; in some cases the craftsman has tried to reproduce an inscription without understanding it and has in consequence produced gibberish.

In two other areas there is little doubt that Egypt took from Sumer ideas of profound importance and lasting significance. These were methods of architecture apparently wholly un-Egyptian, and the art of writing.

The most common building material in Sumer was baked mud brick, though some stone was used by the Sumerians in their early days. The earliest stone-built buildings in Mesopotamia date from the later centuries of the fourth millennium, somewhat earlier than the earliest that are known from Egypt. It is apparent that the use of stone was reserved for the most important sacred buildings, the temples and shrines of the black-headed people whose search for the transcendental, intermittent and unsure though it frequently was, thus was given permanent form and expression in buildings reserved for the immortal gods. However, stone was very much the exception in the hands of the architects of Sumer.

It is interesting to speculate on the means by which the Sumerians came to their discovery of stone, for the land they occupied was virtually bereft of any that could be quarried and used for architectural purposes. They were always cautious in its use, for it was scarce and its general supply depended upon importation from lands far distant from their own. It may be that they discovered the technique outside their own land, or were introduced to it themselves by some other people. At any rate, the early temple buildings at Uruk, Khafajae, and Al-Ubaid, are stone built. But with few exceptions (and those never secular) the Sumerians built in mud brick and, despite the gloomy prognosis of some of their writings which emphasized the impermanence of the works of man, many of their buildings have survived to this age, ravaged but not destroyed by the intervening centuries.

Mesopotamian architecture was to be the inspiration of one of the most important architectural borrowings that the Egyptians effected. It was an acquisition which came to symbolize one of the most exalted of their sacred institutions, the Divine Kingship. Why this should have been so is altogether obscure, not to say downright mysterious.

It is in the representation of the names and titles of the early Kings that this most striking and least expected evidence of Mesopotamian influence may be detected. This is the more remarkable when it is remembered with what sanctity a man's name, let alone a King's, was invested in Egypt. The reason for this view is simple: the notion is that a man's name is full of power; if this is true of all men it must be infinitely more so for the King who was also god. The King was King by right as the Incarnate Horus who succeeded his dead father, Osiris; because he was Horus, he was King. In the earliest times he assumed a Horus name; this name proclaimed the King's divinity and its peculiar and sacred, indeed unique nature, was revealed by the form of its presentation. The often simple hieroglyphs which expressed the King's name, and which are the earliest examples in Egypt of true writing, are enclosed in a rectangular architectural abstraction, known to archaeology as the *serekh*, on which a majestic falcon perches, at once protective and proclamatory. This is the Horus who said 'I am Horus the Falcon, who perches upon the battlements of Him whose name is hidden', the herald of the unknown god, himself a god. Thus, from the earliest times the worship of the King is also linked, symbolically, with that of the mysterious, unknown, and formless one god who, some authorities (but by no means all) have contended, lay behind all the plethora of national and local divinities.

But the *serekh* is more than a convenient perch on which Horus may settle. It appears to represent the front of a fortified palace of the time, with its narrow gateway, floral tracery above the gates, clerestories, and recessed buttresses (plates 31a, 31b, and 31c). This last feature in particular reveals its origins: buttresses of the identical form are known in Sumerian buildings several hundred years before they appear in Egypt. In the second half of the fourth millennium, post-3500 BC, a very distinctive form of building design began to appear in the Sumerian cities, notably in Uruk (plates 32a and 32b). It is evident, particularly, in temple architecture, for it is apparent in the platforms on which the temples were built which eventually evolved into the ziggurats, so typical of Sumerian cities in their full flowering. A distinctive feature of these buildings is the recessed and alternating buttresses which mark the faces of the walls. The alternating recesses and projections produce a pleasing and striking effect, the more so in the brilliant sunlight, characteristic both of Sumer and Egypt, which emphasizes their shape with deep shadow. Several seal impressions from the Jemdet Nasr period, roughly contemporary with the end of Naqada II, show high-walled, fortified palace buildings with recessed buttresses and other details which are repeated on Egyptian buildings of a time only shortly later.

The Sumerians, since their land was entirely bereft of stone, relied mainly on brick for their buildings. The Egyptians, as soon as they were able, took to the use of stone as naturally as a child models in clay. But in the early centuries, in the most important buildings of which they could conceive – the eternal residences of the eternal gods who ruled them, living or dead – they employed a material wholly identified with a distant and alien people and built in baked mud brick.

How distant and alien they were is, of course, the nub of the question. It *is* very odd that the Egyptians should have chosen to identify their Kings with the *serekh* in life and the recessed panel façades of their tombs in death. Yet there can surely be no question that the Kings were of any national origin other than Egyptian; their names and so much of their accoutrements are clearly indigenous to the Valley.

Recessed buttressed buildings served two other, associated purposes, both in that mortuary sphere to which the Egyptian paid so much attention. First, the burial places of the First and Second Dynasty Kings and their great nobles, at Saqqara, Abydos, and other royal cemeteries (plates 33a and 33b), are built in the form of earthly palaces, their interiors painted and decorated to simulate the hangings and furnishings which they would have contained in life: some even contain bathrooms and lavatories, for the convenience of the dead. The exteriors are fretted with buttresses which, since they bear no practical, architectural purpose, are clearly decorative or symbolic.

The second, later use to which the form was put, as late as the end of the Old Kingdom at least, was in the shape of the great sarcophagi which were made to contain the mummified remains of the Kings and great princes, a few hundred years after the *serekh's* first appearance. These represented the *serekh* in three dimensions and again are representations of the palaces in which the 'Great Ones' passed their days.

Though the *serekh's* origins are to be found in the temple buildings of Sumer this does not explain *why* the rulers of what was to become Egypt should have chosen it as their badge. Why an architectural form should have had this profound importance to them is quite obscure; perhaps the shape of the *serekh* or the sound of the word conveyed some other nuance or significance which is lost to us. It is another of the mysteries attending this obscure time.

Eventually, probably during the Third Dynasty, the *serekh* began to be replaced by the unequivocally Egyptian *cartouche*, a carefully plaited and knotted coil of rope which contained the royal names down to the end of Egypt's history. Perhaps the *serekh* (literally, the 'proclaimer') was ultimately thought to be too alien a form; it did, however, continue to be used in certain contexts whenever the designers of a temple's interior wished, for example, to demonstrate the antiquity of a particular motif or the long span of the worship of a particular divinity. That it was dropped from general currency, however, is a rare example of an Egyptian decision to change something which had become established in use; for this decision, too, there must have been some reason. But to the early Kings the *serekh* was of such symbolic potency that, alien or not to Egypt, they chose it to enclose and protect their most sacred names, the names indeed by which they were proclaimed true Kings. The *serekh*s of the early Kings are known from the many seal impressions which have been recovered from tombs built during their reigns. They are amongst the most austere and elegant heraldic designs ever produced (plates 34a, 34b, and 34c).

Although the Egyptians achieved some of the most magnificent buildings that the world has so far seen, like the Sumerians, they never lost their respect for their earliest form of structure, the simple mud and reed hut which, in various forms, was the original shrine, temple, palace, or family house (plates 35a and 35b). Throughout their history they venerated in particular the national shrines of Upper and Lower Egypt, which seem to have been made of reeds. The pavilion of the great *Heb-Sed* festival, the jubilee in which the youth and potency of the King were renewed, was also a simple wooden or reed structure. In this aspect such structures closely parallel the reed shrines of the Sumerian divinities. Enki, for example, is frequently portrayed sitting in his reed house, and when he sought to save man from Enlil's wrath at the time of the Flood he whispered his message not to Ziusudra directly, the King who was the prototype of Noah, but to the walls of that King's reed house in Shuruppak. Perhaps it is not surprising that two river peoples should make use, in their earliest days, of the material that was most readily to their hands: but the symbolic significance of the primitive reed hut was patently strong and highly emotive for both of them, a coincidence less easy to explain without the possibility of the religious identification pursued by both peoples having originated in the same place. Even in their latest temples, immense edifices built entirely in stone, colossal and portentous, the Egyptians recreated the reed shrine as the holiest place in the temple, often locating it deep in the darkened interior where it could be reached only by the highest ranks of the priesthood and the King himself.

The second unique invention which seems to have passed from Sumer to Egypt is that of writing. It must at once be emphasized that, at most, the Egyptians only took the *idea* of making permanent records from the Sumerians for there is little similarity between either the language or the scripts of the two peoples. In the present state of knowledge, the Sumerians appear to be the earlier in making this extraordinary breakthrough, perhaps the most benign and liberating of all man's achievements. The earliest Egyptian scripts, though they demonstrate an easy fluency on the part of the scribes who used them and a sophisticated structure of language, appear first at the time of the earliest Kings of unified Egypt. Certain symbols may have had a widely recognized meaning in even earlier times, when they may have been employed as phonyms, a characteristic never lost to Egyptian writing.

The characters which made up the Egyptian hieroglyphs of the historic or dynastic periods had, many of them at least, their origins far back into Predynastic times. Some of the symbols which the Egyptians employed in their writing may have been in use as early as the beginning of the fourth millennium. Egyptian epigraphy is of course much connected with the process, which the people of the Nile Valley represent so supremely, whereby the expression of deep-seated elements sometimes may be recognized as it wells out of the unconscious itself, cloaked in symbolic form. But the impulse to formulate these profound symbols into a system which could express concepts or sounds and hence provide a system of written records is a step which probably did require external stimulus. Such stimulus, it must at present be assumed, came from some sort of contact with or awareness of the development of systems of writing in Mesopotamia.

Writing in Mesopotamia began as a process of recording the treasure, represented by herds, goods, and slaves, of the temples which in the fourth millennium were the dominant institutions in the polity of Sumer. In Egypt the earliest of what may be called 'documents' since they carry texts or inscriptions are ceremonial or votive objects associated with the Kings – palettes or large mace-heads, for example – or ivory labels which seem to record the important events of a reign or marks which identify royal property. However, in Predynastic times the large pots which were used to store grain, oil, or wine, were marked with signs which may be ancestral to more developed later forms of writing. As in Sumer much of the impetus for Egyptian writing came from the demands of accountancy and the need to maintain accurate and immediately reliable records.

By the reign of Menes-Narmer the distinctive Egyptian script was in full and confident use, albeit in a relatively primitive form, but this was 300 years or so after the date to which the earliest Sumerian pictographs have been approximately ascribed. The earliest tablets in Sumer come from Uruk and Kish, all dated approximately to the mid-fourth millennium BC. Taking into account the flow of new ideas which seemingly poured into Egypt from Mesopotamia at the time of the unification it would seem reasonable to suppose that the concept of writing was one of them.

As with their borrowings of Sumerian architectural forms, the Egyptians quickly transmuted the idea of writing into their own highly characteristic form of script. It would surely be stretching coincidence too far to postulate independent invention of so complex a concept in such close historical and geographical proximity, at the same time in two such substantially different environments. The only tenable assumption is that Sumerian genius fertilized Egypt but what is fascinating is to speculate how the necessary degree of communication occurred between them, to permit sophisticated principles behind the idea of making records, for example, to be expressed by the one to the other, and where it may have taken place. It is not difficult in a rainstorm to demonstrate convincingly the advantages of a stone-built or sun-dried brick structure over a mud and wattle building. Whilst the speculation of how a Sumerian outlined his people's valuable discovery of the art of writing to a thoughtful and attentive Egyptian is a problem of stupendous implications, it is also of a very pleasing humanity. From the evidence such an equation of contact and response, and obviously more than one, must have happened; the coincidences between the two cultures could not have been the result of simple empirical processes.

Structurally there are similarities between some aspects of Sumerian and Egyptian epigraphy. Most of these similarities are to do with the relationship of sounds to the form of the signs: but some authorities have postulated that some Egyptian words are in fact of Sumerian origin. These include the words for hoe, spade, plough, corn, beer, and carpenter; significantly, these all seem to be related to crafts, to the making of things (Asselberghs, 1961). Other authorities would take a much more cautious view and would doubt whether there was any actual borrowing; in the case of the word for 'plough' however, which in Egyptian is *mr*, there seems to be little doubt that the word was taken from the Sumerian vocabulary (Meltzer, 1970). Both peoples also employed determinatives in their writing, to indicate the meaning of a sign which might have several applications or meanings in different contexts.

If the two peoples were in contact, presumably some time after the middle of the fourth millennium BC, the question arises not only as to how that contact might have taken place but where it may have happened. The Egyptians recorded voyages to the Land of Punt – God's Land, the Holy Land – from the time of the Old Kingdom. By the way the journeys are reported it seems likely that the route was already long- and well-established. No certain location for Punt has been identified; later, in New Kingdom times, to judge by the representation of the animals and flora depicted as typical of Punt, it included parts of south Arabia and east Africa but this does not mean that it was always located there. There are many examples of place names changing their actual location, a process which is initiated by a number of different circumstances. As the source of Egypt's supplies of aromatic spices, however – frankincense and myrrh in particular – south Arabia was certainly important. Recent discoveries in coastal south-west Arabia, in the region known as the Tihama, suggest that there was contact with the Valley people in the early periods, certainly during the latter part of the third millennium. It may well also have taken place in still earlier times.

It may have been on such voyages in search of spices that the Egyptians encountered their Sumerian-speaking contemporaries. How they communicated we do not know. How they managed to spend enough time together to learn each other's language is also a question for which no answer is forthcoming at present.

One candidate for the putative meeting place must be the Dhofar province in the south of what is today the Sultanate of Oman. In antiquity both frankincense and myrrh grew there in profusion; indeed all the products and flora associated with the Egyptians' idea of Punt, the Land of God, could be found in southern Oman or could be traded through it.

It is now generally accepted by scholars that Oman was Magan, the source of much of Sumer's copper and the region from which they also obtained much of their stone, including diorite, for the embellishment of their public buildings and the statues which adorned them. Third-millennium copper workings are known in the northern Oman wadis; indeed, the earliest evidence of settlements in the Sultanate, certainly dating from the early third millennium and very possibly from the late fourth, are connected with the copper trade.

That there was some movement at least from west to east, involving regions adjacent to the Nile Valley and Oman, seems clear from the evidence of the cultivation of sorghum in an early-third-millennium site at Hili. This is located in what is today the United Arab Emirates state of Abu Dhabi but historically is part of the northern Oman region. From the copper mines the ore was carried up to the coast, from where the consignments of copper to the Sumerian cities in the north were transshipped. These were often routed, incidentally, through the island of Bahrain which, in the middle of the third millennium, became the centre of the Dilmun culture (Rice, 1985, bibliography).

Sorghum originated in the Sudan, lying to the south of Egypt but always within its sphere of influence; it appears at the end of the third millennium in India and it seems therefore to have been carried across the Red Sea and then across Arabia to Oman where it appears at the *beginning* of the third millennium. Whilst the idea is wholly speculative it must at least therefore be possible that people from the Nile Valley journeyed to Oman and there encountered people from Mesopotamia.

It may equally well be that they did share some common, now forgotten tradition. There are some indications that the language spoken by the Egyptians and the Semitic languages of the people from the desert, like the Akkadians, who came to dominate Mesopotamia after the effective disappearance of the Sumerians at the end of the period with which we are concerned, had some common origin. Egyptian is not a Semitic language though it contains Semitic elements. It is thought that the common stem, the parental Afro-Asian tongue from which the Egyptian and Akkadian languages eventually grew, divided around 6000–5500 BC. It has also been estimated that Old Kingdom Egyptian and Akkadian had slightly more in common than the two modern languages Rumanian and Portuguese; these might seem to be totally disparate until it is remembered that both belong to the family of Romance languages (Edwards *et al.*, 1971).

Of special interest, particularly in the light of subsequent history when the Sumerians' cuneiform in its Babylonian and Assyrian successor scripts became the common form of writing throughout the Middle East for more than 2,000 years is the question why, assuming always that they did in fact know them, the Egyptians so rapidly decided that the Sumerian pictographs (the form from which cuneiform developed) were unsuited or inappropriate to their needs. Seemingly, having grasped the idea of writing in principle, they immediately returned to Egypt and began to set down what they wanted to say through the medium of what later generations have come to call hieroglyphs, a term which reveals the sacred character with which they were invested.

The Sumerians themselves early discarded their pictographs as inadequate and successive stages of the cuneiform script evolved, until it reached its final development towards the middle of the second millennium by which time the Sumerians themselves had disappeared. The Egyptians, who firmly believed that nothing of theirs could ever really be improved upon, never abandoned their hieroglyphs, though they adapted and refined them over the centuries. They did produce two forms of what, by comparison with the monumental hieroglyphs, was virtually speedwriting: these were respectively *hieratic* and, later, *demotic*, which were used in their other than monumental or ritual inscriptions. But to the very end of Egypt's history the people of the Valley kept loyally to their hieroglyphs. The Greeks' astonishment at the extraordinary repertory of characters, symbols, and pictures which they saw, gleaming and redolent of mystery, on the temple walls at the very end of the long and majestic course of Egypt's history is perpetuated in the word which they employed to describe what they believed must be 'sacred writings' as they gazed open-mouthed with wonder at the remains of Egypt's greatness.

In one other aspect of the minor arts in Egypt, one which is associated at least conceptually with writing, there appears to be another definite piece of evidence of contact between the Egyptians and people from the east. This involves the Nile Valley peoples' use of seals, a practice which, at the time it appears in Egypt, was particularly highly developed in Mesopotamia and Elam.

Seals have a very long and distinguished ancestry. The oldest form of the seal is the stamp which impresses a design on clay or other receptive material. It has been suggested that some of the earliest seals of this form, from the Anatolian settlements on the Konya plain, may have been used to impress designs on the bodies of their users, like tattoos, or on textiles.

However, classically the seal evolved as a means of identifying property or certifying the identity of a party to an agreement in largely preliterate societies. The Sumerians and the Elamites developed the seal to a considerable art form. They also pioneered a variant on its form by inventing the cylinder seal which could be rolled out and which therefore made possible a larger, more complex design, and one which could permit considerable ingenuity in its execution. All the peoples of the ancient Near East developed their own form of seal; the variety is dazzling, just as the quality of some of the designs is often of the very highest order.

At around the time of the unification, corresponding approximately to the Jemdet Nasr period in Mesopotamia, which was a time of especially active seal production, cylinder seals appear in Egypt for the first time. Several have been removed from graves and are therefore to be identified with the graves' inhabitants, who are presumably easterners. A little later the Egyptians began to produce their own cylinder seals, sometimes attempting to copy Sumerian designs and inscriptions. Later, of course, they abandoned the cylinder and developed their own distinctive seal form, the scaraboid seal; but this was well into the future.

It is not without significance that the Old Kingdom word for 'noble', which is transliterated as *sahu*, means literally one to whom the King has granted the privilege of carrying a seal. As in the case of the *serekh* it seems incontrovertible, though surprising, that a high rank or distinction in the emerging Egyptian state is identified with a distinctly alien concept, this time the practice of seal-bearing.

The Sumerians, unlike the Egyptians, were formidable travellers. The Egyptians saw little point in moving from their Valley where everything had been ordered for their good; the Sumerians always looked beyond their immediate horizon. It is certainly possible that as a consequence of this restless quality they looked westward and reached Egypt. No undisputably Sumerian burial has ever been identified in Egypt, though graves containing Mesopotamian cylinder seals have been excavated. However, in the British Museum Egyptian collections is a small limestone head of a man wearing what appears to be a Sumerian turban (plate 36), reminiscent of the headdress of the heroic figure on the more celebrated Jebel el Arak knife. It was found in Abydos; it is conceivable that it does represent a Sumerian or one of that people's gods. It is surely possible that in some third, hitherto unrecognized or perhaps forgotten region, the two peoples originally shared more than in historical times they were able to remember.

It must be emphasized that there can be no question of a mass 'horde' invasion of Egypt by aliens from beyond her shores in the time immediately before the start of the First Dynasty. This was once a popular theory, to account for the incursion of foreigners who brought with them the arts of civilization. In the event, the antecedents of Pharaonic Egypt can be discerned far back into the fourth, probably even into the fifth millennium. The people of the Valley in these remote times were the ancestors of those who created the historic land of Egypt, who gave life to the long line of Kings and gods who populated the Valley along with their humbler subjects (plate 58). Contact with influences from beyond Egypt clearly excited and stimulated the native Egyptian genius – but it was essentially native. The origins of the 'dynastic race', so long sought by scholars from Petrie onwards, are quite clearly to be found in the Valley, in its upper, southern reaches.

b

4*a* and 4*b* In three-dimensional figures as well as in media such as rock-carvings and engravings on ivory and bone, the artists of Badarian Egypt portrayed men and women in the dance, with arms raised above their heads, perhaps to imitate the horns of the cattle which were their principal resource at the time. The female figurine conveys a delicious sense of incompetent abandon, as though she had been designed by James Thurber. (Muséum de Lyon, 90000173, 90000174)

5 Badarian pottery is finely made and, though the most common form is the black- or grey-topped red fabric vase, the repertory of Badarian potters was in fact extensive and varied. (Private collection)

6 The pottery of the Naqada I or Amratian people is quite different from that of the Badarians. The designs, often filled-in white on red, are naturalistic and anticipate the brilliant paintings of the next cultural horizon, Naqada II. They are often based on cloth or basket-weaving patterns. (Private collection; photograph, Roger Wood)

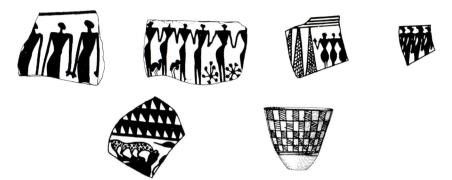

7 The similarity of Egyptian designs in the Naqada period to those from Elam in south western Iran, is striking, and hardly to be ascribed to chance or coincidence. In all other respects the two cultures were very different, but there seems little doubt that Elamite designs did seep into the Nile Valley in the late Predynastic period.

8 Warriors with feathers in their hair (sometimes two or three) are found depicted in Elam, western Arabia, and Egypt. In later times very similar forms are to be found in the Arabian Gulf, particularly in Oman. Often the warriors are shown brandishing a rather primitive-looking bow. This last component is also found on Neolithic rock carvings in western Arabia, which recall the dress and accountrements of warriors on early Egyptian slate palettes. (Winkler: *Rock Drawings in Southern Upper Egypt*, vol. I, pl. xxiii, i)

9 The hippopotamus was a favourite subject for Egyptian artists. Here on a Naqada I vessel, a little procession of the beasts circles its rim, though one breaks off to peer hopefully over the edge. (Reproduced by permission of the Trustees of the British Museum)

10 This alabaster figure of a hippopotamus carved in the round is one of the finest pieces of sculpture to survive from the time of the unification. Despite the animal's ponderous bulk, the artist has imbued it with life, even with a sly and mischievous semblance of humanity. (Ny Carlsberg Glyptotek, Copenhagen)

11 The most typical form of Naqada II or Gerzean pottery is buffware on which is painted a vigorous and often complex design. Naqada II draughtsmen were highly skilled; they are really the first practitioners of drawing on any scale, to be recorded. Frequently they depicted boats with single, double or triple figures – probably divinities – standing on or in them.

12a and *12b* Boats were a dominant theme of Egyptian artists and craftsmen in late Predynastic times. They never tired of depicting them, on rocks, on pottery, and in paintings. In late Naqada II times the native Egyptian boats seemed to have been joined by alien, high prowed boats which are like those depicted on Mesopotamian and Elamite artefacts.

13a, 13b, and *13c* Boats with undoubted Mesopotamian provenance are those engraved on seals from Sumerian and Elamite sites, which show similar high-prowed vessels, often with an animal head on the prow. This form of decoration is also found in some late Predynastic Egyptian drawings.

14 The names of Predynastic kings such as Iry-Hor, Scorpion, and Ka are already shown in the form of the *serekh*, as in this example, indicating the ownership of this vessel. (UC 16947)

15 The making of stone vessels is one of the glories of ancient Egyptian craftsmanship. Even the hardest and most intractable stones were carved with extraordinary precision and assurance. The material also allowed the sculptor to indulge the Egyptian penchant for understatement, allowing the shape of objects and the materials from which they were fashioned to speak for themselves. (Photograph, John Ross)

16 This small pottery boat has no precedent. It contains a representation of the body of a man lying curled up; it is probable that he is dead. The boat seems to be made of skins stretched on a wooden frame: a sort of coracle. It is a remarkable and moving representation of the isolation and vulnerability of humankind. (Rijksmuseum van Oudheden, Leiden, Netherlands, 3.1.6)

17 In the earliest times Egyptian artists, still experimenting with the canons of their art, often produced works of extraordinary freedom and sensuality. An example is this little pottery figure of a man sitting with his head resting on his drawn-up knees; its fluidity and directness were seldom equalled, perhaps not even to the present day. (Memorial Art Gallery, Rochester NY 28.3.83)

19 One of the unsolved mysteries of Egyptian craftsmanship in its earliest manifestations is how artists maintained an even pressure (under the everted rim of a stone bowl, for example) even when employing friable materials like the schist of this bowl. The thickness of the walls seems as consistent over its entire surface as is the perfection of the circle of its perimeter. The final touch of sophistication on this particular object is the delicate line engraved *under* the rim which can have given satisfaction only to the craftsman who made it and perhaps to the god for whose eye it may have been intended. (Private collection)

18 This type of vase in a hard stone, probably basalt, descends from a single-footed form known in western Asia. The engraving on the side of this example is unusual however, and its significance obscure. (Private collection)

a

b

20a and *20b* (*a*) A most elegant goblet of a form which seems to be restricted to the First Dynasty; an example was found in Queen Her-Neith's tomb at Saqqara. Its purity of line is memorable. The holes in the base may have been for attaching leather 'coasters', to maintain the goblet's balance. (*b*) Equally fine, from a slightly later period is this dark stone vessel which demonstrates a powerful simplicity of form which is both assured and compelling. (Private collection)

21 One of the repeated themes in the repetory of late Predynastic artists is a large, rather menacing, black ship, which does not seem to belong to the Valley. In addition to this example a large pottery vessel, the black ship also appears on the wall paintings in Hierakonpolis Tomb 100. (Reproduced by permission of the Trustees of the British Museum)

22 The Sumerians often portrayed their divinities sailing in boats. This was a practice not common in early Egypt (unless some of the figures depicted on the rocks and pottery are intended to be divine) though there are examples from later periods.

a   b

23a and 23b The theme of three figures, usually male, in a boat, is constantly repeated in Predynastic art: (a) large pottery model of a boat with a striped central awning, c.3300 BC (Egyptian Museum, Berlin, DFR); (b) carved schist amulet (found at Gebelein) with three abstract figures, indicated only by their heads, with prominent inlaid eyes (length 8.7cm) (Muséum de Lyon, 1598)

24 Some Predynastic Egyptian representations of boats show them carrying animals, thus investing both the animals and their means of transportation with particular significance.

a

b

25*a* This unusual object, a two-sided plaque carved in shell, is of Egyptian provenance, though it is very un-Egyptian in character. The reverse shows two bulls surmounted by a hieroglyph or representation of a hoe; beneath their hooves runs a stream in which fish are swimming. The hoe is identical to that carried by the dominant figure on the ceremonial mace-head attributed to the late predynastic King Scorpion (*b*). (The hieroglyph represents the phoneme 'mr'.) The designs on the plaque are much more typical of Elamite or Sumerian art than of Egyptian, and the material, shell, is relatively common in western Asia, but hardly ever used in Egypt. Likewise the fish are similar to those found on western Asiatic seals. ((*a*) Stäatliche Museen, Berlin, DDR; (*b*) Ashmolean Museum, Oxford)

26a and *26b* The hieroglyphic determinative for a ram shows an early, and subsequently extinct strain, *ovis longipes palaeoaegypticus* (*a*). The animal is also represented on Predynastic pottery (*b*).

27 The hieroglyph 'ntr' meaning *god*. In this form it is thought that the sign is derived from a staff bound with cloth, a fetish of very early date.

28 Bearded figure from El Amra. (Muséum de Lyon)

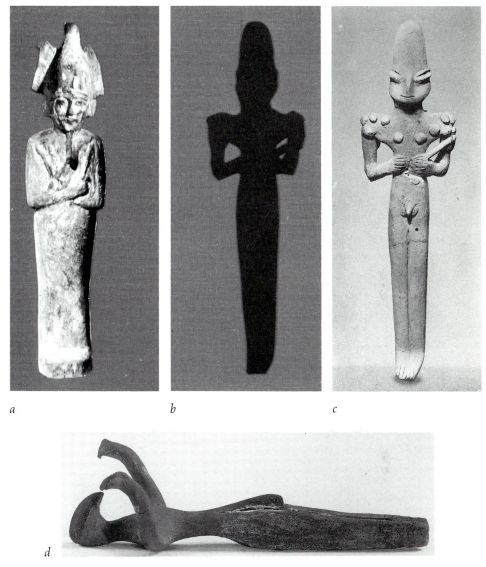

a

b

c

d

29a, 29b, 29c and *29d* Although the earliest references to Osiris, the god of
resurrection and rebirth, do not occur before the end of the Old Kingdom there
is a remarkable correspondence (in silhouette at least) between representations
of him (*a*) and those of the reptilian-headed male figure (*b* and *c*) from Eridu (the
city of Enki) dating from Ubaid times, some three thousand years earlier. The
Eridu figure even carries a sceptre, like Osiris' accoutrements of whip and flail.
Egyptian reptilian (or bird?) headed figures (*d*), reminiscent of the strange Eridu
figures, are known from Naqada I times, though they are rare. (*a*) private
collection; (*c*) The Bahgdad Museum; (*d*) Courtesy Museum of Fine Arts Boston,
Emily Esther Sears Fund (B15557)

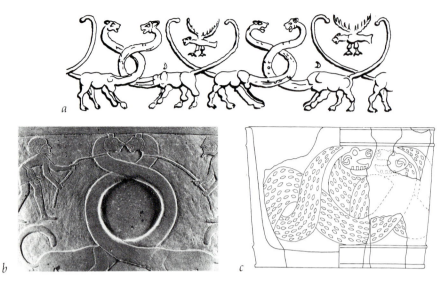

30a, 30b, and 30c One of the most direct parallels between the art of Egypt and that of western Asia is provided by the intertwined necks of the serpopards in these representations: (a) from a seal from Susiana, (b) from the palette of King Narmer, (c) from a chlorite carving from eastern Arabia.

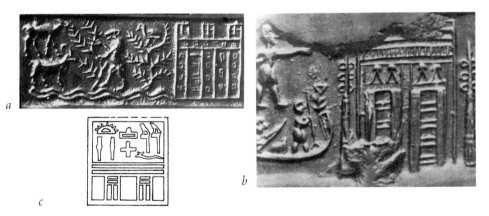

31a, 31b, and 31c The most powerful of all royal symbols in Egypt was the serekh in which the King's most sacred name was enclosed, customarily surmounted by the royal and divine falcon, signifying the King's incarnation as the living Horus. The design seems to have been based on the façade of a Sumerian building of Jemdet Nasr times, (late fourth millennium BC) a palace or a temple. The same panelled façade was to appear for hundreds of years on the architecture of Egyptian tombs and sarcophagi, long after it had been abandoned in Sumer itself.

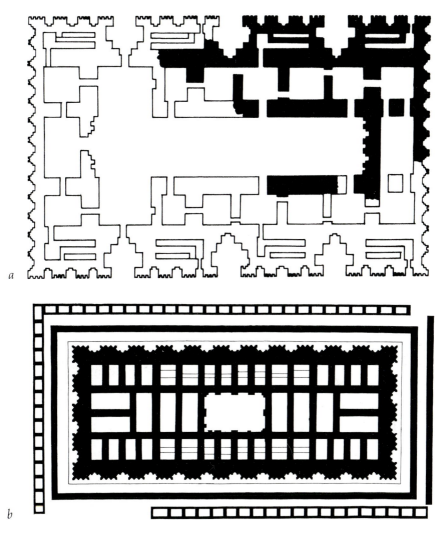

32a and *32b* The ground plans of Sumerian temples (*a*) and of the First Dynasty graves (*b*) of the great nobles at Saqqara in Egypt show significant similarities, particularly in the use of recessed buttressing.

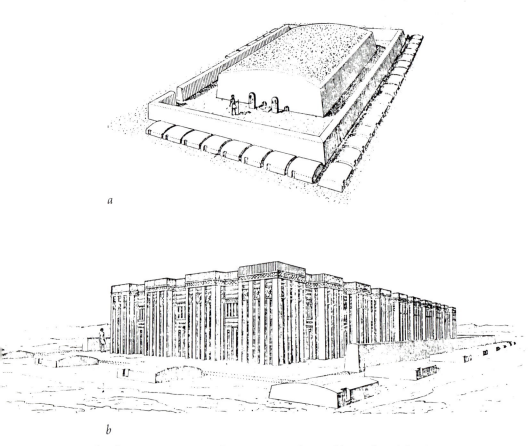

a

b

33a and *33b* Reconstructions of Egyptian royal or noble tombs of the First Dynasty at Abydos and Saqqara.

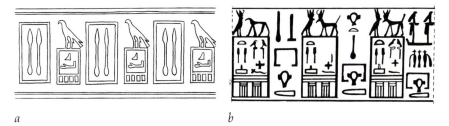

a   b

34a and *34b* As the First Dynasty progressed, the art of inscribing the royal names became more and more refined, until the technique becomes almost calligraphic.

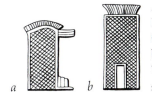

a   b

35a and *35b* The shrines of Upper (*a*) and Lower (*b*) Egypt were always depicted in their traditional form as simple reed shelters, but of distinctive, designs. The shrine of Upper Egypt could be vaguely animal in shape.

36 This very un-Egyptian-looking object is said to have been found at Abydos. It represents a turbanned man or divinity, his headdress not unlike that of the principal figure on the reverse of the Jebel el Arak knife. It is closely paralleled by early Dynastic heads from Sumerian sites, particularly those around the Diyala region. (Reproduced by permission of the Trustees of the British Museum)

37 The perpetual duality of Horus and Set, and the King as Lord of the Two Lands, is symbolized by two royal figures, enthroned together. This serekh is that of King Djer, of the First Dynasty. The standard set up in front of the King shows the dog-god Anubis, here perhaps represented as a wolf. The curious eliptical object in front of the god probably represents the royal placenta, of which there was a considerable cult from the earliest times and throughout Egyptian history. The reverence for the royal placenta is one of the distinctively African elements in the cults of the sacred Kingship.

3

The Lords of the Two Lands

The influences which were abroad in the fifth and fourth millennia BC, the like of which the world had never known before, were powerful indeed and were to change fundamentally the patterns of human existence. The switch from the old stable ways of the hunter-gatherers, to whom the world was a place wholly predictable and which made few demands on its people that they could not very easily satisfy, had been traumatic; quite suddenly the herds began to decline, game grew scarcer, wider territories had to be ranged, and hostile groups, anxious for their own survival, were encountered. The world began to be unforeseeable and, hence and probably for the first time, frightening.

The reaction of some of the groups which survived (and most probably did, one way or another) was to produce a quantum evolutionary leap and change their relationship with their environment, as certainly as if they had become aquatic creatures or learned to fly. They became settled and invented farming. This remarkable creative response, which when it happened probably seemed as obvious and inevitable as all good ideas, happened in many places and at many times. However, nowhere has it been studied more thoroughly than in Egypt and the Near East and nowhere is the evidence more generously available.

So abrupt a transition, to be expressed over a very few thousand years, brought with it a deep sense of insecurity. This is especially evident in the lives of the earliest villagers; it is one of the most significant factors in the development of the curious human practice of living in cities. Cities probably originated as 'central places', serving the needs for defence and communal activity (the latter often directed towards procedures for survival, like the placating by worship of invisible forces, generally thought to be either malignant or capable of altering for the better an otherwise discouraging destiny) of a number of small independent communities. The life of the early villagers was vastly less secure than anything their ancestors, the hunter-gatherers, ever knew, in the warm, closely bonded groups in which they had been accustomed to live. Simply living together in close, permanent, and inescapable proximity introduced tensions hitherto quite unknown.

But cities were of great significance in the development and maintenance of early trade routes. International systems of exchange were an early discovery of post-Neolithic man and many cities owed their foundation to the need to have central places of exchange, collection, and distribution (later no doubt of manufacture) and to this need the early Egyptian cities probably owe their existence. They were, however, a somewhat un-Egyptian construct and the city never really became the dominant element of the society which arose in the Nile Valley, possibly because trade itself never assumed a significance comparable with that which it had in other areas of the ancient Near East. It is probably not without significance that as Mesopotamian influence attenuates, around the middle of the First Dynasty, so the city in Egypt declines in importance, to a level from which it was never really to recover.

Most of the outward forms of the political management of societies derive from, or at least have their remote origins in, this time. One vital element, common to the embryonic societies of both Egypt and Mesopotamia, was the pressing need for a strong, central, unifying belief, the product of a motivation similar to that which produced the proto-city. In Sumer this need seems to have been manifested in permanent archi-tectural forms of great proportions which dominated the living space of the cities and of a powerful, indeed all-pervasive priesthood, whose professional interests rose above the mere individual needs of the city states into which early on, Sumer fractured.

The wish to achieve order and stability was practically expressed by the Egyptians through their invention of the delicious figure of the little goddess Ma'at, who symbolized truth and order. Though she is portrayed as an adolescent girl, Ma'at is an immensely ancient divinity, for her name is compounded in the names of some of the earliest queens.

The need for a focus for belief and unity came to be realized around the person of the divine ruler. This is a very African concept and it is no doubt in Africa that its origins must be sought but the Egyptians appear to have responded in precisely similar terms as did their Sumerian contemporaries when faced with the social pressures arising from sudden population growth. They seem to have devised an exactly similar solution, the development of elites and hierarchies which came to personify, as it were, the stability of the society. Only in detail did they differ; in Sumer the priesthood was first of all the repository of power to be replaced eventually by Kings, who were originally perhaps war-band leaders who became permanent fixtures in the society. In Egypt they adopted the far more inspired concept of the divine King (plate 37).

The powerful urge to create which seems to have seized Egypt in the early years of her unified existence demanded spectacular outlets and responses. Three outstanding achievements must be set to Egypt's account at this time which represent an extraordinary level of creative accomplishment: these are the unified political state, the divine Kingship, and monumental funerary architecture, culminating in the pyramid. Each of these is a supreme achievement in its own sphere, the first in the arrangement of society, the second in philosophical concept, and the third in the making of an artefact that draws to itself a perfection of form and function which is breathtaking.

The apparent permanence of Egyptian society when compared with that of Sumer may be due in substantial part to the reliance by the Egyptians on an *institution* as the focus of their belief, rather than on exterior forms. For the people who produced the pyramids this may sound paradoxical but the Egyptian Kingship, though eventually sadly debased, endured over the millennia whilst the technique of pyramid building (to take that process simply as a convenient example) did not really outlive this initial, most vital period of Egyptian creativity.

Hazard and the vagaries of archaeology may be responsible for what otherwise appears to be the fortunate chance which has made two directly comparable sites, one in Egypt, the other in Sumer, available for study. They are Hierakonpolis, the City of the Falcon and probably the first capital of Upper Egypt, and Uruk in the south-west of Sumer, immortalized as the city from which Gilgamesh its King, initially accompanied by his doomed friend Enkidu, set out on his quest, first to overcome evil in the person of Humbaba and then for the flower of renewed youth. As a consequence of his journey and the death of his friend he found, instead, understanding. He was a contemporary, approximately, of King Djoser of the Third Dynasty.

Both sites are especially interesting as being amongst the first of cities. The populations of both seem to have undergone, in the latter part of the fourth millennium (around 3200 BC), a peculiar syndrome graphically categorized as 'streaming-in'. This denotes a specific phenomenon whereby – and for reasons which are far from clear – large bands of people migrated from a more or less permanent life in the countryside beyond the walls, into the city. This development has been studied particularly in the case of Uruk; it has been suggested that one of the factors in the 'streaming-in' to Uruk was the migration to Sumer of a significant number of people, perhaps moving up from eastern Arabia and the Arabian Gulf. Uruk emerged as a major centre of population in the middle of the fourth millennium, some few hundred years, therefore, before the Egyptian unification; in an area of about two square miles it is estimated that around 20,000 people were living (Adams, 1965).

In Hierakonpolis a similar process seems to have taken place, at about the same time; it is not clear whether the close proximity with the supposed date of the unification of Egypt by the Falcon Prince is coincidence or not. At about this period the population in the vicinity of Hierakonpolis appears to have risen sharply; at the same time there is a notable increase in people moving into the Valley as a whole, marking perhaps the final dissolution of the old hunting way of life in exchange for the settled and, in the case of Egypt, for the abundant life of the Valley.

Hierakonpolis' metropolitan character is demonstrated by, amongst other factors, its great gateway (plate 39). Both as a defensive structure and as a piece of urban grandification, the gateway of Hierakonpolis demonstrates those same niches and recessed and buttressed panelled walls which later became so evident and powerful a symbol as the *serekh* in which the King's Horus name was presented. This architectural style was to dominate Egyptian royal and sacred buildings for the first 500 years of her history as a centralized state. The mid-fourth-millennium site at Hierakonpolis, 113 kms north of Aswan and approximately 650 kms south of Cairo, is one of the most important Predynastic locations in the whole of the Nile Valley: indeed, it may prove to be the most important by far.

First, it is remarkable enough in being a real and unequivocal city. As we have seen, the city was not an institution which really was a natural product of the Nile Valley: the essentially agricultural nature of the society and its dependence on a widely dispersed peasantry, representing the broad base of an enduring hierarchy culminating in the court which flourished wherever the Divine King chose to station himself, militated against the growth of cities in the early centuries. But Hierakonpolis, in ancient times known as Nekhen, called Hawk City by the Greeks and located opposite the modern site of El Kab, was an exception – and a most notable one.

In the fourth millennium it was a large and prosperous settlement, walled about with a real defensive wall and, later, with the high, niched ceremonial gateway mentioned earlier. No other city in Egypt of its time could be compared with it: only, far away in Mesopotamia, lay the city of Uruk which, most improbably, bears such close similarities that it is tempting to describe one as the 'twin' of the other.

Though it seems almost inconceivable that at such an early period two locations as far distant from each other could have been in contact, the evidence that such was indeed the case is strongly suggestive. If such contact was made and sustained, its existence must be seen as a tribute to the power of the elites which were emerging at this time in both societies. The most compelling argument for Hierakonpolis' connection with its Mesopotamian counterpart is the architecture of the city, quite apart from the fact that it was the only place in the Valley at this time which could, in any real sense, be thus described.

Hierakonpolis' wall was huge; it is no less than 9.5 metres thick in places, a really colossal structure. It consisted of a double skin of mud brick, with a void between them (plate 38). Inside the city was an enclosed temple area; this is unusual for an Egyptian city at any period, for the temple or temples were built on acknowledged sacred sites, but the rest of the city, houses, ships, palaces for the nobles, grew up around them in cheerful and random confusion. In Sumerian cities, even from the earliest times, matters were ordered somewhat differently. The temple occupied a specific area which was immemorially sacred; it was marked off from the rest of the city by a *temenos*, a walled area which protected it from the incursions of other, secular buildings. This is what appears in Hierakonpolis, though the wall which now stands is Tutmosid in date (mid-second millennium BC) but the temple area is walled round, cut off from the rest of the city.

Inside the temple area, first excavated in the 1890s and then virtually left untouched until very recent times, was found one of the most remarkable caches of objects ever recorded from an ancient Egyptian site — and certainly the most important group of Archaic works of art ever to be found in one place. The Narmer Palette, the Narmer and Scorpion maceheads, a magnificent seated red pottery lion, the statues of King Khasehem and the great gold falcon which, more perhaps than any other artefact, seems to typify Hierakonpolis, were all recovered from the temple zone (colour plate IV). The remarkable concentration of maceheads, practical weapons as well as monumental votive objects, was so notable that it has led some commentators to propose that they were 'called-in' from chieftains living in the vicinity of the city who came under its suzerainty and that of its princes.

It would almost seem that there was something like a cult of the oversized in Hierakonpolis; perhaps the taste for the gigantic and monumental in scale so often manifested by the later Kings of Egypt had its origins here in their own original shrine. Certainly the huge maces which are matched by immense flint knives, nearly a metre long, suggest that in some of the rituals exceptionally large objects were considered appropriate as offerings (plate 43).

Hierakonpolis seems to have been the centre of a flourishing ivory carving craft (Adams, 1974). Many ivory objects, including seals, human and animal figurines, vessels, wands, carved and ornamented plaques, and inlays for furniture, as well as large quantities of ivory fragments for which no immediate purpose can be identified, have been recovered from the excavations of this most important of early Egyptian centres.

Much of the ivory, notably the plaques, is carved with a vigour and a sort of emphatic naïveté which is somewhat un-Egyptian: though it may seem like special pleading, the ivory's iconography and techniques of the making of the objects fabricated from it are reminiscent of the carving of the chlorite vessels and inlays which are so notable a part of the art of Elam and Sumer at the end of the fourth millennium and the beginning of the third. The elephant ivory from which many of the Hierakonpolis examples are carved is relatively malleable, soft to carve, unlike the less frequently employed hippopotamus ivory. In this respect it would have seemed a reasonable alternative to chlorite, and one with its own obvious attractions, to any craftsman familiar with that relatively soft stone (colour plate III). However, hippopotamus ivory is often used and the point should not be laboured, therefore. The hippopotamus, so often portrayed in the art of the period, was relatively common in Upper Egypt at this time, though later the species disappeared from the river's upper reaches, the consequence of over-hunting.

Amongst the many animal subjects represented by the Hierakonpolis ivories are baboons, dogs, and, in considerable quantity, scorpions. The scorpion, not at first sight the most appealing of creatures, had a powerful appeal apparently to the Hierakonpolitans, one of whose chiefs evidently adopted it as his own symbol. It had an important significance to the people of Elam and the Gulf, in the latter case up to a thousand years later, witnessed by the frequent appearance of scorpions in the design of the Gulf seals.

The Hierakonpolis ivory carvings provide what is perhaps the most remarkable evidence in the minor arts of the transfer of a technique familiar in Elam to an Egyptian context (plates 44a, 44b, 44c). One of the ivories from the Hierakonpolis hoard, recovered early in the century but only recently cleaned and published, displays an identical treatment of the plumage of several of the birds, which are its most notable motif, with that of the plumage of an 'Imdugud' bird – a lion-headed eagle – represented in a piece of chlorite (or steatite) carving from a site on the tiny island of

Tarut in eastern Saudi Arabia (Zarius, 1978), one of the most important centres of the Dilmun culture, later in the millennium focused on Bahrain.

In both cases the plumage of the birds (a mythical one in the case of the Arabian example) is indicated by vigorously incised herringbone or chevron patterns. So similar is the treatment of the two that it is impossible to believe that mere copying or, less likely still, chance, has produced the effect in the Hierakonpolis ivory; much more likely is it that the piece was either made by an easterner or by an Egyptian craftsman who had been trained by (or at the very least, exposed to) those who knew Elamite techniques very well.

The birds on the Hierakonpolis ivories are carved in high relief; the material is carved hippopotamus tusk. The chlorite carvings from Saudi Arabia are in much lower relief. The Hierakonpolis carving also depicts large felines. Their bodies are spotted, with the surface incised to suggest the pattern of the animals' coat. In this the treatment is like that on other Saudi Arabian chlorite pieces from the same site as the Imdugud-bird carving, though the technique used is not so precisely similar as in the treatment of the birds' plumage. One of the most frequent representations on the chlorite carvings is of confronted felines, a theme familiar in Egypt and, less common in the Valley, of confronted snakes.

The correspondences between the Hierakonpolis ivories and the Tarut chlorite pieces are striking. In the period immediately following the unification, in the early First Dynasty, ivory seems to have been used less and schist, a material closely related to chlorite, came to be used on an increasing scale for vessels, as much as for the cosmetic palettes for which it had always been popular. Schist is, however, a good deal more friable than chlorite and it may be that Egyptian craftsmen took a while to perfect their technique of cutting it into bowls and goblets. They never used the more manageable chlorites on the scale that the Mesopotamians did, and by the middle of the First Dynasty were producing schist bowls of remarkable technical precision.

An enthusiasm for exotic materials seems to characterize this period of Egyptian history, when the craftsmen of the little communities and their masters sought more and more unusual stones or more sumptuous metals to produce richer and more splendid objects. These in turn became the reason why merchants and the chiefs of other, more distant or less well-endowed communities came to cities like Hierakonpolis and so contributed to the rise, ultimately, of the family which ruled there to unexampled heights of power and prestige.

Gold and hippopotamus ivory, both products of the Valley, were such materials. But others, like elephant ivory, shells from the coasts of the Red

Sea and even of the Arabian Gulf postulate longer routes for contact and exchange. The most remarkable of such long-distance routes was that which brought one of the most sought after, richest, and most splendid of all materials – gold not excepted – the fine stone known as lapis lazuli.

Lapis is, literally, one of the touchstones of sophisticated early civilizations. It was to be found in large quantities in the cities of Sumer whose people valued it highly. It is also known from Iranian sites of the late fourth and early third millennia; it is found extensively in Egypt, around the time traditionally ascribed to the unification.

The most notable element in the story of lapis, apart from its beauty when it is recovered in its finest state, a marvellous, living, royal blue stone, is its place of origin. The sources for lapis have been carefully studied; it is customarily asserted that the Badakhshan province of Afghanistan is the only source from which the stone derives. In fact there are three other places which can produce stone of something of the same characteristics as Badakhshan but they are either too distant or inferior in the quality of the stone they yield to merit serious consideration as the source of the exceptionally fine stones which found their way to the early Sumerian and Egyptian palaces and shrines. Recently Quetta has been identified as an additional source.

The Badakhshan mines are located in the far north-east of Afghanistan, in the region of the Hindu Kush. It is a remote, rough, and inhospitable country; the mines are located in the Kerano-Munjan Valley. They are some 1,500 miles distant from the nearest point in Mesopotamia, away to the north and west. To reach Egypt the stone would need to travel still further, either traded on by land through the Arabo-Syrian deserts into Palestine and down the coast, or, in this case far more likely, by land down into western Persia and then by sea down the Arabian Gulf and onwards round the peninsula to the Red Sea shores of Egypt. In either event it is a formidable journey, yet it is clear that in the crucial period around the end of the Predynastic period, into the early decade of the First Dynasty, the route must often have been travelled.

Lapis appears in Egypt in graves dated to the early Naqada II period, late in the fourth millennium, often in association with foreign, specifically Mesopotamian elements. It is often found in context with gold or gold-mounted objects and generally and not altogether surprisingly seems to be identified with richer burials, suggesting that its acquisition was a perquisite of the developing elites in the communities which were beginning to assume a formal, hierarchic status in the Valley.

Lapis continues to be found in graves up to the reign of the mid-First Dynasty King Djer; then, abruptly, it stops. It is not known in Egypt again until the Fourth Dynasty some 500 years later; for the remainder of the First Dynasty, after Djer, and the Second and Third Dynasties, no evidence of its import is to be found. That it was apparently not available during the luxurious and magnificent Third Dynasty is particularly telling.

All the great late Predynastic sites have yielded lapis, either in the form of beads, or of jewellery, decoration, and inlays. One of the most notable pieces, almost inevitably, comes from Hierakonpolis (plates 45a and 45b). It is a striking piece with no obviously Egyptian (or, for that matter, Mesopotamian) characteristics. It has been suggested that it was made in the region of the Arabian Gulf and exported thus to Egypt.

Whilst it is virtually impossible to find an exact parallel to this Hierakonpolis figurine in the production of Egyptian artists there is a most remarkable similarity between it and another, smaller lapis figure from eastern Saudi Arabia. This has been ascribed to a date early in the third millennium BC; it comes from the region of Tarut at that time an important trading centre for the Dilmun people.

The Tarut figure is of an old man, wrapped in a cloak, a subject which, a little curiously, is more popular in the art of early Egypt than it is in comparable times in Sumer or Elam. The stone is more skilfully worked than the Hierakonpolis piece but there is little doubt of their affinity. The treatment of the bold, deep-cut eye sockets is similar in both cases, as is the notable air of tension in both figures. It is difficult not to believe that they both come from the same, or a closely related, tradition.

However, it is in architecture that the most impressive parallels between Archaic Egypt and Mesopotamia are to be found. Of these, perhaps the most remarkable is the existence of the Temple Oval in all three regions. The precedent for the Temple Oval structure is to be found in Mesopotamia, Egypt (at Hierakonpolis), and in the Gulf. From the centuries immediately preceding the definite appearance of the Sumerians in what is now southern Iraq (the periods which are identified with Uruk and Jemdet Nasr and are contemporary in Egypt with late Naqada I and Naqada II) there are several examples of what are usually termed 'Temple Ovals', oval or semi-circular walled structures which contain virgin sand and on which the earliest shrines identifiable in the town concerned were raised. Such ovals are known from Khafajae, Al-Ubaid, and Tepe Gawra: there is also an intriguing example in the great Temple complex at Barbar on the main Bahrain island, in the middle of the Arabian Gulf (Mortensen, 1984). But that would appear to be at least a thousand years later in date than a similar structure which appears at Hierakonpolis.

At Hierakonpolis the oval enclosing wall is referred to in the excavators' reports as a 'revetment of rough stones which retained the earth upon which the temple was built. The revetment ran round in a curved or almost circular form' (Quibell, 1898). There is nothing even remotely like it in the whole of Egypt.

The idea behind these oval structures, of which the Hierakonpolis revetment may be the most surprising example, is the ancient Sumerian belief, which seems to have descended from the Ubaid people who were the first inhabitants of southern Mesopotamia and who were probably the Sumerians' ancestors, that certain areas of their cities were immutably sacred, for ever consecrated to the gods. This does not generally seem to have been an Egyptian concept; the gods were everywhere, all pervasive and therefore not to be limited to any space or time. In Sumer the most holy place in the temple was always directly above the first location of the original shrine erected on the site, in the earliest days a simple hut or mud and wattle building. Over the centuries, in the case of a great cult centre like Eridu, sacred to Enki the Lord of the Abyss, more and more complex buildings were erected on the same site, the earlier structures being demolished and the new ones being built on their remains, which were levelled and then held within a containing wall. As this process was repeated, the resulting structure became stepped, a series of platforms, the widest at the base, reducing as it rose. From this process the ziggurat, the stepped temple structure so typical of later Sumerian cities, evolved.

There is another curious survival from Hierakonpolis which is singularly baffling. Several cylinder seals, those most typical products of Sumer and Elam whose use was diffused to Egypt have been recovered from the city; they depict lines of captives, their arms pinioned behind them, being led away by their captors, to whatever fate awaits them. But all the captives are dwarves, little men (they seem to be adults, as they are bearded) with notably angry expressions. Dwarves were a familiar phenomenon in Old Kingdom Egypt where they often were of high rank and held important offices in the state. Several were buried in the retainers' graves at Abydos and Saqqara: they were present in the households of the Kings and nobles and were familiars of the great. What they are doing in such numbers in Hierakonpolis and what the possible implications of their arrest may be are intriguing questions but, like so many others arising from this most ancient and most enigmatic of Egyptian cities, at present beyond solution.

The decline of Hierakonpolis as a political centre at the beginning of the First Dynasty is not yet understood. Its rulers may have become the Kings of Egypt, but if they did they moved first to Abydos, then to Memphis. Abydos became an outstanding funerary centre, a role which might have been thought to be appropriate for Hierakonpolis. At the same time the important centre of the Set people at Naqada, the centre also for

Predynastic Kings, declined in importance, though great nobles, perhaps the descendants of Predynastic rulers, continued to be buried there.

The rulers of the First and Second Dynasties both identified themselves with This, in the region of Abydos whose precise location is uncertain.

In recent years excavation has begun again at Hierakonpolis, for the first time on any scale for eighty years. The work is now directed by American scholars (Fairservis *et al.*, 1971–2); with the exception of a brief and inconclusive survey in the 1930s, no one has worked extensively on the site since the days of Quibell and Green, in the last decade of the nineteenth century and the first years of the present one.

Already the conclusions which the excavations have revealed are significant, confirming beyond doubt the importance of Hierakonpolis and its environs. For the ancient city of Nekhen, the capital of the Hawk people and ultimately of the Egyptian Kingship, is the centre of a larger region, each part of which contributes to an understanding of the profound influence which this distant southerly point on the Nile's course, was to have on the history of Egypt. Undoubtedly it has much more to reveal.

The most arresting discovery which the Americans have made, in the fields below the ancient walls of Nekhen, is what seems to be an exceptionally early burial ground of an indigenous elite, the 'Great Ones' of Hierakonpolis from whom tradition and, on an increasing scale, the evidence of archaeology suggest, the first line of the Kings of Egypt was descended. The burial area which they excavated appears to have been important in the early Naqada I period (*c.* 3700–3500 BC, a range which the excavators state has been confirmed by C^{14} analysis) and again at the time to which the beginning of the First Dynasty is traditionally ascribed, *c.* 3200–3100 BC. It is from this period that the celebrated painted tomb, Tomb 100, which was found – and lost – at the end of the last century, is assumed to descend; however that tomb still remains a unique example.

The group of elite burials at Hierakonpolis included one which seems to be ancestral to the later stream of royal burials, in a way similar to Tomb 100. This is Tomb 1 in Locality 6 (to adopt the terminologies of the excavators) in which a sunken pit was surrounded by triple-coursed mud-brick walls, with wooden planks overlaying it. The walls of the pit were plastered, and it was surmounted by a replica of a temple or palace, made from wooden posts, surrounded by a wooden fence (Hoffman, 1982). It is really not difficult in this structure to see the ancestor, no matter how simple, of the later *mastaba* tombs of the First Dynasty, the great funerary palaces of the Abydos area, and even the supreme funerary complex, built for King Djoser at Saqqara many hundreds of years later still.

Other graves in the complex produced material evidence which illuminates the nascent character of the Egyptian state at this period, and confirms the importance of what was happening at Hierakonpolis in bringing it to birth. A macehead of Naqada I form and the fragments of others suggest that this was a symbol of authority in the earliest times and that the Hierakonpolis elite (it is too early to call them 'Kings' or even chiefs) did not condescend to be parted from them in death, thus anticipating the colossal quantities of material, ceremonial possessions which were to be extracted from later economies and buried with their successors. There were also animal cemeteries, or at least what seem to be the ritual burials of animals at Hierakonpolis, thus giving a still greater antiquity to the animal cults which were always to be such a feature of Egyptian belief. Dogs, baboons, bulls, and goats have been identified and, in one case, what seems to be a sort of family burial of cattle – bull, cow, and calf – suggesting both the beginnings of the family triads which were also always to be a feature of the Egyptian idea of their gods and the exceptional importance of cattle in the Egyptian view of the world. Indeed, many elements in the new evidence from Hierakonpolis seem to point to the people being deeply rooted in the traditions of the Nilotic cattle herders, whose contribution to the ancient Egyptian culture has long been recognized. The Nilotic peoples surviving today in the remote reaches of the Valley and its peripheral areas are probably the living survivors of identical traditions.

Dogs were domesticated at Hierakonpolis. One of the graves seemed to have been reserved for them and contained the remains of five individual dogs. Another grave contained the skeleton of a young man, which bore the marks of butchery. There was, however, nothing to suggest that he was a sacrificial victim; rather the presence of butchering marks might be the evidence either of ritual cannibalism, which some researchers have believed they have identified at other sites or, alternatively, the practice of exhumation, where the corpse is allowed to desiccate or decay and the flesh and tissue is subsequently removed prior to a formal reburial.

That Hierakonpolis was an important industrial centre during the fourth millennium is also confirmed by the Americans' investigations. There was a considerable production of pottery there, demonstrated by the number of kilns which have been found; beads were also made there and Hierakonpolis probably served as an important centre of exchange for exotic goods, some of which, like the lapis lazuli from which the female figure is made, were exported over very long distances. This far-ranging trade brought increasing prestige to the city's rulers, who were able in turn to offer considerable rewards to their followers; hence, it is argued convincingly, their power grew until they were able to bring forth the concept of the Kingship and thus introduce the long cycle of Egyptian history.

Hierakonpolis itself would doubtless have served as a typical 'central place', providing both a ceremonial or ritual focus and a trade and bartering centre for the people living in the surrounding area. An enigmatic stone mound, last described by a researcher before the Second World War, in the centre of the Hierakonpolis ruins, is now recognized as being part of an administrative and ceremonial compound, the seat, perhaps, of a late Predynastic ruler of the city and surrounding countryside. Evidently by early First Dynasty times the ruler of Hierakonpolis was important enough – and susceptible to influence from far away to the east – to build himself a palace with a handsome niched façade. Hierakonpolis was fortified in the late Predynastic period, suggesting that the city's elite was already experiencing some questioning of its right to rule or at least threats to its prosperity. The great wall which was built around the city in the early Old Kingdom may well be the successor of earlier fortifications.

Near the grave fields a small group of rock carvings was identified, which perpetuate the themes so well known from those in the eastern desert. These include boats, which obviously had as much ritual or cultural importance to the inhabitants of the Hierakonpolis region as to their contemporaries to the north and those far to the south in Nubia where drawings of boats also predominate in the early period. The Hierakonpolis boats have amidships a large upright structure of the type which is usually described as a shrine or cabin; however it has also been seen as a forerunner of the later Egyptian sarcophagus. In one case the boat, bearing shrine or sarcophagus, is surmounted by the figure of a bull; it is suggested that the artist's intention was to express a royal burial by depicting the principal figure in the story as a bull, one of the manifestations of the King of Egypt.

The prows of the boats are surmounted with the heads of animals, probably the ibex and the gazelle, in the manner of other Egyptian examples and of boats in Sumer and Elam of much the same period. A drawing of a wounded giraffe, a particularly striking representation, is also included amongst the subjects drawn on the rocks.

The population of the Hierakonpolis region in Predynastic times was probably not above 5,000. This would mean that virtually everyone in the community would be known to everyone else, at least by sight. It would also produce conditions in which, in a period of exceptional change with creative activity being sustained at a high level, the impact of a charismatic leader – or a group of leaders – would be very great, with stories about their prowess being magnified by repetition and embroidery until they assumed the character of legend.

Whilst the 'Main Deposit', found in the temple area at Hierakonpolis, contains some of the most important material from early dynastic Egypt it also represents a grave problem in the chronology of the earliest periods. Since the Hierakonpolis material is regarded as amongst the most crucial in establishing the character and quality of life in the earliest days of the unified Kingship, the consideration is an important one.

The first excavations at Hierakonpolis were conducted by Quibell and Green between 1897 and 1900. They discovered the ancient city site which contained the feature which for Egypt was quite extraordinary – the oval platform or revetment on which a shrine had been built. This was an element which is familiar in the architecture of early Sumerian towns, but it was, and it remains, unique in Egypt. In Sumer, it was the custom to bury sacred objects in the 'fill' of the temple revetment; this practice is also known from Bahrain in the great Barbar temple complex, which also has an oval structure at its centre.

At some time during the Old Kingdom period the temple at Hierakonpolis was rebuilt and many of the most important objects were collected together and placed in a cache which formed the 'Main Deposit', found by the excavators. The treasures of the 'Main Deposit' were of immense importance: probably no other cache of objects, even including the contents of Tutankhamun's tomb, matches them for their aesthetic and historical value. Other deposits and caches were found on the site: the objects in them range in time from the late Predynastic to the late Old Kingdom.

A scarab of the Eighteenth Dynasty was found amongst the objects in the 'Main Deposit' but this was thought by the excavator to be intrusive. But the relatively simple recording techniques of the time, the late nineteenth century, when the thrill of the discovery of a fine object tended to absorb the archaeologist's facilities of judgement and interest, do not provide an adequate provenance for many of the most important objects from Hierakonpolis.

Petrie, who like many archaeologists of his generation influenced to a remarkable degree the thinking and attitudes, not only of those who were associated with him but also of succeeding generations of scholars who seemed disinclined to question his more emphatic statements, was convinced that the Hierakonpolis material was, in effect, *all* Predynastic and based much of his thinking about the chronology of the earliest periods, especially the late Predynastic, on this assumption. It is, however, only an assumption, though virtually all of the chronology of Egypt, down to about 2000 BC, depends upon it. Hence, the chronology of all the ancient world in the third millennium at least, which is fixed to Egyptian chronology, is similarly dependent on this basic assumption of Petrie, for which the evidence, to say the least, is tenuous. More and more of the objects in the 'Main Deposit' are being seen as later in origin than the late Predynastic to which Petrie allocated them. Though the implications of this redating are profound, it does not diminish the importance nor the superlative quality of the objects themselves.

The closing years of Naqada II (or the late Gerzean or Semainean, according to some authorities; to others, more recently, Naqada III) flowed, imperceptibly no doubt to those who lived through them, into the first years of the Dual Monarchy. The actual division is marked by the coronation, if so formal a ceremony occurred, of Narmer as the first King of the Two Lands united. It may however have seemed as if the last day of the Predynastic age was followed by the first day of the First Dynasty, a new dawn indeed, in the world's first fully structured Kingdom.

It is at this point that the person and the office of the King become vital. For most of the next thousand years he was to dominate the scene over which he now towers, the most powerful and majestic potentate yet conceived by man and the unpredictable processes of history. From this time onwards the records surviving from Egypt demonstrate the extraordinary splendour and the complex and carefully managed rituals which surrounded and contained the life of the King, to an extent never achieved by another society of the time and by few of later epochs. The corporate life of Egypt came more and more to be expressed in powerful dramatic presentations designed to connect living Egypt with the unseen world of the ancestors and the gods. One of the most compelling achievements which can be set to the account of those who managed the round of great ceremonies is their apparent recognition of the significance and cathartic effect of role-playing. No other people of comparable antiquity seems either to have developed this understanding to the extent that the Egyptians did, with elaborate, complex, and highly organized ceremonies in which the principal participants impersonated gods and ancient powers, nor to have formalized such role-playing sequences so exactly, setting them down as ritual dialogues of considerable dramatic and literary quality. This faculty was developed to the highest degree in the ceremonies and rituals connected with the King, who now begins to assume his own suprahuman role in the unfolding Egyptian drama.

In the great ceremonies enacted at the court in the presence and with the participation of the King, or in the principal temples throughout the Two Lands, the King and his assistants assumed the roles of the great gods and their attendants; in effect they became those powers whose goodwill was vital to the life, prosperity, and health of Egypt. They actually took on the personae of the powers by wearing masks and elaborate costumes, by means of which the presence and involvement of the divinities themselves could be recognized.

There is something here more than the origins of drama, though the elaborate ceremonies, with the participation of a great concourse of players, with music, dance, dramatic effects, and the generous use of aromatics making the delicate air of Egypt heavy with the scent of incense, would have delighted the directors of many a Hollywood spectacular. The sacred dramas were used to propitiate or to overcome the powers of evil which the Egyptians believed could threaten the prosperity of the King and hence of Egypt; by acting out the collective apprehensions of the society, they sought to make them amenable and capable of being kept in bounds.

Assisting the king in his performance of these ritual dramas were the great officers of state who impersonated the district or *nome* gods and cosmic divinities who attended the Supreme God, whoever he might for the occasion be thought to be: Ra, Ptah, or Atum for example. The chief priests would take the parts of the divinity whom they served, attended by the clouds of assistant priests and acolytes drawn from the temples' extensive staffs, servitors, and retainers.

It is not clear whether women participated in the more general ceremonies: no doubt they had their own rituals in which perhaps the Queen or the Queen Mother (as is still the case in some West African societies) took the principal role. The probability is however that they did take part on the larger state occasions when women closest to the King would have played the goddesses who were members of the Egyptian companies of divinities. In later times ladies of high rank held offices in various of the temples; some were no doubt full-time officiants whilst others were perhaps the equivalents of those medieval ladies who sometimes held honorary or lay positions in the great abbeys or cathedral foundations. There does not seem to be any tradition of boys or young men impersonating female roles, though both boys and young girls had an important function as dancers.

Several of the great dramas of most ancient Egypt survive. One of them is the 'Conflict of Horus and Set', the ritualized version of the mythical struggle between the opposing dualities which made up Egypt's historical personality. The very fact that this conflict is conventionalized into the form of a drama with carefully presented dialogue and action is very remarkable. Then there is 'The Mystery Play of the Succession' of great antiquity for it is known from the First Dynasty. It included a mysterious group of characters called 'The Spirit Seekers' who disappear after the First Dynasty.

At his coronation, likewise, the King played through a complex and numerous series of rituals designed to signify his assumption of the sovereignty over Egypt and all its attributes. At one point he ran a course around what was in effect a microcosm of Egypt, an area marked out in the temple court where the ceremony took place; he also enacted all the roles involved in his assumption of the Kingship of the Two Lands, playing one part in the north of the complex, one in the south. The coronation formula was expressed in highly poetic terms: 'The Rising of the King of Upper Egypt, the Rising of the King of Lower Egypt, the Union of the Two Lands, the Procession around the Wall'. From this it is clear that the King is visualized as the sun or, perhaps more likely in the earliest times, a star.

The coronation ceremonies of a King of Egypt would, in many particulars, have been very much like the ceremonies which have marked the induction of kings in many societies, across the world and in many times. However, since no earlier kings are known than Egypt's it must be assumed that such rituals were invented for or by them. Two are perhaps the most familiar and symbolic of all: the crowning and the enthronement.

The importance of the two crowns in Egypt was very great. They were particularly vital expressions of the Two Lands which each symbolized. When first one and then the other was placed on the King's head, that part of his being from which issued the divine commands or, as the Egyptians put it, 'Authoritative Utterance', it was something more than simple symbolism. In the beginning the King wore his two crowns separately; later, in the reign of Den, the crowns were combined into one splendid abstraction of nationhood and royalty.

The King was always crowned twice, on each occasion in the national shrine relating to the particular Kingdom, either of the south or the north, of Upper or of Lower Egypt. The shrines were immensely ancient, descending certainly from remote Predynastic times. Then they were presumably magical places in which the chieftains who preceded the Kings if, as has been suggested, they were magicians (in the sense that a shaman is a magician), conjured and invoked the power of the hidden gods. The shrines were called, respectively, *per-niza*, the shrine of Lower Egypt, and *per-ur*, that of Upper Egypt. They survived throughout Egyptian history and were always incorporated into the structure of stone-built temples, where they usually became the holy heart of the temple itself. The shrine of Upper Egypt appears to be animal in shape.

The solemn appearance of the King on public occasions was identified with the first glorious manifestation of sunrise; the concept of the sun in splendour is thus, in another conceit of remarkable poetic insight, associated with the rising of the King. The same word is used to describe both sunrise and the King's appearance: the verb $h^{c}{}'$ is written in the form of a hieroglyph ⌒ which denotes the sun rising over the Primeval Hill or the Divine Emerging Island in which the first acts of creation took place. The King is thus identified with the very beginning of things, graphically as well as verbally and philosophically.

At the coronation, after the appearance and the crowning, an act of profound magical importance was the enthronement. The throne was described as the 'mother of the King'; it was, probably later, personified as the goddess Isis, sister and wife of Osiris.

By possessing the Queen, in whom the royal blood descended, the King's title to the Two Lands was made absolute. As he mounted the steps to the throne, in the form of a hieroglyph which again denoted the Primeval Hill ⌂, and took his seat on it he became, as it were, infused with the Kingship, from contact with powers with which the throne was charged. The power of the throne still persists in Africa, in, for example, the stool of the Asantahene, the King of the Ashanti people. Whilst the Asantahene rarely if ever sits on the stool it is the most sacred piece of the royal equipment for it contains the 'soul' of the entire people. Even the sovereigns of England, generally speaking not a very magically endowed class, are crowned seated above a magically charged stone.

The coronation of the King of Egypt marked, on each occasion, a new beginning. Time was itself renewed; the Egyptians counted time from the coronation of each King, to the infinite confusion of later generations of historians. In Egypt, as interestingly enough it was in Mesopotamia, the coronation was postponed until a new cycle of nature began. Charming ancient ceremonies took place at the coronation, such as the releasing of flocks of birds into the air, which carried the happy news of the King's accession to all the creatures of the earth, who thus could share in the universal renewal of life.

One of the greatest occasions for the fusing of ritual, magic, and the drama into one splendid unity was the *Heb-Sed*, the jubilee which the Kings celebrated every thirty years, sometimes more frequently. The origins of the *Heb-Sed* are lost; some commentators have seen the ceremony as a play-acting substitute for the ritual sacrifice of the King which they believed took place when his physical powers began to wane. Whether or not this is the case it would seem that the King at the *Heb-Sed* underwent a ritual 'death' and then was resurrected, once more youthful and recharged and so capable of guiding anew the destiny of Egypt. He was recrowned in both Kingships, sitting under a canopy, on a dais attended by priests representing the Archaic supporters of the King in the process of unification.

Thus the courts of the Step Pyramid provided King Djoser of the Third Dynasty with the ground for these ceremonies in the afterlife and doubtless the same sort of layout served later Kings.

In all the great ceremonies the King was attended by other officiants whose roles seem to descend from very distant times. One was called 'The Herdsman of Nekhen', evidently recalling some significant involvement of cattle people, no doubt originating further south, in east Africa. The King in Egypt was often described as a herdsman, his people 'the cattle of god'. 'The man from Hierakonpolis' also took part in the *Heb-Sed*.

The momentous event of the first appearance of the Lord of the Two Lands is generally thought by historians to have taken place in the thirty-second century BC. This was a time of extraordinary change, of social and political upheaval and rapid advances in several of the principal lands of the ancient Near East, on the edge of what once used to be called the Fertile Crescent. Other than in Egypt, nowhere was the change more profound than in Sumer. There is however a profound difference between the two peoples: the Sumerians never really achieved nationhood in the sense that the Egyptian Kings strove from the outset to impose it on the twin Kingdoms.

The Sumerians were earnest in the recording of long lists of their Kings, organized into city dynasties. They did not set them in a strict chronological sequence, or rather the sequence which they employed is misleading since many of the reigns they record as following one upon the other were in fact overlapping and coterminous.

The Egyptians attempted to keep records of the principal events of each reign, the clearly mythical often shading into the possibly real. They had no concept of chronology; though they were careful recorders of events on which their several calendars might be based and though they kept records in the temples far back, recording, for example, levels of the inundation, each new reign saw time begin again and all dates were reckoned in regnal years. Much of the information which underlies what is known of the earliest Kings, other than the vital, if often only too sparse information provided by archaeology, derives from the records which were set down in the temples at various times throughout the history of Egypt. Some of these, though inevitably fragmentary, were first written down as early as the third millennium, whilst great King lists were set up in the temples of the New Kingdom, in the last quarter of the second millennium in particular.

It has been suggested that the early chiefs, the precursors of the Kings, were also magicians, or at least that they had the reputation of so being; in all probability they were regarded as rainmakers. From this, it is argued, the sacred character of the Kingship is derived and from it also the character of the King as one who is above and beyond the ordinary character of humanity.

One of the most remarkable early Egyptian sculptures in the round, standing nearly 32 cm high, could well be taken as a representation of a man endowed with dark and terrible powers, a shaman or other practitioner of high magic (colour plate II). Carved in dark stone it depicts a sinister figure, completely concealed in an enveloping cloak and a hood with pierced eyelets, which is topped by something which looks very like the peak of the high white crown of Upper Egypt. It is tempting to see in this figure one of the Predynastic rulers from whom the Divine King ultimately descended; there is nothing, however, to reveal its nature or purpose, nor to indicate whether it represents a living man. It comes from El Amra and dates to the Naqada I period. The origins of the mask were clearly very ancient in Egypt.

Somewhat later in date though still, in all probability prior to the beginning of the First Dynasty, is a powerful figure of a ruler (plate 47), an imposing personality by any standards, though with a facial expression (the consequence of restoration) which some might categorize as approaching the ineffably complacent; it has, incidentally, been suggested that the figure is of a woman. But assuming that the figure is male, he is seated with his left arm across his lap in a posture which will be seen hundreds of years later in the statues of Khasekhem and Djoser.

Clearly then, at some point in the Predynastic history of Egypt chieftains first emerged. By late in the Naqada II period (c. 3300 BC) a handsome grave at the falcon capital of Hierakonpolis, the most important centre of southern Predynastic government at the time, shows a degree of furnishing and design not previously encountered in the Valley. This, the celebrated Tomb 100, is one of the crucial pieces of evidence in the evolution of Egyptian political, perhaps also of religious, structures (plate 48).

Tomb 100 (like Tomb 1 at Location 6, more recently excavated) was a large pit with a primitive superstructure, and, more important and so far uniquely, with plastered and painted walls; unhappily it is long since destroyed. It was discovered in 1898 (Quibell, 1900; Kemp, 1973). The scenes depicted on its walls appear to show hunting and the mastery of animals, fights between small groups of men, a sacrifice, and several boats including a very un-Egyptian one. The Hierakonpolis tomb painting shows influences alien to Egypt, which, like the others which have already been considered, would seem to have their origins far away to the east, in Mesopotamia and possibly also in Elam. Several of the elements depicted in the Hierakonpolis painting are included in the repertories of artists in the east, including the later cultures of the Arabian Gulf (plate 47). A number of the elements in the Hierakonpolis painting appear again in the round stamp seals which are a particular feature of the Gulf's trade in the late third–early second millennia BC.

The Hierakonpolis tomb is one late Predynastic artefact whose witness bears very strongly on the history of the period as a whole and also on its presumed foreign connections. In itself it shows that certain individuals were already distinguished from their contemporaries, even in death; indeed the long succession of Egyptian royal tombs seems to have its beginning here, at Hierakonpolis.

At least one of the little figures who appear to be engaged in hand-to-hand combats in the painting seems to be wielding the type of mace or club which, at one time, was believed by some scholars to show that ship-borne foreign invaders from the east had entered the Valley and imposed their rule on the tribes already living there. The invaders were thought to be those associated with the Falcon clan, and as support of the invasion theory, the evidence of the war-maces was introduced. Now it is significant that at the time when the Naqada II culture begins to predominate in the Valley the traditional flat, circular, disc-shaped macehead which was the effective end of the Egyptian club and which is particularly associated with Naqada I, was replaced by a pear-shaped mace, the form which was current in Sumerian and Elamite lands at the same period.

Egyptian conservatism retained the disc-shaped mace as part of the royal regalia but the pear-shaped mace, a much more efficient weapon, became standard issue in the armies of the King. The King himself is invariably shown smiting his foes with the pear-shaped mace and, as these foes are frequently represented as being 'Asiatics', from whom the weapon was borrowed, there is a certain irony in the representations of this demonstration of the King's power.

The flat Naqada I disc of stone, pierced through the centre, with a short neck, was, when mounted on a stick or handle, quite a well balanced, slashing type of weapon (plates 50a and 50b). However the pear-shaped maceheads are formidable 'bashing' weapons, more like the African club. The generous distribution of scenes depicting its use in temples and palaces, abroad as much as in Egypt itself, was a powerful promotional campaign for the King's military prowess and an argument for Egypt's enemies to pursue pacific and deferential policies. In Egypt itself the royal propagandists were even more diligent and the picture of the King smiting his enemies was a popular one throughout the Kingdom's history.

There is a third type of macehead found in Egypt, though with much less frequency than either the disc- or pear-shaped varieties. This is the 'composite' mace, carved from a soft stone and decorated with animal forms. The most significant example was, once again, from Hierakonpolis; it consists of a piece of steatite (or chlorite) carved in the round, centrally pierced and fitted with a copper rod (plate 50c). Both the style of carving and the material are atypical of Egypt but very characteristic of the carving of late-fourth-millennium Mesopotamia and, particularly, of Elam. Carved chlorite vessels and decorative and votive pieces are amongst the most typical products of Sumer's near neighbours on both sides of the Arabian Gulf in the late fourth/early third millennia.

A little later it is possible to see the fusion of the pear-shaped mace and the composite one in the large carved, pictographic maces associated with King Scorpion and King Narmer. The making of such monumental maces seems to have ceased after the latter's reign. In the case of Scorpion the King is accompanied by his high officers who carry a number of standards on which are displayed symbols or fetishes identified with particular districts into which Egypt was immemorially divided. Two of these are Set animals, the hound which identified the god, showing that at this time the Set tribes of the south were already supporters of the royal clan; others represent falcons, a jackal, the thunderbolt of Min, and one possibly representing the mountains. It is significant perhaps that more standards are shown supporting Scorpion than is the case with the slightly later Narmer palette, on which only four standards are displayed.

Before the splendid figure of the King, who wears the high white crown of Upper Egypt, are two most important ideograms. The first is a Scorpion which is considered by most authorities to represent the King's name. It is uncertain how it would have been pronounced; on the evidence of later times perhaps *Selkh*, *Sekhen*, or something like it. The second is a rosette or star, which is only used to identify the Kings at this period. In Sumer a rosette or star indicated a divinity; perhaps in this scene the hand of an immigrant Sumerian scribe or craftsman can be detected.

It is not known where Scorpion's capital was located though the probability is that it was Hierakonpolis. At the time of the unification the two great Predynastic centres of Hierakonpolis and Naqada seem to decline in prestige, at least to the extent that they cease to be royal capitals. They still retain their powerful quality as the residences of the two great gods, Horus the Falcon and Set the Hound, or whatever was the animal sacred to him (see Appendix).

The nature of the Egyptian Kingship, though it is probably the oldest such institution on earth, is extremely complex. The titles of the King reveal something of this complexity and of the careful policy of consolidation and conciliation which the early Kings practised, with eventual total and

103

distinguished success. In all cases in matters which touched their sacred and royal character they adopted symbolisms which were attributed to the two parts of the double realm. The first and most prestigious of the names the King of Egypt bore was his Horus name. This he assumed at his coronation: it was magical and full of power for by its assumption he became not only King of Egypt but the living god. Two of his other titles were established during the First Dynasty; of these the *nesu-bit* or *insibya*, is depicted hieroglyphically by two ideograms, the sedge, growing plentifully in the waterways of Upper Egypt, and the bee, redolent of the hives of the north. At some time there may have been a Sedge King and a Bee King (there was a temple consecrated to the northern goddess Neith, 'The House of the Bee'), though nothing survives to confirm this. They would have been chieftains of congeries of tribes which assembled under their standards; the King of the united Egypt assumed their titles to himself and so demonstrated his paramountcy over the Two Lands. Ever afterwards the *nesu-bit* name of Sedge and Bee was to be read as 'King of Upper and Lower Egypt'. The *nesu-bit* name was introduced during the reign of King Den, the third King of the First Dynasty. Why the bee and the sedge plant, neither of which seems to be particularly characteristic of the Egyptian countryside nor especially majestic, should have been chosen to represent the Kingship is puzzling, however.

The second title which demonstrated the new line of Kings' concern to conciliate their subjects of the two disparate regions of the Valley is the *nebti* name. This was first proclaimed in the reign of King Anedjib, the fifth King of the founding dynasty and is altogether a more cogent and impressive symbol for the supreme power of the god who was also King of Egypt. It linked the two tutelary goddesses of the Kingdoms, hitherto, of course, to be assumed to have been in opposition. They are respectively Nekhbet, the Vulture of the South, and Uadjet, the rearing Cobra of the North. In the titulary of the Kings they perch upon two baskets; they are read as 'He of (belonging to) the Two Ladies', hence the more orotund transliteration 'Lord of the Two Lands'. Always, thereafter, the two goddesses were the special protectors and familiars of the King. No matter to whom amongst the High Gods he might be particularly consecrated nor whose name he might include in his own royal names, the 'Two Ladies' were there. Nekhbet was always to be seen hovering behind or above the King, her great wings spread around his head: she would even extend the power of her protective presence to his possessions or of those most favoured by him. Uadjet, in some ways a more dangerous divinity, was bound around the very head of the King or around his crown (in later times at least) where, rearing up, with her hood spread malevolently, she would release a blast of furious energy to destroy the King's enemies. Both goddesses are powerful and dramatic symbols which, when they are combined, are most formidable.

Further, the combination of these two dominant and hitherto contending goddesses was a subtle act of political judgement. It was also characteristic of many of the actions of the founders of the Kingdom who exercised a sublime and sensitive tact when, coming down river as conquerors from the south, they needed, whenever possible, to subdue the northern part of the Valley and its protagonists by peaceable means, as much at least as by force. That Egypt continued virtually at all times throughout its immense history to be unified (despite the perpetual paradox of the existence of the Two Kingdoms), except for one or two interludes which themselves came to be anathematized as unholy exceptions to a rule of nature, was a tribute to the genius of these men.

In Egypt the idea of the King as god is indistinguishable from the role of art as propaganda. It was an audacious concept to elevate a man, no matter how much endowed with genius or accustomed to the dispensation of power, to the level of the godhead. If it was not to be rapidly exposed as absurd (the god with influenza, a bilious god, the god defecating) this literal apotheosis had to be absolute and uncompromising: from the time of the Scorpion at least the King was depicted as a superhuman figure, towering over mortals, utterly splendid and awesome. In the promotion of the King in this role, a primarily political conception incidentally, and not a religious one, art in all its forms had a decisive function to discharge. It would have been reflected in the organization of the great ceremonies which attended the official life of the god-king and which must have been rich and complex theatrical performances, worthy of the highest state ceremonies. The producers of these divine and royal pageants must have been talented and powerful men, capable of controlling large casts, moving crowds of 'extras' and always ensuring that the breathless attention of the bystanders (themselves highly privileged even to be present) was always focused on the person of the principal player, the King himself. The early maceheads dating from Scorpion's and Narmer's reigns, and the ivory labels of their immediate successors, show ceremonies already highly developed and complex in form. The great theatricals of most ancient Egypt must have been powerful and imposing events, designed to promote the absolute power of the King and the devolved power of his coadjutors.

Unity was not achieved only through political means, however; the King's authority had to be asserted quickly and with devastating effect. Two other documents from the end of the Predynastic period testify to this process; both are amongst the most celebrated and the most important of Egyptian artefacts. Both, too, contribute their evidence to the debate on the nature and extent of foreign influences in Egypt in the Naqada II period, from which they derive, or from the years immediately following it.

The great votive palette of King Narmer, first King of the First Dynasty who is probably to be identified with the near legendary Menes, the Unifier, represents a type of artefact peculiar to Egypt and of considerable significance in the early periods; it was recovered from the 'Main Deposit' at Hierakonpolis. Such palettes, generally made of schist, a grey-green, friable stone often of great beauty, range from small utilitarian plates for grinding kohl (plate 52), the dark-green eyeshadow much favoured by Egyptians, which were customarily included in the kits supplied to the dead and placed in the tomb, to a large, even monumental piece like Narmer's Palette, which was elaborately carved and, from its exceptional size was evidently a dedicatory offering. It was presumably laid up in the Falcon capital as an act of piety by the victorious King.

When this class of palette was first identified in Egypt in the last century archaeologists believed that these 'slates', as they were often called, were Mesopotamian in origin. The mistake is understandable since they often contain so many Mesopotamian design elements; the earlier types have a density of action and detail that is only comparable with the cheerful confusion of the elements of some of the early Susian and Gulf seals. Examples of these palettes with a much more richly endowed field of design than is usual with Egyptian artists are the Hunters Palette (plate 69a) and the Exotic Animals (or 'two dogs') palette from Hierakonpolis (plates 53a and 53b).

This last artefact is a very remarkable production. The entire surface, except for the kohl-grinding area, is filled with animals, some of a very strange appearance. Dominating both sides are two great dogs. A good cross-section of the larger fauna of Egypt is represented but the strangest, most mysterious figure is that of a dog- or jackal-headed creature, reared up on its hind legs, playing a sort of flute. Did Orpheus have his origins in Predynastic Hierakonpolis or is this some masked Master of the Beasts? There can surely be little doubt that it is the enigmatic Set who pipes who knows what strange melodies to the whirling animals (and monsters) which attend him.

The palettes are, however, uniquely and peculiarly Egyptian, though they do begin to appear in quantities at the time of what may have been maximum Mesopotamian penetration. The Sumerians and the Elamites enjoyed carving in soft malleable grey-green stones like chlorite; the schist from which most Egyptian palettes are made is a much less tractable material, requiring greater skill than was usually available amongst Sumerian craftsmen. As in the instance of other artefacts and design elements which seem to be foreign to Egypt, the inspiration for the palettes may, just conceivably, have come from some sort of Mesopotamian precedent or contact, but the genius of the Egyptian artificers quickly made the palettes one of the most distinctive of early Egyptian artefacts.

Schist had been worked for a long time before the unification. Even before the beginning of the First Dynasty it had been used for the making of palettes, originally designed for the preparation of kohl, the ointment with which the ancient Egyptians used to dress their eyes, partly for cosmetic purposes, partly to reduce the glare of the sun, and partly as a prophylactic against the prevalent eye diseases which have always been endemic in the Near East.

The earliest palettes and those which continued to be used by the simpler people are generally rectangular in shape, made particularly elegant by the grinding surface being bounded by two or three narrow, incised lines cut on the stone. This gives these everyday objects grace which is formidable. Even some of the more primitive, like the one carved in the form of a ram, have great charm (plate 54). Marvellous representations are there of the chase; others, as we have seen, record royal occasions. Once again it is chastening to observe the techniques employed: the skill required in cutting away the surface and then grinding it and polishing it to the final state is very considerable.

The schist palettes represent a sort of rudimentary sculpture, requiring considerable skills in the making. After the time of King Khasekhemui, one of the most elevated in the Archaic period, sculpture in the round advanced very rapidly. That stone was beginning more and more fre-quently to be used in architecture is shown by the granite used in a monumental door way in what was probably Khasekhemui's palace in Hierakonpolis. It is a splendid if somewhat sinister piece of carving; used as the base for the massive door hinge it shows an Asiatic captive sprawled on the ground, his face twisted in an expression of hate and rejection.

Narmer's Palette is the largest and most handsome of the votive palettes to survive (plates 55a and 55b). The Temple of the Falcon at Hierakonpolis, where it was found, was one of the principal centres of the family cults of the founding Kings, the meeting place for the followers of the Falcon and for the rites which they practised there, from Predynastic times. The palette is intact. It carries elaborate designs on both sides and seems to be intended to commemorate Narmer's ascendancy over the Two Lands; in that context, it is one of the most important historical documents from remote antiquity as well as being one of the first products of a royal or state propaganda machine. It is designed, with considerable subtlety, to emphasize the King's sovereignty over both Upper and Lower Egypt.

On the obverse the King is portrayed as ruler of the southern Kingdom. He wears the high white crown which was always distinctive of Upper Egypt, just as the curious, inverted, saucepan-like object served as the red crown of Lower Egypt immemorially. The King is attended by his sandal-bearer, a high dignitary, perhaps his son, who is identified by a rosette, the divine or royal emblem. Narmer is shown in the act of striking a kneeling captive, probably one of the defeated princes of the north, whilst above Horus himself brings to the King 6,000 captives from the marshes. The representations are surmounted by two Hathor heads (showing how ancient was the worship of the goddess in that form) and the King's name, its syllables made up of the crude glyphs for chisel and catfish, its unlikely compound. Already the royal name is contained within the palace-façade *serekh*: this will now always be firmly associated with the princes responsible for the unification.

On the reverse the designs are more complex. Here, surmounted by the Hathor heads and the royal name in its enclosure, the King walks solemnly forward, wearing the red crown of the northern Kingdom and carrying his war mace. Behind him walks the same boyish sandal-bearer; another high courtier carries what looks like a bolas, a device used from the remotest times in hunting to bring down the larger game; it may, on the other hand, be a rope for hobbling animals which came to represent the hieroglyph 'tt'. The King and his two attendants have symbols or devices, the ancestors of hieroglyphs, before them. The King's we know; the sandal-bearer, who before was marked by a seven-petalled rosette, now seems to be identified by a throwing stick and a six-petalled rosette whilst his colleague who, unlike him, is shaven headed (perhaps because he is a child) wears a full and heavy wig, and is marked by another version of the object he carries in his hand, suspended above an inverted closed semi-circle.

Before the royal party, scaled down in much the same proportion to the King's two attendants as they are to him, are four little figures carrying standards on which are displayed the symbols associated throughout Egyptian history with certain of the nomes or districts of the Two Lands.

These nome standards are intriguing. They obviously descend from a very early period of Egyptian history; their repetition over thousands of years demonstrates vividly the Egyptian reluctance to change anything that had proved its utility, value, appositeness, or sanctity. Some of them certainly preserve the earlier representations of the divinities of Egypt, fetishes which anticipate the animal and human representations of the gods. The nomes had, in all probability, once represented the tribal or clan areas into which the Predynastic people were divided; the chieftains or princes of the nomes were, with the senior priests, the 'Great Ones' with whom even the most autocratic King found it expedient to consult. When the long, golden time of Egypt's first greatness as a corporate state was shattered at the end of the Old Kingdom, the ancient pattern of the nomes re-established itself and the nome-princes and provincial governors became, effectively, independent sovereigns, until they were put down by the remarkable rulers of the early Middle Kingdom.

At the time of Narmer's Palette, however, all this lay in the distant future. The four little standard bearers on Narmer's Palette carry symbols, two of which are falcons, one is associated with Wepwawet, the dog-fetish of Asiyut, and the fourth is probably the sign of the Royal Placenta, one of the most potent symbols associated intimately with the King.

The cult of the Royal Placenta is one of the more curious aspects of the Egyptians' reverence for the King as incarnate god. It is of immense antiquity, for the cult was well established by the late Predynastic period. By the time of the unification the placenta had assumed the status of one of the gods of Egypt and was thus carried as a standard before the King.

The placenta is the membrane adhering to the walls of the womb in which the embryo is contained. At birth the placenta is discharged and forms what is popularly known as the 'afterbirth'. When it is depicted on the royal standard it retains the elliptical shape it might be supposed to have when it contained the embryo, lying in wait to be born.

For the early Egyptians the placenta was evidently invested with exceptional power. The King's placenta was carefully retained and protected throughout his lifetime; on the evidence of examples in the tombs of lesser figures in the state, it was probably buried with him. If it were to be damaged or destroyed, appalling disaster would result.

No other part of the royal anatomy seems to have warranted the same care and reverence as did the placenta. Not even the royal prepuce was accorded comparable honour, though it, too, might be buried with the King. In any case, circumcision does not seem generally to have been practised in the early centuries, to judge by the evidence of a number of men represented uncircumcised in their statues. Only the placenta was raised to the status of a divinity.

The reason for the placenta's exceptional status is not difficult to find. Because of its uniquely intimate connection with the living body of the god-king, protecting him from the moment of conception, growing with him in the womb and, in a very real sense, giving him life, it was conceived as another emanation of the King himself.

The placenta was thus seen as a form of twin, the witness of the King's *alter ego*, which, at his birth, was born into the realm of the gods. As his twin it coexisted eternally with the King and so the King himself was, at the instant of his birth, two indivisible entities.

The honour paid to the King's placenta is the product of those African values and concepts which were profound and deeply rooted in the Egyptian psyche. The idea of twinship with which it is associated is one of the most basic and enduring canons of the belief of the Egyptians, which manifested itself in the perpetually reiterated theme of duality. The King was the link between the world of the gods and the world of men, existing eternally and equally in both. All his titles were dualized; he was, in a sense, his own twin.

The cult of the placenta is to be seen at its highest manifestation in the earliest periods of which there are documentary records surviving. Then Egypt was still closest to its aboriginal African roots; the placenta is indeed amongst the most powerful symbols linking the Kingship with its earliest African origins. As the long process of Egyptian history unfolded the role of the placenta gradually diminished, though it certainly never entirely disappeared. Even in later times when non-African influences seeped into the Valley and eventually drove out most of the archetypal African traits, the royal placenta was still accorded an honoured place in the company of the King, though probably only the wisest and most astute of seers would have been able to account for its presence in the King's entourage at all.

The standards borne before the King probably represent the chiefs who supported Narmer in his bid to unify the Two Kingdoms. They are leading the King to ten headless bodies, lying on their backs with their severed heads between their feet. Above them Horus stands before what may be his Archaic shrine, made of reeds. Behind him is a high-prowed ship, of the type which has been frequently described as 'Mesopotamian'. This, and the scenes portrayed on the Jebel el Arak knife handle, described below, may be the most explicit recognition of the assistance given by Meso-potamians to the Hierakonpolitan princes when they started out on their programme of unification.

On the reverse, the design is dominated by representations of weird and fantastic quadrupeds with the bodies of lions and huge arching necks on which are balanced feline heads. These confront each other, held on leashes by two attendants or handlers of somewhat un-Egyptian appear-ance. The circular area which they make by the twining of their necks is probably where the kohl would have been ground, if these particular palettes had ever been used for so mundane a purpose.

The motif of confronted long-necked, feline monsters is familiar in the iconography of late-fourth–early-third-millennium western Asiatic designs, particularly those employed in the cylinder seals which are one of the most characteristic products of the Mesopotamian and Susian or Elamite cultures. The device of two serpopards which entwined necks is especially typical of Elamite designs, perhaps the source of much of the western Asiatic influence in Egypt, around the time of the unification. It appears first in Egypt in the Hierakonpolis tomb; it disappears after the First Dynasty. Confronted feline heads are found in the chlorite carvings of the Arabian Gulf, in the early third millennium.

A third register completes the reverse side of the Narmer Palette. A great bull, no doubt a manifestation of the King himself or of one of his principal allies, is 'hacking down' the walls of a fortified city, with his huge curving horns. A naked man, presumably the prince or the governor of the city, lies prostrate beneath its hoofs.

The symbolism of the early palettes is very complex. Most of the examples which survive have animals as their most important protagonists and only the Narmer Palette and those known as the Hunters and the Battlefield particularly emphasize humans (plate 40). The Bull and the Lion are important elements in several of them, though the King seems still to be portrayed either in his own form or as a hawk or falcon. It has been proposed that this fairly notable disappearance from the iconography of royal monuments in the First Dynasty of the Bull and Lion marks their elimination from the politics of Egypt at this still formative period of the unification. Thus, the argument goes, the Bull Prince and the Lion Prince, once powerful chiefs allied to the Falcon Prince, were excluded from power and the animals which symbolized them were largely dropped from the heraldic catalogue. It is an intriguing suggestion for which there is not the slightest real evidence. But a conflict can certainly be detected between the hound and the falcon, the symbols of the two greatest southern Predynastic divinities, Set and Horus.

The Narmer Palette is rich in that symbolism which was to persist throughout Egyptian history: only the serpo-pards eventually disappear. No part of the palette is more potent than those elements which relate to the King and which deal with his power. This indeed was the unique importance of the King, that he subsumed in his own person the entire land of Egypt and everything in it. His overwhelming sovereignty is nowhere better represented than in the royal crowns, the two most important of which Narmer is himself shown as wearing.

The King of Egypt, it might be said, had a crown for every occasion. Their variety is considerable but the two shown on the palette were of special power. They are respectively the high white crown of Upper Egypt and the red crown of the north. Although it is not an infallible principle, gods of Upper Egypt, like Set, tend generally to wear the white crown whilst the gods of the northern Kingdom, like Neith (actually a goddess), wear the red. Often they display the two crowns combined in one, symbolizing the unity of Egypt.

In consequence of their particularly intimate connection with the person of the King, both in a physical sense and because they were first among the more obvious manifestations of his claim to the sovereignty, the crowns represented one of the most enduring elements in the Egyptian belief in the immutability of the world. The crowns were evidence of the special care which the gods had of the people of the Valley and their warrant for Egypt's eternity. When the collapse came it was all the more horrific, because of this sense of unchanging certainty; but the crowns endured.

The crowns, not surprisingly, were themselves divine. They were members, in the early periods, of the personal retinue of divinities which attended the King; their role was the protection of the King and the destruction of his enemies. Special chapels were built for the housing of the crowns, so sacred were they.

The earliest certain representation of the white crown of the south, is on the Narmer palette. Confusingly, the earliest representation of the red crown, traditionally identified with the northern Kingdom which is assumed to have been less significant than its southern contemporary, is on a pottery sherd recovered from a southern site, Naqada, and quite firmly dated to the Naqada I period, in the middle of the fourth millennium, c. 3500 BC (plate 41).

This is rather disconcerting; it inevitably calls again into question the reality or otherwise of the northern Kingdom and whether it really existed at all. Perhaps 'the north' meant that part of the Valley below the Falcon's domains; the red crown may therefore have been part of the regalia of another southern prince whose lands were absorbed by the conquering family of princes from still further south. When it was decided, for political reasons, to identify a northern Kingdom to mirror the southern one, once the unification was securely under way, it is possible that the crown from downstream was adopted as a northern symbol. But this is speculation, nothing more; the decision to use the red crown to 'balance', as it were, the white, may have been yet another coup by the royal propagandists. What is certain, however, is that the red crown always came first in precedence, always enjoyed a more exalted reputation than its white peer, despite the latter's identification with the south, and the origins of the Kingship.

In the early period the crowns were used to reflect the need to unite the two divergent parts of the Kingdom. The three names assumed by the

King at his coronation served the same purpose; the second name, it will be recalled, emphasized the duality of the Kingdom by employing the devices of the sedge and the bee to demonstrate the fact that the King was sovereign of both lands.

Similarly in a dazzling feat of synthesis, an archaic designer of genius, retained by the King a little while after the unification, came up with a brilliant stroke of propaganda, to combine the two crowns into one. This became known as the *shenty* and is a telling and highly evocative symbol of the union; it means 'the Two Powerful Ones'. It was first employed during the reign of Den the fifth King of the First Dynasty, when many of the most notable aspects of the royal administration were first formulated.

One of the most familiar of the motifs from western Asia that crept into Egyptian design at this time is that of the heroic figure wrestling with wild animals, a thoroughly un-Egyptian concept but one which is associated with the countless representations of Gilgamesh in later Mesopotamian times, though Gilgamesh himself reigned in Uruk within the historic period, *c.* 2650 BC. This same motif is dramatically recorded in the Hierakonpolis tomb painting and on a strikingly beautiful ceremonial dagger found at Jebel el Arak in Upper Egypt, a site at the point where the Wadi Hammamat, the dry-course route from the Red Sea, reaches the Nile Valley (plates 56a and 56b).

The Jebel el Arak knife is a remarkable survival because, apart from the documentary significance of its decoration, it is itself an outstanding example of two great ancient technologies. The handle of the dagger is beautifully carved in ivory with an assurance and mastery which requires its maker to have been an artist of high achievement and secure tradition. The figures are carved naturalistically, set into their ground with sensitivity and with no suggestion of the 'primitive'. The blade, on the other hand, is the culmination of the old Stone Age technique of stone flaking, here brought to a degree of precision and elegance which is quite exceptional. The result is exquisite, a 'ripple-flaked' blade of a translucent fineness as far removed from the rough hand-axes of Palaeolithic times from whose tradition it descends, as is the Saqqara complex of King Djoser from the mud-walled hut of the prehistoric chief to whom the knife may have been an object of justifiable pride.

On one face of the dagger's handle is represented a tall and majestic figure, his head turbaned like a Sumerian (and thus like the head in the British Museum collection), wearing a long flowing robe of a type which is familiar from Elam; no Egyptian of the time, as far as we know, would have been seen alive or dead in such a costume. Whoever he is, the protagonist, with a curiously complacent expression on his face, grasps a lion in either hand as he stands on a rock, often the site of appearance of Mesopotamian divinities, as we know from many similar representations on seals and stone carvings. Two dogs, of a distinctly un-Egyptian breed, gaze at him fondly as he subdues the two great felines. The turbaned, robed, and bearded figure is also known from Sumerian contexts of the earliest periods – late fourth, early third millennia – in three-dimensional form. Another Egyptian example is a partially preserved figure wearing a long Asiatic type of robe recorded on the 'Battlefield' palette, where he appears to be leading forward a bound captive.

On the other side of the handle of the Jebel el Arak knife a scene of exceptional historical interest is depicted, for it seems to show the people of the Nile Valley in battle with seaborne opponents whose high-prowed ships, some bearing totems which look like the crescent of Sin-Nanna, the Sumerian moon god, suggest that they may have come from Mesopotamia where such boats were developed. Naked but for penis sheaths the con-tenders are locked together in a battle, real or symbolic, which must in either event have seemed important enough for the Egyptians to record it as they did.

The Hunters' palette, also from the Predynastic period, displays Meso-potamian themes, and the archers and spearsmen whose pursuit of the lions gives the palette its name, have a distinctly Asiatic appearance. The similarity between these hunters, their dress and weapons and those carved on the rocks near Bi'r Hima (Zarius) in western Arabia may be amongst the most important evidence for determining the direction of at least some of the influences which were flowing into Egypt at this time.

Whilst the unification of Egypt is traditionally ascribed to Narmer, it is now generally accepted that he probably *reunified* the Two Lands, restoring the work of an earlier prince of his house, whose name is no longer known. This original unification may have taken place between 100 and 150 years before Narmer's time.

Some of the First Dynasty royal names seem to represent totems or fetishes, peculiar perhaps to the special group or society to which the King belonged. Thus Narmer is 'Catfish-Chisel'; 'The Falcon Catfish-Chisel' is more or less what his name and title mean, and its peculiar character is not diminished by the knowledge that in later times the catfish came to signify an abomination. The situation becomes still more confused when it is recalled that fish were often execrated as the enemies of Horus and his father Osiris, since one of them, the oxyrhynchus, was thoughtless enough to consume the penis of Osiris when his body was cut into pieces and scattered throughout Egypt by Set. In certain rituals, in later times, fish were trampled under foot to signify their fate as Horus's enemies. In the

114

First Dynasty, however, this does not apply; many representations of fish survive and there were fish cults celebrated in the temples. A number of ivory fish were recovered from Narmer's supposed tomb; other representations, particularly in the form of schist palettes, also survive in considerable quantity, but only during the First Dynasty.

The Sumerians, at least in the city of Eridu, were well disposed to fish and to the god who was specially identified with them, the benign Enki. Of him it was said 'When Enki arose, the fishes rose and adored him.' The altars at his earliest shrine at Eridu, dating back to very remote times indeed, were hung about with nets and scattered with the offerings of fish. Of course, fish and fishing would have been much more important aspects of the Sumerian economy, with the products of the Gulf and their richly stocked rivers and lagoons, than would have been the case in Egypt, where fishing never played a very major part in the people's lives. Some Predynastic textile fragments exist which show fishing in progress and occasionally it is depicted on Predynastic pottery.

Narmer, the founder of the First Thinite Dynasty, is said to have reigned for sixty-four years, the term attributed to him by Manetho and it is not intrinsically improbable. This means that he must have assumed the throne as a very young man, the veritable Horus, vigorous and youthful. His 'portraits' show him as a mature man, stately and confident. He is a slender, obviously not tall (though convention makes him tower above his contemporaries), fine-boned, bearded, altogether rather elegant figure. Invariably, he is shown crowned and dressed in the complex royal regalia: lion tail, Hathor bedecked apron and sandals, these last sometimes carried by a young attendant, perhaps his son or some favoured courtier.

One marvellous survival from the early First Dynasty is a small ivory figure of an unknown King, now in the British Museum (plate 57). Though tiny it is powerful and vigorously carved. It depicts the King wearing the Upper Egyptian crown, hunched in his *Heb-Sed* cloak worn at the time of the Jubilee ceremonies. His cloak is richly embroidered.

A distinctly equivocal portrait, however, traditionally attributed to the first King of united Egypt, exists in the Petrie Collection in University College, London (plate 59). This limestone head, from Abydos, is a disturbing piece; the King (or god, for it has been suggested that it is from a statue of the ithyphallic Min) has a distinctly epicene and decadent look about it, not at all like the clear-cut figure who appears on the great palette. However the rather long upper lip and wide-set eyes do strongly recall the portrait of Narmer on his great palette and of the young attendant, perhaps the King's heir, who is portrayed with him.

A very large proportion of the material evidence which survives from ancient Egypt and which provides most of what is known about the life of the people of the Two Lands at all periods throughout its history is supplied by the contents of the tombs in which they caused themselves to be buried, in the forlorn and sadly mistaken belief that their remains would thus be preserved for all eternity. This contribution of the tomb furnishers to history applies particularly in the time of the early dynasties when tomb building, always one of Egypt's most prosperous industries, first assumed real importance.

The monumental tombs of the First Dynasty are, by any standards, very remarkable buildings. They are, after all, amongst the earliest examples of monumental architecture, of any form anywhere in the world, with the exception of Sumer where religious buildings of prodigious scale had been erected in the cities since early in the fourth millennium and probably in the late fifth.

The building of great funerary monuments is the most immediate and obvious change in Egyptian customs which can be attributed to the period of unification. From the time before the accession of Menes-Narmer the most elaborate tomb known is Tomb 100, the decorated tomb at Hierakonpolis which lay in a cemetery of rich burials; certain brick-built structures have been attributed to the last Predynastic kings, but so far without real assurance.

The First Dynasty monuments themselves are without any real precedent in Egypt or for that matter anywhere else. The first to be identified, other than that so disastrously savaged by Amélineau, was found at Naqada, the city of the god Set, by De Morgan in 1896 (plate 60). A little later Petrie began a series of historic excavations at Abydos, one of the most important centres in the whole of the Nile Valley, which was sited in an area which seems to have become of profound importance to the family of princes who now became the first Kings of a united Egypt.

A succession of these great tombs were excavated and described by Petrie. He had little doubt that they were the tombs of the Kings and he published them as such. So matters remained until excavations of comparable structures were carried out on the immense mortuary site at Saqqara, overlooking the ancient capital Memphis, built at 'the balance of the Two Lands'. From the mid-1930s W. B. Emery excavated a series of huge mud-brick rectangular buildings on the escarpment of Saqqara which, as he worked through them, he became convinced were the actual tombs of the Kings (colour plate V); indeed he was able to attribute each huge building with firm assurance to every King of the First Dynasty, bar one.

But where, Egyptologists asked themselves, did this leave the monuments at Abydos, particularly as no actual burials had been found in any of them, a disconcerting absence of material evidence? Originally Emery had ascribed the first Saqqara tomb which he excavated to a high official of the First Dynasty, Hemaka, whose sealings were found in considerable quantity inside the monument. But then doubts arose, for it was questioned whether divine Kings would have willingly accepted the idea of their courtiers, no matter how great, being buried in tombs apparently far more imposing than their own.

The Egyptologists, however, came up with an ingenious solution to the problem of what now appeared to them to be two sets of royal 'tombs', in only one of which, in the nature of things, could the King actually have been buried. Because of their superior size it was decided that the Saqqara tombs were the actual places of burial, a view which was strengthened by the fact that evidence for actual burials had been found in several of them whereas this was not the case in Abydos. It was therefore concluded that, with the Egyptian enthusiasm for dualism, for expressing everything in terms of related or paired opposites, the Abydos 'tombs' must have been cenotaphs, which the King's spirit would have been considered to have occupied. The two monuments thus reiterated the idea of the dual Kingship, with the monuments reflecting the royal duality of the King of Upper and Lower Egypt. In this equation, to Abydos was attributed the southern location whilst the Saqqara monuments were identified as the Lower Egyptian or northern tombs, a not altogether convincing solution since Saqqara itself, like Memphis, is firmly located in Upper Egypt, though in its northern limits. It was argued that the Kings chose to be buried towards the north of their two lands so that the presence of their sacred remains would confer the ineffable merit of their sanctity on the still fragile union of south and north. Thus two schools were established: those who believed, following De Morgan and Petrie, that Abydos, because of its special holiness and its proximity to the place of origins of the Thinite house, was the more likely place in which the Kings would have been buried and those, like Emery and Lauer, the French archaeologist who worked at Saqqara for some fifty years, who contended that the size, the nobility of design, and the splendour of decoration of the tombs there could only have housed royal burials.

Subsequently, however, another factor emerged which changed the view of the situation once again. The monuments at Abydos are strung out along an area known as the Umm al-Qa'ab; beyond the town and behind a temple dedicated to the very ancient canine god Khentiamentiu (a forerunner of Anubis) the remains of very large structures with panelled and buttressed walls have been identified (plate 61). These appear to be comparable with some of the most remarkable of all Archaic survivals in

117

Egypt, the so-called 'Castles of Khasekhemui', one of which is also located at Abydos and another at Hierakonpolis. Both of these date from the end of the Second Dynasty. These are colossal, towering structures built of mud brick, now sombre and menacing in their ruin, but once gleaming brilliantly white. However it is now reasonably certain that to call these structures 'castles' is misleading.

It seems likely that the First and Second Dynasty Kings built these huge structures as 'funerary palaces' (as they have been well-named) and located them close to their tombs, which are themselves comparatively modest, representing only a part of the whole enormous complex. They contained magazines, shrines, and, perhaps, dummy buildings like those which later graced the Djoser complex at Saqqara and earlier, the 'model estate' in the great Saqqara tomb attributed to the reign of King Hor-Aha, probably the second King of the First Dynasty. The courts were probably the locations of great religious or commemorative ceremonies.

These buildings were, it has been suggested, dwellings for the spirit of the King, attended by the spirits of the courtiers, artisans, women, and even dogs, all of whom were sacrificed in various quantities throughout the First Dynasty. The buildings were almost certainly replicas of the palaces in which the Kings lived; their walls rose at least thirty feet and in their day must have been magnificent and imposing structures.

Once again it is the fact that these buildings are virtually unprecedented that astonishes even the most blasé observer. The readiness to build on a scale never before attempted was a phenomenon which was to manifest itself often throughout Egyptian history; it begins with these great structures at Abydos and those also at Saqqara for the tombs there, even if they are only built for officials and for members of the royal family other than the King himself, are complex, richly appointed, and vast in scale.

There are notable and curious differences between the two types of funerary monument, in their differing locations. The substructures were not dissimilar but their superstructures were quite different. In some cases the monuments at Saqqara appeared to contain a small tumulus or burial mound inside the tomb, encased in brick. Sometimes this casing was stepped, leading some authorities to see here the origin of the Stepped Pyramid of the Third Dynasty. In Abydos and indeed in most important Predynastic burials a tumulus was built up over the burial pit. This was the tumulus mound incorporated even in the most extravagant tombs.

Other than their size the most notable feature about the buildings in both locations (and the others at Naqada, Abu Rowash, Tarkhan, and Giza which can be compared with them) is the repetitive design of recessed panelling and buttressing on their façades. This, it is generally agreed, is borrowed from the façades of temple buildings in Sumer, particularly those built in the Jemdet Nasr period at the end of the fourth millennium, when the unification of Egypt was achieved; indeed, the tombs at Saqqara are altogether very reasonable representations of Sumerian temples, a circumstance that could hardly be the consequence of chance.

It can only be a matter for wonder that at so very early a date there were men in Egypt capable of designing buildings of this size and of this complexity, supervising the construction processes involved, and carrying out the interior designs and furnishings. It is difficult to see how they acquired their skills, other than by contact with the only people of the time who did have experience of large-scale architectural projects, the Sumerians who had a tradition of sophisticated architecture reaching back for nearly a thousand years.

What Sumerian architects would have been doing in Egypt is another matter. It can hardly be that travelling merchants brought with them the idea, for example, of recessed temple façades, persuaded the local Egyptian chiefs (with whom it is presumed they had commercial relations) to adopt them as the façade decorations of their palaces, subsequently of their tombs, and, simultaneously, as the most important element in the royal badge, the *serekh*. The fact, too, that there are so many of these great monuments suggests a matter of royal policy firmly applied and not the casual borrowing of a random idea from a distant and alien culture.

The precision with which the great tombs are built is as striking as the scale on which they were planned and executed; with other examples of early Egyptian craftsmanship there seems to be little tentative about even the earliest monuments, rather the buildings and the materials from which they are constructed are handled with a vigorous assurance and élan. Development of technique and of architectural form can indeed be observed throughout the First and Second Dynasties but these are again always redolent of an assured tradition. The lavishness with which every detail of the tombs' decoration was executed is breathtaking; the pilasters are covered in goldleaf, and there are rich paintings on the walls, imitating the interiors of the palaces. Some of the tombs had their interior walls whitewashed, and coloured paint was applied to the surface, recalling the painting of the Hierakonpolis tomb. However, the style of painting in that case, a narrative clearly depicting incidents which would have been intelligible to a contemporary observer, remains unique.

It is unrewarding to look to the native Egyptian domestic architectural traditions of the fourth millennium for any understanding of the remarkable revolution in form and design which is represented by the royal funerary monuments of the First Dynasty. Something is known of the houses for the living in both the Naqada I and Naqada II periods. In the first, the huts which the people constructed were flimsy affairs, little more than 'hides'; in Naqada II times more extensive building techniques were acquired and quite substantial structures came to be built, to judge from the models of houses which have been recovered from Gerzean sites. Nothing is known of palatial buildings – if such existed – or temples, other than the little reed or wicker shrines which appear to represent the cult centres of the north and south.

Although Narmer's probable successor, Hor-Aha (perhaps his son), proclaimed his martial qualities in his name, which means Fighting Hawk, he seems to have been a notable conciliator, the reconciler of opposing factions. He ruled long and wisely. He was a great builder, always one of the proudest activities of a King of Egypt. He honoured in particular the creator god, the supreme craftsman, Ptah of Memphis: it seems that Ptah was particularly linked with the Thinite–Hierakonpolitan house. So profound was his memory that Manetho recorded that the Egyptians maintained that from him (or rather from the King in Manetho's list who is identified with Hor-Aha) they learned to worship the gods and to live together in a civilized manner. It is recorded that he died in the sixty-third year of his reign, from injuries which he received in a hippopotamus hunt.

It has been suggested that Hor-Aha's queen bore the charming, if rather winsome name, 'Sweet of Hearts'. She was buried close to the great King's funerary monument at Abydos.

Another great monument of Hor-Aha's reign is to be found at Saqqara. Two features mark this tomb from others in the same place; on one side was laid out a small model estate, showing farm buildings, granaries, and other agricultural structures, to remind the owner of the tomb no doubt of the pleasures of the Egyptian countryside (plate 62). Close by was the first of what was to become a long line of an enduring aspect of Egyptian funerary cults, the burial of a boat for a King or great prince, to enable him to travel to the eternal realms, beyond the imperishable, ever-circling stars. The boat burial of Hor-Aha's reign is the earliest surviving example of this practice.

Hor-Aha's name is written with a falcon grasping a mace, with a pear-shaped head; this ideogram is supported by a shield. The macehead may stand for the new weapon with which the Falcon and his followers imposed their will on the people of the Valley. His name appears on a faience plaque, early evidence of one of the most long-lasting Egyptian crafts.

King Djer was the third King of Egypt, succeeding Hor-Aha at his death, however caused. Djer's reign marks the further consolidation of Thinite rule over the Valley; if later legend is to be believed it was a time when the sciences flourished, for Djer was commemorated, far into Egyptian history, as a great physician. It is curious that a ruler of such superlative power as the King of Egypt should be remembered as practising a calling that was certainly not so highly regarded in antiquity as it is today. However, Djer's writings on anatomy and the treatment of diseases were said still to be in circulation in late antiquity, nearly 3,000 years after his lifetime. One of his prescriptions, incidentally, was said to be for strengthening the hair, suggesting that incipient baldness was a concern to the people of Egypt 5,000 years ago, as much as it is to modern man.

However, one of the few documents to survive from the early First Dynasty, and which comes from Djer's reign, casts a more equivocal light on the King's reputation as a healer, at least if the general interpretation of one part of it is correct. The document in question is an ivory label from Saqqara (plate 63). It is in three registers and seems to depict some important state or religious ceremony. A proud hawk, surmounting the *serekh* on which the King's name is blazoned, stands at the end of the first register. Towards him advance little figures carrying offerings (one of which looks disconcertingly like a television camera mounted on a ladder), whilst a mummy or perhaps a statue follows it. Other bearers bring a fish, a bird, and a great ceremonial spear to the falcon: at the end of the register however, a more sinister scene seems to be enacted. Two figures face each other and one seems to be plunging a knife into the other's breast; he holds ready a vessel, of a typically elegant First Dynasty form, in which, presumably, he will catch his victim's blood. It seems certain that what is shown here is a rite of human sacrifice; there are other similar representations of the same ritual. There is little doubt that the passive figure in this strange and rather chilling little drama *is* a victim, for his arms appear to be drawn back in the manner which always represents a pinioned prisoner in Egyptian iconography. The ladder which appears in the first register was an important and probably a primitive element in Egyptian ritual. It conveyed the idea of the King mounting to the stars. The spear, too, was an immensely ancient component in the cults associated with the early Kingship.

Djer is also shown on a rock-carving in the far south, beyond the second cataract. Here in his falcon guise, the King is shown reviewing his defeated enemies. In another scene, this time on an alabaster palette from a monument at Saqqara, he is shown in what was to become the immemorial gesture of a King of Egypt dealing with those who set themselves or their people against his authority. Though the picture, an effective piece of propaganda no doubt calculated to discourage any other stirrings of rebellion, is damaged, it is probable that Djer is wielding a pear-shaped mace, the weapon which was always to be represented in such scenes. One record from the reign of Djer speaks of 'the year of the smiting of the land of Setjet'. Setjet was the land to the east of Egypt and is usually taken to mean western Asia.

The reign of Djer was remarkable for the rapid advance of all the arts of civilization. By a singular chance a marvellous cache of jewels was found in the King's tomb at Abydos still adorning a human arm, wrapped in linen, which had been thrust into a cranny in the tomb's walls and missed by the robbers who otherwise pillaged it thoroughly. A rich hoard of copper vessels, tools, and weapons was found in Djer's monument at Saqqara, together with a superb gold-handled knife, evidence of the sumptuousness of the King's accoutrements and the opulence of his court.

There is still a confusing variety of ways in which the often harsh, rather barbarous-sounding names of the First Dynasty kings are transcribed. Thus *Djer* is also rendered as Zer. Uadji is also known as *Djet* whilst *Den* is also transcribed as Udimu. Those italicized are the variants adopted here.

After Djer's reign, the throne of Egypt seems to have been assumed by a woman. Meryt-Neith compounded her name with the great goddess of the north; her northern affiliations may have contributed to the Thinite family's policy of conciliating Lower Egypt, as their dynastic succession became more and more established as each royal generation passed.

Women were important in Archaic Egypt, most particularly because they bore the succession to the throne. Only by marrying the heiress could the King take possession of the sovereignty, even if he had been born of a queen. The queens were called 'She who unites the Two Lands', recalling by this title perhaps the event early in the dynasty when a southern prince possibly married the heiress of the north and so brought the two Kingdoms into association. The queen was also 'She who sees Horus and Seth' as though to her was reserved the privilege of the actual manifestation of the two perpetually counter-balanced gods.

To find a queen ruling apparently with all the power and pomp accorded to a King of Egypt is, at this early time, mildly surprising. The Egyptian traditions stated that it was only decided that a woman could occupy the throne when the Second Dynasty was well advanced. But there is no doubt that Meryt-Neith was buried with the solemnity accorded to a King: her tomb at Abydos and the building associated with her reign at Saqqara are buildings of considerable grandeur. The Saqqara monument was memorable for the subsidiary burials of menials and artisans who were, willy-nilly, obliged to accompany the inhabitants of the tomb to oblivion or the promise of eternal life. The burials included a maker of pots, a painter supplied with his pigments and the reeds whose crushed ends constituted his brushes, a shipmaster, indeed an entire household of upper servants.

All the royal monuments at Saqqara and Abydos are surrounded by the subsidiary burials of servants and lesser figures in the court. No one can speculate with any hope of certainty about the attitude of those Egyptians who were obliged to go down into the grave with the great men or women whom they served. No trace has been found of resistance amongst these subsidiary dead, no sign of dreadful struggles as, centuries later, in the mass graves at Kerma, far to the south (in what was, for the average Egyptian, deepest Africa), nor the chilling if faintly farcical element shown by one of the characters in the drama of the death pit at Ur in Sumer, who seems to have been a little late for her own funeral and who slipped in after her companions, to join the ranks of those about to die. The Egyptians were buried in orderly tombs, neatly laid out with appropriate offerings; presumably they had administered to them some sort of tranquillizing drug or swift-acting poison, to carry them out of this world into the promise of the next. The argument which most scholars advance to account for what appears to be the placid acceptance of premature death is that by this means only would they expect to achieve immortality, as part of the retinue of the eternal King, as at this time there was no belief in the general application of eternal life beyond the King and his immediate entourage. It is as good an explanation as any.

Next in line after Meryt-Neith came the Serpent King Djet or Uadji, whose name commemorates the great serpent goddess of the south. Uadjet was always one of the divine attendants of the King, with her northern counterpart, the cobra goddess, Nekhbet. Djet's reign marks another high point in the early First Dynasty. After more than a century of the rule of the Thinite house, life in the Valley had developed at an unprecedented degree, in affluence and in the assurance which affluence brings. The power of the Kings is increasingly manifest in the splendour of their possessions and the richness of the establishments which they maintained. During the central years of the First Dynasty crafts such as carpentry, joinery, carving, and inlay, advanced rapidly, becoming very skilled and sophisticated.

The building at Saqqara which is attributed to Djer's reign is colossal, measuring 56 by 24 m. The central chamber in which the occupant's body, in all probability, lay or which was to be visited by his *Ka* is particularly remarkable, for the room was originally panelled in wood, inlaid with strips of gold plating. It is one example of the Saqqara monuments which seems to warrant Emery's attribution of royal burials to them – or at least renders that attribution still more understandable.

Around the great building was a low platform on which were mounted an astonishing display of some 300 bulls' heads modelled in clay with the actual horns set into place (plate 64). This practice is not unique to Djet, though his tomb is the first known to demonstrate it; another example is the tomb of Queen Her-Neith, perhaps the consort of King Djer, who was buried in the reign following Djet's. The *mastabas* which display bulls' heads in this way seem to connect these early Kings with the great bull cults which were so much a part of the emerging culture of post-Neolithic societies.

The Egyptians always supported bull cults, but it is only in early times that the bull is a primary royal symbol. The bull was regarded as the herald of the gods; the animal was particularly associated with the ithyphallic god Min, who was also identified with the bee, a creature which was part of the mystical persona of the King. The King always bore the title 'Bull of his Mother' but the royal iconography generally did not portray the King with 'bullish' attributes in later centuries; bulls in fact are particularly associated with the First Dynasty (plate 65). The most accomplished and impressive representation of the King as bull is undoubtedly the fragment of a slate or schist palette which shows a royal bull goring his fallen enemy. The carving is exceptionally fine, technically of a very high standard; the stone has a wonderful plasticity and the animal's body is beautifully rendered. The carving has a curious dream-like quality about it, almost a suggestion, though it is paradoxical, of slow motion with the great bull's head slightly turned towards the spectator, being presented as if it were engaged in some ritual act.

Bulls were associated with the heavenly bodies, the planets and con-stellations, from very early times both in Egypt and in Sumer as well as in Elam and later in other parts of the ancient world. Earlier still, bulls had been portrayed on the painted walls of the shrines at some of the earliest of all 'towns', at Çatal Hüyük in the Konya plain in Southern Anatolia. The 'bucranium', the bull's skull or its head in outline, which appears painted on Egyptian pottery of the early period, is an immensely ancient design, appearing on the earliest Near Eastern pottery, from northern Iraq, at sites like Hassouna and Sammara; in Egypt the bucranium seems from early times to have been associated with the cow-headed goddess Hathor. In the third millennium the bull was a powerful symbol in Elam and, later, in the Gulf, where the island of Failakah seems particularly to have been a centre of bull cults. Later still, of course, the Cretans were to raise the running of the bulls to the level of a national pastime.

It is not clear how the Egyptians managed so early on and with such little experience on which to draw, to demonstrate that most rare and exalted ability in design, to refine and reduce a design to its bare and simple essentials and in doing so produce works of art which transcend mere greatness. It is a pretty speculation, how the Egyptians acquired their aesthetic sense. It might be expected that early artists, revelling in the discovery of their burgeoning skills, would introduce every sort of element of which they could conceive – and still retain their vision – into their work. There are enough examples of this process: the products of the South American empires or the early Chinese states, all of Indian art throughout its long and repetitive history, are typical examples. Yet the chaste elegance of an art reduced to exquisite proportion, as, for example, that which the potters of the later Song Dynasty in China achieved, is demonstrated by Egyptian artists thousands of years before their Chinese counterparts. Unlike the Chinese, too, the Egyptian craftsmen were working at the beginning of their tradition and not after many centuries of innovation, rejection, and experiment.

The finest works of art of the period display a distinctive blend of austerity and elegance which is almost arrogant in its demand to be recognized on its own terms: it is an art which is wholly aristocratic, produced by members of an elite for the most exalted members of society, both human and divine. It is moving and quite extraordinary to see Egyptian artists so very early on reducing their works to their essential components of mass and form. Once the experimental forms, exotic and eccentric as they often are, either become adopted into the canon or disappear, artists and craftsmen of genius in the Archaic period seem already capable of stripping out all inessential elements in a design and retaining only those which express its deepest character. The stela of King Djet is a magnificent memorial of the King and of his reign, expressed by the rearing serpent, suspended in the sky above the battlements of the fortified palace whose façade forms the *serekh* in which the King's name is written. It is one of the masterpieces of Egyptian art (plate 66).

Djet's stela was recovered from his tomb or cenotaph at Abydos where it would have been one of two set up in front of the mastaba. It is a superb object and its design, of an exceptional elegance and refinement, prompts some speculation about the remarkable aesthetic sensibilities of the practitioners of the arts at this early date. Above all else, what Djet's stela demonstrates is restraint, exceptional refinement, and an understanding of form which is not to be repeated by artists of other nationalities until the coming of the Greeks, 2,500 years later. Even then, the Greeks hardly ever

125

achieved the monumental simplicity that the unknown master of the stela of King Djet produced with such divine assurance.

Everything associated with the King was of the finest quality. Carving, not only on the scale of the stela, but even in minor pieces such as those used in the games which were frequently put into the tombs of the noble dead, now achieved great elegance and precision. The reign of Djet was one of those times when all the influences seem to conspire to produce high art and the evidence of life striding forward to excel; Egypt was to experience many such times, more often perhaps than any other nation. The reign of Djet is one of the first. Like his predecessor, King Djer, Djet recorded a campaign as 'the smiting of the easterners'.

Djet had his servants buried in both his monuments at Abydos and at Saqqara. It was said that a great famine took place during his reign and that he built a pyramid at a location now identified with Saqqara. No pyramid is known to survive from so early a period, however; the first pyramid, the Step Pyramid of King Djoser, dates from the beginning of the Third Dynasty.

Djet was followed on the throne by Den (also known as Udimu). This was another high point of the First Dynasty when all the advances in the arts and the prosperity of Egypt, whose beginnings were evident in Djet's reign, came to their full flowering. The royal administration developed considerably during this reign; the King, ruling through his chosen assistants, the most powerful of whom were probably members of his family (though this was not invariably the case in First Dynasty times), extended his control over the whole Valley. He led campaigns against marauding tribes on the frontiers, to ensure that such barbarians would not disturb his Kingdoms.

Chance and the unusual incompetence of the robbers who plundered the monument at Saqqara dated to Den's reign preserved an immense cache of objects, many of them of spectacular quality. Weapons, tools, an enormous variety of stone vessels, including examples in rock crystal, alabaster, and schist, were preserved. So too were the games which would help the occupants of the tomb to while away eternity.

The lid of the box which contained the King's gold seal was also preserved, a witness to the sophistication of the royal government at this time. Den was long remembered by the Egyptian people and records purporting to descend from his reign were quoted in the New Kingdom, including a prescription which was included in the Ebers medical papyrus, for Den, too, was remembered as a physician. One of the medical studies thought to descend from this time dealt, in a remarkably objective manner, with the nature and treatment of fractures. It was during his reign that the double crown was said to have been adopted for the first time. It seems also that during this King's reign all evidence of the 'Sumerian connection' ceased and from this time onwards Egyptian forms exclude alien influences until the end of the Old Kingdom.

More retainers were despatched on the death of King Den. Also Queen Her-Neith was buried in a great tomb at Saqqara during Den's reign. She was a survivor from Djer's reign and was buried with many fine objects, but without the usual holocaust of servants. The burial chamber still contained the remains of a large wooden sarcophagus and the scattered bones of its one-time occupant. Her tomb, like Djet's, was supported by lines of outward-facing modelled bull-heads.

The fact that she was buried without any retainers at all is very striking. Her lonely distinction is emphasized by the fact that only her dog accompanied her on her last, dark journey (plate 67). It was laid across the threshold of her tomb, to guard its mistress through eternity. It is a curiously touching survival; the dog appears to be of that most ancient of all breeds, the prick-eared, long-skulled hunting hound, for long centuries the companion of the Great Ones of Egypt. It was described by Emery, who excavated the tomb, as a 'saluki-type' breed. However, there is no doubt that it was an Egyptian hound (see Appendix).

After Den came Enezib, according to the list of Kings. Manetho maintains that son followed father throughout the First Dynasty but Enezib seems to be the first King accorded by later authorities with sovereignty over the Two Lands, suggesting that up to his reign the Thinite assumption of the Kingship was still disputed by the northerners. Enezib, however, is named as the first King of the united Egypt in the Saqqara king list, but he was usurped (or at least his monuments were desecrated) by his successor Semerkhet, which suggests that the dynasty was not wholly secure and that there was some residual resistance to them still abroad. Enezib introduces a new style with the titulary of the Kingship. He adopted the title 'The Two Lords', suggesting that he was concerned to fuse the interests of the two great rival gods. In this he is anticipating Khasekhemui of the Second Dynasty. Enezib's reign marks a notable falling off in standards compared with the prosperity of his predecessors, a falling off demonstrated by the relatively modest size of his tomb when compared with those of Den, Djet, and certainly of the dog-loving Queen Her-Neith. However, for his Abydos monument he could afford to install sixty-four retainers in subsidiary graves around it.

The design of the tomb at Saqqara attributed to his reign is very remarkable, for *within* the superstructure of a familiar *mastaba* format there was found hidden what is in effect a buried stepped pyramid structure; this feature has been noted in the comparison between the Saqqara and the Abydos type of monument. This was entirely unexpected when it was discovered though it is known now not to be unique; Queen Her-Neith's tomb has the same feature though, in her case, in what is clearly a more primitive form. It has been suggested (not altogether convincingly, though the concept is quite Egyptian) that the combination of the two forms of tomb represents the stepped mound or tumulus of the south contained within the rectangular panelled structure of the north (Emery, 1961). There is certainly nothing to suggest that the panelled structure *is* northern; after all it was chosen by a southern line of princes to contain their royal names in the form of the *serekh*.

In any event, the stepped structure finally conquered, bursting out of its concealment magnificently in the burial monument of King Djoser, several hundred years later. Then the Step Pyramid swallows the *mastaba* which was the original form of the tomb conceived by Imhotep, Djoser's architect.

The First Dynasty was now moving towards its end. King Semerkhet, the fifth of the line, ruled, it seems, only for nine years; the only funerary monument to have been found which might be attributed to him is at Abydos. It was said that in his reign 'a very great calamity' befell Egypt: Manetho does not describe it, but it has been suggested that Semerkhet was a usurper, with only a dubious title to the Kingship. He was followed by the last King of the dynasty, Ka'a, who reigned, according to Manetho, for twenty-six years. Ka'a had two great funerary monuments, the Saqqara monument being particularly impressive and of great size. The interior walls of this great building were found to be painted imitating, it is thought, the gaily coloured matting which hung upon the walls of the royal palaces.

Though they brought an entirely unprecedented degree of civilization and prosperity to Egypt there is undoubtedly a sense of strangeness, almost of the bizarre, which surrounds the reputation of the Kings of the First Dynasty. The transition from a relatively simple, barbaric chieftaincy, demonstrated by the Predynastic Kings, to a high and fully articulated monarchy is marked with absolute suddenness. To those accustomed to the splendour of the Kings of Egypt as their image has descended to the modern world, there is something disconcerting and strange, almost alien indeed, about the customs and rituals which attend the Kings of the First Dynasty and of several of the Second. Although much of the immemorial legacy of Egypt descended from their times and many of the attributes associated with the Kingship were laid down in their reigns, there is an uneasy quality about their occupancy of the thrones. Even their origins are mysterious.

Then, too, there is the distinctly ambivalent way in which they were regarded by later generations. They were honoured greatly as the founders of the Kingly succession, but their memories seem also to have been feared. At some time after the end of the dynasty all the tombs in which the Kings and high officials were buried, on the escarpment at Saqqara looking down on Memphis, at Abydos, and at Helwan, were destroyed in immense conflagrations. The fires were intense and the destruction of the houses of these great dead was without doubt deliberate. Their memory seems to have been so abominated that all trace of them had to be obliterated. Somehow the customary explanation, of dynastic upheavals and the vindictiveness of their political opponents, seems inadequate for so violent a manifestation of hate and rejection carried out with such ruthless determination over the whole country.

One reason for the somewhat sinister reputation which the earliest Kings of Egypt seem to have borne in the minds of the later generations may be associated with the cults of ritual death. The Egyptians were obsessed, as no other people has ever been, with life and its perpetuation. All their beliefs centred on the need to extend life beyond the frontiers of death. To this end also was directed their love of and identification with the living world they saw around them.

In apparent contradiction of this principle there is the undoubted fact that the Kings of the First Dynasty, and a number of the Second, took with them companies of retainers who were sacrificed and buried with their royal master or, sometimes, mistress.

There is something cruelly disturbing about the neat rows (their very neatness is chilling) of subsidiary burials which surround most of the great burials at Saqqara and many at Abydos. There is no doubt that these interments took place at the same time as the principal was laid in his tomb; the same mound usually covers them all.

Sometimes the occupants of the subsidiary graves were courtiers or undifferentiated attendants of the King. In some cases they were craftsmen and specialists who might continue to provide their master with their eternal services.

The degree of specialization of craft and trade indicated by the inhabitants of the subsidiary graves in the Royal Tombs suggests an incipient class structure or emergent hierarchical society in Egypt, even in the earliest times. Of course, the King must have maintained a similar view of hierarchies as did Louis XIV, when he assured the dukes of France that, as King, he was placed as high above them as they were above ordinary men, a view which it is difficult to feel the dukes heard with any satisfaction. The King of Egypt was god; hence, all men, merely as men, must have been equal in his sight. However, it is evident that hierarchies existed, perhaps even in Predynastic Egypt, as witnessed by the differing relative sizes of the attendants on the maces of King Scorpion and King Narmer and the palette of the latter. The status of the craftsmen, singled out for the particular honours of ritual death in the service of their master or mistress, suggests the existence of an elite, other than the nobility or the upper class of official. Throughout Egyptian history and particularly in the early periods there was a developing class of middle-rank people, who occupied an increasingly important place in the fabric of the state and who often penetrated its highest courses. Binding all these influences together was the King. In Frankfort's brilliant phrase, he moved through the fabric of Egyptian society 'like a shuttle in a great loom'.

The practice of the immolation of servants was eventually discontinued; by the end of the Second Dynasty it had attenuated and was allowed to fall into disuse; it was in any case, a most un-Egyptian custom, in conflict with their sublime humanity. It is, however, wholly in character that ever afterwards a well-founded Egyptian, royal or simple, went on his last great journey attended by quantities of little servant figurines, in wood, faience, pottery, stone, or metal, which would serve as his 'answerers' and undertake any disagreeable or distasteful tasks which he might be called upon to discharge, during his progress to the light of perpetual life.

There is only very tenuous evidence for the practice of the ritual killing of servants *before* the First Dynasty: it seems to have been a custom peculiar to and introduced by the princes of This. What prompted this harsh concept is beyond speculation. If we knew more of the ancestry of the Thinite Kings we might be able to determine why they followed a custom which, in later periods, came to typify the more barbarous African monarchies; it will, of course, be recalled that the occupants of the great tombs at Ur, dated to a period not long after the Archaic dynasties of Egypt, were also attended by sacrificed retainers. The Kings of the First Dynasty were the first to go into the ground in such grand and richly appointed monuments, the first not only in Egypt but so far as we can tell in the whole wide world. The low rectangular brick structures in which they were buried, called by the Arabic word *mastaba* because of their similarity in form to the low benches built outside the house of the *fellahin*, are based on the design of the palaces in which their earthly lives were spent. The architecture becomes more complex as the dynasty progresses, just as the size of the tombs increases, almost reign by reign. The architects who worked on these superb edifices seem to have been experimenting with their materials and the scale on which they could deploy them; they obviously worked with assurance and it is exciting to recognize evidence of their stretching their resources further and further as their experience grows. The interiors of the tombs, honeycombed with magazines and store rooms as the palaces themselves must have been, were richly decorated, gleaming with gold, and filled with the opulent products of armies of artificers. The exterior walls, recessed and buttressed, were painted white. Interestingly, the buttressing itself is more complex in the earlier part of the dynasty.

The prosperity which the unification brought to Egypt and in particular to the northern part of Upper Egypt where Memphis, the capital, was situated is nowhere demonstrated more dramatically than at Helwan. There upwards of 10,000 graves have been excavated; they are the burial places of officials and others of what might be called the upper bourgeoisie who must have provided much of the administrative class of the capital area. Some of the people buried there were no doubt nobles, close to the King and probably his familiars, but none of them seem to be royal personages. The quantity of pottery and of personal possessions buried at Helwan is prodigious; for a society to be able to extract at such an early date so much of its material wealth from circulation, generation by generation, displays a remarkable degree of economic confidence in the future. It must also have been good news for the artists and craftsmen who, also generation by generation, would have been required to supplement the wealth of what had become, to a substantial degree, a grave-oriented society.

Amongst the graves at Helwan are examples of the burials of dogs and donkeys; as these do not seem to be the subject of cult or religious observance, it may be that they were family pets, since the Egyptians always kept animals about them, as members of their households. The burial grounds at Helwan are of great importance for what they reveal about the quality of life enjoyed by relatively modest people, the officials, courtiers, and those who served the court, during the first flowering of the Kingship in Egypt. It must be presumed that the dead buried at Helwan served their royal masters at Memphis which was then in the first phase of its existence as the capital of the Two Lands, and at the great religious centres nearby. These would have included Heliopolis which, even in the very early period, and probably in Predynastic times as well, was established as the centre of the cult of the sun, a cult which was only to assume a national status in the Old Kingdom.

Over 10,000 graves, ranging from extensive and complex structures comparable with those at Saqqara to relatively modest interments, have been excavated at Helwan, principally in the 1940s and 1950s (Saad, 1947, 1969). They are of great importance in assessing the character of life in Egypt during the early centuries, both because of the quality of the objects and architecture which they contain and because their evidence makes necessary the reversal of a number of otherwise long-held ideas about early Egyptian religious belief and funerary practice. Despite this, some of the ideas which Helwan calls into question are still quoted in reviews of these earliest periods of Egyptian history.

It must however be said that recently some doubt has been cast on the general dating of the Helwan tombs (Wood, 1987). A number clearly are early; others, however, date from as late as the Third Dynasty when many of the architectural techniques which would seem remarkable in an early Archaic context have become almost commonplace. However, the interest of Helwan lies in the fact that it is a cemetery of the non-noble, at least in the main. As such it shows both the development of tomb-building, reaching down, at a relatively early date, into the middle ranks of society and the comparative luxury of the goods with which such people were able to surround themselves in death as in life.

Thus, some of the tombs revealed at Helwan (as at sites like Abydos and Saqqara) that First Dynasty Egyptian architects were confident in the use of stone for walls, ceilings, and staircases. It is frequently asserted that the earliest use of stone was in the late Second Dynasty but quite apart from the revetment of Hierakonpolis, the First Dynasty tombs at Helwan (as well as some of the larger, contemporary tombs at Saqqara) demonstrate that this is not so. Some of the blocks used to wall and floor the burial chambers are huge, suggesting that they are already the products of a long-established and assured tradition.

Many of the artefacts recovered from the tombs at Helwan are of fine quality. Pottery, some copper wares, and stone vessels predominate, but a number of handsomely made boxes were found in the tombs. Boxes, made from wood, ivory inlays, or sometimes from basketry, presumably for holding valuables or other personal possessions, were always popular in Egypt (plate 68).

Helwan has also provided evidence of the advanced nature of the textile industry in First Dynasty Egypt. Wool was used widely, in particular for making the cloaks in which early dynastic men are often portrayed. Linen, too, of exceptional delicacy, equalling the most exquisitely fine, gossamer-like fabrics the like of which have only been made in modern times, was also produced. Such fabrics were evidently available on a generous scale and hence, presumably, were made industrially by skilled craftsmen working either on the great magnates' estates (as is attested from somewhat later times) or, as was probably the case for the fabrics used by the rather less exalted occupants of some of the Helwan graves, produced by craftsmen working on their own account, in studios like those which existed for the production of stone vessels and pottery containers. An endearing characteristic of the burials at Helwan is that a relatively high proportion of the graves, when compared for example with the contemporary but rather grander tombs at Saqqara and Abydos, contained objects which had been broken during the time of their use and then, thriftily, repaired. This was done, in the case both of pottery and of stone vessels, by drilling holes in the vessel and its broken part and then binding them together, either with copper wire or with cord.

Most of the Helwan tombs seem to have been destroyed by fire, the same great conflagrations which were so notable a feature of the destruction of the First Dynasty tombs at Saqqara and Abydos and which demonstrate such apparent hostility, not to say loathing, by the Egyptians of the Second Dynasty for those of the First. It is really very strange, this wholesale posthumous destruction which was evidently practised across the land of Egypt, not only of the tombs of the Kings and the 'Great Ones' but also of the relatively modest inhabitants of the graves of Helwan.

Helwan is a pleasant place, some 20 km south of the modern capital of Cairo. It is celebrated today for its medicinal waters and its less salubrious steel plants. Something must have drawn the First Dynasty Egyptians there, to populate such considerable tomb fields. Whatever it was, that impulsion is lost, but the existence of the large numbers of tombs, with their substantial architecture and their rich furnishings, calls for a reassessment of another of the long-held beliefs about religious ideas in Archaic Egypt, namely that the prospects of eternal life were first reserved exclusively for the King, then for his closest attendants, and only later for members of the court.

The evidence of Helwan seems to make it clear that such was not invariably the case. The large numbers of people buried there and the character of the tombs suggests that their occupants went into them with the same assurance of some form of life after death which the people living in the Valley in later times so firmly maintained. Many of the dead of Helwan, like those of even earlier, Predynastic burials, seem to have been laid in a foetal position, as though anticipating rebirth. Whilst nothing could diminish the King's claim to divinity, in this life as much as in the life after death, it appears that his subjects, or at least those who were buried at Helwan, had quite considerable expectations of immortality.

The invention of the Kingship is one of the most enduring of all Egyptian achievements, one with universal significance, from whose forms all successive great kingdoms in the Near East (and perhaps others more distant still) drew their inspiration. Few, if any of them, however, achieved any part of the majesty which the Egyptian Kings seem so easily to have assumed.

133

The nature of the King is well expressed in an inscription which, though it dates from the relatively decadent period of the New Kingdom, probably summarizes the Egyptian view of the Kingship from its earliest appearance. 'What is the King of Upper and Lower Egypt? He is a god by whose dealings one lives, the father and mother of all men, alone, by himself, without an equal.' It will be observed that here the King is 'a god' and not 'the God'; the dual, in this case the bisexual nature of the earliest gods is reiterated also.

If human ingenuity or ambition were to set out consciously to create such an institution as the Kingship, the Nile Valley would have been amongst the least suitable locations which it would have been possible to choose on which to launch it. The narrow river banks, with the occasional wide expanse of cultivation drawn out and extended over a length quite disproportionate, with two (at least) distinct cultures and traditions, would surely seem to be the least favoured ground for such an epoch-making innovation, the invention of the first nation in the history of the world.

It is difficult perhaps to imagine a time when there was simply no precedent for the idea of the nation state. The individual's loyalty was to his clan, perhaps to his lord, and no doubt principally to his land and family. To persuade a man or, as it must have been in this case, many men to follow him into an expedition into unknown lands ruled by unknown gods, was at least as remarkable an achievement on Menes-Narmer's part as was Alexander's triumphant progress through the lands of the Persian Empire and beyond its confines to India when, by force of his genius and his godlike capacity for inspiring total devotion, he swept his soldiers far from their Macedonian homeland to the very edge of the world.

That Narmer and his followers even conceived of uniting all the Nile is the measure of the Thinite princes' ambition. They were southerners yet they became convinced of the necessity of uniting their land with one totally dissimilar in most respects, other than that the same river washed its banks as it did their own. That the differences between Upper and Lower Egypt, south and north, in custom, culture, beliefs, and rituals were profound is demonstrated by the fact that throughout Egyptian history such differences were insisted upon and it was only the King that provided the link between them: he alone was Lord of the Two Lands. At a less elevated level it was said: 'The speech of a man of the Delta with a man of Elephantine? No man can unravel them.'

The extent of this achievement in welding the entire Valley into one state can be measured, paradoxically, by the fact that the Egyptians maintained the fiction of the separate identities of the two kingdoms throughout the long sweep of Egyptian history. The essential differences, in custom, ritual, belief, even in all probability in language at least in the beginning, always persisted between north and south. The union of the Two Lands was really an unnatural construct which at various times throughout Egypt's history, when the central Kingship faltered, for example, or when the threat of foreign invasion became a reality, came apart at the seams and the Valley fragmented, north and south and even into small principalities centred on the administrative districts into which both Egypts were divided. Yet, despite this tendency to fracture, the vision of the early Kings was so powerful and enduring that always a heroic figure, usually and most significantly from the south, would emerge to impose once again the ancient Thinite concept of the united lands.

This extraordinary sequence of events which so changed the life of third-millennium Egypt was triggered off by the decision of a young Thinite prince to set himself on a course never before attempted, so far as we know, by any man. Aided by a group of his peers and a mêlée of his and their tribal and clan supporters he instituted a programme of conquest and diplomacy to weld Egypt into a nation under his rule.

His partners in this enterprise, to judge by their standards which he was evidently proud to depict being borne before him on various of the documents which survive from his time, were important chieftains like himself; however, he seems to have been accepted as being supreme over them or quickly made himself so. Whether the paramountcy was by some ancient right attached to the eponym of the Falcon clan or whether it became his as the consequence of some irresistible charisma that he possessed, the Falcon he was and the united Egypt which he was to create was, *par excellence*, the Falcon's land. At least one of his great peers, the Lord of Ombos, eponym of the federation of clans which honoured the swift hound as its totem, must have nurtured some reservations about the Falcon's claims to the sovereignty. But the dissension which the ancient affront to the status of the Set tribes was eventually to precipitate was, for the moment, in the future.

On a day, then, probably in the first quarter of the thirty-second century (*c.* 3180 BC) the Falcon prince set out on his annexation of the land to the north of his patrimony, accompanied, as the stories afterwards told, by the Spirits of the Dead, the demi-gods who were to be immortalized as the Companions of Horus. Thus the royal propagandists skilfully suggested that he was attended not only by the living 'Great Ones' of Egypt but also by a ghostly retinue of heroic figures from the ancient past. An appeal to this powerful myth by Menes-Narmer and his advisors suggests how

135

well they understood their people and those whom they sought to absorb by identifying his advance to the northern Kingdom with the shades of long-dead chieftains, whose legends evidently were still current and still capable of exciting a loyal response from the people.

This decision to set about conquering the whole extent of the Valley and to bring it under the control of one sovereign had one profound and lasting consequence. This was, indeed, to be the single factor which, more than any other, determined the character of Egypt throughout the third millennium.

After the years of spasmodic and, it must be presumed, frequently localized rebellion the strong central government of the King eventually produced a deep and lasting peace throughout the Valley. The Two Lands were, as a consequence of the Valley's topography, wholly secure and easily capable of efficient defence.

To east and west ranged the great deserts. The route through the mountains to the east could be policed with relative ease. To the west the seemingly limitless Libyan desert provided its mantle of protection to the Valley.

To the south only the area below the cataract could provide entry to the barbarous hordes from Africa; the gates to Egypt could be closed against them by the expedient of building guard forts in the gorges of the Valley and, from time to time, by sending punitive expeditions to put down the Nubians and others welling up from Africa, if they seemed minded to intrude upon the Valley's tranquillity.

Egypt's relations with Nubia, and indeed with all of black Africa to the south, have only in recent years been reappraised. Historians have tended to assume that the African south was significant to Egypt only as a source of labour, soldiers, precious metals, ivory, and rare woods. What was not appreciated until more recent research was the relatively high cultural level achieved by the Nubians from an early date; to what extent their culture was derived from Egypt or to what extent Egypt drew into itself influences from Africa is still disputed (Williams, 1980).

Some spectacularly rich burials of the late Predynastic period have been found in Nubia. At Sayala, Nubian chiefs were buried with a fine panoply of imports and very rich objects: copper axes, ingots of copper, chisels, two enormous bird shaped palettes, and two monumental maces with gold handles. The maceheads are pear-shaped and on one of the handles was depicted a series of animals (plate 72), magnificently engraved. This is a superlative object and would have been a prized possession in the Treasury of an Egyptian King; in fact hardly anything quite so fine has been recovered from Egypt of the same period. Sadly this majestic object disappeared from the Cairo Museum soon after its discovery in the early years of this century.

At Qustul a group of graves has been excavated which, from the luxury of their contents, prompted their excavator to describe them as the burial places of Kings of the Nubian A Group people who were contemporaries of the Egyptians of the late Predynastic and Archaic periods. Certainly the contents of the Qustul tombs are very fine: some of them show an elaboration of design and concept which is remarkable for what has hitherto been regarded as an outlying province of Egyptian culture in the latter part of the fourth millennium. There seems to be a preoccupation with boats at Qustul, as there is on the rock walls of the many lower Nubian sites which are decorated with rock drawings. Whether or not the graves are of Kings, the peers of their colleagues to the south, there is little doubt that the Nubian chiefs of the late fourth millennium were able to sustain an extensive trade with their contemporaries to the north. Trade was evidently active and considerable; during the early dynastic period, however, relations between Egypt and Nubia seem to have declined and the A Group Nubians disappear by the Third Dynasty. It may be suspected that the Kings of Egypt, who frequently record punitive expeditions to Nubia even in the earliest times, were responsible for the destruction of what might have become a rival to their power (Williams, 1980, 1986).

In the north, the defensive situation was complex. There it was necessary to keep watch on the long Mediterranean shoreline, though throughout most of the third millennium no other power was really capable of mounting a substantial seaborne invasion against Egypt. Only the corridor to the north-east, reaching up to Sinai, through Gaza to the Levantine coast, and, further east still, across the northern Arabian deserts, presented a real hazard. From these regions, as from the eastern deserts of Egypt itself, there constantly flowed tribesmen from the unsettled Semitic-speaking groups who moved around this vast and inhospitable region. They preyed upon the outposts of the infinitely superior Egyptian state whenever they sensed they could get away with the seizure of herds, cattle, or goods. Constantly the King set out to destroy them and as constantly the nomads vanished, withdrawing to their own uncharted wilderness. When the collapse did come to Egypt, on at least two occasions the impulse for it came out of the Arabo-Syrian desert wastes.

The terms which the Egyptians used to describe their eastern neighbours are various, often offensive, and frequently confusing. The term which is usually rendered as 'Asiatics' is *Aamu* and implies people coming from the east. It seems probable that first and foremost amongst the people so described were the nomadic inhabitants of Egypt's own eastern deserts,

137

whom the Valley people always feared and disliked. The term was also used to include the peoples of Sinai, notably in the south, who shared, particularly in the late fourth and early third millennia in the general culture prevailing in southern Palestine and also, to a degree which cannot yet be fully assessed, in the cultures of ancient north-western Arabia.

It is a matter of speculation to what extent the Egyptians were aware of or had any real contact with the tribes who lived in the western part of the Arabian peninsula. The peoples who lived to the west of Sumer, the barbarous, illiterate, and savage tribes (in the Sumerians' minds at least) who inhabited the Syrian and Arabian deserts, were generally called *Martu*. They were the ancestors of the *Amuru* who ranged across much of the northern, central, and eastern Arabian deserts, moving through the oases over immense distances.

Recent archaeological research in south-western Arabia has revealed contact with Egypt at the end of the third millennium. Contact is *suggested* at a much earlier period by the iconographic similarities between the hunters depicted on the Hunters Palette and on western Arabian rock carvings at Bi'r Hima (Zarius et al., 1980) (plate 69a and 69b).

Connections with Sinai and Palestine have been suggested from a study of one particular detail in the design of Narmer's Palette. This is a curious object which has been identified as a 'desert kite', an enigmatic category of structure which is certainly found in the Sinai and in the Palestinian deserts but which is also typical of the northern Arabian desert. The 'kites', long lines of stones which have been interpreted as the remains of corrals or traps for animals, are thought to date from as early as the end of the fourth millennium. In Arabia, particularly in the north-west, structures of this sort and also rather larger ones which sometimes even assume almost monumental proportions, seem to be associated with early copper-working regions.

For a thousand years, then, even the potential conduit of danger represented by the 'Asiatics' was kept securely closed. Peace reigned as securely in the Valley as the King reigned in Memphis. Nothing obtruded to disturb the peaceful development of Egypt, nothing clouded the tranquil progression of day following day, King succeeding King.

By the time of the Old Kingdom, from the Third to the Sixth Dynasties, (c. 2868–c. 2181 BC), the effect of these long and tranquil centuries on the psychology of the early Egyptians may be imagined; it may also be appreciated in the reliefs of ordinary life carved on the tombs of nobles and court functionaries and in the literature of the time. The Egyptians developed a profound sense of certainty, of the order of the world, and of their place in it. They could not doubt, living in their secure, tranquil, richly endowed land that theirs was an existence ordained by a beneficent providence and that, as it had been, so would that life always be. The conservatism which is so often described as one of the most innate characteristics of Egyptian culture comes from this time, laid upon the profound conservatism of the peasant, no matter where he lives.

At this time, from the late Predynastic in the latter part of the fourth millennium, through the early phase of the dynastic period at the beginning of the third, the vast preponderance of the Egyptian population was engaged in simple agriculture. The population has been estimated, variously, at between 1 and 2 million people, though the estimate depends largely on guesswork and is probably much too high. They lived, in the main, in small communities scattered over the Valley floor and, as they became increasingly habitable, in the marshlands of the Delta. Their lives would not have been harsh or unduly arduous: the river and the land were generous and sustained the people relatively comfortably. For the vast majority life would have gone on its tranquil progress, uncomplicated by contact with the court, the Great Ones, or the King.

The Egyptians from the earliest recorded times sustained a lively interest in two other human corporate pastimes, which, typically, they invested with their own particular qualities. These were games playing, particularly board games, and organized sports.

In most tombs, from the First Dynasty onwards at least, are to be found a variety of board games. Many of these have animals as the counters: dogs, gazelles, jackals, lions, and bulls all have their turn in different games. The games, so far as it is possible to reconstruct them, are dependent on the throwing of sticks or other equivalents of dice to effect progressive moves. That they were so frequently placed amongst the funerary equipment of a well-appointed Egyptian setting out on his last journey to the west, suggests that they may also have had some ritual significance. However, as the affluent dead of the early dynasties filled their graves with all manner of evidence of their earthly wealth (in the certain belief that they *could* take it with them) this point need not be argued too exhaustively.

In the First Dynasty the dead were sometimes buried with circular discs on which, carved in relief, hounds pursued gazelles for ever, in a perpetual fruitless chase (colour plate VI). It is not so fruitless, however, as the hole which pierces the centre of the disc is fitted with a spindle by which the mounted disc is spun. Then the hounds seem to leap on the heels of the quarry; thus, perhaps by means of sympathetic magic, if the device is revolved, to while away eternity, the owner of the tomb might be guaranteed a good supply of game.

So much of the evidence for the ancient way of life in Egypt comes from tombs that it is difficult to reconstruct what the buildings of the living were like. However, there are occasional glimpses of architecture other than the funerary, from contemporary and later references, for in such matters the Egyptians were conservative, preferring to retain forms, over immensely long periods, even if sometimes they were effectively disguised, like the mound within the pyramid or the wattle shrine, built in stone, in the heart of the later temples.

Very little can be said with certainty about the earliest temples to be built in Egypt, or of the ceremonies which were practised in them. The names of some temples of the First Dynasty may be known from the inscriptions on several ivory labels, if the inscriptions have been correctly deciphered. Some temple structures appear to be depicted on First Dynasty labels; from these representations the buildings would seem to be flimsy and unpretentious, probably made from reeds or light timber (plate 70).

The temples and shrines of Archaic Egypt were probably much more like the cult places of later central and west African tribes, dark and heavy with magic. The soaring, majestic temples associated with Egypt throughout its later history had to wait for their introduction by the Third Dynasty and until the Fourth for their most splendid manifestation in the Valley of mortuary temples associated with the pyramids, a tradition which was continued, though in somewhat different form into the Fifth.

Despite Herodotus' remark, admittedly made at least two and a half millennia after this time, that the Egyptians were the most religious people in the world, it is more likely that the timeless, unchanging, tranquil, and, essentially, happily integrated life in the Valley in the early centuries of a united Egypt was precisely the consequence of an absence of specifically religious commitment or involvement. Religion, even in the special sense that the word must be used in early Egypt, was the business of the King and his immediate colleagues; at least this would be the case in respect of national cults. These, in any case, had as their focus, and indeed their whole point and purpose, the person of the King as intermediary between Egypt and the gods.

Local and tribal (or even perhaps clan) cults were a different matter of course. Each part of Egypt had its complement of greater and lesser divinities; there were, too, the primordial forces of nature like the storm which were to be worshipped or, more likely, placated. There were shrines which contained the numinous essence of local cults; sometimes these might be advanced to a greater status.

The preoccupation of the theologians putting forward, for example, one system of philosophy concerning the origin of Egypt (and hence of the cosmos) against another, Memphis *contra* Heliopolis as it might be, would have touched the Egyptian in the fields or on the river bank not at all. Only much later, as one of the marks of decay in the Egyptian state, did the priesthoods which emerged in part as the result of the sort of mild ancestor worship to which the cult of the King eventually led, begin to require a formal power base, rooted in the temples, which, like the distasteful manoeuvrings of the Christian orders in the later Middle Ages, sought to advance the worldly interests of one group above another. The rise of ritual and the power of the temples were signs of the beginning of the end for the pristine Egypt. The joyful life of the countryside, broadcast so vividly in the reliefs of so many Old Kingdom tombs but drawing on a tradition greatly older, was replaced by solemn processions of gods with their mortal and immortal attendants.

It is not certain that there was an actual dynastic disruption following the death of Ka'a, the last King of the First Dynasty, and the reign of the next King, though Manetho shows a new dynasty beginning. That King is Hotepsekhemui who is acknowledged as the first King of the Second Dynasty; his line is, however, still identified as Thinite and it may well be that the Kings of this dynasty were related to those of the First Dynasty. To judge by later Old Kingdom cases, the line may have been transferred by a princess as heiress of the Two Lands. The first Kings of the Second Dynasty are obscure figures and little is known of their reigns. We can only presume that the period of their sovereignty was marked by a continuation of that same unrest that marked the final years of the First Dynasty Kings. It cannot be certain that the Second Dynasty actually followed the First; they may, in part at least, have been contemporary, ruling different parts of the Valley simultaneously.

Hotepsekhemui, whose name means 'the two powers are at peace' suggests the hope of the people of the time for a conciliation between the adherents of Horus and Set, the 'two powers' identified in his name. Hotepsekhemui was followed on the throne by Raneb, whose name is the first in Egyptian history to introduce the name of the Sun-god Ra, and then by Nynetjer. Clearly, Egypt continued to develop her institutions and her culture during their reigns; the evidence, however, is very scanty and the sequence of these Kings is only known because their names appear in order on a statue of a kneeling official, of a slightly later date (plate 71). After the dominant and forceful sovereigns of the First Dynasty their early Second Dynasty successors seem pale figures by comparison. Indeed, after the majestic enterprise of the Kings of the First Dynasty it is difficult to consider those of the Second Dynasty, or at least the early members of the dynasty, as being in the same class of monarch at all. It is difficult to resist the idea that they may have been a small local dynasty, of which there must have been many in pre-First Dynasty times, which somehow got itself acknowledged as national rulers.

As the Second Dynasty unfolded it is evident that some of the ancient influences in the Valley, dormant or repressed during the First Dynasty, began again to stir. Some sort of reaction against the Falcon clan seems to have occurred and this found its focus evidently in the deep-rooted honours paid by the southern people to the god Set. The most perplexing of all the early cult figures involved in this period is that of Set. He is a southern god, associated with the desert, storm, and violence. He is portrayed as an enigmatic creature, with a strange, canine, and long-muzzled head, with sharply pointed ears (plate 73). As was earlier remarked, there is little doubt that he is an Egyptian hound, of the same breed as the numerous dog-gods of Egypt, including Anubis and his predecessor Wepwawet. Set seems to have been the god of the people of the south, whereas Horus is an aristocratic totem, associated with the princes of This. It might have been expected that the Thinites would have attempted to reconcile the divinity of their house with that of the people on whom their power would ultimately come to rest; there is in fact clear evidence that the early Kings reverenced both Horus and Set particularly in the titles of the queens, who alone conveyed the right to the Kingship. None the less, the early dynastic conflicts were mythologized as a conflict between Horus and Set, when the two antagonists were locked in a titanic struggle for the Kingship of Egypt after the alleged murder by Set of his brother Osiris, who was, if only in mythological terms, the primeval King. Throughout the first two dynasties the partisans of Set seem frequently to have opposed the Thinite settlement, though the princes of This were southerners, like the god. Gradually, the evidence suggests that the supporters of Set gained the ascendancy and, in the latter part of the Second Dynasty, after the reign of Neteren, King Sekhemehet suddenly changed his name to Peribsen, and instead of his name in its monumental *serekh* being surmounted by the victorious falcon he displayed his new name surmounted by the animal of Set, that noble and imperious hound whose swiftness was, in the words of an Egyptian poet, 'one with the sharp arrow, who is more powerful than the gods' (plate 74).Clearly, under Peribsen Set became paramount to the extent that the King felt able to discard the loyalties to Horus for what was perhaps the even older allegiance to Set. In his inscriptions Peribsen declared 'The Ombite (Set was Lord of Ombos) has given the Two Lands to his son Peribsen.'

But the later stages of the Second Dynasty, no matter what were the political realities in the Valley, marked another high point in Egyptian creativity. Large-scale, formal sculpture, often executed in the hardest stones, is one of the glories of Egyptian art and amongst the most splendid legacies to be passed by the ancient to the modern world. Here it is possible to detect something like a beginning and then a triumphant progress to the great works of the early Old Kingdom, than which there may arguably be said to be no finer works of the hands of man. The transition between the reigns of Sekhemib-Peribsen and Khasekhem-Khasekhemui may have come about as the result of an uprising of the Set peoples against the followers of Horus in the latter years of the Second Dynasty (Newberry, 1922). Sekhemib, coming from the deep south, proclaimed himself Set-King, a title which he alone assumed. To mark his adherence to Set, the ancient patron of his people, he took the name Peribsen, along with his new (or perhaps very ancient) title. So, just as the Horus Kings were, each of them, Horus incarnate, so he *was* Set, the personification of the very ancient god of the south.

Though Peribsen may have been a usurper in the view of the prevailing Horus faction, he may equally have been the scion of a still older line from which the chiefs of Upper Egypt, in times before the Kings, descended; at any rate he placed himself in opposition to the Horus Khasekhem who, early in his reign, had gone south to put down a rebellion of the Nubian tribes. This rebellion defeated, Khasekhem returned to the frontiers of Egypt to find Set, in the person of Peribsen, in possession of what he, the Horus, saw as his patrimony. A series of fierce engagements took place, up and down the Valley; the outcome was victory for Khasekhem and defeat for the Set-King. Khasekhem, it is then suggested, assumed a modified throne-name, 'the Horus Khasekhem*ui*'. This meant 'In him the Two Powers are reconciled', a significant and majestic assertion indeed, in all the circumstances.

This concept of what might have happened in such immensely distant an epoch is, in many ways, merely an attractive thesis, but it provides a plausible reconstruction of events as they may have happened in the Valley so long ago. This version of the conflict of Horus and Set, on which it is based, presented in terms of the rightful (or accepted) claimant (Horus) returning from an excursion beyond the frontiers to find his kingdom usurped (by Set), depends on a long hieroglyphic text inscribed on the walls of the great Horus temple at Edfu, one of the most important centres of Old Kingdom Egypt. The version which survives is only derived from Ptolemaic times; it is likely, however, that it preserves much older material.

The text purports to be a *historical* record of the rebellion of Set against Horus and is represented as being declaimed by Imhotep, the chief minister of King Djoser, and the most powerful magus in Egyptian popular legend.

He is depicted standing before a nameless king, probably Djoser himself, and recounting the story of the rebellion.

Djoser reigned in the early Third Dynasty; he may have been directly descended from Khasekhemui, though this is not certain. The Set rebellion would have taken place, in historical terms, in the closing period of the immediately preceding Second Dynasty. It is indeed a speculative interpretation but one which has much appeal in explaining what was clearly a crucial and profoundly memorable experience for Egypt in Archaic times.

Whatever else it may do, the story of the conflict of Horus and Set confirms the essentially political character of the two protagonists. Peribsen became Set; Khasekhem-Khasekhemui was Horus, and the long saga began. However, it is not without point that Khasekhemui, the victorious incarnate god, saw his role as conciliator as the most important of his qualities. Far from rejecting Set, he assumed to himself the *personae* of both gods and set them up as equal supporters on his royal badge. In subsequent years, probably after Khasekhemui's death, the protagonists of Horus asserted themselves and achieved the total denigration of Set, to the point, eventually, when a prince who may have been the descendant of the ancient and true line of chiefs of Upper Egypt became identified as a monster, the embodiment of evil. It is an interesting case study in the power of religious belief to corrupt reality and to pervert history to serve the ideological ends of an entrenched priesthood.

Perhaps the earliest attempts at portraiture in the round to have survived are amongst the most exceptional and come from the end of the Second Dynasty: two statues, one in limestone, the other in schist of King Khasekhem, King of the Second Dynasty, the last probably to be identified with Khasekhemui (colour plate VII).

For works made very nearly 5,000 years ago, the statues are remarkable. One, in Cairo, has been oddly bisected: the other, in the Ashmolean Museum, Oxford, is one of the supreme masterpieces of Egyptian art. It shows the King seated on his throne, wrapped in his cloak and wearing the high crown of the south; beneath his feet the enemies of Egypt are trampled. The King is tranquil, his eyes placid; already he has assumed his full divinity and sits enthroned above all creation. The technique of carving is assured and highly skilled; the sculptor works the stone with absolute mastery and without any hint of uncertainty. The carving of the cloak as it stands away from the King's throat for example, is quite brilliant. However, it is difficult to imagine in what *atelier* the master learned his craft so early on, for no comparable statues from an earlier time survive.

According to Manetho, the King, who corresponds to Khasekhem, was a giant, standing, if it is to be believed, some eight feet tall. He is said to have ruled Egypt for forty-eight years; then the last name in the list appears, the mysterious reconciler of the opposing factions, Khasekhemui who may also be Khasekhem. He was said to have been a great military leader; but Khasekhemui's genius as conciliator is graphically demonstrated, in yet another evidence of the early Egyptians' genius for synthesizing a whole spectrum of experience in one brilliant design motif, by the presentation of his royal name, in the *serekh* enclosure, surmounted by the two gods, Set standing at peace with Horus (plate 75). It is one of the most perceptive pieces of political propaganda graphics in the history of men and states; it is also quite unique in all the long history of the Egyptian royal formulary.

It is a pity that we do not know more of Khasekhemui; it is probable that he, at least as much as Menes-Narmer, deserves the name of the Unifier of Egypt. If he was a giant in stature he remained a giant in the recollection of the people, for his memory was venerated profoundly over many centuries. The two statues from Hierakonpolis, the first from Egypt to show the King enthroned, are amongst the greatest works of art to survive from the earliest period.

At Shunet ez-Zebib, outside the holy city of Abydos, there is a huge, towering brick structure, dark and enigmatic, built of baked brick though once white painted like the royal tombs. This is the building which used to be known as the 'Castle of Khasekhemui'; it now seems more likely that it was a First Dynasty funerary palace; but, extraordinarily, neither this building, nor most of the others like it, have ever been properly excavated. Only in a land so richly endowed with splendid and monumental buildings of high antiquity as Egypt could such a survival have escaped either the depredations of the treasure hunter or the trowel of the archaeologist (but see plate 76). It is one of the most remarkable ancient buildings in the world and by association, however tenuous, may stand as a monument to a great and mysterious king whose reign was long recalled with gratitude by the people of Egypt, as the time which marked the placing of the final seal of peace and unity upon the Valley, the culmination of a process which was begun by the founding Kings, to one of whom the monument was first dedicated.

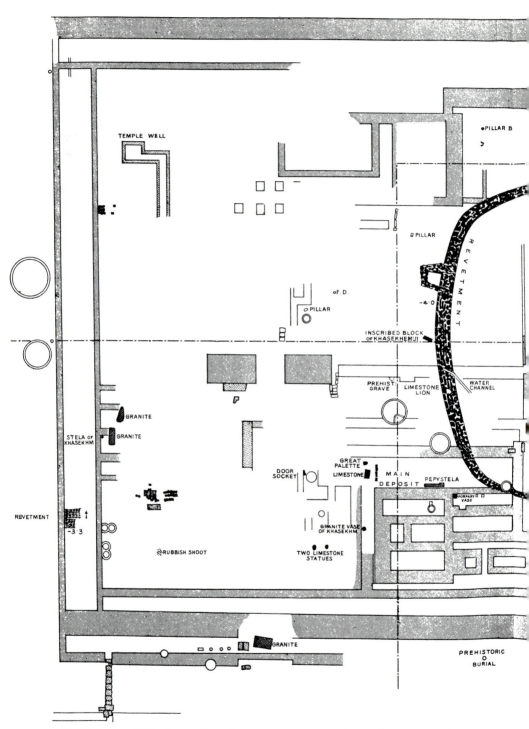

TEMPLE WELL

PILLAR B

PILLAR

REVETMENT

F. D.

PILLAR

—4·0

INSCRIBED BLOCK
OF KHASEKHEMUI

PREHIST.
GRAVE

LIMESTONE
LION

WATER
CHANNEL

GRANITE

STELA of
KHASEKHM

GRANITE

GREAT
PALETTE

DOOR
SOCKET

LIMESTONE

MAIN
DEPOSIT

PEPYSTELA

PORPHRY
VASE

REVETMENT

—3·3

RUBBISH SHOOT

GRANITE VASE
OF KHASEKHM

TWO LIMESTONE
STATUES

GRANITE

PREHISTORIC
BURIAL

38 The plan of Hierakonpolis within its protective walls reveals a semi-oval revetment in the enclosed temple area, an architectural element unusual in Egyptian cities, though found in several examples in Sumer (southern Iraq) and also at Barbar in Bahrain. (From Capart)

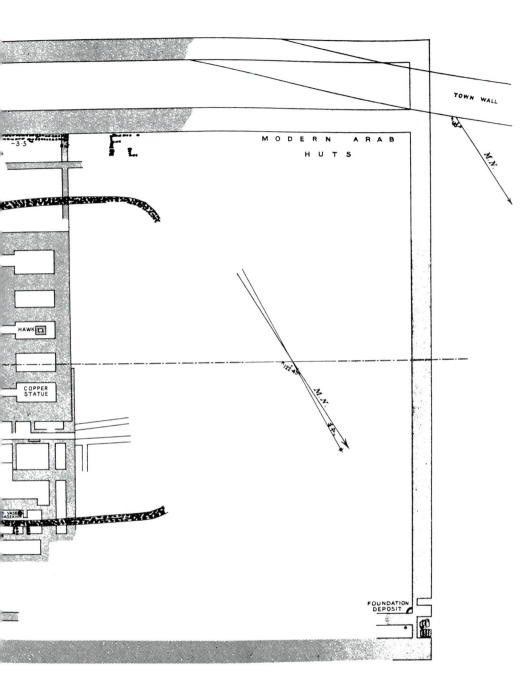

TOWN WALL

M.N.

MODERN ARAB

HUTS

-3.5

F.

HAWK

COPPER
STATUE

M.N.

VASE
ASEKH

FOUNDATION
DEPOSIT

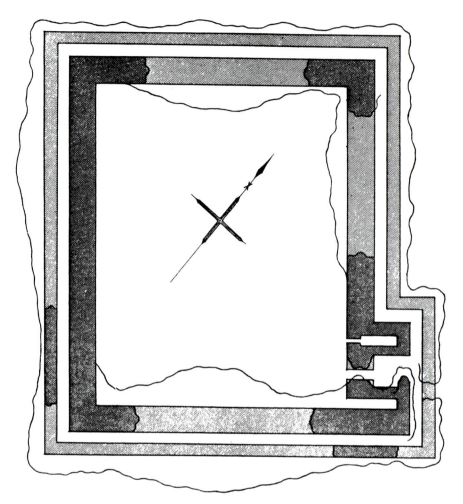

39 Hierakonpolis, perhaps the 'capital' of the line of princes who provided the first Kings of Egypt, was notable for its huge surrounding wall and monumental gateway. The gate is well designed to baffle raiders and to permit a vigorous defence, a witness to the instability which it must be assumed threatened the city and its environs in the late fourth and early third millennia. (From Vandier)

a   *b*

40a and *40b* The 'Battlefield' palette, is dominated on the obverse (*a*) by a great lion, perhaps representing the King or one of his allies in the process of imposing single rule in the Valley. At the extreme right a figure in a long robe (possibly Sumerian or western Asiatic in style) leads forward a captive. Birds scavenge the corpses of defeated enemies at the base of the palette. On the reverse (*b*) is a design more Asiatic in format than Egyptian. The bird beside two caprids divided by a palm tree is a design to be found on seals from Elam and, much later, the Arabian Gulf.

41 The 'red crown' is traditionally associated with the Lower Egyptian Kingdom. However, this sherd which shows the Crown is dated to Naqada I times, c.3500 BC, long before the white crown of Upper Egypt appears. It was recovered from Naqada, an Upper Egyptian site. The Red Crown was always regarded as more exalted than the White, despite the latter's identification with the southern princes who unified Egypt. (Ashmolean Museum, Oxford)

42 The lion of Hierakonpolis, though possibly later than its past ascription to the First Dynasty (it may date from later in the Old Kingdom period) is a fine example of a difficult technique, the firing of large-scale and intricately moulded pottery objects. The lion seems to have been one of the animals particularly associated with the rulers of Hierakonpolis. This superb object is in many ways a curious piece. It is in no way typical of Egyptian work, nor is it similar to the work of any other contemporary artists in other cultures. (Ashmolean Museum, Oxford)

43 The late Predynastic rulers of Hierakonpolis seemed to have identified themselves with votive offerings of objects remarkable for their exceptional size. Great knives, almost a metre long, of which this is an example were deposited in the temple. They could have had little practical use. (Ashmolean Museum, Oxford)

a

b

c

44a, 44b, and 44c There are some remarkable similarities between the techniques of the chlorite carvings from eastern Arabia, Sumer, and Elam and those of the Hierakonpolis ivories. The treatment of the plumage of birds is almost identical; compare (a), with colour plate IV. Many themes are common, too: lions (b) are popular subjects in both traditions, as are confronted felines (c).

a   b

45a and 45b Lapis lazuli comes principally from Badakhshan in north-eastern Afghanistan. It disappears from Egyptian sites in the middle of the First Dynasty. A female figurine in lapis, quite uncharacteristic in form of Egyptian work, has been recovered from Hierakonpolis (a). It may have been imported into Egypt from the Arabian Gulf. A comparable figurine (b), an old man wrapped in a cloak comes from Tarut in eastern Arabia. ((a) Ashmolean Museum, Oxford; (b) Museum of Archaeology and Ethnography, Riyadh, Saudi Arabia)

46 This figure, carved in ivory in the round, seems to have some of the characteristics of the little men on the large seals from Hierakonpolis. The arms are drawn back in a way which in both Egyptian and western Asiatic art, represents the pinioning of a prisoner.

47 A statuette which may represent a Predynastic ruler from Hierakonpolis, though the figure has also been interpreted as a woman. The long robe is not typical of later Egyptian forms, though the posture, with the left arm lying across the lap, and what could be the first portrayal of the royal wig cover, or nemes, are repeated in royal statues until the reign of Djoser (limestone: height 24cm). (University College Museum, London, UC 14878)

48 The famous 'painted tomb' (Tomb 100) at Hierakonpolis, perphaps the burial place of a Predynastic ruler. Excavated in 1898–9, it was subsequently lost. This photograph, from the records kept by F.W. Green, the discoverer of the tomb, was taken at the time of its excavation. (Reproduced from the *Journal of Egyptian Archaeology* vol. 59 (1973), with the permission of the Egypt Exploration Society and the Faculty of Oriental Studies, Cambridge University)

49 The most remarkable feature of Tomb 100 was a large painting on its subterranean walls. This is unique containing elements common to both Egyptian art of the late Predynastic period and to that of western Asia. These include the hero wrestling with lions, the whirling animals, and warriors facing each other holding spears and bucklers. Some of the designs, such as the warriors also appear in the much later iconography of the Arabian Gulf, particularly in that region's distinctive stamp seals.

50a, 50b and *50c* The original Egyptian mace, typical of Naqada I times, is a flat circular disc (*a*), not, it might be imagined, a particularly dangerous weapon. Much more formidable is the pear-shaped mace head (*b*) which replaced it in Naqada II times and which probably originated in Western Asia. (*c*) A mace-head recovered from the Main Deposit at Hierakonpolis is more typical of Sumerian or Elamite carving; it is certainly untypical of Egyptian forms. (Approximately 4.5 cm wide; Ashmolean Museum, Oxford)

51 Captives on the base of King Khasekhemui's throne (*a*) seem to be thrown about in a way similar to those depicted on early Western Asiatic seals

52 The simplest palettes found in the tombs, those originally made for the preparation of kohl, a cosmetic for the eyes, none the less have inevitable elegance of design in the parallel lines of the margins. (Private collection; photograph, Roger Wood)

a   *b*

53a and *53b* This palette, variously called 'The Exotic Animals', 'The Oxford' (from its location in the Ashmolean Museum), and 'The Two Dogs', is one of the most complex and strange of this type of artefact. The obverse (*a*), dominated by the cavity in which the kohl would have been ground, shows two fantastic creatures, with long saurian necks and feline heads and bodies, licking a prone caprid. This creature is surmounted by a bird and the undulating necks of the saurians seem to be holding off two jackals from the animal which lies between them; another jackal is depicted below the grinding area. Beneath the long clawed feet of these two fantastic creatures more horned beasts are represented, beset by hunting dogs. The difference between the representations of the dogs and the jackals is clear. The dogs are the usual slender Egyptian hunting breed, the *tesem*, though shown here with their ears down, rather than pricked up as usual.

On the reverse (*b*) more fantastic creatures, including a griffin and another long-necked beast, mingle with predatory lions in harrying the horned game. A stately giraffe observes the scene whilst, in the bottom left hand corner a dog- or ass- headed figure, evidently a masked man, pipes, as if directing some wild bacchanal of the animals. He may be one of the earliest representations of an animal-masked priest or officiant, and as such may be the ancestor of the priests and notables who donned masks to impersonate the great gods in the temple and state ceremonies. It is possible that he represents this great god Set, here the Master of the Dance and of the animals.

The palette, a work of art of the highest quality, derives one of its names, 'The Two Dogs' from the two animals which act as supporters to the complex scenes depicted on its two faces. There are, however, not dogs but jackals, as is clear from their rounded ears and long, thick, bushy tails. (height 42 cm; Ashmolean Museum, Oxford)

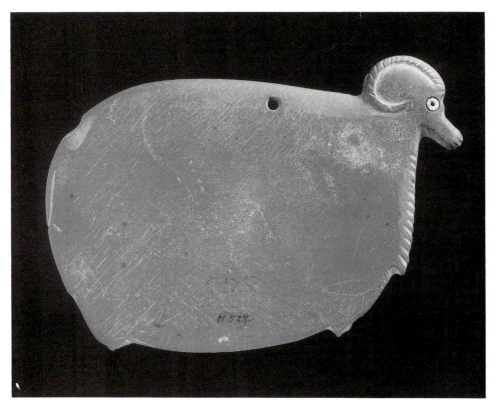

54 A palette carved in the form of a ram. Sometimes craftsmen produced amulets depicting animals in the schist. This example has a pleasing naivety of form and execution. (Museum of Archaeology and Anthropology, Cambridge)

a   *b*

55*a* and 55*b* The votive palette of King Narmer, deposited in the temple of
Hierakonpolis, shows for the first time the King crowned as ruler both of Upper
(*a*) and Lower Egypt (*b*). The high ceremony which was always an integral part
of Kingship, is clearly depicted with the King inspecting his slain enemies,
processing in state, and surrounded by a series of dramatic events celebrating
his victories. The two long-necked serpopards on the reverse are a common
theme in Egyptian art at this time, as they are in the art of Sumer and Elam.
(Egyptian Museum, Cairo; photograph, Roger Wood)

a   b

56a and 56b The Jebel el Arak knife is one of the most important documents
from the time of the unification, frequently cited as evidence of the presence of
armed invaders in Egypt at this time. Certainly two groups of men seem to be
fighting, in the presence of a boat which has a distinctly Mesopotamian look
about it (a). But though it clearly does record an incident of some notoriety,
perhaps a purely local one, it cannot give conclusive evidence of invasion. On
the reverse (b) is a distinctly Sumerian-looking figure subduing two great, heavily
maned felines; the hero dominating lions is a theme popular at this time in Egypt
(it appears on the Tomb 100 painting at Hierakonpolis) and in western Asia,
where it is often anachronistically associated with Gilgamesh (King of Uruk in
the 27th century BC). The form of the herdsman's turban should be compared
with that of the 'Sumerian' head from Abydos (plate 37). (Egyptian Museum,
Cairo; photograph, Roger Wood)

57 This small statue in ivory of an aged King, robed for the *Heb-Sed* festival, anticipates later sculptural forms; it could be enlarged to a monumental scale without losing its proportions or precision of design (probably First Dynasty). (Reproduced by permission of the Trustees of the British Museum)

58 A favourite motif in the art of the Archaic period, repeated in a great many different forms, is a man, usually old, standing wrapped in a great enveloping cloak, often leaning on a stick. Sometimes, though more rarely, the figure is female. The cloaked man appears again in Middle Kingdom sculpture.

59 A white limestone head of a god, perhaps Min, or of an early First Dynasty King; it might be a portrait of Narmer himself. The head bears some resemblance to the portraits of the King on the Narmer palette; it is also like the young sandal bearer who follows Narmer and who may be his son. The features suggest a distinctly African ancestry. (University College Museum, London)

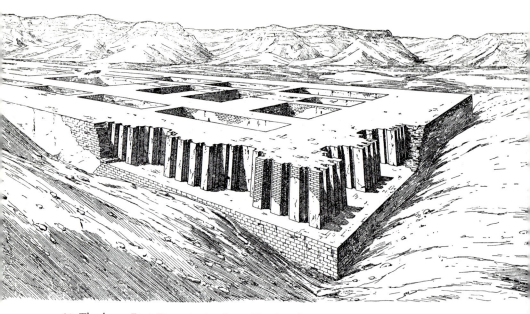

60 The large First Dynasty tomb at Abydos, first excavated by De Morgan and ascribed by him to Narmer, was subsequently re-excavated by Petrie, who concluded that it was in fact the tomb of his queen, Neith-hotep. The name of King Hor-Aha has also been found there, as well as that of a high official whose name is elegantly represented by three birds. (From De Morgan)

61 Umm al-Qa'ab – 'the mother of pots' – a region near Abydos, is the location for a number of enormous mud-brick structures, the walls of which once rose as high as thirty feet. This is the building that used to be known as 'the castle of Khasekhemui' (the last king of the Second Dynasty), though it is probably of First Dynasty date and is all that remains of one of the large funerary palace complexes built to house the burials and to perpetuate the cult of the Kings. (Photograph, Michael Rice)

62 Beside the tomb at Saqqara dated to the reign of the second king of the unified Egypt, Hor-Aha, is a model of an estate showing cultivated lands and model buildings, cattle byres, granaries, and the like. The same tomb also contained the first recorded Egyptian ship burial.

63 An ivory label, probably recording an important event, or series of events during the reign of King Djer. The scene of what seems to be a human sacrifice is to be seen at the extreme right of the upper register. (The Egyptian Museum, Cairo; photograph, John Ross)

64 The architecture of the early tombs, at Saqqara and at Abydos as well as other sites, is remarkable and perplexing. One of the most striking and unusual features, are the lines of bull-skulls mounted around the perimeters of two of the great Saqqara tombs. This, the most remarkable example, with over 300 skulls, is dated to the reign of King Den (Tomb 3504). (From W.B. Emery, *Great Tombs of the First Dynasty*, Vol. 2)

65 Early statues of bulls in the round are rare, but this one, attributed to the Archaic period, has affinities with the treatment of bulls in the sculpture of Sumer at the time. (Museum of Archaeology and Anthropology, Cambridge)

66 One of the two stele erected outside the tomb of King Uadji at Abydos. It represents one of the high points of Egyptian monumental sculpture. (Musée du Louvre)

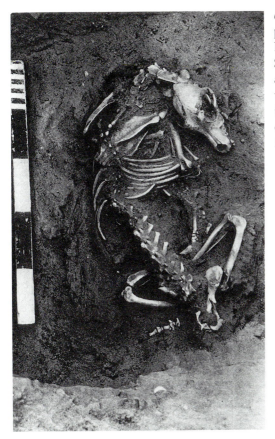

67 Queen Her-Neith, probably the consort of King Djer, was interred alone at Saqqara except for her dog, an Egyptian hound, which was buried by the threshold of the tomb. (Photograph by courtesy of the *Illustrated London News*)

68 The Egyptians manufactured small decorative boxes, presumably to hold their more cherished possessions, since their society was largely an open one. They are often found in the First Dynasty, for example at Helwan, but the tradition is older, as is demonstrated by this painted pottery box from late Predynastic times. (Reproduced by permission of the Trustees of the British Museum)

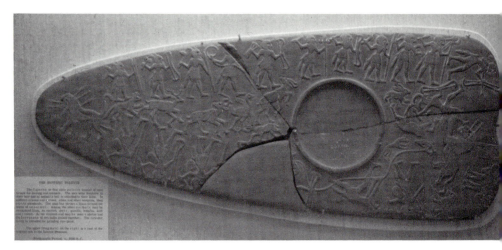

a

69a and 69b One of the most celebrated visual references from late Predynastic times is the 'Hunters Palette'. An exceptionally complex scene is shown, mixing highly realistic elements with elements of fantasy. Evidence drawn from rock carvings in Western Arabia (*b*) shows that the weapons, hairstyles, and dress of the hunters is closely paralleled by similar figures in the region north of Jeddah, at Abdur ash-Samailiyah. (Photograph, John Herbert)

b

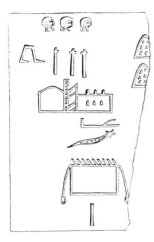
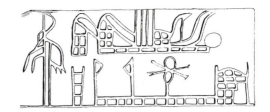

70 The earliest representations of Egyptian temples are to be found on First Dynasty ivory labels.

71 The only reasonably secure evidence for the Kings attributed to the early Second Dynasty is the sequence of their names engraved on the shoulder of this kneeling official, made probably during the latter part of the Dynasty. (The Egyptian Museum, Cairo; photograph, John Ross)

72 At Sayala in Nubia, in the southern reaches of the Valley, a rich burial of a local dignitary yielded a finely worked, gold mounted ceremonial mace. On its baton beautifully executed lines of animals are depicted. Unfortunately the mace was lost soon after its discovery early in this century.

73 This superb representation of Set, though very late in date, shows the persistence of the god's image throughout Egyptian history. Here the god is given a composite head, wearing a dog-mask with the Set animal's long hound muzzle and the curving horns of a caprid. He wears the Double Crown. At some time the head has been altered to give it the appearance of a ram. (Ny Carlsberg Glyptotek, Copenhagen)

74 The Set-King Peribsen,
who first ascended the throne
under the name of Sekhemib,
changed his name and with it
adopted the animal of Set, the
swift hound, as his badge and
in doing so discarded the
Horian symbolism of the
Falcon. For some reason, a
later hand has attempted to
deface the King's badge.

75 The great King
Khasekhemui adopted as his
royal badge the serekh
surmounted by both the royal
falcon *and* the animal of Set,
here clearly represented as the
Egyptian hound. Their
association symbolizes the
unity brought to the Valley
by the King who, perhaps
more than any other, deserves
the title 'Unifier'.

76 By late in the Second Dynasty metallurgy was well advanced and craftsmen were able to produce finely fabricated copper vessels, such as this from the tomb of King Khasekhemui. (Reproduced by permission of the Trustees of the British Museum)

77 The burial complex of King Djoser, the second king of the Third Dynasty, at Saqqara, is the most remarkable of all the world's monumental architecture, representing the first experiment in stone in this genre: it is entirely successful. The complex consists of the six-levelled Step Pyramid in its centre (colour plate VIII), surrounded by ceremonial courts and buildings symbolizing the land of Egypt, all enclosed within a wall, approximately 30 feet high and running unbroken for some one and a half miles. Thirteen entrances are set into the walls, which are recessed in the 'Sumerian' style but only one of them is real, giving access to the complex. (Photograph, Roger Wood)

4

Fulfilment and decline: the end

It is difficult to exaggerate the achievements of the Archaic Kings of Egypt and their assistants. They were true innovators, creating new forms, processes, techniques, and concepts in virtually every department of life. The extent of their innovations is not only itself astonishing; it is bewildering to consider the degree of organization of bureaucracy and government control which must have gone into the planning and management of the projects which they achieved. Later on, in the time of the great pyramid builders now approaching, huge projects of building, design, and decoration became almost commonplace. But even in the earliest times the control of the royal enterprises must have been exceptionally complex and, like virtually everything else in Egypt, without apparent precedent, as much as the products that the craftsmen made often had no precedents in their use of materials and the forms in which they created.

The reigns of the Kings of the Archaic period introduce an entirely new dimension into human experience through the deployment of exceptional creative talent and an abundance of materials expended on the invention of more and more elaborate funerary monuments. This process, one which typifies the social mores of societies through the ancient Near East in addition to Egypt, culminated in the lifetime of King Djoser Neterikhet for whom the Step Pyramid complex, that non-pareil of all the world's architecture, was raised at Saqqara.

The middle of the third millennium in Egypt is forever commemorated by the towering monuments built on the low sandstone plateau at Giza not far from Memphis, by three Kings of the Fourth Dynasty, Khnum-Khufu, Khauf-re, and Men-Kaure, known to Herodotus and hence to posterity as Cheops, Chephren, and Mykerinos respectively. The material wealth and luxury which the pyramids indicate, quite apart from their intimations of supreme political and religious power, are well nigh inconceivable to the modern age.

A colossal expenditure of energy, wealth, and organization was required to bring to this point in central Egypt the armies of men, skilled and unskilled, high professionals and simple, who were to work on constructing these most enduring of all the works of man. The splendour of what was laid inside the chambers prepared for the royal dead must have been beyond description.

The Sumerians (if indeed they *were* Sumerians) buried with the inhabitants of the Royal Tombs at Ur some of the finest products that were made by goldsmiths of any time and which are singularly unlike the usual run of the craftsmanship of Sumer, whose creative artists were more secure in the expression of ideas in poetry and in literature than through the plastic arts. In Egypt relatively little of that time survives; that which does is so magnificent, in form and technique, that the richness of those objects which the robbers of the tombs must have acquired in the course of their ancient and notorious profession can only be guessed at.

The supreme royal substance, in Egypt as elsewhere, was gold. It is extraordinary how across the world this yellow metal, not in itself so excessively rare, as witness the vast extraction of it over the past 5,000 years, has always been associated with Kings. In Egypt not even silver, which was considerably rarer than gold, could displace the supreme rank which gold occupied in the estimation of the people: a position which indeed it has never lost, despite the competition of rarer metals and more precious stones.

The third millennium, that brilliant springtime of modern man's experience, used to be categorized by an earlier generation of archaeologists as the Bronze Age. Seldom has a term of convenience, of academic shorthand, been more inept. Bronze, the product of annealing copper with tin to harden it, came into general use in the Near East only late in the millennium; for most of the period covered by the centuries from 7000 BC to 2000 BC the manipulation of copper represented the highest achievement of metallurgical technology.

Copper and gold, a sumptuous combination by any standards, encapsulate the epoch much more precisely than bronze: but more immediately still the high culture of the third millennium is represented by the rich funerary cults and the elaborate monuments associated with them. These seem to have been seized on by the creative energies of the peoples of the time, so representing a vast absorption of the wealth of the nations and the labour of uncounted hordes of workers.

Really, the third millennium might better be called the Age of

Extravagant and Complex Funerary Monuments, not a term which rolls lightly off the tongue perhaps, but one which is certainly more pertinent to the character of the time than is a simple identification with metal. If the culmination of this curious obsession with great tombs appears to be represented by the pyramids, they are in fact only one form of monument designed to provide an eternal living place for the great dead.

For reasons which are still very largely obscure peoples with no apparent contact with each other, separated by enormous distances and with totally unrelated cultural traditions began, early in the third millennium, to build more and more complex structures in which to house the remains of their chiefs and Kings and, increasingly, a substantial part of the community's movable wealth. Often these monuments were enclosed in mounds, or were themselves mound-like in structure, though built of stone. In the history of human obsessionality the practice represents a curious chapter. From the Orkney islands in the most remote north-west, across Europe, through Egypt and Mesopotamia, down the coastlands and islands of the Arabian Gulf, in Oman, and away into the Indian subcontinent and beyond, elaborate tombs of this type were constructed at this time. In the Arabian Gulf, for example, an extraordinary concentration of mound burials is to be found on the principal Bahrain island where it is estimated that some 170,000 tumuli are to be seen still, the vast majority dating from the late third to the early second millennia. Examples of similar mound fields can be found in eastern Arabia: Oman has its own, even earlier type of mound, constructed often from finely made ashlar blocks of brilliant white limestone. The pyramids, stupendous though they may seem to later generations, must be seen against the backcloth of the long development of Egyptian funerary monuments on the one hand and, on the other, of the much more varied range of tomb structures devised for the great ones of a substantial part of the ancient world during the third millennium. Even the pyramids, incidentally, contain the more simple tumulus or mound, as do the great *mastabas* of the early Kings; it obviously had a profound and pervasive significance.

One of the earliest architectural uses of stone in Egypt was in the flooring of some of the Archaic tombs built during the First Dynasty at Saqqara, though the main material of these remarkable monuments was mud brick. They were strung out along the skyline, looking back to the capital city, Memphis, on the plain below. Stone was also used in the building of some of the early tombs at Helwan. But it was not until the beginning of the Third Dynasty, around 2680 BC, that the titanic complex that was to preserve for all eternity the body of the second King of the dynasty, the Golden Horus, Djoser Neterikhet, was suddenly to appear on the Saqqara escarpment, built entirely of stone, on a scale never before contemplated on the face of the earth (plate 77). Djoser was the successor, perhaps the brother of the dynasty's first King Sanakht who was renowned for building a great temple named 'The Goddess Endures'. A *mastaba* which is thought to be his contained the remains of a very tall man, nearly two metres in height. Of such relatively trivial information the magic of Egyptology is surely made.

The central and most important feature of the Djoser complex was the ziggurat-like stepped pyramid, six platforms placed one upon the other, making a stairway to the heavens. Beneath his monument the mummy of the king was buried in a deep pink-granite chamber, sunk into the rock. The rooms which abut the actual burial chamber are decorated with tiles of an exquisite blue faience, some showing the King in the celebration of the rituals which by this time hedged the divine sovereign about, determining his every action as much in death as in life. The tiles, in a material whose colour and finish was always to be one of the glories of Egyptian art, show the King as a young and vigorous man running in a ritual race as part of the great cycle of ceremonies associated with the *Heb-Sed* festival which itself recalled the events of his coronation; others reproduce, in exquisite detail, the hangings of the palace walls in which he passed his earthly existence.

The Djoser complex is unique. Once again, it is totally without precedent, not merely in Egypt but in the entire world. For centuries its high white limestone curtain walls and the elegant, superbly proportioned kiosks, magazines, and shrines which were built within the walls made it the most remarkable building in the world; perhaps indeed it remains the most remarkable ever built. This mighty structure is constructed with an assurance and a mastery that is breathtaking. The supreme achievement of the Third Dynasty of Egyptian Kings was to preside over the transition from mud-brick architecture to building in stone.

It is not to be wondered at that for thousands of years afterwards the pyramid of Djoser was a place of awe-struck pilgrimage, not only to celebrate the memory of the King for whom it was built but to recall the man who built it, the first universal genius known to history, whose name was Imhotep. It was he, 'the greatest of magicians' as he was hailed, who designed and built Saqqara, not to his own glory but to that of his divine master. But in later centuries Imhotep, too, was worshipped at Saqqara as a benign and kindly divinity, a healer and the god who granted the prayers of the most humble petitioners. Just as the stepped pyramid and its subsidiary buildings together make up the most remarkable single structure yet designed by man, so the man who designed it must rank amongst the very first of those who, by their genius, transformed mankind. It is entirely possible that no more remarkable creative talent ever lived.

Though it is difficult to resist drawing a parallel between them, the temptation to connect the Sumerian ziggurat directly with the Eygptian pyramid, even with the stepped pyramid of Djoser at Saqqara which bears a close, superficial resemblance to the Mesopotamian terraced sacred mountain, must be put aside. The origins of the pyramid have been well traced back through the rectangular brick *mastaba* to a sand-piled tumulus mound. The ziggurat emerged as a consequence of a combination of factors, the need to raise sacred buildings above the level of the flood plain, the necessity to repair and rebuild mud-brick structures with frequency, and the predisposition of the Sumerians to regard certain areas as irrevocably sacred, requiring new temples or shrines to be rebuilt directly on the site of their predecessors. The pyramid's final form, on the other hand, may well have been the result of a solar inspiration. This may be confirmed by anyone who has observed the phenomenon, and suggests that an Egyptian architect with heightened awareness saw, towards the time of sunset in the area to the north of Heliopolis, particularly in the winter months, the rays of the sun breaking through low cloud and forming a perfectly triangular shaft of light over the flat and largely featureless countryside. It is a remarkable sight and one which might well be calculated to inspire an artist contemplating a fitting monument for a king who was beginning himself to be identified with the sun; few natural events look quite so like the direct and evident intervention of a divinity.

It is unrewarding to seek for other explanations of one of the most perfectly satisfying shapes in relation to its environment that architecture, sacred or profane, has ever evolved. The Greeks, who had a faculty when dealing with the works of foreigners of reacting either with superstitious awe or with absolute banality, called the pyramids (in Egyptian, *mer*) 'little cakes', *pyramidoi*, a description of quite overwhelming inappositeness but one which has given them their name today.

None the less, the fact that the first of all pyramids is stepped or terraced and, moreover, built of small, largely rectangular stones reminiscent of the mud bricks of the *mastabas* from which originally it evolved, is, in the context of possible Sumerian–Egyptian connections, a coincidence that cannot wholly be disregarded. Against any direct attribution must be placed the fact that no true ziggurats survive from Mesopotamia earlier than those built at the end of the third millennium, later than Djoser's pyramid by some 700 years. But the origins of ziggurat building can probably be traced back to the White Temple at Uruk in the thirty-fourth century BC raised on a series of platforms and unlike most Sumerian buildings, built in stone.

It has frequently and quite properly been observed that the purpose of the pyramid and the ziggurat are quite different. In Egypt the pyramid was a tomb, to house forever the body of the god-king and to ensure his passage back to the celestial regions whence he had come. A separate temple complex lay at the foot of the pyramid and there the priests, supported by grants of land to ensure the temple's revenues, chanted the liturgies and made the sacrifices essential to the perpetuity of the dead King. In Sumer the ziggurat was simply the platform on which the city god's most sacred shrine was placed, where, at its summit, the ceremony of the *hieros-gamos*, the sacred marriage, was enacted, commemorating the Inanna-Dumuzi myth of the death and rebirth of the god whose blood fertilized the earth. In Egypt, all this was accomplished at the *Heb-Sed*, the festival of jubilee, in quite different circumstances, and, even after death, in the courts of the pyramid temple rather than in, and certainly not on, the pyramid itself.

There is however one point of contact between pyramid and ziggurat. Both were obviously forms of the 'sacred mountain', a concept of the highest antiquity, representing the place on which divinities were accustomed to manifest themselves. It is notable that neither Egypt nor Sumer are really well supplied with anything that could be dignified with the term 'mountain', other than Egypt's Red Sea mountains and the Zagros range, to the east of Sumer. It may well be that the reverence with which both peoples regarded the idea of the mountain represents the recollection of a land which had a special significance – it has been suggested that it was their original mutual home – which was itself mountainous; again, the question must remain entirely speculative at this stage. It is interesting none the less that the hieroglyph for 'foreign country' was a sign showing mountain peaks.

Of the ancestry of Imhotep, the supreme Egyptian architect, nothing is known for certain. By the high titles that he bore, it might be presumed that he was a close connection of the King, possibly even by birth, though some have thought him to have been a commoner who, with the court's recognition of his exceptional genius, rose quickly in the royal service. This was indeed a process frequently encountered in the biographies of successful men in Egypt. In the Third Dynasty, although there is evidence that the old hereditary nobles kept some of their power and influence, the administration of the Kingdoms was placed in the hands of 'new men', competent and forceful individuals, practical men who served the King well. A later tradition asserted that Imhotep came from Upper Egypt and that his father was Ka-Nefer, the director of works, so there may have been a family tradition to account for Imhotep's architectural genius.

At any rate Imhotep was the chief minister, advisor, companion, physician, sculptor to the King, a high priest, and a hereditary noble. The recital of his titles and offices is impressive: 'Chancellor of the King of Lower Egypt, First after the King of Upper Egypt, Administrator of the Great Palace, Hereditary Nobleman, High Priest of Heliopolis, Builder, Sculptor and Vase-maker in Chief'. He was the bearer of the King's seal and 'seal-bearer', it will be recalled, signified 'noble'; he is credited with the building of the first temple at Edfu, the repository of much of the early history, or perhaps more accurately, of the legends of origins of the Egyptian people.

Commissioned by the King to design his burial place Imhotep began, simply enough, by building a substantial version of the *mastaba*-type tomb in which most of Djoser's predecessors had been interred. The *mastaba* was to be a large one and it was to be built in limestone blocks, itself an important innovation. Approximately 10,000 tons of stone needed to be quarried for the *mastaba*, in itself a great quantity. It was, however, to be as nothing when compared with the final extent of the material required for the King's monument. At some point, as this first structure was completed, daring inspiration seems to have seized Imhotep; of course, it could have seized Djoser, but there is no evidence on the point. As a result the resources of Egypt were harnessed to undertake a project the like of which had never before been attempted anywhere (colour plate VIII).

In essence what Imhotep proposed was that the King should occupy for ever a central place in a great rectangular shrine, built of blocks of limestone finely, even exquisitely, worked, which would simulate the land of Egypt. Its centre was to be a great tower (the result of several developments itself) which would rear up, in six stages, each stage stepped up from the one below it, a veritable stairway to the region of the Imperishable Stars, beyond which the King would reign for all eternity. A stellar orientation for buildings, rather than a solar one, is a characteristic of the Third Dynasty and represents the culmination of what may have been one of the most important aspects of aboriginal Egyptian cults, soon to be subsumed by the worship of the sun.

The dimensions and quantities of what Imhotep eventually created for Djoser are immense. The wall which surrounded the stepped pyramid complex measured 536 metres in length by 272 metres in breadth: it is 10.5 metres high, built of fine limestone, 1 million tons of which were quarried, dressed, and laid in courses of spectacular precision and enduring beauty. At first Imhotep planned to build a pyramid raised to four steps; then he took the final decision to raise the steps to six. This decision increased the volume of stone from 200,000 tons to 850,000 tons. It should be remembered at this point, that we are in Egypt around the year 2650 BC.

Of fine white limestone, brilliantly polished, to cover the outer courses 70,000 square metres were required. These had to be cut, trimmed exactly, polished, and fitted into place over the monument's entire surface. Within the courtyard Imhotep built dummy buildings, granaries, and store houses, not unlike those on the model estate built during Hor-Aha's reign not far from the Step Pyramid, but infinitely finer in conception and execution, and of course immeasurably greater in scale.

Around the colossal central mountain of stone blocks, beneath which the King's body and those of his closest family would lie forever in splendid pomp, the land of Egypt, north and south, would be laid out, that the King might review it when he chose and, at the same time confer the ineffable benevolence of his presence over the lands for ever. Granaries, storerooms, temples, places for 'the great ones', the ancient gods, stations for the enactment of the sacred dramas were all laid out – and all built in the same glorious, exquisitely worked stone which, in the brilliant sunlight of Egypt, now takes on a wonderful golden hue.

Imhotep, with the confidence of genius, created this unique building in one lifetime on the rocky escarpment which overlooks the ancient capital of Memphis. His confidence was not overreaching. Throughout the complex, one of the largest as well as one of the earliest consciously designed artefacts of man, Imhotep was inspired by natural forms: the tall-standing papyrus, the lotus closed or open, the palm trunk. These he modelled in stone with a divine plasticity; none the less he was working with materials the properties of which must largely have been unknown to him. What stresses might a stone lintel bear? How to convey the sense of half opened timber door, or a roller blind, pulled down against the sun, in stone?

The boundary wall enclosing the complex is itself a remarkable and sophisticated construction. It has only one real entrance, located in the same place as the entrances to the funerary courts of the First Dynasty at Abydos. In addition, however, there are fourteen other dummy gateways. There are 196 simple bastions decorating the walls; between each bastion are two recessed panels, and two recesses on each side of the bastions. In the courtyard contained by this extravagant surround, as well as all the cultic and ritual buildings, was found the burial of a bull's head, perhaps an echo of the many bulls slaughtered in the First Dynasty so that their heads could decorate the exterior of a Great One's *mastaba*.

Imhotep solved virtually all the problems he set himself, brilliantly. Only in one place did his assurance, perhaps, falter. At the single entrance to the whole complex the visitor, even today, passes through a peaceful colonnade, a small hypostyle hall. Imhotep here wished to use columns, to support the roof, and sought to simulate the bundles of reeds which served the purpose of strengthening walls and doorways in reed or wattle buildings. He built his columns of elegant rose brick, facing them with finely carved skins of limestone, imitating reeds. But then — who knew what weight the columns might support? If Imhotep was in touch with colleagues in Mesopotamia he may well have received discouraging reports of the effectiveness of columns in, for example, temple structures which showed a disappointing tendency to fall down, slumping inelegantly into rubble heaps, to the peril of both the users of the buildings and the architects' reputation. Did Imhotep know, perhaps, of the fickleness of columns?

In any event Imhotep supplied his own solution. The columns stand in Djoser's hall to this day, 5,000 years later and with some assistance from archaeology. They were originally bonded to the walls on either side of the entrance area by solid blocks of limestone: they still endure, if a little apprehensively, clinging to the supporting walls.

It is this element of dilemma, even more than the sublimity of the design and the construction of the complex as a whole, which demonstrates both the humanity and the genius of Imhotep. Freud once described the frankly rather sanctimonious Akhenaton as the 'first individual in history'. It was an unwise judgement, for the line before Akhenaton is long indeed and close to its head must surely be the incomparable Imhotep.

The mind reels before the splendour of Imhotep's conception and his ability to carry it into reality. How did he find craftsmen capable of working the stone, train them, devise tools for them, work out the complexities of the spatial divisions, design all the details (or at least, supervise their design) and be on site every day to see that the huge number of men engaged on the project was properly deployed? We may ask the questions but we cannot supply the answers; we may doubt that we ever will, but perhaps the essential genius of the high Egyptian civilization and the arcane secret for which so many have so hopefully sought, was for organization, for planning, for the orderly expression of the notebooks of a genius. That the state had planners of such genius in its service as Imhotep may still be recognized by anyone with eyes to see; extraordinarily enough, he was not alone, though he may well have been the greatest.

The Step Pyramid complex miraculously held one supreme masterpiece, surviving, against all the odds, the depredations of nearly fifty centuries.

This is the seated life-size statue of the King, old and robed for his jubilee, which was found in its little *serdab* or enclosed chapel set before the northern face of the pyramid and to the east of the entrance to Djoser's mortuary temple (colour plate XI). There Djoser was left to sit, his eyes aligned with a narrow vantage point through which he could observe, for all the eternity he had no doubt confidently expected, the service of perpetual rituals designed to give him life forever and, with that life, prosperity for Egypt.

Djoser's statue is one of the world's great masterpieces, a work for all time; in it indeed lies Djoser's immortality. It is carved from a block of limestone: the King sits heavily, for he is old, his head massive under the weight of a great wig and its cover. His cloak is wrapped round him; one arm lies awkwardly across his thighs, the other at his side. His feet are enormous.

Djoser's face, despite the damage which was done to it when his rock crystal eyes were gouged out, is arresting. It corresponds well with the young King shown on the faience tiles but with one notable difference: the young King has an almost Semitic cast of feature, as though somewhere in his ancestry a Bedu strain from the desert people had entered his blood. But with the old King his ancestry is suggested as something more African; indeed, Djoser's features in old age are distinctly negroid.

His statue is the most perfect expression of the majesty of an Egyptian god-king to survive. His power is not merely absolute: he is power itself. The nobility of his countenance is supported by the dignity of his body, old though he is. He needs to make no further statement; he can only be approached with awe.

Even when viewed from behind, the power that Djoser exudes is still formidable (plate 78). The great head is like a mountain top; the wig cover making it seem still more immense, adds to the dimension of might and splendour which Djoser inhabits.

Not only is the survival of Djoser's *serdab* statue miraculous (it was discovered only in this century) and the statue itself a supreme work of art, it is the ancestor of all royal portraits, the archetype of the King enthroned in majesty. It deserves to be recognized as one of the wonders of the world.

The reign of Djoser saw Egyptian society begin its ascent to heights never before achieved in human experience. The immanent presence of the god as King released a great surge of creative energy; for the best part of the next 500 years Egypt seems to be dedicated to the production of splendid works celebrating the divinity, power, and magnificence of the King, and so giving life to Egypt. All the nation's efforts are dedicated to this end, to the life, prosperity, and health of the Two Lands through the medium of their divine master. Though Khasekhemui's legend carries with him a sense of the power of a conciliating and benign monarch and the healing of divisions in the state, Djoser, perhaps his grandson (though this is far from certain) is the first archetypal divine King of Egypt. With his reign the centuries of Egypt's splendour begin.

There is a notable élan about much of the work of the Third Dynasty which suggests a vigour and a delight in the processes of creation on the part of the artists and craftsmen working at the time. It has been suggested that this characteristic of vigour is 'barbaric', but this is to mistake its character and to ignore the increasing sophistication and cumulative experience of the first two dynasties, a period which in total represented some 500 years. There is rather a lightness, an elegance of spirit, demonstrated by many of the details of the great complex which Imhotep built to enshrine his divine patron. The quality of the carving of small details for example, in the extremely hard, brilliant white limestone which was employed for some parts of the complex is exquisite and quite amazing.

From a few tantalizing fragments in the Saqqara complex we know that sculpture in particular advanced rapidly in Djoser's time. Life-size and larger statues flowed from the sculptors' workshops, anticipating the great works of the Fourth Dynasty to come. Statues of private men, retained in the intimate service of the King, began to be made. One of the pieces found at Saqqara reveals the name and titles of Imhotep himself. Emery, who worked in Saqqara for so many years, would have it that his tomb is nearby, waiting discovery; it is probably as unlikely, alas, as the discovery of Alexander's tomb in his city of Alexandria.

The essential characteristic of Egyptian creativity in the early centuries, at least, was not repetitious variation, as so often seemed to be the case in later periods, but innovation and dynamic change; in one sense the Archaic period represents a sort of continuum of change, over the span of half a millennium. The accession of individuality, in itself a process so profound that it can only be detected through the influences which it exerted, almost imperceptibly, on all aspects of the society, induced a desire for experiment, a joyful matching of capability with imagination, often of fantasy. The creation of the Djoser complex early in the Third Dynasty is expressed horizontally, despite the noble stepped tower which has given the complex its alternative name. It follows the towering walls of the great courts at Abydos and Hierakonpolis associated with the burials of the early Kings. As Imhotep was a southerner apparently, it is not impossible that he knew well the monuments at Abydos and Hierakonpolis and determined to outdo them, in stone.

The *mastabas* of the early dynasties had within them a sort of embryonic stepped structure, concealed inside the eternal fabric of the building. It was almost inevitable, therefore, that later generations should express their creative spirit in a shape of pure force, colossal but surging upwards, resting with absolute confidence on the earth, immovable but expressing that reaching out for the firmament – and beyond it, to the realm of the Imperishable Stars – which is so typical of the spirit of early Egypt. It would have been more extraordinary, perhaps, if the Egyptians had *not* produced so perfect a shape as the pyramid, at this particular point in their development. That they did so sets the final seal on their achievement; after that supreme expression of creative energy it was only to be expected that they would decline. It was not a performance that could ever be repeated, nor one that could even be sustained; indeed, it may be argued that it could not be matched.

The pyramid, the supreme artefact of the age which was now approaching, represented in stone the summation of all that early Egypt was seeking to express. In every aspect of life, particularly those which touched the King in any way, the early builders of the Egyptian state were attempting to reconcile the cosmic with the societal, to identify their society with absolute values and with concepts which otherwise defied articulation.

Egypt's ability to create in freedom was the product in part of its isolation and the abundance of its resources. The massive influence of the deserts of Arabia weighed only slightly, if at all, upon her in the early centuries. The desert demands conformity, if for no other reason than for survival. The Semites, who came from the desert, have always been slow to accept change. For them the purity and simplicity of desert life was immutable and ordained.

For the Egyptian the abundance which surrounded him led him on ineluctably both to innovation and to change. Although it would be dangerous to press the analogy too far, the contrast between the formal conservatism of the desert and the rococo experimentation of early Egypt is not unlike what happened when the people of the desert escaped from its confines and largely from its influence in the early years of Islam. Colliding then with the riches of the ancient cultures whose remains lay on the paths of their zealous conquests, they produced the extraordinary flowering of the arts and the material splendour of the Islamic empires. If there are Semitic influences to be detected in late Predynastic Egypt (as seems unequivocally to have been the case at least as far as language is concerned) perhaps those who introduced them were as swift to respond to the promise of Egypt as the carriers of similar influences surely did nearly 4,000 years later.

180

Some might see elements in the Djoser complex as the last flowering of the 'Mesopotamian connection' in Egypt. The great wall, running for a total length of over 1,600 metres, is recessed in a way reminiscent of the recessing of *mastaba* tombs which are an evidently Mesopotamian feature. This similarity with the exterior of a *mastaba* is in line with the monument's rich and complex symbols, and it probably deliberately recalls the earlier structure.

It is, of course, just possible that Imhotep knew of the monumental buildings of Sumer. Alternatively, it has been suggested that Djoser's pyramid is to be seen as the spontaneous invention of a divine stairway by which the King's ascension to the skies might be effected, though he hardly had need of a staircase to leap up to the sun, beyond the Imperishable Stars, for this was his true domain, the rulership of which was his by inalienable right. In any case the idea of a free-standing staircase was hardly one of general significance in Egypt at the beginning of the Third Dynasty, though the ladder, as we know, played some part in the earlier rituals associated with the divine Kingship.

The explanation for the similarity of the pyramid and ziggurat may be that they both originated in the same, now forgotten archetype, common to peoples in the Near East 5,000 years ago at an early stage of societal and urban development. There are many such symbols: the familiar triangular pyramids are clearly a more particularly Egyptian form though even these were to be repeated coincidentally in other cultures, distant in time and clime. Perhaps at the beginning of the third millennium men felt they had, for whatever reasons, to build imitation mountains and to give them a markedly terraced appearance. In Mesopotamia the idea stuck; in Egypt it did not and the familiar colossal stone triangles evolved.

Our eyes are accustomed to seeing the monuments of Egypt as they are now: shattered ruins, ravaged by time, neglect, and pillage. What we see now are the lifeless hulks of once tremendous organisms, as vibrant with life as was, say, a European cathedral in the Age of Faith. Nevertheless, despite the ravages of fifty centuries, it is not difficult to imagine the effect that the Djoser mausoleum and its vast surrounding structures, glittering white in the brilliant light of Egypt, or shimmering magically when the moon was high, would have had on those succeeding generations to whom it would have been a familiar but no less wonderful landmark, as it rose on its remote escarpment, at the very point where the cultivation ends and the limitless desert begins. To the Egyptians, with their belief in the divine order represented by the King, it was a witness to the unique bond which existed between their land and the heavens. Indeed, mysterious and gleaming, it must have seemed like part of the immortal mansions brought down to earth. So the complex seemed to tourists who visited it during the New Kingdom, more than a thousand years after it had been built. The buildings were still then, it seems, intact; visitors left admiring graffiti on the walls which can still be seen, recalling perhaps some second millennium Memphite family's outing to this amazing and numinous place.

From time to time, during the early centuries of its existence when it was still a living temple, the sound of chanting and of music, essential components of all rituals in Egypt, would have been heard across the silent spaces between its lonely eminence and the city of Memphis which lay below it. The sounds must have seemed like the echoes of the stars singing as the priests went about their business of perpetuating the life of Egypt through the ceremonies of giving life to Djoser. Its mystery would have been compounded by the fact that all but the King, his courtiers, and the priests would be excluded from the temple precincts.

The achievement represented by the Djoser complex is far greater than that for which the later pyramids, of Khnum-Khufu, Khaufre, and Menkaure stand. They are remarkable, certainly, though only the first is really formidable: even so, it shows a clear line of descent from other monuments, including this first pyramid of all at Saqqara. Khufu's Pyramid is not *sui generis*; that of Djoser undoubtedly is. Every element in it is original; it is a sort of compendium of architectural invention. It is also remarkable for what it reveals about the development of large-scale sculpture, a technique which began with the statue of King Khasekhem. Djoser's complex contained evidence of large statues of the King and, no doubt, of the gods. Most of these are lost but one unfinished limestone figure of the King survives (plate 79).

There is no doubt of the piety which caused such tremendous structures as the pyramids to be erected; the idea of countless slaves dying under the overseer's lash is the product of the perfervid imaginations of nineteenth-century romantics and Hollywood movie moguls. An example of the Egyptians' power of organization and of the Kings' concern for the welfare of their subjects (like their Sumerian contemporaries, Egyptian Kings often liked to think of themselves as the shepherds of their people, though surely of a somewhat elevated class) is to be found in the levy system used to mobilize the farmers of Middle Egypt during the inundation when they were unable to work their land. Their attitudes are well expressed by the graffiti scrawled on many of the blocks praising one gang, disparaging another, and generally presenting a remarkable demonstration of group loyalty.

The control of large masses of men engaged in hard, demanding, and often highly skilled work called for organizational skills of an exceptionally developed order. Herodotus maintained that Khufu's Pyramid was built in about twenty years. It contains 6 million tons of stone, brought from the Mokkatam hills, finely cut and fitted into place, course by course. Two and a half million blocks were cut: over twenty years this means manhandling an average of 125,000 blocks each year. Averaged out this means that 300,000 tons of stone had to be worked and put in place, year by year. It is difficult to imagine a modern contractor being prepared to accept such an assignment today, even with a twenty-year completion date for the project.

The architects engaged on these enormous public works seem from the outset to have used the plateaux at Giza and Saqqara as though they were gigantic drawing boards. We must assume that they did produce preliminary drawings, perhaps even scale models on the lines of examples known from later periods, probably adopting the technique of the sand model; however, they seem to have been prepared to change direction quite cheerfully in the middle of a huge enterprise or even to introduce entirely new features into it when it was already well advanced.

Thus Imhotep started with the idea of a large, grandiose, stone-built *mastaba* for Djoser, enlarged it, built a series of four steps over it, enlarged these again, and then extended the stepped structure to six stages. These changes resulted in an enormous increase in the requirement of stone and, one suspects, in the exasperation of the building supervisors on site. They, after all, had themselves to learn techniques for handling these vast quantities of stone. All the great pyramids demonstrate a sort of improvisatory element where it seems that the architect was still prepared to experiment, despite the scale on which he was working, devising some of the largest buildings ever conceived by man.

The internal mathematics of pyramid building are immensely complex: they have been well studied and such studies demonstrate clearly that, despite this improvisatory element in their design, the architects were fully in command and were intensely conscious of the challenge which mass and quantity presented to them. Even when there was a major disaster, as may have been the case with the collapse of the Maidum Pyramid, the lessons which it offered were quickly learnt and the architect concerned went on to build other, more successful monuments.

The sophistication of the building techniques employed in Fourth Dynasty architecture is quite remarkable. To excavate and then pile up the enormous quantities of stone required to produce a pyramid requires careful control and a fine mathematical sense: these the Egyptians presumably acquired empirically, just as they seem to have had a knowledge of the properties of π (or something very close to it) which were obtained from practical experience but which had a profound influence on their ability to design complex structures.

The recessed buttresses which were so notable a part of the exterior presentation of *mastabas*, palaces, sarcophagi, and even the walls surrounding buildings like the Step Pyramid, were also built into the interior structures of the larger *mastabas* and the pyramids to strengthen them and help them to bear the immense weights involved. They are present in the earlier *mastabas* too, and can be found in the one originally built for Djoser.

The relieving chambers inside Khufu's Pyramid are rightly celebrated, demonstrating a keen and subtle awareness of the dangers of stress when dealing with great masses of stone. But more subtle still is the employment of saw-tooth edging to the blocks which go to make up the pyramid, to prevent them splaying out under the tremendous weights pressing down upon them.

The Pyramids of Giza must have been astonishing sights when they were new (plate 81). They would have gleamed white as magically as their ancestor at Saqqara a few kilometres away, and have inspired as much wonder and awe. The architect who made the Great Pyramid for Khufu, probably his kinsman and the co-ordinator of the whole colossal enterprise who so built a structure which has penetrated the consciousness of succeeding generations like no other, was called Ankhaf, probably a royal kinsman. He has about him the look of an assured, decisive man who, given a task, would complete it. What he did is there for all to see (plate 82). Ankhaf was probably a son of King Sneferu by one of his minor queens; he was not therefore a contender for the throne and he seems to have served his half-brother loyally.

One consequence of the immense organization needed to build the pyramids, and the recruitment and training of the hosts of artists and craftsmen necessary to work on all the various divisions of the project, was that in the later decades of the Old Kingdom, when the King no longer absorbed virtually all the available labour and talent in the construction of his pyramid, a pool of highly skilled men existed from which the nobles and indeed even the merely prosperous could draw-to-build and decorate monuments for themselves. The process of the apparent 'democratization' of Egyptian religion has often been commented upon. The argument proceeds that first the King alone was guaranteed immortality; then his attendants, family, and most intimate courtiers were brought in the scope of the afterlife by being buried close to him. It may seem a naïve view for a sophisticated people, but there is little doubt that the fact that a minor self-made official or tradesman could afford to commission a handsome tomb led quite quickly to the insistence that such a tomb was worth commissioning and that the individual concerned could expect to enjoy an eternity once reserved exclusively for his betters. This was to lead ultimately to a sort of democratization of death and the loss of the primordial Egyptian attitude to the gods and the world beyond death. Later in the Old Kingdom we see the King himself acknowledging the change and giving his favoured courtiers 'houses of millions of years', tombs which were intended to serve as estates for eternity, comparable with the lands, herds, and servants with which he would reward those who served him in their lifetimes.

There is little enough known of the ways in which the royal government of Egypt worked, how decisions were taken, to what extent projects were planned before being started, or how instructions were transmitted from the source to the place where the action was. It is evident that there must have been an orderly process for the consideration of affairs of state, for the recording of decisions, and for the inspection and reporting of progress and results. No doubt some element of royal (or divine) whim played its part in advancing a particular idea or project, but generally speaking the quality of work which has survived from Old Kingdom Egypt is so high that neither its planning nor its execution could have been haphazard. The Egyptian respect for order, for the interconnections which they saw existing between all things, animate and inanimate, would have tended towards seeking an assured structure lying beneath the projects which they undertook.

Many of the titles of senior officials of the earliest periods have been recorded. They suggest the complexity of a developed bureaucracy, the long usage of title which had become florid and orotund, and a clear recognition of how enthusiastically all officers (and no doubt others) respond to titles of honour. Thus there was 'The Controller of the Two Thrones', 'He who is at the head of the King', 'the Master of the Secrets of the Royal Decrees', 'He of the Curtain', in addition to the less specific 'Sole Companion to the King' and other marks of distinction which were evidence of the royal favour. There were offices called 'The House of the Master of Largesse', the base from which the royal bounty was distributed to those in need or to those whom the King wished to reward or favour. There was even an 'Overseer of the Foreign Country', though why only the singular form was used is not known. 'Hereditary Prince' was an important and ancient rank. It had its origins, rather surprisingly, in a term which meant 'Mouth of the People', suggesting a responsibility rather like that of a Tribune in Rome.

The collection and husbanding of the royal revenues by means of taxes levied on provinces, towns, individual landowners, and farmers was the responsibility of the Treasurers, of whom there were two, one for each Kingdom. They worked from the White House in the case of the southern Kingdom and from the Red House for the northern. Even in so practical a task as the control of the exchequer, the characteristic duality of Egypt was still maintained.

The Egyptians, especially in the Old Kingdom, had a particular concern for the record of a man's career appointments in the formal security of his tomb, which thus presented a sort of petrified obituary. There was a multiplicity of such appointments with which an ambitious official might be favoured during his lifetime: directorships of the royal administration, supervisory functions, inspectorates of outlying posts in the bureaucracy, temple ranks, and appointments at the court. Some of the most exalted appointments, those which were particularly identified with or brought the holder into personal contact with the King, tended to be honorific and ceremonial and were reserved largely for the high nobility. A King's descendants would, in succeeding generations, tend to move down through the upper reaches of the bureaucracy as new generations, closer to each new monarch, filled the highest places. There must have been considerable sources of power in the awarding of office and its emoluments.

However, later in the Old Kingdom (as indeed at its beginning) princes of the royal line do not seem generally to have occupied the highest offices. Presumably they represented a danger to the succession; like the Tudors, the Kings of Egypt tended to seek out and promote their own men who thus would look to them only as the source of favour and fortune.

One of the sources of Egypt's strength in remote antiquity was undoubtedly the King's ability to identify able newcomers in his entourage, even in its humblest ranks and, even further, to encourage his nobles to watch out for exceptionally talented youngsters who, early on in their lives, could be singled out for the state's service. The rewards were great for such men.

In the Old Kingdom there existed an elaborate system of social dependencies ranging from the King downwards. Officials and members of the great households were rewarded with gifts of jewellery and furniture, clothing, metal ware, vases, pottery, and land; first these descended from the King, then the recipients would be expected to pass on some part of their benefits to their dependants in turn.

The tombs of the Old Kingdom, those superb biographical monuments filled with the bustling energy of everyday life in Egypt and the worldly concerns and achievements of some quite exceptional administrators, provide many examples of men who achieved great eminence in the society of their day, despite modest or even humble antecedents. However in the practice of the temples and the service of the gods, the King was, theoretically at least, alone in his relationship with the divine. In theory, therefore, the King, as principal immanent divinity, conducted every ritual in every temple throughout Egypt: the officiating priest was merely his surrogate. In reality, however, the companies of priests attached to the great temples were powerful, sometimes even representing a degree of opposition to the royal authority.

The power of the temples was exercised by these professional priests who lived in them and on their endowments, which could be very considerable. Their duties were various. First and foremost they were responsible for the sacrifices, for maintaining the proper honours appropriate to the god-king. They might be attached to a temple or attached to a tomb, endowed to keep alive the *ka* of the dead King: they might conduct the huge and colourful ceremonies which took place in the great temples, year in and year out.

One of the most agreeable characteristics of early Egyptian society is that, whilst it is intensely autocratic in character, it is none the less flexible, permitting men of talent, no matter what their racial or social origins, to move into the highest reaches of the administration. When the King is god, differences in degree amongst his subjects are of relatively minor significance. The selection and training of artists, however, demands a more subtle system, a more precise schedule than the recruitment of officials to administer the royal estates or to officer the levies.

The scale on which the pottery, stone-carving, and copper-casting industries were organized was considerable; when the demands of monumental and funerary architecture are added, the extent of the need for experienced craftsmen in all these fields is obviously formidable. The number of workers in what might be called 'craft industries' must, on the evidence of their surviving products, presumably only a fraction of their real output, have been very high, as significant a percentage of the Egyptian population as that, say, employed on the land.

It is rare (though not entirely unknown) to encounter a badly made stone vessel or wasted pot; quality-control standards in early Egypt were exceptionally high, befitting the technical ability of the craftsmen. Standards, by and large, were maintained over hundreds of years and the ability to do that was itself remarkable.

It is intriguing to speculate what sort of administration existed to ensure that the remarkable consistency of design was maintained. We know that royal officials were given, nominally at least, responsibility for the supervision of the making of royal statues, or for the architecture of the royal tomb. However, it is difficult to believe that these great officials, often with many appointments to discharge, were more than the presiding figures over groups of less exalted officials who actually co-ordinated and supervised the work.

It is impossible, however, not to wonder how the Egyptian artificers managed even to meet the demands of their royal clients. In Djoser's time, for example, tens of thousands of jars, plates, vases, and vessels of every conceivable shape and size would be placed in the King's tomb with lavish prodigality. Presumably some, if not all, of these objects had been used in the palaces of the King; it is possible, however that many were made for funerary purposes alone. To have produced this quantity of stone vases a prodigious industry must have existed, yet so far little trace of extensive industrial workings has been discovered. This is the more surprising when it is considered that there must have been manufacturing centres or, at the very least, collection centres where the products of what must have been an army of outworkers were assembled. Once again, the logistics baffle and respect for the organizational powers of the ancient Egyptians must soar. An antiquarian note is struck, incidentally, by the contents of Djoser's tomb. The names of virtually every King who preceded him on the Two Thrones is found inscribed on the stone vessels, which were piled up in his tomb in such enormous quantity, filling the subterranean magazines.

The products of different craftsmen, perhaps of particular workshops or studios, can be detected in different parts of Egypt; there seems, therefore, to have been some sort of national distribution system for the products of studios to use. This is particularly true of pottery products, where it is also easier to detect. In the case of stoneware however, there is a notable consistency over the years and over the whole land between the various types of vessel manufactured. There is, of course, an amazing medley of forms and sizes: the much vaunted Egyptian conservatism in art (a conservatism which in fact is more apparent than real) did not prevent them from adding new shapes to the catalogue of vessels which they produced (plate 83). But once a shape or form became accepted it was adopted apparently over many hundreds of square miles, sometimes over the whole country.

If the temples, particularly those consecrated to Ptah, were the repositories of the corpus of approved designs and forms of products manufactured either for the royal service or for the rituals of the temples (a considerable assumption but certainly not entirely insupportable), there must have been some system of information exchange or flow from the temple to the many different and widespread workshops which would have carried out their manufacture. It may have been simply a matter of handing on the techniques from generation to generation, from father to son. Those lines in the normal course of nature must sometimes have been interrupted, yet the forms often survived over very long periods. The traditions of the craftsmen's work seem to have been living traditions, not merely the work of copyists. Nothing has survived to indicate how the central authority passed on its design instructions: the medium may have been entirely perishable, of course, but some such system must surely have existed.

The principles that apply to the making of stone vases apply equally to most objects of Egyptian manufacture. In the Old Kingdom the walls of tombs and their associated buildings belonging to the royal family and distinguished nobles were customarily decorated with scenes of daily life in Egypt, in the palaces, and in the countryside. Many variations exist and certainly it is often possible to detect the hand of a master in one set of carvings and a more provincial, less talented hand in another. But the designs are broadly consistent and the conventions employed by the artists, the curious distorted frontality, for example, which is so odd a feature of Egyptian portraiture of humans when compared with the absolute literalism often employed for animals, is consistent everywhere in Egypt from the Fourth Dynasty onwards, when seemingly someone had determined that this was how it was to be done.

The ability of Egyptian artists to handle frontality with perfect assurance is demonstrated by their development of stone sculpture in the round. This was a slightly later form in its development than the making of stoneware vessels; for example, Predynastic artists do not seem to have attempted monumental statuary on any real scale, contenting themselves with enchanting miniatures which, none the less, are often the ancestors of the later, greater forms. There is some evidence that in the early days they worked in wood for the large-scale statues which adorned the temples; a face which survives demonstrates the superlative quality of such work (plate 84).

In late Predynastic times ivory was frequently carved in formal, rather rigid shapes. Generally these objects are modestly domestic: combs, ladles, and spoons for example; some of these are already of a formidable elegance. The Egyptians were always enthusiastic board-game players, and developed a variety of games with counters in the form of animals; some of these, the lions and dogs for example, are especially fine and seem to have within them already the promise of the towering monumental forms to which in the distant future they will be expanded. These will eventually become the adornment of the temple colonnades of massive sphinxes with which later, more pretentious ages loved to ornament the land of Egypt.

Pottery figurines, as well as those carved in ivory, were made in large quantities in early times. Some were clearly votive objects: others are less clear in their purpose but they want nothing in appeal. It may be, however, that the apparently less durable substance of fired clay was not considered so significant by whatever authorities actually determined the form that more significant objects were to take, for there seems to be more random variety in the early decades in the objects made from clay. However, pottery once it is fired has an unequalled capacity to survive and in consequence a wealth of pottery objects has come down to the present time.

The key to this consideration of early Egyptian manufacturing industry may lie in the shadowed interiors of the great temples dedicated to the supreme craftsman-god, Ptah of Memphis. Of all the great Egyptian divinities Ptah is in many ways the most mysterious. Yet he was to survive throughout Egyptian history, from the earliest times to the latest, a powerful influence in the creative life of the country.

Ptah's origins are obscure. He seems to have been associated with the Kings of the First Dynasty; whether this means that he too originated in This (somewhere in the region of Abydos) or in Hierakonpolis is not known. It does appear, however, assuming the legend to be correct, that when Menes-Narmer established his capital at Memphis Ptah was swiftly recognized as the city's presiding divinity and the earliest temple in his name was established there.

The high priest of Ptah at Memphis was one of the greatest of the 'Great Ones' of Egypt, an immensely powerful member of the ruling elite and a close confidant of the King. His was the supreme directing intelligence of the armies of sculptors, potters, craftsmen in jewels, copper, gold, silver, and wood; he, no doubt, was close by whenever a decision affecting the royal tomb or the creation of a great temple was required in the innermost councils of the King. Through the undying traditions of Ptah's priests the survival of Egyptian forms in architecture and manufacture were doubtless realized.

In the early centuries the High Priest of Ptah was the nearest to the concept of pontiff (other of course than the King himself) that Egypt knew. Later the high priests of Re in Heliopolis and, later still, of Amon in Thebes became dominating influences in the religious life as much as in the political economy of Egypt. But by these times the character of the Egyptian establishment seems profoundly to have changed, from the days of Ptah's supremacy.

This change in the relative status of the gods of Egypt seems to be associated with the collapse of the Kingship after the first thousand years of its existence. When the Old Kingdom fell apart in the twenty-second century BC at the end of the Sixth Dynasty, Egypt was experiencing part of the general distress and upheaval which seized the whole ancient Near East, in the closing decades of the third millennium. At this time, in the Mesopotamian valley as well as in the Nile Valley, there seems to have been a strengthening of the influence of Semitic-speaking, desert-dwelling peoples, who hitherto, whilst they had always been there, had generally been kept in check. They were in any case mainly nomads, 'sand-dwellers' who could be kept at bay by the superior military character of the peoples of the great cultures of Egypt and of the city states of Sumer. Gradually, however, they became more aggressive, more adventurous; they also became more skilled, as they absorbed more of the knowledge of the dwellers in the valleys. In the north of Mesopotamia as in the desert regions of Syria, Palestine, and Jordan, they early on became dominant; these societies were semiticized from their early days, not exclusively, but certainly predominantly. With the rise of Semitic-speaking peoples to positions of power the old establishments were undermined and began to crumble; in Egypt the form remained but much of the substance was gone.

The character of the priesthoods of Egypt also seems to show a similar process of change at work. The system of theology originally associated with Ptah's temple at Memphis was notably spiritual in character and of a nature which most philosophers would recognize as refined, even exalted. It was gradually overturned or at least substantially reduced in influence by more materialistic, certainly more forceful priesthoods like that of Heliopolis where the cults of Re, the personification of the sun, were centred. The priests of Re were careful observers of the skies and no doubt employed their knowledge of eclipses and other natural phenomena to amaze the simple and so increase their power in the state.

At the same time the exalted position of the King as supreme god incarnate seems to have begun to decline, as Ptah's supremacy declined. Whether the two were in any way connected is not known. The certainty of the Egyptians of their election as the favoured children of the gods seems at this time to be hastening to disillusion. But this lay in the future still, when the pyramids were new.

The accession to the throne of Egypt of the second King of the Third Dynasty was an occasion of profound importance; Djoser Neterikhet was the first King to assume that most splendid of all Pharaonic titles, 'The Golden Horus'. The Third Dynasty seems to have been connected lineally with the Second; it is generally thought that the great Khasekhemui left as heiress to his state a daughter or granddaughter and that she bore the Kingship, as it were, within her. She was venerated in later times as the ancestress of the Third Dynasty. A princess of Egypt was always the bestower of the title of King on whomever she might marry; in this sense the succession was matrilinear, though the sovereignty was, with very few exceptions in early times, held by a King.

For several reasons the accession of Djoser marked a new turn in the destiny of Egypt. First, it inaugurated a long sequence of prosperity and tranquillity, unequalled in the Two Lands' experience. Though the reign of Khasekhemui was recorded as a time of reconciliation and unity it was only in Djoser's time that the resources of the state could be organized on a scale which permitted the undertaking of public works of such positively titanic proportions. These great enterprises allowed for the employment of workers and craftsmen on an immense and generous scale. With them came an increasing liberation of the Egyptian creative genius, permitting the threshold of art to be pushed further and further out from its original plane in the centuries which were to follow. Architecture on a monumental scale became a preoccupation of the state which was to endure to the present day; it had its beginnings in Djoser's time.

For the first time, too, individuals other than the Kings begin to be identifiable. Imhotep is, of course, the most notable, the supreme genius of the Egyptian creative experience, but others, though lesser men, in all departments of life and activity begin to emerge, to take on clear and often engaging shapes and even make known their names.

Thus as our field of vision of Egypt opens out at this time, around the twenty-seventh century BC, we come to see more and more clearly the role played by ordinary men and women in the state. The Third Dynasty itself was a relatively brief interlude, seventy years or so in duration; the amazing burst of creative energy which marked Djoser's reign and the genius of Imhotep could hardly be expected to be long sustained at the same level of art. However, the arts of sculpture and the making of large-scale statuary developed steadily; technique also advanced, in some cases very remarkably. For example, the manufacture of plywood is first detected in the Third Dynasty, and the means of the cutting of large stone blocks for architectural projects became better understood, leading the way to the building feats of the Fourth Dynasty. The arts of the metalsmith and the jeweller also become more and more specialized and refined.

Of other works of art of the Third Dynasty, apart from those associated with Djoser himself, those left by one of his contemporaries and high officers, Hesy-re, are perhaps the most notable (plates 85a and 85b). A series of panels carved in relief in sycamore survive from his tomb at Saqqara. The reliefs have a spare austerity, proportion, and balance which is startling; they forcibly suggest the splendour in which the lives of such officials were passed. Though when they were new they would have been vividly coloured they also suggest dramatically the quality of taste which, even at this early time, marked the perceptions of cultivated Egyptians.

Hesy-re's career is of interest in that he is identified as a physician – ever an honourable vocation in early Egypt – specifically as a dentist. Dentistry was practised extensively by the ancients and evidence from the Arabian Gulf (actually from Bahrain) in the centuries after Hesy-re's time also shows considerable application of dental care, at least to the extent of extracting carious teeth. The extraction was probably effected by the technique of 'elevating' the tooth, working it loose with metal probes. Though the method must have been scarcely agreeable the short-term discomfort would have been well worth enduring for the relief of the toothache. The Sumerians, with their considerable reliance on the date as an item of diet, suffered piteously from the toothache. In witness of this, they even personified toothache and made it an object of their poetry. Not so the practical Egyptians; their answer to toothache, like that of the Dilmunites of Bahrain, was extraction. In respect of dental care, at least, life in third-millennium Egypt and even in the distant Gulf at the same time must have been preferable to life in late Victorian England where itinerant toothpullers exercised their calling with none of the care or professional concern which the biography of Hesy-re, for one, suggests was demanded in Egypt.

Not long ago another Third Dynasty pyramid was identified and was found to be of one of Djoser's successors, the King Sekhemkhet; his complex is also 536 metres long (presumably there is some significance in the figure) but only 187 metres wide. When the pyramid, or what remained of it, was excavated a beautifully made sarcophagus, evidently unopened, was found in the tomb. The flowers which had been laid on the stone from which the sarcophagus was carved were still lying there. The opening to the sarcophagus when it was found, sealed as the priests had left it, was a curious portcullis type of device; nothing quite like it had been found before. It may be imagined with what tense anticipation and excitement the opening, and the intact burial evidently contained within it, excited: alas, for nothing. The sarcophagus was empty. What was more it had evidently always been empty; no dead man was ever lain to rest within it. The reason why this should have been so is an enigma. Djoser did have two alternative burial places available to him apparently, though both were contained within his great funerary complex. The complex itself was a microcosm of Egypt; it is possible that this is also the explanation for Sekhemkhet's otherwise rather weirdly empty coffin, in an empty pyramid.

The central building in the complex at Saqqara, though it is by far the most majestic and extensive, is not the only stepped pyramid in Egypt. There are several other examples, of which those at Zawyet el-Aryan,

Abydos, and Elephantine are well recorded. It is not clear why there should have been this crop of stepped structures erected at just this particular time in Egypt.

The great sunburst of creative genius represented by the erection of the Djoser complex is an extraordinary incident in the life of man. Nothing could have prepared the world for Djoser's monument; yet those who later followed him on the thrones of Egypt managed to universalize the burial of Egyptian Kings to the extent that they have become a virtual commonplace, familiar to generations who would never see them, as expressions either of the triumph of the human spirit or as monuments to wilful self-aggrandizement.

Yet, whilst these mountains of stone were being reared up on the plateau at Giza, life in the Two Lands continued in its habitual rhythms. The Nile returned each year, the crops were planted, the animals were husbanded, the King and the other gods were celebrated with appropriate ceremony.

The life of the King must have been absolutely and immutably circumscribed. To be an immanent divinity is no doubt profoundly satisfying, even to the most fractured ego; it must, at the same time, often be deeply exasperating. Every act of a living god takes on a universal import; unless the god follows, in the most absolute obedience, the rituals proscribed for the welfare of the Kingdom and hence of the visible and invisible worlds, chaos and old night must descend as surely as night would cease to follow day, or the sun to rise. No act of the King could be performed without profound ceremony; it is more surprising that some of the great series of Triad plaques of King Menkaure of the Fourth Dynasty, as remarkable works in their own way as are the pyramids themselves, show him with an expression of anticipation, even of eagerness. There must have been very little that could really excite a King of Egypt. No wonder that Sneferu, deeply bored, is recommended by one of his advisors to take to the waters of a nearby lake, rowed by a team of maidens, clad only in fishing nets. Even this charming concept seems little calculated to raise the spirits of a despondent god.

The opinions of the fish-netted handmaidens, inevitably, have not been recorded. But much of the life of the ordinary people (and often of the less ordinary) of Egypt in the later centuries of the Old Kingdom has been. This record is in the form of a sort of petrified movie film extending over acres of tomb walls. It was carved in relief by journeymen craftsmen of genius who immortalized in stone the daily life of third-millennium Egyptians so that their patrons, the princes and Great Ones of the Lands, could go on enjoying the idyll of life along the Nile banks for all eternity, since no more beautiful or fulfilled existence could ever be imagined.

194

The scenes depicted on the walls of tombs throughout Egypt, but especially the later Old Kingdom period, particularly at Saqqara in the shadow of the royal monuments, are vibrant with life. This indeed is their purpose: they are part of the supreme third-millennium national industry of Egypt, the celebration of life and its prolongation into eternity.

No aspect of life is overlooked. Work in the fields, counting the cattle, entertainment in the family, pastimes of all sorts, the arts, building, cultivation of the vine, fishing, building boats, harvest time, all manner of work and involvement is represented. The trades are represented, as are some of the learned professions: the scribe, the doctor. Not much is shown, at this period, of ritual and the worship of the gods: this is still principally a matter for the King, the great priests, and their immediate entourages. Their practices might ensure the ever repeated rounds of birth and plenty but they seem distant from the preoccupations of ordinary men. Man was master of his own world and could conceive of no more perfect existence. All was for the best, indeed, in the best (or in a sense perhaps the only) of all possible worlds – always excepting, of course, the transfigured world of the gods, but even that was only Egypt existing in the celestial dimension.

The immense document which is represented by the tomb reliefs is often punctuated by captions, by the words of the participants in the activities which the reliefs depict. Egyptian was a language rich in metaphor and in cheerful insult: the language of the ordinary people recorded on the walls is earthy, uninhibited. It is also joyous: the fisherman, wading into the water, politely says 'Good Morning' to the different types of fish swimming at his feet.

The gradual intrusion of the ordinary folk into the world of the Great Ones begins, tentatively, in the Fourth Dynasty, increases in the Fifth, and becomes characteristic of the Sixth. It coincides with other, perhaps more significant, and doubtless related, changes in the nature of Egyptian beliefs, in the monarchy, and in monumental architecture.

Some authorities have proposed that the early royal religion in Egypt, up to and including the Third Dynasty, was linked with the stars. The evidence, either way, is slender but certainly the Pyramid Texts, assuming these to be more ancient than the time in which they were first inscribed on the walls of the Sixth Dynasty pyramids, seem to identify the divine King as a star and it is amongst the stars, or even beyond them, that he seeks his eternal habitation. The stars are valuable instruments for measurement and the Egyptian engineers and architects of even the earliest periods seem to have been capable of making complex and sophisticated empirical observations which they used to align their buildings. The precision with which the monumental buildings of the Archaic period and the early Old Kingdom are aligned is legendary; that precision was achieved by careful sitings on selected stars and the skilful use of water channels, the consequence of the careful observation of the behaviour and properties of water which large-scale irrigation projects and techniques had made familiar. With the advent of the Fourth Dynasty, however, the sun cult, the prerogative of the hierophants of Heliopolis, began to rise above the other cults of national or royal status.

As a general principle gods and their adherents dislike, and energetically resist, change: sensibly so, since an enthusiasm for change amongst their followers seldom bodes well for divinities. Similarly, the priesthoods which purport to serve the gods represent a substantial investment, often built up over many generations. They always formed one of the most powerful corporations in ancient society, hierarchic and carefully institutionalized. They were ready to use every device to maintain their power and influence.

They were not always successful, however. In Sumer the temple corporations were evidently the repositories of state and economic power in the late fourth and early third millennia. Their influence was reduced and, in part at least, replaced by the secular power of the war-band leaders who gradually institutionalized their positions and eventually became Kings. The royal power, and the court which surrounded the Kings was more open, more accessible to ambitious outsiders than the temple priesthoods which were, by definition, arcane and exclusive.

In Egypt the neat equation of King and god relieved much of this potential area of antagonism. Even so it is possible to detect, in the early centuries, several shifts in the nature of the cults which were practised in the Valley and in their relative influence. Once the unification was adopted as state policy, national cults began to emerge, gradually to rise above the local cults which had kept the loyalty of the ordinary folk over the millennia. The decline in the star cults associated with the King, the reduction in the status of Ptah, the corresponding rise of Re in Heliopolis, and the inversion of the role of Set with his consequent presentation as a malignant influence, who once was the god of a large proportion of the Valley dwellers, all demonstrate the way that, even in Egypt, the political influence of temple cults was employed to satisfy the need for power.

The centre of the royal administration was firmly fixed, and had been for generations, at the apex of the Delta, where Upper and Lower Egypt meet, south of Cairo, at Memphis. This name is anachronistic, being a Greek form of the name of the pyramid of Pepi II, which was not built until quite late in the Sixth Dynasty. In earlier times the city was called

Ity-tawy; Pepi's pyramid was called Men-nefer and the Greek corruption of this praise-name produced 'Memphis'.

Memphis, to retain the familiar form of its name, was not only the royal capital; it was also the centre for the cults of the artificer god, the supreme creator, Ptah. As was noted earlier, Ptah was particularly associated with the creator Kings of Egypt, those who laid down her foundations so securely in the First Dynasty and, to a lesser degree, in the Second. In the Second Dynasty however, the cult of the sun begins to edge its way into official religion; the names of several of the early Kings of the dynasty bear names which are compounded with that of Re, the personification of the sun-in-splendour. Re's main cult centre was at Iwun, now Heliopolis (the city of the sun, like 'Memphis' another Graecism, though a more acceptable one), today a suburb of Cairo. At some time the idea of the sun began to dominate Egyptian models of thought and then virtually to exclude the star-cults; the gods were still identified with stars, but now in a role increasingly subservient to the sun. With the emergence of the worship of the sun as the principal state cult (to encapsulate a sequence which in fact took a number of generations to be realized) the burial chambers of the Kings changed their shape.

The soaring terraces of the Step Pyramid represented a sort of apotheosis of the rectangular brick *mastaba* of the early Kings. The creation of the true pyramid, the three-dimensional linked triangles, which is so perfect and so satisfying a shape, coincided with the beginnings of the solar cult; as was suggested earlier, the pyramid's shape may well have been inspired by the shafts of sunlight piercing through the winter clouds in the vicinity of Heliopolis, in the startling triangular formation that they sometimes adopt, thrusting downwards from the heavens to the earth. The pyramid reverses the process, reaching up from the earth into the heavens.

The last King of the Third Dynasty was Huni; it is not clear what, if any, relation to him was the next King, Sneferu, who was acknowledged as the founder of the Fourth Dynasty. His mother, though, seems to have been a minor wife of Huni, but we do not know if Sneferu was his son; evidently the annalists did not think so, for otherwise there would not have been a new dynasty commencing with his name. He did, however, marry the Princess Hetepheres, 'the Daughter of the God', who presumably brought him the thrones of Egypt as her marriage portion. He was revered throughout the length of Egyptian history; his reign was always regarded as one of the high points of the Egyptian Golden Age. Virtually uniquely amongst the Kings of Egypt he was remembered by a sobriquet: he was 'the Beneficent King' and his cult was sustained down to Ptolemaic times, more than 2,000 years after his death.

His cult was practised as far away as the mines of turquoise in Sinai, and as late as the Middle Kingdom a little shrine to his memory was maintained at Dahshur. A simple dish with the charcoal for an offering of incense, was found still on the modest altar which was consecrated there to his memory.

There are three important monuments which may have been of Sneferu's foundation: the Bent Pyramid at Maidum (plate 80) and two some distance away at Dahshur. It is possible that the one at Maidum, though finished by Sneferu, was begun by Huni; it was certainly attributed to Sneferu in later periods. In the New Kingdom a scribe visited Maidum and recorded that he 'came to see the beautiful temple of Sneferu. He found it as though heaven were within it and the sun rising in it.' The pyramid was restored during the Middle Kingdom, one of the earliest recorded examples, as it might be, of the conservation of an ancient monument.

The founder of the Fourth Dynasty was also a considerable warrior. He led campaigns both to the south and west to put down troublesome uprisings of Nubians and Libyans on the frontiers. He, or one of his officers, left behind a powerful example of Pharaonic propaganda in the form of a rock carving showing the King striking down some luckless chieftain in the Sinai peninsula. Such carvings, the earliest of which date from the First Dynasty, were displayed on prominent rock faces, no doubt to impress the natives in perpetuity with the extent and implacable power of the King. The presence of Egyptian forces in Sinai was occasioned by the need to garrison the mines of turquoise and the routes to the sources of copper which the King sought to control.

Sneferu also maintained more peaceful contacts with distant peoples. He built a series of exceptionally large ships, constructed from cedar wood, and brought loads of cedar by sea from the great Levantine port of Byblos, with which Egypt was long to sustain trading relations. Cedar was found in one of the pyramids of his foundation.

The quality of life for the rulers of Egypt in Sneferu's time can be gauged by the extraordinarily sumptuous elegance of the furnishings found in the tomb of his consort Queen Hetepheres, the mother of Khufu, Sneferu's successor. Once more it is not only their richness of materials and precision of craftsmanship which amazes: it is, overwhelmingly, the certainty and restraint with which they are designed.

The hoard of objects from Hetepheres' burial, a fraction of what originally it contained, are amongst the most splendid to survive from the Old Kingdom, or indeed from any period of Egyptian history. Hetepheres' tomb was robbed, evidently soon after her death and burial; it appears that this desecration was discovered and what remained was hastily reburied in a deeply cut pit. The queen's body however, seems not to have survived. What did survive however, was a magnificent alabaster sarcophagus, a carrying chair, exquisitely inlaid with gold, a gold-encased bed and gossamer-fine canopy, gold implements, and silver bracelets inlaid with butterflies (colour plate XII).

Though only a few hundred years separate her time from that when Egypt was in a state of a preliterate and still experimental society, her familiar objects, the objects which were, by custom, the companions of Hetepheres' living days, are of an austere but sumptuous splendour, matched with a dignity, restraint, and perfection of design that is allied with gold, silver, and rare inlays. The delicate gold cups, the razors also of gold, golden blades honed to a highly efficient cutting edge, pottery vases of a usual type but of extraordinary refinement, these, added to the more familiar furniture, including what must surely be one of the most elegant chairs ever designed, take the breath away. The quality of life which must have supported and produced such wonderful things can only be a matter of speculation. Fortunate indeed is the society which can produce objects of this perfection and simplicity; these two words perhaps best express what life may have been like in Old Kingdom Egypt, when, reaping the harvest of the years which had gone before them, the people of the Valley raised up a culture of such superlative achievement. The integration of ideal and actuality can surely be sensed in the quality of those products which have survived and which, in an altogether remarkable way, convey not only the sense of great riches and a sumptuous court but a degree of tranquillity, profound enough for artists and craftsmen to produce objects which betray no sign of tension or anxiety. The products of Egyptian craftsmen at this time ask only to be taken on their own account; it doubtless did occur to those who made them that they also had to please a patron, but that patron was one who shared the ideals and collective understanding of the society from which they came. A portrait of the patron survives (plate 86), an elegant and handsome lady, seated, holding a life-giving lotus to her fine-boned nose, which, by the accident of slight damage to the surface on which she is portrayed, has a most engaging tilt.

Khufu, known generally by the Greek version of his name, Cheops, was evidently the undisputed heir to Egypt, by virtue of being the son of his mother, the heiress Hetepheres. He reigned, like his father Sneferu, for some twenty-four years. Though he is reputed to have built the greatest and most enduring monument ever erected by man, there is only one surviving portrait of the King (plate 87). This is a tiny piece in ivory, its very minuteness contrasting ironically with the huge pyramid. The King is shown seated on his throne, wearing the crown of Egypt. Although the scale of the portrait is so small, Khufu has a disagreeable face, rather plump with an expression of dyspeptic ill-temper. He was not remembered warmly by the Egyptians, though there is no reason in fact to suppose that he was a particularly harsh or tyrannical ruler. It has been plausibly suggested that Khufu was trying, in building the Great Pyramid on the scale that he did, to outdo his father, Sneferu. If so, this is to be Oedipal to a titanic degree.

Of all the artefacts to descend from the Fourth Dynasty, with the exception of the pyramids themselves, Khufu's funeral boat is a survival which is little short of miraculous. Its burial beside the Great Pyramid may serve as the example of a custom which is frequently encountered in royal burials of the early periods. The boat is a wonderful creation, slender, elegant, and beautiful – even today, locked for the present in a greenhouse of a building thrown up with quite extraordinary insensitivity beside the pyramid itself, it is a moving, dramatic, and most precious inheritance. It is unique, having survived over 4,500 years in pristine condition, even, when it was found, with some of its ropes intact.

The lines of Khufu's boat are exquisite and on the water she must have been a glorious sight. Until the present day no larger boat had sailed the Nile. She has one notable feature which, however tenuously, may link her with more modest sisters in the distant Arabian Gulf: every plank in Khufu's boat is sewn, not nailed or riveted. The technique of sewing craft is immensely ancient; it is still practised in the remoter reaches of Oman's coast where it may have possibly originated. (As an aside it may be noted that if the boats shown on the rock carvings in the Wadi Hammamat, for example, represent those on which the carriers of Sumerian or Elamite influences travelled across the Red Sea and were, as is most likely, sewn boats, it would be perfectly possible for them to be broken down, carried overland, even across the desert to the western Arabian coast, reassembled, and sailed across to the Egyptian coast.)

An elegance of line and a strict regard for minimal decoration in monumental sculpture and in architecture are amongst the glories of this age. Throughout the Old Kingdom Egyptian art at its best always demonstrated these qualities; it was only much later, particularly in the New Kingdom when alien influences, especially those from northern lands, had penetrated Egypt, that the florid, extravagant, and over-luxuriant style of decoration became predominant. Even then, in some of the finest New Kingdom sculpture for example, it is possible to observe artists striving to return to the purer style of the earlier periods. In Saite times, much later still, there was a deliberate archaicizing tendency where pastiches of Old Kingdom forms were conscientiously produced, a rare and remarkable example of the artists of a nation paying deliberate homage to their predecessors of nearly 2,000 years earlier.

The elimination of inessentials can be seen in works like the marvellous triad groups made for King Menkaure, the builder of the third pyramid at Giza (plate 88). The King, now presented not only as the ruler of the gods but as a man of great and vigorous physical beauty, is shown as it were coming out of the stone itself, supported by two divine companions. The King is depicted as smiling, almost it seems welcoming the observer, his head lifted confidently, assured both in his divinity and in his beauty. Incidentally the distinctly African cast of the King's features, like that of Khufu in the tiny ivory piece which is his only known portrait and of Djoser in his *serdab* statue, prompts the speculation whether the pyramid builders were not, after all, black Africans. This question has often been put, and as quickly suppressed, except by African historians who have perhaps been too enthusiastic in their espousing of this possibility. But the Giza Kings of the Fourth Dynasty do share a notably African or negroid cast of feature.

The consideration should not be overlooked that a royal funerary monument on the scale of a pyramid is a concept which would be entirely at home in Africa proper. Many of the forms of Egyptian sculpture, mostly in the round but also much of it in relief, are probably African in inspiration. The same awareness of mass and the assertive frontalism of much later African art seem to be shared by the works made by the first great producers of art in Africa, the people of the Nile Valley.

The later reigns of the Fourth Dynasty Kings, particularly of Khaufre, the builder of the second pyramid at Giza, and some of those of the Fifth Dynasty, highlight another remarkable ability of those Egyptian architects who were responsible for the planning and decoration of the temples or the other immense public buildings which are amongst the principal achievements of that age. This was the careful siting of statuary within the monumental buildings that contained them and the conditions under which they were displayed for the eyes of the dead King and his companion gods who, theoretically at least, were those for whom their presentation was alone intended.

It may seem that such considerations are relatively slight; it may also appear that to talk of statuary being deliberately sited or of the deliberate presentation of the sculptor's work is fanciful, imputing to the artificers of the past considerations which depend upon the application of the criteria of today to such distant times. Yet such is clearly the case.

There is plenty of evidence, particularly from Khaufre's temple at Giza, that the monumental statues of the King were designed to be seen largely in isolation from each other, though in the case of the triad figures of Menkaure, for example, there were probably originally forty-two of them, representing every nome in Egypt. More than this, special consideration was given to the lighting of the great statues. In the case of Khaufre's statues there is evidence that they were top-lit by illumination from clerestories, allowing the sun or the moonlight to move down the line of figures, each set into its niche, in a majestic progression (plate 89). More subtle still, it seems likely that the statues were also sited so that, at certain times, the light would strike the rose-granite floor at the feet of the great figures and reflect upwards, giving the statues the hues of something like living flesh.

It seems likely that lighting techniques of this order were even employed in Djoser's great mortuary complex at Saqqara; slits in the upper reaches of the colonnade which led into the courtyard may have lit statues there. It is a brilliant testimony once more to the Egyptians' power of observation that some phenomenon in nature, light reflecting on a pool perhaps or piercing through a breast in the upper levels of a reed structure, was absorbed and transformed into the light pouring down from a clerestory and forming a pool of reflection or from a slit in the upper levels of a building's walls which allowed the light to focus on to a particular piece of statuary.

Khufu and his successors, Khaufre (Chephren) and Menkaure (Myker-inos), are each the possessor of a name which, of all those people who lived during the third millennium, are known to the greatest number of those who lived after them. As the repetition of a man's name was thought by the Egyptians to be one of the means of ensuring his prosperity in the afterlife, this must, presumably, be a matter of continuing satisfaction to them. The colossal effort of raising the pyramids at Giza, if they did not in fact ensure the protection of the King's mummified remains (for it must be presumed that they were long ago desecrated and destroyed), at least have kept alive their names, as no one else, living in their time, could possibly claim.

However, it must be assumed that the pyramids are gigantic machines designed to subdue eternity: any other explanation seems still more fanciful. Their purpose is to annihilate death. That they failed to achieve at least part of their objective must be presumed by their ruined state, empty interiors, shattered sarcophagi. The immense ingenuity which went into their creation was matched by the cunning of those who penetrated their most secure sanctuaries.

But there always remains that most tantalizing of archaeological possi-bilities, the offchance that somewhere, deep inside the pyramid or far below its lowest masonry course, its principal inhabitant still lies in secret, surrounded by the treasure of a King of Egypt in his last great ceremony, his gold masked face smiling with the *rictus* of death and the satisfaction of having outsmarted posterity; it is an intriguing vision. Over the years during which scientific excavation has been conducted in Egypt there have occasionally been hints that 'hidden chambers' may survive in some of the pyramids. Curious noises, sudden rushes of air, or the disappearance of rain-water after a storm have all contributed to the idea that somewhere a chamber may be hidden in which an intact burial might still survive. It is, to say the least, unlikely; but it would be unwise to deny the possibility entirely.

During the reigns of Khufu's successors the scale of pyramid-building in fact declined somewhat; Menkaure's pyramid is really quite modest, at least when projected against Khufu's. But the art of the sculptors of Egypt advanced wonderfully. No work surviving from this period has excited so much speculation, admiration, and wonder as the Great Sphinx at Giza, carved from the living rock with the face of Menkaure surmounting the body of a colossal lion.

The really remarkable observation about the Great Sphinx, apart from the fact that it is perhaps the most famous piece of sculpture in the world and one of the largest ever made, is that it is virtually unique in the entire canon of Egyptian art. There are sphinxes in abundance, to be sure, particularly those made by the Kings of the Middle Kingdom, which are particularly powerful and often rather baleful creations. The type reached a sort of overstated culmination in the Avenue of Sphinxes (though ram- and not human-headed) which still gives an especially operatic look to the approach to the Temple of Karnak. But, singularly, there are virtually no other examples in all the length of Egypt of the sculptural adaptation of boulders, standing rocks, or cliff faces. Opportunities abounded, after all. To this day many rocks along the river and in the Libyan hills seem to be trying to give birth to a gigantic human or animal shape. The ingenuity of Egyptian engineers would certainly have been equal to the complex tasks involved; they would, one feels, have relished the challenge. The temptation for the living gods who occupied the throne to perpetuate their images amongst the living rock of the Egyptian landscape must have been well-nigh overwhelming. Yet they did not do so.

There must, presumably, have been some constraint, though certainly not ones of modesty or diffidence, which prevented them from doing this. Only Rameses II, a man with an unerring sense of the meretricious and overscaled, caused effigies of himself and his consort to be carved in the rock face of their temples at Abu Simbel. Yet this is not quite the same thing as the adaptation of a standing rock outcrop such as a planner of genius in the Fourth Dynasty seized on and in doing so immortalized his King, through its sculpted monumentality. Rameses' work is simple architecture; the creation of the Great Sphinx on the Giza plateau is art on a heroic scale, involving the adaptation of a landscape. The Great Sphinx is one of a kind; despite the depredations resulting from Turkish artillery practice, his enigmatic smile suggests that his creator knew that he would remain, aloof and unique, though why that should have been so is altogether quite obscure.

Consider, for a moment, the pyramids when they were young and brand, sparkling new. First one must visualize the plateau at Giza, empty, without the Great Pyramid, or indeed any other pyramid for that matter. The Libyan desert would run, limitlessly, to the west. Then, as if watching a stop-action film of a flower germinating and growing, the pyramid rises, course by course, on the flattened plateau, levelled by the skilful applications of techniques learned in the management of water, the sides of the huge structure were aligned to the cardinal points with the most perfect precision, as the consequence of the most elegant observation of the stars. The Egyptian architects made the stars their assistants in the task of laying out the pyramids, temples, and all manner of complex buildings, whose solemn presence depended as much on measurement as on the inspiration of the design and the skill of the building techniques employed.

When the Great Pyramid built by Ankhaf, a royal kinsman with the look of a substantial and decisive executive about him, for Khnum-Khufu was completed, it was like no other building in scale and splendour. When the pyramid was new it gleamed brilliantly, with its casing of polished white limestone which reflected the sunlight which poured down on it. It must have been as taxing to the eyes to look on 'Khufu is belonging to the Horizon' (the pyramid's own name) as it was to look at the sun itself in splendour. At dawn the eastern face of the pyramid would be washed with golden light as the sun rose; at nightfall all the imaginable colours of an Egyptian sunset (especially in wintertime) would suffuse its western face with crimson, gold, purple, and tender pinks. When the moon was high it would glisten as silver as the moon itself, then, seen from the western elevation, it would seem to hang above the desert miraculously. By starlight it would appear, like Djoser's monument a few miles away, as a fragment of the apartments of heaven, brought down to earth.

Gradually, as the generations passed, the plateau around Giza filled up with its royal dead and their extraordinary monuments. Every part of the great buildings was covered with polished stone; the temples, built in darker stones, contrasted with the pyramids, which towered above the other burial places which clustered round them, their occupants hoping thereby to draw to themselves some part of the vicarious immortality which proximity to the mountains of stone of the Kings' tombs promised for them. Laid in rows the *mastabas* of the courtiers and the small pyramids of the queens and the royal children have a forlorn and touching quality, even now. Then, they must have constituted a well-planned, orderly city of the princely dead.

When it was completed the complex of monuments at Giza, polished in the perfection of an ideal form, must have sat like a diadem on the brow of earth. From every face of the pyramid, through the night as much as in the day, light must have been thrown back into the immensity of space as from a colossal jewel.

Herodotus relates a curious story about the burial of Khufu at Giza. In Book II he says 'the underground chambers which Cheops intended as vaults for his own use: these last were built on a sort of island surrounded by water introduced from the Nile by a canal' (Rawlinson's translation). This proposition has been universally discounted by scholars; there is no evidence whatsoever of a subterranean lake and it is generally reckoned that the chambers beneath the pyramid have, like those within its actual fabric, been fully plotted. This is not to say that there can be no other chambers, as yet undiscovered, but there is certainly less evidence to suggest that such might be the case with Khufu than there is in some other pyramids.

However, in the case of the Herodotean story there is one later precedent at least for a type of subterranean lake burial that he seems to be describing; its existence prevents perhaps the absolute dismissal of what might otherwise seem a fairly typical Herodotean canard. In the cenotaph at Abydos of King Seti, the distinguished father of that Nineteenth Dynasty megalomaniac Rameses II, the sarcophagus was placed on an island with a double stair, which was the hieroglyph for the primeval hill or island on which all creation began. The island was surmounted by a channel filled perpetually with subterranean waters. These were 'the waters of Nun' from which the supreme creator god had first risen. They are the waters of the nether world over which both the sun during the hours of darkness and the dead on their journey to the west had to pass.

It is unlikely that Herodotus had heard of Seti's cenotaph. It is however possible that these subterranean islands, recalling the island of origins, the land of the beginning, did feature in some burial rituals and the priests, who seem to have been Herodotus' principal and often wildly inaccurate source of information, had conflated the practice with the most august sepulchre which they knew. But it is notable none the less how often in

205

early antiquity hidden waters beneath the earth are invested with special sanctity and mystery.

Whilst it is known that it was King Djedefre who completed Khufu's burial and laid down the great ship (or ships, since another probably awaits excavation) beside his pyramid, there is considerable confusion at this point about the succession of the Kings. It appears that factions formed within the royal family, probably the consequence of rival queens backing the competing claims of their respective sons. Whether any of this was apparent to the people of Egypt is unknown; certainly the annalists of the royal house must have been aware of what was going on, for it was their task to record the names of the Kings in proper order and to set down the principal events of their reigns.

It was apparent that the Sun God and his devotees had been making significant advances of position throughout the Fourth Dynasty. Khufu's name was compounded with that of Khnum, a ram-headed creator god from the Aswan region; most of his successors took names compounded with that of Re, the sun god, ruling in Heliopolis. The priests were gaining power and asserting themselves at the expense of the King's divine absolutism.

The last King of the Dynasty gives some evidence of what might well be interpreted as an attempt to reject the domination of Re and his cult. His name was Shepseskaf (plate 91); he seems only to have reigned for four years. He rejected, too, the idea of the pyramidal funerary monument and instead reverted to something like the earlier form. He built a great low-lying rectangular structure with a rounded top and sharply angled ends which gave it the shape of a gigantic sarcophagus. This is the Mastabat Faraon which, though it is badly ruined, may still be seen at Saqqara.

It is only a matter of speculation whether Shepseskaf's reign was curtailed by the intervention of the priests, fearful of the possibility of his limiting their power. There is one rather touching piece of evidence which suggests that his qualities as a man were as notable as his acts as a King, concerned to restore the power of his house. His queen was called Bu-nefer; she it was who conducted the ceremonies at Shepseskaf's funeral, a responsibility usually carried out by a brother or a son. It must be presumed that she loved him.

Throughout his earthly life the King was surrounded by ritual and richly symbolic ceremony; it was also intensely formalized. The degree with which this formality must have dominated the King's life and even the lives of those closest to him is demonstrated by an act of King Shepseskaf, by whose time the absolute divinity of the King was beginning to be conditioned by an increasing recognition of his human nature. The event in question is one in which the King decreed graciously that his principal minister, adviser, and friend, a high priest and the King's own son-in-law, Ptahshepses, could kiss his foot as a mark of singular favour, rather than kiss the ground before the King's feet, as custom would otherwise have demanded. So overwhelmed was Ptahshepses with this act of royal condescension that he recorded it in his tomb, with pride and gratitude. What life must have been like in the days of the earlier Kings, for example in the time of Djoser or Khufu, can only be imagined. But the loneliness of the King's office is recalled in the sad advice, given to the occupant of the throne: 'fill not thy heart with a brother: know not a friend'.

Above all other considerations the Egyptians were obsessed with the prolongation of life and with enabling the King to do honour to the gods who were considered to be living entities. Much Old Kingdom statuary, for example, is vibrant with life: no subsequent culture, nor even the Greeks at their best, achieved quite the perfect simulacra of living beings that the Egyptians brought off so completely in the early centuries of their history.

The Egyptians believed that life could be prolonged beyond death by a mixture of magical incantations, spoken or carved on the tomb's walls, the provision of food and the appurtenances of living, either real or simulated, and by the careful preservation of the body and the body's appearance, the last being effected by the making of statues. The immense quantity of statues which survive from the Old Kingdom make it clear that they are, or are certainly intended to be, portraits of the subject represented. They may be idealized, to the extent that most subjects chose to have themselves represented as younger, rather than older. To this rule the great seated statue of Djoser is a majestic exception.

Egyptian sculptors brought to the making of statues the same genius for observation which they deployed in their delighted recording of the ways of animals and of the countryside. There is no mistaking an Old Kingdom statue for one from a later period. Old Kingdom figures stand or sit four-square; the planes of their faces tend to be broader than those of their successors, their eyes fixed on eternity.

The sculptors of the Old Kingdom devised the 'archaic smile', later to be identified so firmly with Greek *Kouroi*, two thousand years before those ambivalent statues were made, celebrating the ambiguous beauties of young Hellenes. But whereas the Greek smile frequently hovers on the edge of a simper, the Egyptian model is exalted, essentially anticipatory, as at the approach of a vision of glory (plate 94).

The production of statuary was extensive and the studios which produced them must have been large and busy institutions. Not all the

207

statues made at this time are of the finest quality; some are distinctly provincial whilst others, though they have come from securely documented excavations, are sometimes bizarre or simply incompetent to the extent that were they to appear on the antiquities market in Cairo they would be dismissed as counterfeit. But these lapses from a vigorously controlled production quality are comparatively rare.

It is not only amongst the great or the monumental statues of the Kings that the superlative standard which is the mark of the Old Kingdom is to be found. 'Reserve heads' of private individuals are often works of remarkable power; these were placed in the tomb to act as replacements should the full portrait statue be lost. Almost at random it is possible to select examples of artists' work which demonstrate the glories of this period of Egyptian art: a young sandal-bearer, nude and graceful with a charming air of diffidence, becoming to his youth, or an old man, wrapped in a heavy, rather un-Egyptian cloak (perhaps he is a foreigner) and leaning on his cane, who somehow conveys the sense of being surrounded by night and silence: these are quite humble works but of remarkable power.

The finest Old Kingdom statuary was, so far as we know, produced with the simplest tools, though often the sculptors chose to work with the hardest and most intractable stones. Pounding, abrading, and cutting with copper bits and stone tools produced some of the greatest works of art ever made, fashioned with a quality of detail and finish which is so often miraculous.

Closely allied to the Old Kingdom genius in sculpture is that of carving in relief. The ability of such artists of this period is quite uncanny; on the one hand they could sustain a dense and complex sequence of images, of scenes from daily life for example, over an extensive surface, without ever losing the coherence and vitality of the whole, whilst on the other they could produce an immediacy of impression which can really only be compared with drawing in stone, with the assurance of the placing of a line around the jaw or the suggestion of the fullness of a cheek which would hardly be approached by an Italian master.

To judge by later evidence reliefs on this scale were produced on a sort of production line procedure. The area to be covered would be marked out first of all with a grid of squares so that the design, of which a miniature version or a drawing would first be prepared, could be worked out on the grid, in an enlarged format. The master would direct the drawing. At successive stages craftsmen would incise, cut, polish, and colour the relief, all under the master's supervision and that of his closest assistants. The technique would have been familiar to Leonardo or Michelangelo in their creation of a mural or a complex piece of statuary.

After Shepseskaf's death the dynasty changed again, though there was still probably some familial connection with the previous line. Now, however, the cult of Re emerged supreme: the King is hailed as 'son of Re'; whereas before he was the great god immanent, he is now merely a divine son, content to carry out quite menial tasks in the service of his father, who sails supreme above the Egyptians' world.

The King who heads the Fifth Dynasty is Userkaf; it is probable that he married a senior royal daughter, perhaps the sister of Shepseskaf, who bore the right to the Kingship. Userkaf may have been a member of a branch of the royal family, though not the ruling one. He was followed by Sahure and Nefer-ir-ka-re. Their commitment to the sun cult was absolute; according to legend all three were brothers, all fathered on their mother by Re. The influence of the priests of the sun cult, centred at Heliopolis, now became dominant; their propaganda becomes pervasive and very effective.

The Fifth Dynasty, like those that had gone before it, had a distinctive style of royal funerary monument: the sun temple, built close to the Nile and notable for a proud-standing obelisk in the temple's court. Beside the temple, in several cases, a stone solar barque was built, recalling the boats which had been lain beside the dead King, in various forms, since the First Dynasty.

International contact was now widespread. Even distant islands in the Aegean such as Cythera received evidence of the Egyptian King's existence, in this case a small marble cup inscribed with the name of Userkaf's temple.

Sahure, who succeeded Userkaf, built the royal cemetery at Abusir, from whose ruins much of the evidence for the character of life in Egypt and the royal courts in the Fifth Dynasty has been recovered. From the reliefs of the Sahure sun temples it is clear that Asiatics to the east of Egypt, the Badu of the Arabo-Palestinian deserts and their cousins inhabiting the eastern Egyptian desert, were now becoming increasingly troublesome. It was necessary for the King to take punitive action against them. But he also traded with the easterners, sending ships to Byblos and to the mysterious land of Punt.

One of the most remarkable mysteries of twentieth-century archaeology involved Sahure. The 'Dorak Treasure' was said to be a hoard of richly wrought jewellery, figurines, and regalia, including a number cast in gold, which an archaeologist from London reported that he had been shown by a beautiful girl in the small Anatolian town of Dorak (Mellaart, 1959). He was allowed to draw many of the pieces of what would certainly have been a stupendous and important hoard of royal gold. One of the pieces was a superb cylinder seal, cast in solid gold, which bore the cartouche of Sahure; the whole hoard seemed, from stylistic considerations, to be of the period of the King's reign, in the first half of the twenty-fifth century BC. Unfortunately when the archaeologist returned to Dorak to seek the mysterious girl and her equally mysterious treasure, only a blank, featureless wall was to be found where he had believed the house in which she lived to be. Of the girl and the gold there was equally no trace, nor has there been to this day.

However, there is *another* collection of gold objects from the same period, with the cartouches of two successors of Sahure, which is sometimes known as the 'Boston Hoard' since this splendid group of objects found its way to the Boston Museum of Fine Arts, where it now rests (plate 96) (Vermeule and Vermeule, 1970). This was also believed to have originated in southern Anatolia.

The two hoards (if indeed the first existed) appear to be similar in their style and details of design. They have a sort of barbaric splendour, a massiveness which is not actually characteristic of the best work of the Egyptian craftsmen of the period; but the similarities and the apparent association with Kings of the Fifth Dynasty are suggestive. It is certainly not impossible that in the time of this dynasty, when the country was enjoying one of the most prosperous periods in her history, Egypt could have had contacts with Anatolia, which had long been one of the most important sources of raw materials in the third-millennium world. It was also an important destination on the trading routes for the export of manufactured products.

One of the finest artefacts from Sahure's reign, which shows the quality of work which could be produced almost as a matter of routine in the later Old Kingdom, is a group portraying the King in the company of a nome god. This has been described as provincial work, lacking the highest qualities. If it is, it is a tribute to the master craftsmen of the Egyptian provinces: in fact, it is the equal of the very finest work which survives. Its massive quality is particularly notable, imparting a remarkable sense of strength and power to it (plate 95).

Sahure was succeeded by his brother, Neferirkare; a number of the Kings of this and the succeeding dynasty were to compound their names with the word 'Nefer' which means, variously, 'beautiful', 'good', 'white', as well as with the name of the sun god. From this time most of the names of Egyptian Kings are praise names of each King's particular dynastic or personal divinity.

Throughout the dynasty it is possible to see a continuous increase in the number of inscriptions and written records with which the Kings set down the principal events or preoccupations of their reigns. So extraordinary is the legacy of the visual arts which the Egyptians of the Old

Kingdom have left that their literary output can easily be overlooked. It is, however, a remarkable production and is as much a manifestation of the Egyptian spirit's search for expression and fulfilment as is the other artists' work in stone or metal. From this time onwards writing, one of the noblest of the Egyptian arts, may also be recognized as one of the most rewarding to study.

The Egyptians developed to a unique degree the art of both visual and verbal punning: they delighted in the games which words and characters can be encouraged to play with each other. For such games hieroglyphs are exceptionally well suited; because the characters represent actual objects as well as suggesting concepts they are many-levelled and the inscriptions which they make are, in consequence, exceptionally rich and complex. They often, too, sustain a particularly close, sometimes almost a mystical relationship with other aspects of the society from which they sprang, notably belief and custom. In this way the written language becomes another means to perpetuate the life of the society and make it accessible visually, interacting with, for example, the architectural detail of a pyramid or the expression of the ceremonies attending the appearance of the King.

This Egyptian genius for graphic synthesis is shown to special advantage in the variations that they developed in the hieroglyphs which expressed concepts relating to horizon, mountains, and sunrise. The hieroglyph ⌒ denotes a mountain, covered with sand; it means 'mountain'. With the addition of another peak it signifies 'foreign land' ⌒⌒. The horizon, 'the place where the sun rises' is represented by the same ideogram, with the addition of the sun's disk rising between the two peaks of the mountain ⌒⊙⌒ . A third variation shows the hill lit with rays of the rising sun ⌒ . This is the 'hill of the sunrise'; and like the others is an early hieroglyph recorded in the Pyramid Texts. In a stroke of creative genius and by the addition of another element, the hill of sunrise, now suffused with sunlight, becomes an ideogram meaning 'to appear in glory' and is used to mark the appearance of the King, the son of the sun from the Old Kingdom onwards, on occasions of high state ⌒ .

The same intriguing ability to develop symbols of a penetrating perception appears in another context in Egypt in early Archaic times and then repeats itself in several different manifestations; this is the representation of the stepped or terraced mound. It signifies the Primeval Hill, the mound of creation on which the creator god settled himself when it first appeared above or out of the waters of the Abyss and on which he performed the first acts which inaugurated the cycle of creation itself.

The most spectacular manifestation of the terraced mound is, of course, the Step Pyramid and its companions, all of which were built in the Third

Dynasty. Like the hieroglyph the pyramid consists of six steps, but it should not be forgotten that when Imhotep started to build an eternal resting place for Djoser he began by constructing a huge square *mastaba*, which is still to be seen at the base of the pyramid. Only after work began did he alter the design and create the great monument by which both he and the King he served will always be remembered. Whether he had the concept of the pyramid mound in mind originally it is of course impossible to know; it seems a more likely explanation that the shape was already invested with a numinous or mystical significance for Imhotep and his master, than the alternative view which considers the Step Pyramid as a sort of celestial staircase by which the King is enabled to mount to the stars. If it is the Primeval Mound which it symbolizes, then it would permit the King to fulfil the role of the creator god in the perpetual renewal of the life of Egypt, which the whole complex at Saqqara encompasses.

Clearly the stepped mound meant something very special to the powers of the Third Dynasty and, so far as we can judge, particularly to them. Their successors began at once to break away from the stepped form in the experimental structures which Sneferu developed at Dahshur and Maidum and which achieved their consummation in the pyramids which *his* successors raised up on the plateau at Giza. Evidently, the influences which were current in Egypt in the Fourth Dynasty were quite different from those which had moulded Imhotep's genius in the Third. None the less, it should not be forgotten that the 'true' triangular pyramidal shape was already one of great antiquity in Egypt, for it appears on many Naqada II drawings as the hills or mountains, sometimes represented singly, sometimes in groups, which are indicated by infilled triangles.

But there is a more mysterious form of the terraced mound, again from times earlier than the Third Dynasty, one that is, in a quite literal sense, more occult still. Hidden in the core of the brick enclosed rubble superstructures of several of the great First Dynasty *mastabas* at Saqqara the terraced mound is buried, as though waiting for its ultimate liberation or rebirth in the soaring terraces of the Third Dynasty pyramids. Its presence in these, which are some of the earliest monumental structures in Egypt, suggests that it had a very special significance to the Egyptians as early as the time of the unification.

The terraced mound is to be found in all periods of Egyptian history, even in its latest, most decadent days. In this it is one of the most enduring and persistent images developed by the genius of the Egyptian spirit.

The glory of the Fifth Dynasty must be the reliefs and the portraits of the Kings and great men of the realm that the sculptors produced. Both these categories of works of art show subtle but distinct variations with the forms that preceded them. The reliefs are more intimate in the scenes which they depict, frequently humorous and often with elements of stylization and formality which are remarkable. This may be demonstrated by, for example, the papyrus screen which is laid down on some of the stone-cut reliefs of hunting in the marshes – a favourite subject which suggests that the Delta in northen Egypt was becoming a more familiar place for the nobility and King to visit, a consequence, in all probability, of an increasing ability to drain the marshes which would otherwise have been too water-logged to allow for much settlement, or even penetration. These reliefs have something of the elegance and formality of Chinese painting.

More and more from this time, too, there survive the records of the careers of quite ordinary men who achieved success in the service of the Kings. In several cases it is possible to trace a line of such successful men, forming a small dynasty of builders, civil servants, or the priests of a royal temple foundation. Many of the recitals of their services and the appreciation which they were accorded by the King reflect that complacency (some might say smugness) which seems to be fairly typical of the prosperous Egyptian of this period.

Ka-Hay was a singer in the household of King Nefer-ir-ka-re. The story of his son will serve as an example of a man of relatively modest origins who lived to become one of the 'Great Ones' (or very nearly) of Egypt. Ka-Hay was a member of a family which had long provided musicians to the court to play and sing in the constant round of ceremonies and for the solace or delight of the King and his companions. Ka-Hay was evidently exceptionally gifted musically and his voice attracted the King's notice. He became something of an intimate of the King and, to show him particular favour, the sovereign gave the order that Ka-Hay's son should be educated with the royal children. For an Egyptian of modest origins this was roughly equivalent to his son being given a place at Eton, with the promise of a fellowship at a senior Oxford college, followed by entry into the upper ranks of the Treasury, the certainty of a peerage, and the affectionate familiarity of the royal family. Fortunate was the boy to whom such a prospect opened; the boy in this case, Ka-Hay's son, was called Nefer.

The one essential element to Nefer's success was that he should become the intimate friend of the King-to-be, the heir to the throne of Egypt, the prince, who in all probability was to reign as Ne-user-ra. All was well; eventually Nefer was named Sole Companion to the King and was the perpetual recipient of his bounty. He progressed in the administration, becoming, eventually Overseer of the Court. It is estimated that he died around the year 2400 BC.

His tomb is a joyous celebration of his life and good fortune. Nefer did not forget his family in the days of his prosperity: when the King gave him his tomb, 'the house of millions of years' so that, as the inscriptions charmingly declare, 'he might grow very beautifully old', Nefer brought his family with him. Numerous adults were buried there, his wife and his father and mother, most of whom seem to have been singers. One of them was even a prophet of the goddess who had charge of ritual music.

The wall reliefs are still gaily painted, rich in colour. They are less sophisticated than the finest work of the time, a shade provincial, it must be admitted, but their charm is in no way diminished by their naïveté. They show life continuing for ever on Nefer's estates in Lower Egypt where the grape harvest is underway and a family pet, a handsome and vigorous cynocephalus baboon, himself helps the workers turn the wine press (plates 97, 98 and 99). In another scene the same baboon stands proudly on the prow of one of Nefer's ships, which is being loaded for the journey to his estates in Upper Egypt, and directs the sailors loading the ship with imperious gestures, a magisterial *baton de commandment* gripped in his paw. We even see carpenters preparing Nefer's sarcophagus, a handsome coffin made in the time-honoured style of a palatial building with recessed walls (plates 100a and 100b), a concept which had thus endured for the best part of a thousand years. Nowhere, in the whole of Egyptian art is the delight in life celebrated so joyfully as in Nefer's tomb; nowhere, too is the humour of the Egyptians, a kindly and generous-hearted humour, so well recorded. An engaging feature of Nefer's eternal mansion is that the workers on his estate, the fishermen, sailors, gardeners, and household servants are all named, so that they may share in their master's immortality.

Nefer, his wife Khensuw, and their dog — one of the race of prick-eared hunting hounds — watch all the activity with evident satisfaction. As is fitting for someone who, despite his eminence, was the scion of a family of musicians, Nefer has a small orchestra included amongst the amenities that he took with him into the tomb. All in all, his tomb portrays a late Old Kingdom idyll.

But the most extraordinary survival in the tomb lies deep in a recess of a rock-cut shaft. It is the mummy of a man, one of the very few known from the early period: it seems not to be the remains of Nefer, however, since a wooden box laid close to the body bears the name 'Waty' (colour plate IX). He lies on his back as though asleep, a sleek and well-fed gentleman, naked, lying as though taking his siesta. His body is perfect. Even the soft tissues of eyelids, lips, and genitals, for example, remain intact and unblemished. He has a small moustache; the outline of his mouth is full and firm.

The technique by which this perfect mummy was made is not known. It seems that the body, presumably eviscerated, was not pickled in natron like the later, New Kingdom examples, a process which reduced them to the consistency of leather and the appearance of creatures of nightmare. The body seems to have been wrapped in gossamer-fine linens, every part of it, and then bathed in some fine plaster-bearing liquid which when dry, shrank very slightly to provide a perfect outline for the body which was within it. The effect is miraculous.

Nefer was a priest. There was no distinction between the religious and the secular life, as it might be understood today. Most high officials also acted as priests of a particular order, the lector priests, *sem* priests, or some other category of officiant in the temple ceremonies.

It is difficult for anyone living in the modern world to imagine with what confidence, with what certainty indeed, a gentleman of the Fifth or Sixth Dynasties, looking out across his estate as evening came on, must have faced life. Order prevailed, the Two Lands were in equilibrium, and the King was secure at the centre of the universe. Not even the assurance of a landed gentleman in nineteenth-century England could quite have equalled it. The tranquillity and order of life in the Valley is demonstrated by the way in which the ordinary daily concerns of the people, the great ones as well as the simple, begin to predominate on the walls of the tombs.

Sports of various kinds were practised by the Egyptians, who clearly enjoyed both participating in them and watching them on high days and festivals. Water sports were common, but seem to have been reserved for the lower orders; indeed, to call them 'sports' at all may be overstating what seems, often, to have been little more than good-natured competitions between rival groups of boatmen to see who might throw the opposing crew into the river. Hunting in the marshes was clearly felt to be a more appropriate pastime for a gentleman and many are the representations of Old Kingdom nobles, their families, retainers, and, not infrequently, their pet animals, hunting with spear or throwing-stick the fish and birds with which the Delta teemed.

The Kings and the great princes hunted the large animals – lion, giraffe, hippopotamus. These occasions were evidently attended by as much protocol and ritual as a hunting excursion by Louis XIV; they were probably as carefully stage-managed and no doubt the King returned to his palace after a hunting trip with a gratifying 'bag'.

In the later years of the Old Kingdom some nobles chose to decorate their tombs with scenes of sports and recreation. One of the favourite motifs was to show sets of naked boys dancing, flinging themselves about in acrobatic and energetic programmes. These, the original *gymnopaedie*, are matched by other groups of youths wrestling, running races, or leaping over poles held by their companions (plate 102).

The round of ceremonies in the temples of the Two Lands, the never-ending rituals of the worship of the high gods, were intended to keep in constant equilibrium the security of Egypt and to effect the service of the divinities who determined its life and prosperity. The most essential purpose of the temple rites was to provide the King with his proper context as the incarnation on earth of the first of the gods. Only when Egypt was first in decline, during the descent into anarchy after the collapse of the Old Kingdom, did the King begin more and more to be recognized as mortal and his attributions of divinity become merely conventional, the expression of what once had been, rather that the extraordinary appearance of reality which the combined genius of the propagandists, the artists, the priests, and the King himself conspired to create in the early centuries of dynastic rule.

The rise of the powerful court and official families, to be matched in the next dynasty by the increasing power of the provincial nobles and their consequent detachment from the centre of royal power, contributed to the gradual erosion of the position of the King. It may well be that originally the rise of ordinary men to positions of power was, to some degree at least, the consequence of a calculated decision by the Kings to try to limit the influence of the great nobles. In the Fourth Dynasty most of the power and the significant offices of state had been concentrated in members of the King's close family. As these circles increased as the generations went by, and as the bureaucracy became more complex requiring more officials to manage it, the King was obliged to relinquish, little by little, his absolute control of the state machine. No doubt the rise of the priesthoods and the extent to which the temples acquired the revenues of the land, by endowment and by the sort of pious coercion which religious communities have always exercised on the credulous, also contributed to the shift of power away from the King, making it more difficult for him to balance one interest against the other and so allow the royal or state interest to ride supreme over the rest.

The Fifth Dynasty ended on another note of high achievement. The last King of the dynasty was the Horus Wadjtawy Unas; in the subterranean chambers of his pyramid at Saqqara, a relatively modest one when compared with the great prototypes at Giza, were found inscribed on the walls, in finely cut hieroglyphs, decorated with a blue paint whose brilliance matches that of medieval heraldry or the illustrations in one of the better

Books of Hours, the texts of spells, incantations, and all manner of sacred mutterings which were designed to facilitate the King's journey from this life to his perpetual life beyond the ever-circling stars.

The Pyramid Texts, as they have come to be known, are unique: no other ancient culture has anything even remotely like them. They are presented in the form of 'Utterances', declarations either in the voice of the King or of the gods and spirits who attend him. Many are obviously of immense antiquity, descending from Predynastic times. Then, it will be recalled, the chieftains of the Predynastic people may also have been regarded as magicians; the texts are full of magic to bursting point.

Much of the texts is written in the form of dialogue, antiphonal exchanges between two or more participants in the ceremonies, the language of which they record. This again suggests the importance which the Egyptians attributed to dramatic utterance and to the forms of play-acting; the Pyramid Texts are a sort of performing script for the King and his attendants on his last great journey to the stars. Their almost wilful obscurity may be judged by Utterance 352, 'A vulture has become pregnant with the King in the night at your hour, O contentious cow'. It may be that they do not render well into other languages.

The complexity of the language of the texts is multiplied by the Egyptians' enthusiasm for punning. This punning is achieved not only verbally, by using words of similar sound or meaning in differing or related contexts, but also visually by the use of hieroglyphs which convey a meaning by their pictorial form as well. For this reason, quite apart from the immense distance of time over which they have reached us, the Pyramid Texts are literally (and in a special sense, visually) untranslatable.

It is not known when they were collected in the form in which they appear in Unas's pyramid; certainly it must have been long before his lifetime. They survived throughout Egyptian history, one of the people's most important pieces of cultural impedimenta. In the Middle Kingdom they were inscribed on the interiors of the decorated coffins which replaced the more monumental enclosures for the dead which the Old Kingdom so prodigally employed. In later times still they formed the basis, though often corrupted, of the various forms of what is generally called the Book of the Dead. This took the form of papyrus scrolls buried with the dead, inscriptions in the tombs, and extracts painted onto sarcophagi and mummy wrappings. The texts have another dimension: they form a sort of continuous hymn through all the rooms of the pyramid on the walls of which they are engraved, so that the reader (or the spirit of the dead King) moves through them adding the dimension of space to the others in which the texts exist.

The Pyramid Texts are amongst the most complex and certainly the most arcane of the survivals of the minds of the men who lived in Egypt at this time. They are largely impenetrable to the contemporary mind: were they fully comprehensible they would, with little doubt, tell more about the Egyptians of the early dynasties than any of the material remains of their time.

Again, the dynasty changed after Unas died, presumably fortified for his journey by the efficacy of the texts; once again in all probability, continuity of the line and the blood was ensured by a princess, perhaps Unas's daughter, who married Teti, the first King of the Sixth Dynasty. If the annals are to be believed, women had ensured the continuity of the royal line since the end of the First Dynasty; setting aside the possibility of a *mésalliance* or unlicensed dalliance by one or more of the royal mothers of the Kings, the genes of Menes and his bloodline may still have been handed on to the new dynasty, almost a thousand years after his lifetime – or at least such was the royal fiction.

It was a very different Egypt to which Teti succeeded from that which Menes-Narmer knew. Since Djoser's time, over 300 years before, King after King had created superb monuments, raised them up, cased them in glittering white limestone or other brilliant stone, and laid them about with temples and pavilions, pools and gardens. Everywhere the ordinary Egyptian cast his eyes he would have seen wonders, the whole a concentration of material splendour unexampled in human experience and probably never to be repeated in quite this prodigality and density. For a man born in Unas's reign and living on into the early years of King Pepi II, seventy years or so later, Egypt must have seemed as eternal and unchanging as she had done since Khasekhemui finally achieved the reconciliation of the Two Powers and made order supreme. But in fact the end was approaching.

There was still much grandeur left, still great works to be done and marvels achieved. The most energetic of the early Kings of the dynasty seems to have been Pepi I, who reigned long and built extensively. He was a vigorous administrator and a skilful politician who allied himself in marriage with some of the great provincial dynasts, hoping perhaps that by doing so he could restore the loyalty to the throne of that caste. The erosion of the nobles' support of the throne had come about, ironically, as a result of earlier Kings' generous grants of land and power to the provincial magnates. Now there was simply little left to give them.

The most remarkable survival from Pepi's reign is the large, standing copper figure of himself, supported by a smaller figure of his son, probably his successor Merenre. The statues are made by beating sheets of copper over a wooden core, a technique pioneered in Sumer, many hundreds of years earlier. They come from Hierakonpolis, which demonstrates that the ancient Falcon capital of the Predynastic Kings was still honoured, long after it had ceased to be the focus of the cults which had initiated the drive to unite the Two Lands.

Merenre did not long succeed his father; there is some evidence that he was in his teens when he died. He was succeeded by the remarkable Pepi II who, according to the annals, came to the throne when he was six years old and reigned for ninety-four years, dying as a centenarian.

Though ninety-four years sounds improbable, the weight of evidence, in the opinion of most authorities, suggests that Pepi's was in fact the longest reign of any King known to history and that there is nothing inherently implausible in the figures attributed to his life span. What is quite certain is that his long life marked the effective end of the Old Kingdom and hence of that great experiment which had been begun so long before by the Thinite Kings.

Pepi's reign began well. In all probability he was the child of his father's old age. The well-known record of young Pepi's delight at the impending arrival at his court of a dancing dwarf from Nubia is charming and shows that Egyptian Kings were engagingly mortal when they chose to be. Indeed, mortality, or perhaps the want of it, was the principal problem of Pepi's interminable reign. He must have outlived all of his contemporaries and most of their children. The state atrophied; the power of the magnates grew. The King was still powerful enough to cause a splendid pyramid to be built for his tomb with its attendant and magnificent monuments; he was able also to commission appropriate burial places for his wives and family. Pepi seems to have tried to contain the power of the great nobles, which was increasing rapidly throughout the Sixth Dynasty. But the corruption was already too deep; the spark was burned out. Egypt was exhausted and on Pepi's death a long and dreadful night began to descend over the Two Lands.

It will be apparent that the society which grew up in Egypt in the third millennium was entirely god-directed: it was thus both theocratic and theocentric in a quite literal sense. The prosperity and survival of Egypt was the dominant concern of the Egyptian state; indeed the King, who brought together in his own person all the diverse elements of humanity, nature, and divinity, was a god precisely because only thus could he, with absolute assurance, determine the fates and ensure that the Egyptian state was protected from all harm. There is thus really no such thing as 'Egyptian religion': to an Egyptian of the early third millennium the concept of *religion*

219

would be meaningless. The integration of identity, survival, the state, and the rituals recognizing the gods' (or perhaps a sole divinity's) concern for Egypt was absolute. The most disastrous consequence of the revolution at the end of the Old Kingdom, when even the shrines of the gods and the eternal mansions of the Kings were ruthlessly destroyed by the mob, was the separation of religion into a distinct function. The rulers of the Middle Kingdom, who reimposed order on Egypt, were, as it were, gods only by courtesy. The priesthood, already emerging as a power in the state in the middle of the third millennium, grew more powerful still and contributed in large part to the collapse of the Old Kingdom. The priests had, however, sunk their claws so deep into the body of Egypt on which they grew, that they emerged at last with a significance almost equal to the Kings's. Gradually religion (as we might understand the term) became separated from its exclusive relationship with the Kingship and became something to whose benefits all men might individually aspire. By the time of the New Kingdom, in the second half of the second millennium, Egypt was hopelessly and irrevocably corrupt.

With this corruption went the rise of the peoples of the deserts, particularly those to the north and east of Egypt. Most early Semitic-speaking societies seem not to have believed in the survival of the individual after death; paradoxically the ancient character of Egypt had been undermined by the emergence of the individual. Corporate identity and corporate faith no longer survived as the distinctive Egyptian 'way'. What Jungian analytical psychology would call individuation is ultimately defeated (or perhaps, ultimately brought to full realization) by the appearance of the individual (see Chapter 6).

The experience of individuation undergone by early Egyptian society is no doubt the key to the extraordinary vitality and endurance of the Egyptian creative experience. With few exceptions, and none of these from the earliest periods, Egyptian artists and craftsmen are anonymous; their work is, in a sense, the product of the community which they so powerfully represent. The creation of the pyramids is itself an expression of the sense of identity of the community: these great projects were necessary to bring the community together not in the old unity of the Stone Age bands but on a scale raised to the level of the state. Of course, the experiment failed but the grandeur of the attempt and its consequences in the production of some of the finest objects ever made by the hand of man surely mark it ineluctably as one of the highest points of the human condition. The exceptional creativity of Egyptian craftsmen, the artists and the planners of the great architectural enterprises which were undertaken almost from the very earliest days of the Thinites' rule, was the product of their environment, of the nature of life in Egypt in the third millennium BC. They lived in a particularly favoured, isolated world; their genius was such that they did not atrophy but, over hundreds of years, developed their distinctive culture phase by phase until, in the later years of the Old Kingdom, with the weight of experience and achievement of the early centuries behind them, they could reasonably believe that their way of life was ideal, unchanging and ordained by the gods and that in the security of their state and its beliefs as much as in the material prosperity of the lands, no better life was conceivable.

The early reigns of the Fifth Dynasty Kings probably represent the most potent example of this condition and of the attitude of mind which it bred. Throughout that dynasty and for most of the Sixth the same tranquil assurance, the same belief in the eternal unchanging certainties, prevails.

The culture which grew and flourished in the Nile Valley was wholly autochthonous. It grew out of the lives and preoccupations of the cattle-rearing African peoples (black Africans, it must certainly be acknowledged) who were the true ancestors of the Pharaohs, in all their majesty and power. The Egyptians long held on to the recognition of their essentially African character, incidentally: even in the Middle Kingdom the King could be portrayed in all the barbaric splendour of an African chief, a notably powerful representation which recalls something of Djoser's great portrait.

Egypt's decline began when these essentially African characteristics became diluted by incursions from outside the Valley. For many centuries Egypt was able to neutralize those influences which did seep in from the lands to the north and east, but eventually the African strain became too weakened and a more classically 'Oriental' character began to emerge, which eventually was to dominate the subsequent centuries of Egypt's history.

The Fifth and Sixth Dynasties were the culmination of the long sequence which started with the little communities which began to cling to the Valley in the fifth millennium. The supreme elegance and confidence of Fifth and Sixth Dynasty art is the most emphatic statement of this triumph of the Egyptian spirit. Paradoxically − and Egypt is ever the land of paradox − the seeds of change, even of destruction, were already germinating, soon to flower and smother the true, native spirit.

The end, when it came, came quickly, it seems, with a terrible and shattering force, at least to the assured and confident rulers of the Two Lands. The reasons for the collapse were various.

Ironically the power which had bound the Two Lands together and which had set the whole course of Egyptian history in motion, the Kingship, was one of the principal, if unwitting contributors to the dissolution of the

Old Kingdom. The monarchy reached the height of its autocratic (perhaps more properly, theocratic) power in the Third and Fourth Dynasties. From the Fifth Dynasty onwards it is possible to detect the increasing influence of the priesthoods, particularly that of Re in Heliopolis. The priests, as always advancing their own and their order's interests above all others, began to circumscribe the King's authority, by the combination of cajolery, coercion, and the exploitation of superstitious awe in which priesthoods the world over have ever been expert.

However it was achieved, the absolute role of the King was diminished. From being something very like the immanent manifestation of the supreme divinity, he became merely one of many little gods; he was content to row in the barque of Re or to act as his scribe, a far cry from his earlier unique divinity. As the King's power declined and that of the temples' rose, the great nobles were not slow to assert their interest and that of their families.

The King needed allies: it is evident from the reign of Shepseskaf that the advance of the priests was occasionally resisted. More and more, there is evidence, the king rewarded his courtiers and officers with grants of land, drawn from what must at the outset have seemed an inexhaustible bank, from the royal domains. But as the prosperity of the magnates increased, so did their arrogance; over the generations they lost their loyalty to the crowns, other than in the increasingly merely formal recognition of the King's sovereignty. The position was still more acute in the case of the nomarchs, the governors of the provinces into which Egypt was immemorially divided: there were generally forty-two of them. In the later Old Kingdom these governorships, once the gift of the King conferred on those servants on whose service he could rely, became more and more frequently regarded as hereditary fiefs, descending from father to son with only a passing nod to the royal prerogatives. The nomarchs became, in effect, independent princes, ruling their districts with little concern either for the central authority or, it may be suspected, for the welfare of their subjects who, in earlier times, always had recourse to the justice of the King if ever they had cause to show oppression or exploitation either by their masters, if they were workers on the land, or by the officials of the state.

As the pride of the provincial nobles increased, the state which they maintained becoming more and more superb, at the expense of the dues which should have been applied to the royal and central government, another force began to emerge which likewise demanded recognition and reward. This was the class of 'new men', artisans, craftsmen, and specialists whose particular skills, practised in a trade or a vocation, brought them prosperity and the desire for advancement for themselves and their families.

All of these influences, wholly alien to the original social structure of the unified Kingdom which the Thinite or Hierakonpolitan princes had made, began to wear away the foundations of the state. Further down the scale still, though this must be speculation, it is not unreasonable to suspect that similar pressures for advancement (in the next world as much as in this one, for this was, after all, Egypt) began to affect even the lowly amongst the population; that most potent of political motivations, envy, no doubt was already manifesting itself. It would be contained for long centuries because of the nature of Egyptian society but beneath the surface it must have been suppurating furiously.

The diminishing of the royal authority and its decline from the status of absolute divinity must have allowed these influences to grow and to gain a hold from which they could not be uprooted. The King might for the while attempt to limit the power of the priests as Shepseskaf did: the incitement of the pious mob and some effective religious sleight of hand would soon set the balance in the temples' favour once again. Similarly Pepi, whilst still in command of his powers, would try to hold back the arrogance of the nobles, but to no avail. They could continue to assert themselves and to ride roughshod over every interest but their own, no doubt excepting the interests of the priesthoods, for those of a recalcitrant nobility and an avaricious clergy have always found a common cause.

But there was a still greater menace facing Egypt, from beyond the hitherto secure frontiers with which she had surrounded herself. The phenomenon which now bore down in Egypt was one which had been piling up, like a dense and threatening storm cloud on the horizon, and which had already brought destruction and black ruin to other lands around.

The threat which now faced Egypt, no less fearful for the fact that it had long been anticipated, was probably as dreadful to the people of the Valley, secure in their centuries of long-civilized tranquillity, as nuclear war or the prospect of an invasion from distant space is to a modern advanced and peaceable community. The menacing entity which now came down on the Valley, and in doing so unleashed all the tensions and dissensions which were ready to tear the fabric of Egypt asunder, emerged from the desert. The menace was represented in real terms by the tribes and savage hordes which had always lived in the heartlands of the deserts, alternately looking with envy and contempt (to judge at least by later, similar cases) at the mighty civilization which they now saw lying open and vulnerable to them.

The people of the deserts to the north and east of Egypt (to the west and south of Sumer) were Semitic-speaking. They were, in all reasonable probability, the ancestors of the peoples living today in much of the Arabian peninsula and in the deserts on its northern periphery. To describe them as Semites is to do no more than employ a linguistic term to differentiate them from the Sumerians, whose language bore no relation to any other language at all, and from the Egyptians whose language belonged principally to the Hamitic family, though in Egypt's case there had for long been an important Semitic component in the spoken tongue.

The way of life of the desert people was markedly different from those of the Sumerians and the Egyptians. They eschewed the cities which were so typical of Sumerian society, and they did not attempt to create the highly centralized nation state which was Egypt's particular and unique contribution to the history of politics. Some had, of course, come to settle around the coasts and in the oases but many were in all probability nomadic though closely linked by the complex but enduring network of familial and clan ties which have always bound the desert peoples together.

In Sumer, as in Egypt, there had always been *some* integration between the Semitic-speaking elements in the population and the rest; thus, Kings with Semitic names are known from Sumerian city states, from early times onwards. But to the Sumerians the majority of the desert people were those 'who know not grain', just as to the Egyptians they were 'the sand-dwellers' and other, less restrained, sobriquets.

The desert people had long standing and mutually supportive relationships with the settled people. The nomads, to use a term which is probably anachronistic in that they did not necessarily display the cohesion and accepted customs of those to whom the term may be applied today, were important in the exchange systems on which so much ancient trade depended and for the provision of livestock from the herds which they managed. However, towards the last quarter of the third millennium this relationship began to change and the Semitic-speaking desert folk began to scent the prospect of political power and, hence, access to the wealth and sophistication of the Valley peoples.

The rise of the desert peoples to power in Mesopotamia and the beginning of the process over a still larger area of the ancient Near East is convincingly signalled by the appearance of the first great Semitic leader whose name is known. It is doubtful if one man could intervene in the processes of history and effect such a degree of total change as now ensued throughout what once was called 'the Fertile Crescent'; none the less, an official in the court of the King of Kish called Sharukhin, and known more familiarly as Sargon, was a leader of exceptional authority and charisma. He swept to power over the fragmented and divided city states of Sumer which after more than a thousand years of brilliant flowering were now showing signs of exhaustion and incipient collapse. The Sumerian cities had always feared the desert people; indeed it is possible that the first walled cities in southern Mesopotamia were built to keep out the desert hordes. Sargon, a civilized member of the desert-bred people, now established a glittering capital at Agade (whose whereabouts is still unknown) and a dynasty which endured for more than a hundred years – a creditable duration for any political construct in Sumer. He absorbed most of the culture of Sumer, only pausing to semiticize the names of the gods, and to adapt Akkadian cuneiform to Sumerian, to which in fact it was particularly ill-suited. He, or his grandson and most important successor, Naram-Sin, is said to have fought a battle against and defeated a king called Manium. It was once believed, before the dating of the Akkadians was brought down to the period that it occupies today, that Manium was Menes, the founder of the First Dynasty of Egypt; by modern chronologies this is, of course, impossible.

It is, however, perfectly possible that Sargon and his Egyptian contemporaries Unas, Teti, and Pepi I may have known of each other's existence for Sargon *may* have conquered or at least traded extensively with Cyprus, with which island the Egyptians certainly had contact at this period. Doubtless too Sargon's claim that his empire ran from the Lower Sea (the Arabian Gulf) to the Upper Sea (the Mediterranean) would have meant that the Levantine cities where his agents and armies were active would have made his name known to the Egyptians. Sargon's empire even penetrated to the Holy Land of Dilmun, but whether the Egyptians either knew of this or cared if they did, is not known for certain.

Within a century or so of Sargon's reign and during the lifetimes of his immediate heirs, Egypt too experienced a collapse which must have made the fall of even the more populous Sumerian cities seem trivial events in comparison. It was the dreaded 'Asiatics' who brought down chaos on to the tranquil Valley and, in doing so, probably encountered social and political conditions which assisted in the destruction of the grandeur of the Old Kingdom society.

The last quarter of the third millennium was as decisive in the course of history as was the last quarter of the fourth. Whereas, however, the earlier period had seen the introduction of a time of exceptional creativity and achievement the end of the third marked the appearance of darker influences, of flames flickering at the edges of the glorious cultures which were swiftly consumed.

It is really not at all clear why this cataclysm should have hit so extended a region as it did, embracing Egypt and much of Iraq, and reverberating up the eastern Mediterranean coast. It may be that it was provoked not only by those influences which have already been listed but also by another of those relatively minor climatic changes which it is now recognized have

225

had so profound an effect on man's social progress so frequently. It is known that there was a series of low Nile floods, of failures in the inundation, towards the end of the Old Kingdom. In normal circumstances the Nile served its children well but occasionally an exceptionally high or an exceptionally low Nile could bring, on the one hand, devastating floods, on the other unassuageable drought; in either event, it meant tragedy on an immense scale to the people of the Valley.

The low Niles at the end of the Old Kingdom and the hardship which they would have produced amongst the whole population of Egypt which depended upon assured production from the fields, would have been the cause of unrest throughout the Two Lands. The extortions of the feudal nobility (which are clear, if only from the occasional inscription of one who recorded the fact that he stored grain and resources to be distributed to his people, contrasting this with what otherwise might be considered the customary depredations of those of his rank) would have added to the unrest. The King's power was reduced; the army was probably disaffected and the temples were no doubt extracting whatever advantage they could. The Asiatics and other barbarian tribes sensed the time was right and with devastating effect they fell on Egypt.

Remarkably enough, there are several of what appear to be eye-witness accounts of the calamity which befell Egypt; one of these survives in the form of a text which has come to be known as 'the Admonitions of Ipuwer'. In this long, mutilated poem, one of the treasures of Egyptian literature and amongst the oldest known surviving texts, Ipuwer, a wise man, laments that the king is old, secure in his palace, unaware of Egypt's sufferings which are kept from him by the lies of venal courtiers. The catastrophes which have struck Egypt are twofold: the incursion of foreigners who have flooded into the Valley unchecked and the total reversal of the established social order. This aspect of the disaster is indeed the most complained of; servant girls can usurp the places of their mistresses, officials are forced to do the bidding of uncouth men, and the children of princes are dashed against the wall, all inversions of the order of nature profoundly shocking to the observer, who records the events of this melancholy and unprecedented time.

As the relationship of gods and men changed, so inevitably did the relationship of the King and his subjects. After the last quarter of the third millennium the King is mortal; no complexity of ceremony or ritual can conceal this essential fact. The divine condescension by which a Fourth Dynasty King might favour one of his intimates by permitting him to kiss his foot thus earning the unbounded and immortal gratitude of the man he so honoured, would be unthinkable in this later age.

The Egyptians themselves looked back to the third millennium as a Golden Age. They identified it with the rule of the great god Re, identified in turn with the sun by the theology of Heliopolis, with Saturn in other philosophies. Re however grew old: the poet described his bones becoming silver, his flesh gold, his hair and beard lapis lazuli. Even in describing the decline of an age the Egyptians could not disavow poetic imagery which recalled their predilection for sumptuous and costly materials, brought to them from distant lands with arduous toil.

There is one small irony in the collapse of the Old Kingdom and all for which it stood, which reveals itself now when considering the direction from which came the final impetus which toppled the established structure of the state. At the end of the fourth millennium influences from Sumer or Elam (and perhaps from the Gulf) reached Egypt and seem to have acted as wholly benign stimuli, contributing to the acceleration of the rate of growth of the embryonic Pharaonic state prodigiously. A thousand years later it was once again influences from the east which entered the Valley but this time, to destroy and not to build.

All well-meaning attempts to find the original Paradise Land, a quest which dominated one minor bypath of scholarship for several centuries past, are, in all probability, doomed to failure. But if it is necessary to postulate a land where there was something approaching a harmony of all natural things, Archaic and Old Kingdom Egypt will provide a better than average option. When that particular phase of the human experience came to its end man never again enjoyed that childlike joy in creation and the world around him which is the particular mark of the Egypt of this time. It was as if the Egyptians really had glimpsed the *tremendum* (to borrow a term from medieval times) and were always striving for the renewal of that experience. The age of innocence ended when the Old Kingdom collapsed, when god and King were divided and hence man was cut off from his direct access to the divine. In one sense, at least, he has ever since been trying to recapture that enchanted time.

Certainly, after the end of the third millennium matters in Egypt were never wholly the same again. The upheavals of this time continued for the best part of two centuries; it was remarkable enough that anything at all survived. This time of trouble is known to Egyptologists as the First Intermediate Period; during it there is evidence of increased contact with eastern lands, not all of it the consequence of conflict. Trade obviously continued, with some vigour; surprisingly enough the times produced some of the finest literature to survive from Egypt, of which the Admonitions of Ipuwer is an example but by no means the only one.

227

It is during this period that the Egyptians began to make in notable quantity one of their most typical products, the scarab seal. In the same late third millennium and early second the Gulf people also developed a highly distinctive form (as distinctive indeed as the scarab was to be), a circular domed stamp, its reverse often quartered and pierced with one or more dotted circles with the designs, often of exceptional liveliness, being incised on the face or obverse. Occasionally scarab forms of the seals are found in the Gulf at this time, suggesting direct contact with Egypt; it is fair to speculate, in view of their often remarkable similarities of design, which one came first and whether the Egyptians adapted the circular Gulf seals (which seem to have originated in Bahrain) and, typically, turned them into something utterly Egyptian or the other way about. Occasionally there are suggestive correspondences between the design of the Gulf seals and Egyptian forms which cannot altogether be explained by chance or the common response to similar needs or occasions.

But if trade continued between the centres of power in Egypt, however much as these had changed and the world outside, the soul of Egypt, if a nation may be said to possess so intangible a faculty, was changed still more. When stability was restored the forms and eternal marks of Egyptian society survived, miraculously, virtually intact, but its essential god-ordained nature was never more to be recalled, as it had been during the first glorious millennium when Egypt was young. The process of growth was complete: Egypt was now mature, a vehicle as every individual must be, for every influence and stimulus from outside.

The individual in the state now began to assert himself, just as the state began to assert itself as an individual entity. The corporate nature of the Egyptian state, unified under the immanent divine ruler, shattered, and the interests of the individual rose supreme. The fierce independence and individuality of the desert people may have been responsible, at least in part, for this transformation in the nature of Egypt. The idea of the society being devoted wholly to the promotion of the divine now began to fade; though other peoples would proclaim themselves 'chosen' or suggest that their society's rulers were determined solely by reference to the divine, no society after the collapse of the Old Kingdom in Egypt ever approximated to its unity of the human and divine, or demonstrated so absolutely the indivisibility of the two.

The world beyond Egypt's borders was stirring into life; the course of the next 4,000 years was beginning to be set. The states which were emerging belonged, more evidently than ever Egypt did, to the world of modern man. Old Kingdom Egypt really was the ultimate sophistication of the late Neolithic state, written not only large but in hieroglyphs.

The identity between man and god which was one of the essential elements in early Egyptian belief was swept away by the changes which supervened in the aftermath of the Old Kingdom's eclipse. When the King was recognized as the god he drew all humanity into himself; through him it was renewed and perpetuated. But now man and god were separated, forever.

At the same time, from the same sources, another terrible uncertainty began to manifest itself. In the Semitic mind there was no certainty of the survival of the individual after death; indeed, most Semites who had considered the question at all clearly believed that at death the individual was extinguished. This concept, of course, struck at all the accepted canons of Egyptian belief; if, at one time, the King alone had been certain of immortality, for hundreds of years all Egyptians above the humblest levels of society had believed in the prospect of a well-endowed and agreeable existence in a sort of eternalized Nile Valley, where the crops grew more lushly even than they did in the Valley itself. Egypt clung to the outward form of her rituals and observances but increasingly the centre of her belief was hollow. The glory, quite literally, had departed.

The institutions of Egypt were restored by the Kings of the Middle Kingdom, founded by the first Amenemhat of the Eleventh Dynasty. Like the unification more than a thousand years earlier this reconsolidation of the Two Lands was achieved by a southern family. They were princes of the region around Thebes which for the first time now comes to prominence. Sucessive Amenemhats and Montuhoteps vied with one another in the complexity of their throne names and in their dedication to the restoration of the unity and grandeur of Egypt. The Twelfth Dynasty was one of the high points of the Egyptian experience; it will also serve as the witness of the change which had come over the Two Lands. One of its greatest sovereigns was Senwosret III who reigned at the beginning of the second millennium BC. He was a remarkable ruler, wise, compassionate, and brave; he was long remembered. He caused himself to be represented in a series of portraits which are quite unique, for their time and provenance. Though he was indisputably still the most august sovereign in the world, Senwosret chose to have himself represented naturalistically, with none of the trappings of divine authority with which it had hitherto been considered appropriate to invest a royal portrait in Egypt. But by his time, the gods had gone from Egypt. Whereas Menkaure could face the world smiling with divine assurance, attended by divinities, Senwosret shows himself as a man full of years, weary and haggard with the awareness of the responsibilities of rule. His face is drawn, careworn but sensitive, almost suffering; it is the portrait of an incarnate god who has looked into the innermost sanctuary and found it to be an empty room.

78 Even viewed from behind where the mass of the King's great wig cover is revealed, the statue of Djoser (colour plate XI) still radiates a formidable power. (Egyptian Museum, Cairo; photograph, Roger Wood)

79 A statue of the King, roughly blocked out in the early stage of carving, lies unfinished on the ground inside Djoser's burial complex. (Photograph, Michael Rice)

80 The so-called Bent Pyramid at Dahshur, probably built by King Sneferu.

81 The plateau at Giza as it appeared early in the excavations carried out by the University of Pennsylvania.

82 Ankhaf may have been the architect of the Great Pyramid built for King Khufu at Giza in the Fourth Dynasty. He has the air of an assured and competent executive. (Museum of Fine Arts, Boston, C.14249)

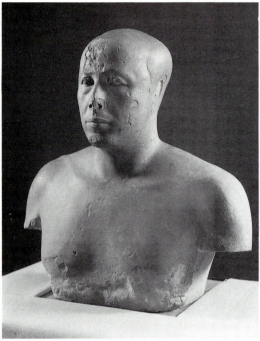

83 The Egyptian genius in the manipulation of stone is demonstrated by their frequent choice of exotic stones, such as this, with marked striations, out of which to carve a dish. (Private collection)

84 The nature of the material means that few wooden carvings survive from the earliest periods. However, this mask, from a virtually life-size First Dynasty figure, shows with what mastery Egyptian artists carved in wood. Fragments of life-size wooden statues have been found in the tombs of the nobles of Saqqara. (Egyptian Museum, Cairo; photograph, John Ross)

85a The portrait of Hesy-re, a contemporary of King Djooser, shows a fine-boned, distinctly aristocratic cast to the features. (Egyptian Museum, Cairo; photograph, John Ross)

85b The elegance to which hieroglyphs can attain is well demonstrated by the inscriptions which record the name, titles and career of Hesy-re. (photograph, John Ross)

86 Hetepheres, the mother of Khufu (builder of the Great Pyramid), is portrayed here in a fragmentary relief in gold, originally overlaid on a piece of furniture. (From Stevenson Smith, *History of Egyptian Sculpture*)

87 King Khnum-Khufu, known also by the Greek form of his name, Cheops, was the son of Sneferu and Hetepheres. This is the only portrait of the King, a tiny ivory piece whose survival seems to mock the Great Pyramid itself. It was found in two pieces; the head was recovered some three weeks after the body, through Petrie's devoted sifting of the 'fill' from the site at Abydos. (Egyptian Museum, Cario; photograph, Roger Wood)

88 In the temple below Menkaure's pyramid were several stone groups representing the King, his consort, and the gods and goddess of the districts of Egypt. These are amongst the most splendid artefacts of any age or provenance. The King and his attendant figures, eternally youthful and vigorous, seem to spring from the stone alert and welcoming. Though the King is undoubtably still portrayed as a god, he has about him a sense of life, a hint of the warmth of human flesh. (Egyptian Museum, Cairo; photograph, Roger Wood)

89 The assurance of a man raised to the level of divinity is captured with certainty in this statue, in immensely hard diorite, of King Khaufre; 4th Dynasty. (Egyptian Museum, Cairo; photograph Roger Wood)

90 A head of a King or prince, once thought to be Shepseskaf, but now generally agreed to be Khaufre. It is one of the finest surviving royal portraits from the Old Kingdom. (Courtesy of the Museum of Fine Arts, Boston)

91 King Shepseskaf, the last King of the Fourth Dynasty. This highly individualized portrait conveys a slightly sinister expression, as well as being a close examination of the man who stood against the incursions of the priests into the Egyptian state – but lost. (Freer Gallery of Art, Washington, DC)

92 One of the very few Old Kingdom temples to survive is the Valley Temple of King Khaufre at Giza. The massive square-cut columns and lintels are in marked contrast to the usual style of Egyptian architecture, with soaring columns. Khaufre's temple expresses itself laterally and more massively. (Photograph, Roger Wood)

93 The ability of the Egyptian sculptor to 'draw' in stone is well demonstrated by this relief from the tomb of Ti at Saqqara. The extraordinary plasticity of the great, placid bovine with his handsome collar is contrasted by the grace and delicacy of the cranes in the lower register. (Photograph, Roger Wood)

94 There is an intriguing quality about much later Old Kingdom work, in particular the sculpture. Whereas earlier examples represent a delight in life, an intense sense of living, some later works suggest a remarkable exalted state, with a sense almost of transcendentalism. This quality is manifest in statues of young men with markedly exalted expressions, who look as if they might be in the presence of some tremendous power. They do not, however, display the apprehension typical of their Sumerian counterparts. Figures such as this, from the Fifth Dynasty c.2350, anticipate the Greek 'kouroi', which first appear nearly two thousand years later in the sixth century BC. The similarity extends even to the position of the hands, and the right leg advanced. (Kunsthistorisches Museum, Vienna)

95 Sahure, whose reign was one of the most productive in the Fifth Dynasty, is shown here in company with one of the nome gods. The King is no longer the unique Great God, master of the Universe, but merely the companion of a relatively minor divinity, one indeed of forty-two, personifying the districts into which Egypt was divided. (Metropolitan Museum of Art, New York; photograph, John Ross)

96 A gold cylinder seal from a hoard of richly fashioned objects believed to have originated in Anatolia. The seal bears the cartouches of Djedkare and Djed-Kaw, two of the successors of King Sahure c.2400 BC. (Courtesy of the Museum of Fine Arts, Boston: centennial gift of Landon T. Clay)

97 Nefer, the son of Ka-Hay a court musician, rose high in the service of the
King and was rewarded with a fine tomb for himself and his family, amongst
other privileges. Here he is seen inspecting the activities of his retainers on his
estates, attended by his wife Khonsu and their dog. (Deutsches Archaologisches
Institut, Cairo)

98 Befitting one whose family were distinguished musicians Nefer ensured that even in the wine-pressing his men were encouraged by attendants with their instruments. (Deutsches Archaologisches Institut, Cairo)

99 A handsome cynocephalus baboon, perhaps a family pet of the Nefers or of one of their relations buried in the tomb, assists the workers in the wine-harvest. (Photograph, Michael Rice)

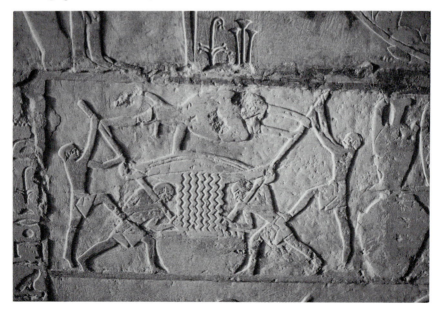

a

100a and *100b* Nefer records the making of his sarcophagus (*a*) which, dating from around 2400 BC, still retains the form of the Sumerian temple façade (though its origins must long have been forgotten) which first appeared in the royal tombs of the First Dynasty, more than six hundred years earlier. His tomb, as represented here, also perpetuates the Sumerian temple façade form (*b*). (Deutsches Archaologisches Institut, Cairo)

b

5

Eastwards from Egypt

The evidence indicates clearly that a degree of contact existed in the late Predynastic period between the Egyptians and Sumerian and Elamite ideas and concepts, though the nature and extent of that contact and how and where it was achieved is still very obscure indeed. It remains, then, to consider this issue further, for its resolution is important if only because of the influence which both the Egyptians and the Sumerians had on the world which came after them and which, in substantial part, descends from them. There has been intermittent interest in the question from well back into the last century, but a reappraisal is now timely, in the light of new evidence and the new methods which are now available to archaeology. Some of this new evidence has emerged only over the past decade or so; it stems in particular from the opening up of Arabia to archaeology, a phenomenon essentially of the postwar period and, specifically, of the past twenty-five years. Some of the material evidence and the inferences which may be drawn from it has already been described, in its appropriate context.

Egypt has a long coastline due west of the Arabian peninsula; they share the Red Sea. As a consequence of Egypt's geographical location, lying at the precise point where influences from north and south, east and west tend to converge and comingle, the Valley was, particularly in historic times, a sort of cultural sump into which these many diverse influences flowed. The extraordinary factor was that the Egyptian personality remained pristine and distinct in its earliest manifestations despite this infusion, a tribute to the enduring qualities of its African roots.

The Egyptians, from the evidence of their earliest records, took every possible precaution to insulate the Valley from foreign incursions and from alien pollution. They employed terms of execration when speaking of foreigners: 'beastly', 'vile', and 'unspeakable' were some of the more restrained epithets which they employed when describing their neighbours.

Many scholars of an earlier generation believed that Egypt and Sumer had a common ancestry, whilst others attributed the impetus for the later phases of Egypt's civilization to the efforts of Sumerian colonists. Some have believed in a 'dynastic race', representing them as invaders following the standards of Horus, who came into the Valley as conquerors. Similarly, the primacy of Egypt, as the heartland of the sun Kingdoms, began to be argued forcefully by the diffusionists, who saw all the great historic cultures of the ancient Near East and ultimately of Europe (and even of South America) having their common origins in Egypt. Mopping and mowing in the train of the diffusionists came the proponents of the theory of the Atlantean origins of the ancient Egyptian priesthoods, to be joined by the later generations of eccentrics, those who seek for the origins of ancient cultures among travellers from the stars and distant galaxies.

Commentators in recent years have been guarded in accepting the direct involvement of the Sumerians in Egypt, however, because of the formidable barrier of the great deserts which lie between Mesopotamia and Egypt and the equally formidable distance represented by the sea route, which is the only alternative access to the Nile Valley. However, the most recent developments in the study of the archaeology of Arabia, particularly of its eastern and western seaboards, have begun once again to focus attention on the issue and to suggest some new directions from which enlightenment may come.

The Arabian peninsula is virtually virgin territory, archaeologically speaking, and it is vast, a small continent with a wide variety of different environments and societies within its borders. Those borders are the natural ones of sea, mountain, and desert, and whilst much of its land surface is harsh and inhospitable, around the edges of the deserts, on the coasts, and in the great oases, life has flourished, in all probability for as long as man has been a bipedal hominid.

One of the characteristics of the archaeology of western Arabia is the proliferation of designs carved on rock faces in the desert. Many of these, of a style associated with a group first identified around Jubba, to the south of Jeddah, are of great antiquity, the oldest perhaps dating from as early as the sixth millennium BC. The carvings' chronology ranges, however, from this very high dating down to the present day. Virtually every culture that has been present in western Arabia has left evidence of its passage on the desert rocks.

However, far more research has been carried out in eastern Arabia and on the islands and the western coastal states of the Arabian Gulf than in other regions of Arabia. This work has centred on successive seasons of survey and excavation carried out by Danish teams, working there since the early 1950s. The results of this work have often been dramatic and farreaching; outstanding amongst them has been the revelation of a considerable culture flourishing in eastern Arabia, on the islands of Bahrain, Tarut, Failakah, and Umm an Nar, and in Oman in much of the third millennium and down to the early second millennium BC. Bahrain is now generally identified with Dilmun, the otherwise legendary Sumerian land of the creation and primeval innocence. Dilmun was also the centre of a wide-ranging and long-lasting mercantile tradition, which is extensively documented in Sumerian sources and in the records of their successors, the Akkadians and the Old Babylonians.

Whilst several of the surviving references to Dilmun celebrate its island character it appears that the centre of Dilmun shifted over the centuries from what may have been its earlier location in eastern Arabia, with important settlements on the island of Tarut and inland near Abqaiq; only later, it appears, did it come to mean mainly the principal Bahrain island. There a city was established on the northern shore late in the third millennium, which was continuously occupied and rebuilt down to post-Alexandrian times and beyond. A monumental temple site, also on the north of the island near the village of Barbar, was rebuilt three times between 2300 BC and 1800 BC approximately. This appears to have been consecrated to a divinity associated with water and the probability is that the god honoured at Barbar is Enki, the Sumerian god of the sweet waters under the earth, the Lord of the Abyss, though the possibility remains that Ninhursaq, the Sumerian mother goddess, Enshag (the son of Enki), or Šamaš/Utu the sun god, may also be commemorated there; Enki is the most likely candidate, however. In the vicinity of the Barbar temple site and indeed in much of the northern reaches of the island are extensive and so far largely unexcavated remains, many of which are probably temples or cult structures. Dilmun was exceptional in its reputation for sanctity and there is little doubt that many great divinities were honoured there.

Bahrain is remarkable for the extraordinary density of its fields of grave mounds. Something over 170,000 very well constructed mounds have been recorded in Bahrain, the majority dating from the late third/early second millennia and thus matching the time of Dilmun's special importance to the people of the Mesopotamian cities.

The reason for Dilmun's commercial importance was that it acted as the entrepôt for the business conducted by Mesopotamian merchants and their counterparts from the great, bleak, brick-built cities of the Indus Valley, like Moenjodaro and Harappa. Dilmun's trade routes also encompassed the hinterland of Arabia, Iran, Afghanistan, Anatolia, and most important, the major resource of copper located in what is today the Sultanate of Oman.

One of the principal reasons for the importance of the Gulf in the third millennium, when it was the veritable highway of the world's trade, was the movement of copper, from the rich mines of Oman to the Sumerian cities, which were almost entirely without raw materials. It has now been established that ancient mine workings are to be found in northern Oman and that communities concerned with copper's extraction, smelting, and marketing, were established along the coast of what is today the United Arab Emirates, particularly at Umm an-Nar, a small island just off the shore of the modern state of Abu Dhabi, at Hili, a settlement in the great Buraimi oasis, and at Bat and Ibri in the Sultanate.

It is one of the most notable characteristics of the early civilization of the Gulf that it was in large part dependent upon the various habitable islands which nestle close to the western Arabian coastline or, in the case of the most northerly, the island of Failaka, in the Bay of Kuwait. The Gulf islanders, the Dilmunites whose far-ranging exploits took them not only to the Indus Valley but northwards, deep into Syria and Anatolia and, in all probability, to the Levantine coast, were intrepid seamen and adventurous in the search for new markets. They were undeterred by distance; their ships were versatile, seaworthy vessels. They, or their Sumerian contemporaries were, indeed, the first to devise sailing craft capable of cutting across the ocean.

The archaeology of Dilmun and of the island of Bahrain in particular, though it is yet relatively little known, in fact has a history extending over more than one hundred years (Rice, 1983). The first report on the antiquities of Bahrain was the work of Captain E. L. Durand, a British civil servant employed by the Viceroy's office in Calcutta, who visited the islands in 1878–9. He was followed by the well-known nineteenth-century travellers Theodore Bent and his wife in the 1880s and then, in 1906, by Colonel F. B. Prideaux, who conducted the first scientific excavation of Bahrain's most notable antiquities, the grave mounds, particularly a group at Aali, which had also attracted Durand's interest. Subsequently these structures, many of which are very large, became known as the Royal Tombs, the putative burial places of the ancient Kings of Dilmun, dating from the late third millennium BC.

It was probably Prideaux' report which came to the notice of one of the age's outstanding scholars, Sir Flinders Petrie, who throughout his immensely long life was deeply concerned with the origins of Pharaonic Egypt. Indeed it is his view of those origins and his researches into the Predynastic cultures which still colour most of whatever is written about the earliest phases of Egyptian history today. Only Petrie's observations about chronology, which he tended to put back to what is, by the standards of modern scholarship, an unacceptably early range of dates, are questioned vigorously.

Writing in the magazine *Ancient Egypt*, which he founded to popularize the study of the Pharaonic civilization, he wrote of the alien, non-Egyptian influences which he, like others, felt could be detected in the late Predynastic cultures.

> The strong Mesopotamian suggestions of the design have, as we noted before, no exact parallel in the East. They seem rather to belong to a people of Elamite or Tigran origin and ideas who had progressed on their own lines. The presence of shipping as an important factor would be against their having come to Egypt across the Arabian desert. The probability seems that they branched off to some settlement in the Persian Gulf (such as the Bahreyn Islands) or on the South Arabian coast and from their second home had brought its style and ideas into Egypt.

In another article, charmingly called 'The geography of the gods', in which he examines the geographical origins and associations of the principal divinities of Egypt, he writes:

> The general diffusion of the worship of Hathor and her identification with many other deities or genii points to her belonging to the Dynastic people, as already stated. The movement of the dynastic people appears to have been by sea round from the Persian Gulf and up the Red Sea into Egypt.

Later, in one of his works of popularization, *The Making of Egypt*, he returned to the same theme. Speaking of the 'Falcon tribe' which he believed had conquered Egypt prior to the beginning of the First Dynasty, Petrie says:

> This Falcon tribe had certainly originated in Elam, as indicated by the hero and lions on the 'Araq knife handle. They went down the Persian Gulf and settled in 'the horn of Africa'. There they named the 'Land of Punt', sacred to later Egyptians as the source of the race. The Pun people founded the island fortress of Ha-fun which commands the whole of that coast, and hence came the Punic or Phenic peoples of classic antiquity.
>
> Those who went up the Red Sea formed the dynastic invaders of Egypt entering by the Qoceir-Koptos road. Others went on to Syria

and founded Tyre, Sidon and Aradus, named after their home islands in the Persian Gulf.

Petrie speaks of the prospect of Gulf as well as Elamite influences being present in Predynastic Egypt with an assurance which might be taken for an expression almost of certainty. It is not clear why he considered that the Gulf islands were involved at all, though, as was remarked earlier, nineteenth-century commentators seem often to have believed that the Egyptians and the Sumerians had either a common origin or were influenced in their formative periods by some other, third party. Evidently Petrie saw the people of the Gulf islands fulfilling this role; perhaps he took his Herodotus more seriously than other scholars have done. His reference to the Gulf people's role in the founding of the Phoenician cities of the Levant coast, derived from Herodotus and so dismissed by many scholars in the earlier years of this century, has recently received support as a result of researches arising from renewed interest in the archaeology of Bahrain.

Another scholar of a time slightly earlier than that in which Petrie was active, who toyed with the idea that Bahrain might have had some special, insular significance to the Egyptians, was Cecil H. Smith of the British Museum. In a discussion following the presentation of a paper by Theodore Bent to the Royal Geographical Society after his visit to Bahrain in 1889, Smith suggested that 'To Nefer', the Egyptian name for the land of Punt, one of the most frequent loci cited in later times as the home of the gods, might in fact mean 'the holy island'. Earlier still, in the first scholarly analysis of ancient Dilmun in modern times, Sir Henry Creswick Rawlinson in his commentary on Durand's report 'On the antiquity of the Bahrain Islands' in 1880 observed that 'Dilmun' might convey the meaning 'The Blessed Isle'. This attribution of holiness to Dilmun is crucial to an understanding of its character. It was the primeval, archetypal Holy Land to the Sumerians and, it may be suspected, perhaps to other still earlier peoples who may have lived in the Gulf and eastern Arabia.

In Sumerian texts which celebrate Dilmun various epithets are customarily attached to it, by which it is represented as a paradisial place where the gods dwelt and in which numerous acts of creation took place. It is called the Land of Crossing, the Land where the Sun Rises (for the Land is situated in the Sea of the Rising Sun) and throughout its literature particular emphasis is placed on Dilmun's purity:

> The Land Dilmun is a clean place,
> That place is clean, that place is bright.

Above all else, Dilmun is a pure place, perhaps even *the* pure place. Dilmun was *Meskillag*, 'the land of pure decrees', and one of its tutelary goddesses was named *Ninsikilla*, the Lady of Pure Decrees.

From the earliest times the Egyptians seem to have maintained the idea that many of the beliefs and events which characterized their 'culture' – to employ a term which, of course, they would not have recognized – had their origins in a far distant island. The evidence for this belief is contained in various collections of texts and inscriptions including the Pyramid Texts, some of which certainly descend from Predynastic times, the inscriptions of the Horus Temple at Edfu, which, though Ptolemaic in date, incorporate much earlier material, and the inscriptions of the Thoth Temple at Hermopolis, which may also contain early records or recollections of the Egyptian people. It would appear from these texts that the Egyptians preserved, however faintly, memories of an island, far distant towards the east, on the edge of the world, where the first and most crucial acts of creation occurred and where the first and second generation of gods had their home.

One of the most frequent symbols for the first land to emerge at the creation is the Primeval Hill or Mound. Its location is sometimes explicitly marine in character: thus in the Pyramid Texts, Utterance 484 speaks of 'the Primeval Hill in the midst of the sea'. The land here is specifically a sea-girt island and not a hillock of mud revealed by the withdrawal of the waters of the inundation which has so often been described as the first land to appear at the Creation. The Primeval Place was the Island of Rest, or of Peace.

The Island of Peace was associated with the rising sun; then it became 'the Island of Flame'. It was the Divine Emerging Island which appeared from the Abyss of primeval waters, personified as *Nun*, the oldest of the gods according to some theologies. In this context the Primeval Hill sometimes was called Ta-Tanen; Tanen was the god of the Primeval Mound in Memphite theology and a recursor of Ptah. He was also regarded, like his Sumerian counterpart, Enki, as a god of the depths. From the Island of Flame (or Fire) came, in the very beginning, *Hiké* the personification of the vital essence which to Egyptians was the basis of life. The island was a magical place, far distant to the east, beyond the limits of the world, a place of everlasting light where the gods were born. As King Pepi remarks, 'I go up this eastern side of the sky where the gods were born' (PT, Utterance 265). In the great incantation which forms Utterances 273/4 of the Pyramid Texts, in which the deified King leaps into Heaven and consumes the other gods in a celestial cannibal rite, the text proclaims the magical nature of the Island of Fire:

The King is the Bull of Sky,
who conquers at will,
who lives on the being of every god,
who eats their entrails,
Even of those who come with their bodies full
of magic,
From the Island of Fire.

The gods are said 'to give an island' to the justified Osiris and Egyptian legend spoke of 'Middle Island', an unknown, distant locality which was reached by the boat of Anty, the ferryman, who carried passengers to the island like Sursunabi, Ziusundra's ferryman, who carried Gilgamesh to seek the Ancient who had been translated to Dilmun by the gods after the Flood. Anty plays a somewhat equivocal role in the dispute of Horus and Set, for when the tribunal hearing the evidence of the two gods' contention decides to remove its hearing to a remote and distant island, Anty the ferryman is instructed not to provide Isis with a passage to the island. The goddess bribes Anty, however, and by a deplorable piece of trickery secures the verdict in favour of her son, Horus, at the expense of Set. Set incidentally was the Lord of Asia and particularly of lands to the east of Egypt. There were many ferrymen who feature in the Pyramid Texts; several of them are associated with regions to the east. Thus Utterance 359 observes:

O Re, commend me to the ferryman of the Winding Waterway, so that he may bring me his ferryboat ... in which he ferries the gods ... to the eastern side of the sky.

One of Horus's titles is 'Horus of the Land of Sunrise'. He is often saluted as Horus of the Horizon (Harakhte) in which the horizon signifies the land of light, the mountains to the east of Egypt, at the eastern edge of the earth.

The island was repeatedly identified as a place of reeds; the land there was marshy. One of its names, as we learn from the Book of the Dead, was the Field of Reeds of the Blessed. This, too, is said to be located on the eastern edge of the world.

Both the Egyptians and the Sumerians sustained the most affectionate memories of their earliest shrines or temples, which were built of reeds. Thus the Edfu temple, in its innermost recesses reproduces the archetypal reed shrine in stone; the Sumerians, on the other hand, immortalized in their poetry Ziusundra's reed hut, to the walls of which Enki whispered the warnings of the Deluge to come.

249

At the creation, according to the Edfu inscriptions, the creator spirits brought into existence a number of sacred places of which the first two were 'the Mound of the Radiant One' and 'the Island of Re'. Others included the High Hill, the Oil-Tree, and the Place of Ghosts.

The land contiguous to the original island was called Wetjeset-Neter. Other names by which the island was known in the beginning, as well as the Island of Peace, were the Island of Trampling and the Island of Combat. The island first lay in darkness surrounded by the primeval waters called Wa'ret. Its original inhabitants and sovereigns were falcons. Horus, who was saluted as Lord of the Land of Sunrise, was represented as a divine falcon.

Adjacent to the Wa'ret were several sacred places: the pay-lands. These included the Island of Fury. The island was the site of the archetypal temple and is to be recognized as the Homeland of the Early Primeval Ones.

According to the Hermopolitan myths the sun god himself was born in a pool which existed on the Primeval Island. In the Edfu texts the island itself is called the 'Pool which came into existence at the Beginning'. The island was the nucleus of the world. The gods who emerged in this period were the Most Aged Ones of the Primeval Time. The pool stood on the edge of the island; it was surrounded by reeds. The island was known to be the realm of the falcons.

It seems that the island was associated with the idea of the death of an early generation or company of gods; the gods were killed, it appears, in some form of battle. The island may have become their tomb. The falcons who were the island's original rulers became associated with its funerary customs, this recalling the early generation of gods who met their deaths there. The idea of islands as numinous places and of their funerary nature seems thus to be particularly ancient.

The lands in the vicinity of the island were known, as we have seen, as pay-lands. The creator brought them into existence by drying up the water around the place of origins and so exposing the land. He went on to create the world.

Then the creator, who is now revealed as Tanen and his companion, the Falcon, seem to have made a journey through the Wa'ret which took in some of the pay-lands. They appear to have set out on their journey from the island. There is no indication at this point that the Falcon is divine; it seems that he assumes or is granted divinity at a somewhat later stage. Tanen, however, is a god.

The island is the Place of the Ancestors. In the Edfu tradition the ancestors came from places far distant from Edfu itself, which is concerned to present itself as the home of the Egyptian people. Indeed, the assumption of such ancestor gods as their own was part of the Edfu's campaign in asserting its claim to be recognized as the Egyptian homeland.

The first temple of the Falcon is recognized as originating in the Blessed Island of the Child. The temple itself is identified with the Primeval Mound, the Divine Emerging Island. The Primeval Mound is, as we have seen, identical with the Pure Land, one of the most frequently employed epithets of Dilmun.

There is another curious parallel, or perhaps it is simply a coincidence. One of the most frequently repeated glyphs in the iconography of, for example, the seals which are perhaps the most important artefacts to survive from the Gulf settlements of the late third/early second millennium BC, is the foot or footprint, a symbol which indeed also appears in Meso-potamia in the earliest times. In Egypt, by contrast with Mesopotamia and the Gulf, the hieroglyph which represents the foot is shown in profile; it means 'place' or 'position' and also represents the consonant 'b'. However, there is a special usage of the hieroglyph in the Pyramid Texts, though employed very rarely, according to Gardiner, the compiler of *Egyptian Grammar*, where it appears as a compound. The compound consists of the foot with a jar from which water is pouring. The meaning here, accord-ing to Gardiner, is 'Pure', 'Clean', as in Utterance 513 from the Pyramid Texts:

> Be pure: occupy your seat in the Bark of Re: row over the sky and mount up to the distant ones: row with the imperishable stars, navigate with the Unwearying Stars.

One of Enki's shrines is described as 'the clean place' and 'pure' and the idea of distant journeying (albeit to the far-off stars) is compelling, at least in the context of a review which started out on this voyage through the Egyptians' perceptions of their island connections. The association with purity and water is also notable.

There is, at present, no archaeological evidence to support the idea of direct contact between the Gulf people and the early Egyptians before the end of the third millennium; but the newly developed study of the early Gulf cultures, in which Bahrain-Dilmun plays so essential a role, will perhaps produce such evidence. It may even be that the common denominator between the Sumerians and the Egyptians will prove to be the people who became the Dilmunites. It is possible that the texts' concern with the pay-lands, the process of their drying up, the wanderings of Tanen and the Falcon, and the repetition of the island motif might represent the memory of a disturbed and precarious period in the people's history, when they were living in the Arabian peninsula, near the Gulf, perhaps around the perimeter of the al-Rub al-Khali or in its vicinity. Late Neolithic populations (who were very skilled workers in stone) flourished there and lacustrine conditions persisted well into late prehistoric times around the edges of what is now the Empty Quarter; eventually the waters of the Gulf withdrew, leaving the land the desert it is today.

Whilst, as several scholars have suggested, the Mesopotamian mace may have played a part in the unification of the Two Lands (if the Two Lands actually existed) by the Falcon prince from This in Upper Egypt, there is no evidence for an invasion or anything like it in the period immediately before the unification. In the light of later history it seems more likely that what Mesopotamian influences there are in Egypt and, perhaps, what recollections there may be of the Primeval Island in the Egyptian consciousness, were implanted by relatively small bands of men, traders perhaps or refugees from a dying environment. It probably only needed one of them to be an exceptionally accomplished and persuasive raconteur for his stories of life in the far distant Land of the Sunrise to make a profound, even a lasting impression, on his hearers, particularly if his audience comprised the able chief of a lively congeries of clans and his close associates.

Finally, the mention of the power of story-telling prompts the recollection of the Enchanted Island, of which the shipwrecked sailor told so marvellous a tale. He had been voyaging to the mines (where were those mines located, one would like to ask, that he had to sail so far to reach them?) when a storm destroyed his ship and, alone of all his companions, he was cast up on the shores of a lonely island. There he was most graciously received by the island's divinity, a human-headed serpent of a notably kindly disposition, who was bedecked in gold and lapis lazuli. The serpent-king introduced himself as one of the rulers of Punt; this appears to be the only occasion when Punt is identified as an island. The serpent-king courteously declined the offer of the sacrifices of asses, which, rather surprisingly, the sailor proposed to him. Well he might refuse it, if Punt proves to be located in or adjacent to east Arabia, for the asses of the Hasa province have long been famous.

When the sailor eventually left the island he was loaded with treasures by the generous serpent. To anyone acquainted with the customary merchandise of Dilmun's traders the gifts make familiar reading for they are all products for which the island's trade was later celebrated: perfumes, ivory, rare woods, and, very strikingly, baboons, though what an Egyptian was to do with such animals in which his own land abounded is not clear. The sailor was also presented with hunting dogs. This too is remarkable in that Anubis, who, in certain of his manifestations was undoubtedly the prick-eared, fleet Egyptian hound, is proclaimed as 'Anubis who presided over the Pure Land' (PT, Utterance 437). Since, in several of his forms, Anubis is a god of the dead, this utterance seems to link a funerary divinity with the Pure Land of myth. The serpent-king returned the sailor safely to the residence of the King of Egypt, which he reached after a *sea-voyage of two months*. Even in the Middle Kingdom, when this engaging story was first written down, magical islands in far-away seas still exercised a fascination for the Egyptians.

It would be foolish to assert that *all* references to islands in Egyptian religious or mythological texts must refer to Dilmun; indeed it may be that none refers specifically to it. Even such references as there are, are certainly not precise; the island probably existed in the dimension of myth more often than being fixed anywhere on the earth's surface. But it is not impossible that the recollection of a sacred island, which may have become Dilmun, was a direct inheritance or was handed on to the Egyptians by a third party. Then it was conflated with the natural tendency of a riverine people to think in terms of the great waters of their river withdrawing to reveal an island at the beginning of the sequence of creation.

It is, however, difficult to identify any island with a reputation for special sanctity, of great significance as a burial place, lying far away to the east of Egypt which so precisely matches the required topography as does Bahrain. If Bahrain is Dilmun, the Sacred Pure Land of later Sumerian myth, then Bahrain's topography, its central mountain, a large natural pool, reed-lined shores, and its proximity to Arabia's *sabkha* (all of which are indeed elements of Bahrain's topography) may be something more than merely suggestive in the context of the emerging of the earliest Egyptian community and its own ideas of its origins. None the less there is one serious reservation which must be made about Bahrain's claims to be 'To Nefer', the Egyptians' land of origins. This has to do with the chronology of Arabian Gulf archaeology.

Dilmun, the Sumerian land of primeval innocence and abundance and the focus of much of the cities' overseas marketing campaigns, features in Sumerian records as early as the latter part of the Uruk and the Jemdet Nasr periods. Uruk is comparable with Naqada I, whilst Jemdet Nasr, at the very end of the fourth millennium, coincides with Naqada II. However, it seems likely that at this time Dilmun really meant eastern Arabia, which was often embraced within Dilmun's dominion in later times. Thus far at least no unequivocal fourth- or early-third-millennium material has been excavated from Bahraini sites. One Jemdet Nasr seal was recorded from a grave at Al Hajjar, an important burial site in Bahrain, but it seems likely that this was some sort of heirloom or talisman; it had been recut since its original making. Early-third-millennium material has been recovered in considerable quantities from east Arabia, and numerous Ubaid sites, dating back into the fifth millennium, are well known there.

There seems to have been an important early settlement near Abqaiq in eastern Arabia and another on the island of Tarut; the settlement of islands is one of the most characteristic models of early habitation in the Arabian Gulf. Tarut has not yet been excavated extensively, but the Danish expeditions which first visited the sites there in the 1950s and 1960s reported significant evidence of early periods on the *upper* levels of the principal mound in Tarut itself, suggesting a long history of occupation.

Later, without doubt, Bahrain *was* Dilmun and was celebrated throughout Sumer for its sanctity and for its numinous character. By then, of course, the time of the foundation of Egypt had long passed and it may be that the earliest recollection of the Egyptian people was of an otherwise undifferentiated island in that distant, eastern sea.

All of this, of course, does nothing to explain the mechanism by which the several and in so many ways crucially important influences from Mesopotamia actually reached Egypt. The rich repertory of designs featuring high-prowed Mesopotamian-style boats on the knife from Jebel el-Arak and on the walls of the great tomb at Hierakonpolis were obviously very significant to the people who were active in recording their preoccupations at the end of the Predynastic, in which influences from Mesopotamia came flooding into the Valley.

It is clear from the archaeological evidence that trading contact had been established between the Valley people, the proto-Egyptians, and people who had dealings (though at how many removes must be unknown) with others who had access to shells which are only found in the Arabian Gulf and to lapis lazuli, the wonderful blue stone so much favoured by the ancients, which comes only from a site in the province of Badakhshan in what is now northern Afghanistan. Both of these exotic materials are found in Predynastic Egypt; the Gulf shells are known from Badarian times and lapis from Naqada I. The question is how they got there.

The Mesopotamians, Sumerians, and Gulf people alike were adventurous and far-ranging seamen. The Egyptians were not, sensibly preferring to stay in their well-favoured Valley. Trade never achieved the sophistication or the extent in Egypt that it did in eastern lands; so much was easily to hand in Egypt anyway that there was no need to explore unknown regions in search of metals, stone, or other materials, other than, to a degree, timber for their larger vessels and the fine woods which, from the earliest times, were used in the decoration of their mansions, of daily living as much as of eternity. The Egyptians generally seem rather to have despised trade and those who practised it. Their naturally aristocratic predisposition seems to have inclined them rather to farming and the harvesting of the Valley's natural abundance.

The crucial question is whether the products of the east reached Egypt by a sea route, or over land. The sea route, though the run from the head of the Gulf to the central Red Sea looks formidable, is entirely feasible. Sailing south from Sumer the prevailing winds would carry the craft, which were quite substantial and capable of bearing, for example, twenty tons of merchandise, down to Bahrain, on to the northern Oman coast, skirting the copper port of Umm an-Nar, round the towering headland of Ras Musandam, down the Omani coast, and out into the Arabian Sea. The currents prevailing in the northern Indian Ocean would now take over and carry the craft along the southern Arabian coast to the Bab al-Mandab, at the entrance to the Red Sea. Here the temptation must have been strong to leave the open sea and beat up the enclosed waters of the Red Sea, heading north. The eastern shore (the west coast of what is now Saudi Arabia) must have been less favoured than the western or Egyptian littoral though the fact that the 'western Arabians' portrayed in the Jubba-style rock carvings found near the west coast, at Bi'r Hima north of Jiddah (plate 69b) carry weapons which are not only like those of their Egyptian contemporaries but are also markedly similar to those depicted in the art of late-fourth-millennium/early-third-millennium Sumer, suggests that contact of some sort had long existed (Zarius *et al.*, 1980).

The frequency of representations of boats and seamen with Meso-potamian connections has inclined observers always to favour the sea route as the most likely means of access for Sumerian ideas and influences to have reached Egypt. This is supported by the enthusiasm with which the divinities of both peoples, the Egyptians and the Sumerians, identified themselves with sailing. The 'sacred barque' was an important component of the rituals of both peoples: Sumerian gods are constantly shown sailing the marshes and rivers of their land and representations of sacred boats are frequent in Egypt from the earliest times, where, as has already been noted, the Mesopotamian type of boat, distinct in profile from the Egyptian, is early regarded as worthy of particular representation. Both sets of gods were accustomed to visit each other by boat, in Egypt's case sailing on the Nile, in Sumer's often traversing the canals which linked the cities. Water was profoundly important in the mythology of both peoples: in both cases, creation began in the deep and the creator god was, in various manifestations, the god of the Deep or the Abyss, Atum or Nun in Egypt, Enki in Sumer.

Though the sea route appears the easier, in fact a land route across

Arabia, from east to west, is just as feasible, given the circumstances of the late fourth millennium, as one by sea skirting the coast. It would also be a good deal shorter. Nor is it necessary to think exclusively in terms of a route which would run across the northern Arabian deserts, from the headlands of the Gulf or from the extreme southern Mesopotamian cities towards Gaza, then permitting the traveller to drop down through Palestine and enter Egypt from Sinai and the northern gates of the Two Lands.

In the sixth and fifth millennia BC, and perhaps from much earlier still, there was, all the evidence now suggests, a significant population in eastern Arabia and particularly in the south-eastern quadrant of the peninsula. Then lakes and substantial marine transgressions, running inland from the Gulf, allowed a larger faunal population, including man, to flourish. It has been suggested that the people of this region were ancestral to the people who made Ubaid pottery in Mesopotamian centres like Ur, called, for convenience, the Ubaidians; they, in turn, were probably ancestral to the Sumerians. They were in all probability well established around the periphery of the Rub al-Khali and especially in what is now northern Oman. But gradually, perhaps through excessive hunting, perhaps through the destruction of trees by the action of the domesticated goat or by human agency, the climate began to deteriorate and the desert, represented in Egyptian mythology by Set, the god of confusion and Lord of the East, began to move in towards the areas which previously had been able to support a population of men and animals. It probably happened quite quickly and in its happening is an object lesson for the present day. In a generation or two, certainly well within the memory of men who could recall the stories of their grandfathers, it is possible that the people were forced to move, some eastwards and then north, others westwards along the edges of the dying lakes. These would reach the Red Sea; then the journey to Egypt would once more face the people of south-eastern Arabia as it had perhaps already faced some who had gone on the long sea route.

In addition to whatever significance the islands of the Gulf may have had to the proto-Egyptians and their Ubaidian contemporaries it is possible that Oman was an important location for them both. The funerary architecture of Oman is the most developed at this date of any comparable culture in the Gulf. Many of the elements which are known from the Wadi Hammamat rock drawings can be detected in Oman; so they can in south-western Arabia. It may be speculated that the people who produced them moved westwards, from the Omani fringes of the Empty Quarter.

Some of these elements, like the tall high-feathered headdress worn by warriors, are also found in fourth-millennium Persia and, later on, in Oman.

Influences from Elam abound in early Egyptian art and there is no doubt that the people of south-western Persia, too, made a contribution to the rich culture which was then soon to develop into dynastic Egypt.

There is another factor in the putative history of relations between these embryonic states, in the time before history: this is the part played by trade and the agents of trade, the travelling merchants.

Trade, in the form of the exchange of goods and the acquisition of raw or source materials, is of immense antiquity. Tools and artefacts of the high Stone Age were traded over considerable distances. Once man in the Near East had developed his economy, as a consequence of his management of water resources, animals, and plants, to the point at which it produced surplus and the leisure in which individuals could practise their particular skills and develop crafts, the conditions for sophisticated trade came into existence.

The Sumerians lived in a land largely bereft of natural resources. Their cities, from at least the early fourth millennium onwards, were flourishing communities whose inhabitants were lively, creative, and acquisitive people. To the Sumerian, as ingenious as a bedouin in his ability to survive in a hostile environment and to condition it, the world around him – deserts, sea, and mountain – was his market place. In reaching out beyond the confines of the Valley of his twin rivers to find the wood and stone which it lacked, he made contact with all the peoples around him and, no doubt, astonished them by the sophistication and subtlety of his manners, conditioned already by a first flowering literature of incomparable quality, as much as by the products which he brought with him on his travels.

In historic times the Gulf played the major role in international trade, particularly in the third millennium and the early centuries of the second. The lapis lazuli and the Arabian Gulf shells found in Egyptian Naqada I and II contexts were presumably the products of this wide-randing trade in still earlier times.

Several seals of Mesopotamian provenance and attributable to the Jemdet Nasr period at the end of the fourth millennium have been found in Egypt and are no doubt also to be associated with the presence of traders in the Nile Valley. Seals were devised, originally in all probability in Anatolia, as a means of identification; the seal is cut with a design in negative or intaglio and, when pressed or rolled out on clay, imprints a positive impression. The Mesopotamians and the Gulf people were great makers of seals and many of them are of outstanding beauty and interest.

The Egyptians were relatively late into seal production; when they did produce them, typically, they devised a most individual, even idiosyncratic format. This was the scaraboid seal, a stamp seal with its reverse in the

257

shape of the dung beetle, in hieroglyphs a potent image for 'being'. The scarab, though it is known during the Old Kingdom, really only came into its own after the Old Kingdom's collapse and appears in quantity during the hiatus in Egyptian history known as the First Intermediate Period towards the end of the third millennium. During this time there were considerable incursions into the Valley from the east and Asiatics, including no doubt Arabians, began to infest Egypt. This is, perhaps coincidentally, the time of the greatest mercantile activity by the Dilmun merchants and the Mesopotamian and Indus Valley traders based on the Bahrain Islands. Egyptian scarabs, probably dating from this period or a little later at the beginning of the Middle Kingdom, have been found in Bahrain although unfortunately these have not yet been published; they are in the keeping of the Bahrain Museum. Some Dilmun seals (plate 105), normally a most distinctive type, the reverse being a raised, domed boss, criss-crossed with sets of parallel lines, with pierced circle ornament, have been found in Kuwait with scaraboid reverses, though with their faces engraved with customary Gulf designs. Clearly there was some contact, probably through the medium of the merchants, with Egypt at this time at least.

Whether such contact represented the continuation of a longer two-way trading relationship is unclear, however. There is as yet no certain evidence of Egyptian artefacts or influence in Sumer or the Gulf at the time when the eastern lands were evidently making so profound a contribution to Egypt. This negative evidence may in fact support the idea that the Mesopotamians' principal route was by sea; the prevailing currents would carry ships westwards along the Arabian coast but the return journey, if it were attempted, would be hazardous and very difficult.

The early traders of Mesopotamia, India-Pakistan, Anatolia, and the Levant were quite prepared to found small colonies, perhaps little more than ethnic or linguistic ghettos, in the cities with which they traded. There seems to have been a long-lasting tradition of the merchant houses establishing branches in foreign cities, which acted both as buying and selling agencies and as bankers, providing facilities, for example, for the bearers of letters of credit from the head office.

There is no definite evidence of such a practice in Egypt; trade was never the consuming interest to the more aristocratic Egyptians that it was to their more commercially-minded Sumerian contemporaries. Egypt was richly, even abundantly supplied with every gift of the gods; she rarely needed to import materials excepting those, like lapis lazuli for example, that by some divine oversight had been omitted from her own catalogue of riches, or the merely novel products like those of Cretan or Asiatic craftsmen whose exotic charm would add another dimension to the home of a well-placed official or the palace of a prince.

But there is no reason to doubt that Mesopotamian traders or their agents reached Egypt, nor that, equally likely, they established permanent or semi-permanent bases in the Valley. Egypt must have seemed an exceptionally favoured region of the world to people accustomed to the much less well-endowed lands of Sumer and the east.

Clearly close contact with Mesopotamia and with Arabia or the Gulf did not last long; it may have been spasmodic during Naqada I and more frequent and extensive during Naqada II. In the decades immediately around the traditional date of the unification of the Two Lands, in the thirty-second century BC, these contacts seem to have reached their climax, then diminished, ultimately ceasing entirely. It will already have been seen that the trade in lapis may be the benchmark for the contact and its absence for its cessation. Lapis does not appear again in Egyptian contexts after the middle of the First Dynasty until comparatively late in the Old Kingdom.

Much of the evidence for contact with western Asiatic ideas that does exist is visual and is connected with the Kingship. It must at least be possible that the princes who created the unified Kingdom out of the Two Lands into which Egypt was perhaps notionally divided were supported by migrants from Sumer. It seems unlikely that the early Kings were themselves Sumerian or indeed any sort of aliens. Though their names are strange they are not un-Egyptian; most of them are representative of animals, whether totem or fetish. The possibility must not be entirely dismissed, of course, that they are aliases concealing non-Egyptian identities, but there is no evidence to support this suggestion.

Amongst the more prominent of the bearers of Sumerian ideas into the Valley must have been at least one with a notable architectural bent, for he was able to persuade the Kings to adopt a Jemdet Nasr fortified palace façade as their badge and to introduce a very un-Egyptian style of recessed and panelled façade on their most important buildings, palaces, and tombs. These elements are the most extraordinary of all the assimilations by Egypt of Sumerian forms, suggesting a really profound degree of influence by the easterners.

The practice of the ritual holocausts of attendants at the burials of the Kings has already been noted as fundamentally un-Egyptian. The practice is, of course, well known in Africa, that singular continent from which Egypt drew most of her vitality, inspiration, and mystery. It is also known from Sumer, where the death pits of Ur and Kish contained rich burials of royal or sacred personages attended by dozens of retainers, guards, and courtiers. But the Sumerian examples are from a time long after the custom had died out in Egypt, late in the Second Dynasty. The Ur burials are dated *c.* 2500 BC by which time the humane and life-rejoicing Old Kingdom was in full and splendid swing. There is evidence from the Epic of Gilgamesh, that towering monument of Sumerian literary genius, of the practice existing in still earlier times in Sumer, for the death of Gilgamesh, King of Uruk, in the twenty-seventh century BC seems to have been the occasion, at least as it is recorded in verse, for the sacrifice of many of his intimates. The possibility cannot be dismissed that the custom had far earlier antecedents still in Sumer, reaching back into the fourth millennium, but for that the evidence has disappeared or has simply not been found. Such, indeed, are the hazards of archaeology.

If the custom was another Sumerian importation it may be appreciated why it was eventually discarded by the Egyptians, though with their usual caution and dislike of change they took their time about doing so. It might also explain the execration which marked later generations' attitudes to the First Dynasty Kings and also, perhaps, why their tombs and those of their officers, were burned in such intense conflagrations.

Poised at the point where the late Predynastic period emerges into the First Dynasty is the great tomb at Hierakonpolis. The painting which decorates the tomb's walls is justly celebrated; its iconography, however, is obscure. What is clear about it, however, is that many of the elements in the painting are part of the common currency of the designs which, from the earliest times to the end of the third millennium, were typical, not so much of Mesopotamia (though they did indeed feature there), but of the Gulf. The confronted animals, the bovine turning back its head, the whirling birds, horned beasts, and the two warriors with the bucklers are all typical of the art of the Gulf, Elam, and Oman (plates 106a, 106b, and 106c). But although the Gulf, its islands, and the Arabian mainland were certainly identified with funerary cults and monuments of remarkable complexity and scale there is no evidence that they practised the killing of attendants in the burials of their Kings.

Recent research in the Arabian Gulf states has begun to bring into question one of the previously held assumptions about contacts between Mesopotamia and Egypt, even when they were admitted to have existed. On the basis of all the available evidence it appeared clear to earlier scholars that the influences ran in one direction only, from Sumer westwards to Egypt, by whatever route. The only objects of clear alien provenance were found at Egyptian sites whilst the Sumerian (or, strictly speaking, in terms of the favoured chronological parallels, the late Uruk or Jemdet Nasr) influences in art and architecture were there for all to see in the years immediately before the generally accepted date of the unification of Egypt and the beginning of the First Dynasty. Now the situation is beginning to change; it is no longer so clear cut.

In addition to the Egyptian or Egyptianizing seals described earlier a most important site in the north of Bahrain has yielded evidence of what was at least contact with Egyptian products if not with Egypt or Egyptians. This is the remarkable site of Barbar, where three temples superimposed one upon the other, dating from the late third to the early second millennia have been excavated. A group of fine alabaster jars found in Temple II have long been recognized as Egyptian (plate 107). However, they have been considered again by the scholar who has studied the Barbar site most extensively and analysed its chronology and associations; he remarks that 'the rim of one is not only rare but also restricted to the Fifth and Sixth Dynasties in Egypt' (Mortensen, 1971).

In the courtyard of the second temple at Barbar, which is now dated to the last years of the third millennium, were found three large, roughly hewn stones, with rounded heads. These were originally thought to have been used for tethering the sacrificial animals; the stones were pierced through and the holes showed wear, caused, it was thought, by the ropes by which the animals were held. However, an earlier suggestion has recently been resuscitated: that these stones are, in fact, anchors (plate 108). Those most immediately comparable to the examples found in Bahrain, amongst a type of artefact which is common to the seafaring nations of antiquity, are similarly to be dated to the end of the third millennium. It is reported that 'almost identical anchor stones have been found in Egypt, where they have been used secondarily in connection with bull offerings, e.g. at Saqqara in front of the tomb of Mereruka, dating to the Sixth Dynasty (2320–2160 BC)'. The association with bulls is suggestive, for bulls seem to have been of special importance in the cults of the ancient Gulf.

It is of course far too early to claim any convincing proof that these latest findings indicate an Egyptian presence, or, at the least, any form of contact between the Dilmunites of the late third/early second millennia and the Egyptians of the late Old Kingdom and the First Intermediate Period. Yet this is precisely when one would expect to find the evidence of contact, for at this time the Dilmunites were in control of a powerful and wide-ranging trade network which touched, if it did not include, most of the principal trading routes in the known world. The appearance of the scarab seal in substantial quantity at this time *could* be further evidence of this contact.

A further enigma remains to be resolved at Barbar. The most important features of the site throughout its long history, extending over 6–700 years, seem to have been the various holy wells which were sunk there and which evidently formed one of the principal elements both in the site's architecture and in the rituals which were practised there.

The well of the Second Temple is the best preserved on the site today, though that of Temple III has not yet been excavated. The well of Temple II is a handsome square chamber, built of finely cut limestone blocks, none of which is particularly large. It opens to a flight of processional stairs leading up to the main terrace of the temple from the waters which rise from a perpetual spring in the chamber's floor. The spring is still active today (plate 109).

The limestone blocks of which the chamber is constructed are quite atypical of the architecture of Dilmun-Bahrain at the time, to the extent at least that it is known. It is equally quite unlike the construction of buildings in Sumer, at this period late in the third millennium. Sumerian architects in the third millennium tended always to work in brick and rarely in stone; stone was used in sacred buildings in Sumer in earlier times, conventionally dated to the fourth millennium, a thousand years before, apparently, the date of the second temple at Barbar. The same small well-cut blocks can be seen at Barbar in the revetted oval retaining wall which supports the platform on which the temples were built (plate 110).

It can only be a matter of speculation as to the origins of the men who built the Barbar temple. It is tempting, however, to see in them men who shared the same tradition as those who built the great, eccentrically shaped tomb for Khasekhemui at Abydos (plate 111), where the stone courses of the tomb chamber look remarkably like those at Barbar. But again chronology suggests a hiatus of nearly a thousand years between the two structures.

Most remarkable of all, of course, is the fact that at Barbar an oval mound lies at the heart of the temple structures, just as it does at the temple site at Hierakonpolis and in several Sumerian sites. If the implications to be drawn from these apparent coincidences in form are substantiated, they would be quite staggering. The problem of chronology in the case of Barbar remains, but the similarity in the architectural technique in the walling of the Barbar chamber and Khasekhemui's, the oval mounds at Barbar and Hierakonpolis, and the 'anchors', begins to present a formidable case for the presence in Bahrain of builders who shared their traditions with Egypt.

What is becoming certain, however, is that contrary to what was earlier believed there *is* material Egyptian evidence to be found in the Gulf; it cannot yet be said that this suggests an Egyptian presence but there can be no doubt that either the people of the Gulf and the Egyptians of the late third millennium were in touch with each other, or each with a third party. As excavation on the many Gulf sites which remain to be investigated is undertaken it may be expected that more evidence of contact with Egypt will appear. If it does, it will no doubt cluster around the late third/early second millennia; in which case it may throw some further light on to the chronology of Egypt itself.

The evidence for contact and inspiration between Sumer and Egypt, though tending to become increasingly definite, is still amorphous and often obscure. Any consideration of the role which the Gulf and the Gulf islands may have played must be totally speculative at this stage. Yet there seems still to be for the Egyptians the memory of a distant land, an island on the edge of the world, God's land, the Land of Sunrise where, in the mist-enshrouded days of fable and folklore memorable events occurred which, with their repetition over generation by generation, acquired the characteristic of the marvellous and the mysterious. The recollection spills out from that deep well of the human psyche, the unconscious, at its most potent and enduring when it encounters events or individuals who contribute to its own archetypes. Such may have been the case in the days when men were still in a highly experimental stage of societal living and, in Egypt and Sumer, harnessing what they identified as powers of limitless potency. For we are dealing, after all, as both peoples testified, with that time before time, the time of the gods.

101 Lion in ivory.
(Fitzwilliam Museum,
Cambridge)

102 Boys' games

103 The triad of three standing figures constantly occurs in early Egyptian art and, in forms such as the father, mother, and child, throughout Egyptian history. This group, representing perhaps the products of a late Predynastic sub-culture (since in form they are quite unprecedented) are male, female, and sexually undifferentiated. The male figure has been thermoluminescence dated to 3200 BC.

104 The three figures again appear on this seal from Failaka in the bay of Kuwait in the northern Arabian Gulf. The two large figures seem to be wearing long robes: the smaller one, leaping out of the boat, is evidently nude. (Seal impression)

105 Stamp seals, dating from late in the third millennium BC to early in the second, from Bahrain in the Arabian Gulf. (The Bahrain Museum)

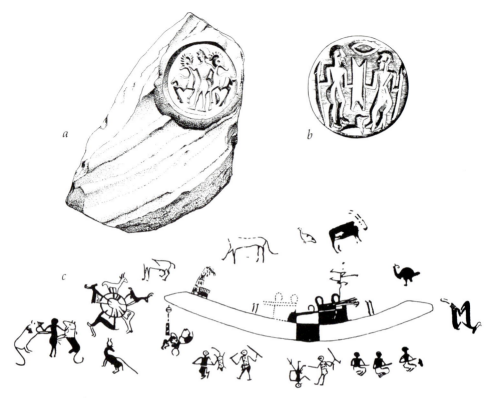

106a, *106b*, and *106c* Certain elements in the Tomb 100 painting from Hierakonpolis are particularly identified with the art of Elam and, later, of the Arabian Gulf. These are the warriors with the buckler and the hero subduing animals.

107 These alabaster jars were excavated from the great third millennium temple site at Barbar, Bahrain. The largest of the three is of a type which is known from Egypt in the late Old Kingdom.

108 On the terrace of the second temple at Barbar (c.2200 BC) were found these
rounded, pierced stones. It has been suggested that they are anchors, presumably
with some cultic significance. Similar examples were found at Mereruka's tomb
at Saqqara. (Photograph, Michael Rice)

109 The use of small stone
blocks in the lining of the
lustral basin or sacred well at
Barbar, Bahrain is typical of
early third millennium
monumental architecture.
(Photograph, Michael Rice)

110 The central mound at the Barbar Temple is enclosed by a semi-circular retaining wall or revetment. It is reminiscent of the earlier and very distant structure at Hierakonpolis. (Photograph, Department of Antiquities, Bahrain)

111 The stone walls in the tomb attributed to King Khasekhemui at Abydos are surprisingly similar in shape, size, and alignment to those in the Barbar temple (cf. plate 109).

6

C. G. Jung and the Egyptian experience

At various times during his long and remarkably creative life C. G. Jung seems to have felt himself strongly drawn to Egypt. As a boy he had ideas of becoming an archaeologist and developed a precocious interest in Assyriology and Egyptology; however, there was no faculty at that time for the study of archaeology in his local university of Basle and so he turned to one of the two professions which had always engaged his family, medicine (the other was the Church and hence, perhaps, his lifelong concern with the religious motivation). It is difficult to imagine that Jung would have made so universal a contribution to the understanding of the nature of man as he did, had he become an archaeologist rather than a doctor, who turned his attention early to the yet infant study of the human psyche. To this study he was to give a particular direction, specifically in the field which has become generally known as 'analytical psychology'.

Jung's contribution to the development of a science of human nature was many-levelled. In particular he identified and defined the role of the collective unconscious, the common psychological inheritance of all men living, from all men of the past. He was, of course, profoundly aware of the importance of dreaming but he saw the dream as a repository of the unconscious heritage; he was as strongly moved by the repetition of identical or directly related symbols in different ages and cultures. Although he came under Freud's influence early on in his career as an alienist, he broke with him over the older man's insistence on the paramountcy of sexuality in determining psychological characteristics or disturbances. Jung did not undervalue the importance of sexuality but preferred to relate it to the whole persona, seeing it as a part, not as the whole. Throughout his career he explored regions of human experience which he believed came out of the unconscious. To the Freudian and the rationalist many of these seemed arcane, even bizarre: alchemy, astrology, the foreshadowing of the future by events or dreams, even the phenomenon of unidentified flying objects, all came under Jung's serene but penetrating and inspired scrutiny. But of course Jung's use of such material did not necessarily imply either his acceptance or even his belief in it.

Much more directly than Sigmund Freud, Jung seems to have understood that there was a deep and very special stratum of experience underlying the familiar stereotype of 'ancient Egypt'. Even in the early years of the century this stereotype was already well formed and it tended to prejudice an understanding of the unique nature of the Egyptian experience, certainly of the experience of the earliest periods. To Freud, responding naturally to his own Jewish cultural heritage, Akhenaton and Moses were the most arresting figures of pre-exilic times. To Freud, Akhenaton was the initiator of the concept of monotheism, which seemed, in the intellectual judgement of the time, both to anticipate and to find its fullest flowering in the Old Testament version of the intervention of the divine in human affairs.

But Akhenaton was not 'the first monotheist'. The idea of the one, all-pervading divinity, the first cause, is deeply ingrained in Egypt, having its origins in times long before the Eighteenth Dynasty and probably having its roots in the Predynastic cultures of the Valley.

Jung, descended from solid Swiss Protestant stock (his father was a parson) was not so God-driven as his Viennese colleague and his recognition of the deep levels of the human consciousness and, in particular, of the collective unconscious drew him on to speculate about pre-conscious levels and the nature of the 'primitive'. This was a word which Jung employs perhaps a little too freely for today's taste when speaking of societies which had still, in his time, escaped the full consequence of western cultural expansionism. However that may be, Jung came closer to apprehending the nature of pristine societies than any observer before him. Not only did he appreciate the quality of such societies and of the people who comprised them, but he also appreciated, with exceptional insight, the significance which the understanding of such societies had for the world of his own day.

Jung seems only to have visited Egypt on one occasion, in 1925. This was towards the end of his journey to Africa, an experience which was evidently of great importance to him, undergone at a time of his life when he was under great stress and in need of psychic renewal. The impact of Africa on him was evidently profound, though he does not seem to have written of his Egyptian visit, other than in letters to some of his correspondents, until *Memories, Dreams and Recollections* was published in 1959. Of course, he too was a creature of his time and of his own cultural heritage, which inevitably influenced, though it did not imprison him. One consequence, however, of the attitude which characterized African society as 'primitive' was to think of the experience of the Africans whom he met (as well, evidently, as the Arabs) as being on a level of cultural development less advanced than that of his own European background. In setting out for Africa, he recalled in *Memories, Dreams and Recollections*, 'The desire then grew in me to carry the historical comparison still further by descending to a still lower cultural level.' This was to be sought in 'Africa where one meets men of other epochs'.

When he actually set off for Egypt he came to the country from the south, travelling up from east Africa, observing that he wished 'to approach this cultural realm ... from the South, from the sources of the Nile. I was less interested in the complex Asiatic elements in Egyptian culture than in the Hamitic contribution.' Jung's remarkable perception of the essentially African character of Egypt is clearly demonstrated by this observation, but he does not appear to have written further about his actual experience of Egypt during his journey there.

However he continued to meditate on Egypt and on the particular nature of the Egyptian psyche. The most extended consideration is recorded in the *Collected Letters*, in which many of his references to Egypt are contained; this deals with that special nature of Egyptian psychology in high antiquity. Writing to Frau Johanna Michaelis he said:

> Your questions are not easy to answer. Your conjecture that Ancient Egyptian psychology was somehow fundamentally different from ours is probably right. Those millennia had indeed different problems. On one side a torpid impersonal unconsciousness reigned, on the other a revealed consciousness, or a consciousness inspired from within and hence derived directly from the Gods, personified in Pharaoh. He was the self and individual of the people. The spirit came from above. The tension between above and below was undoubtedly extreme, hence the opposite could be held together by means of equally rigid forms. The duality of the ruler is based on the primitive belief that the placenta is the brother of the new born child which as such often accompanies him throughout life in ghostly fashion, since it dies early and is ceremonially buried. (C/f Levi Strauss 'Primitives and the Supernatural'). The Ka is probably a descendant of the placenta.
>
> White and red are sacred colours in India too, for instance the temple walls are painted with white and red stripes. What they mean is not clear to me. Your interpretation as light and blood is extremely probable but one should have historical proofs.

The tension between above and below in ancient Egypt is in my opinion the real source of the Near Eastern saviour figures, whose patriarch is Osiris. He is also the source of the idea of an individual (immortal) soul. The purpose of nearly all rebirth rites is to unite the above with the below.

(vol. 1, pp. 259–60)

This letter, written in 1939, seems central to Jung's view of Egypt. The idea that the King represented the individuality of the Egyptian people, their 'self', is telling, as is Jung's awareness of the balance of opposites which was always one of the most important marks of the Egyptian psyche in social organization, religious belief, and art. The suggestion that the placenta represents the King's twin would provide a reasonable explanation for its place in the line of royal standards borne before the Archaic kings; indeed, it is the only wholly convincing explanation for the appearance of the placenta in Egyptian rituals of the Archaic period.

However, Jung overestimates here, as he does in other contexts, the role of Osiris; far from being the 'patriarch' of 'Near Eastern saviour figures', Osiris is a relative latecomer, for whose cult on any extensive or national scale there is no evidence until late in the Old Kingdom times. Atum, Geb, or even Ptah and Re would be more convincing candidates in Egypt, whilst there are more formidable contenders still, if one is looking for early patriarchal figures in Sumerian myth.

Jung was much impressed by the figure of Osiris as the dying god, reborn in his son; he saw him as the father god who brings into being his own son and successor. The King of Egypt was not identified with Osiris until after death and then only from late Old Kingdom times; he could hardly have had such an identification any earlier and there is no evidence that the King was linked with any of the native Egyptian divinities with whom Osiris was later equated, like Wepwawet and Khentiamentiu. Jung justified his belief in the influence of Osiris by attributing the origins of his cult to approximately 4000 BC. In this, of course, he was out by some 2,000 years, the consequence of relying on the very high chronologies popular in his younger days. In another context he gives the same date for the beginning of writing.

One result of his African journey was the observation that the cult of Horus was that of the 'newly risen divine light', the first light at dawn, the glimmer on the eastern horizon. This is the worship of Horus of the Horizon, Harakhte, though its significance in Egypt was probably greater later than it had been in earlier times. In the New Kingdom, for example, it was believed that the Sphinx represented Harmachis, another manifestation of Horus in the Horizon, and it was worshipped as such. Jung observed the remarkable phenomenon of the Nile baboons who seem to wait for the first rays of the sun and then rise and greet its glory. This moment is brilliantly captured in the great temple of Abu Simbel (one of the few commendable details about that otherwise overblown structure) where a line of cynocephalus baboons is depicted on a frieze at the top of the temple's façade. The baboons sit on their haunches, their paws raised, clapping the sun's rays as they strike them when the temple is bathed in the first light of dawn. The allegorical significance of the baboons' action is not in the least diminished by the knowledge that their response is primarily physiological, for the animals are in fact wakening themselves and boosting their circulation, torpid after the night's sleep. Jung identified the phenomenon with the worship of Horus, an entirely accurate observation, in fact.

The sensitivity of the Egyptians to the world around them and their capacity for synthesizing disparate phenomena into a single poetic image is nowhere better demonstrated than in this celebration of the first light of dawn, the importance of which was so instinctively, even intuitively, understood by Jung when he visited east Africa. The Egyptians were, in a quite literal sense, enchanted by the band of light which appears at the eastern horizon heralding the appearance of the sun each day. They told themselves that the god was returning after surviving the perils of the night as he travelled in his divine barque through the Underworld. As they were pragmatists as well as poets it is not essential to think that the Egyptians actually believed this, or, indeed, any of their engaging myths.

The moment when the dawn spreads up the eastern sky is a magical one in Egypt, to this day. The whole world falls silent, all created things seem poised and motionless, the very air, no matter how balmy, is palpable. The light on the eastern horizon is strange, milky white, tinged with saffron and pale violet, spreading its radiance rapidly, intensifying in colour as it does so. Then, with the impact of a shout breaking the silence, the sun surges up from the horizon, swinging rapidly into the sky to begin his progress in daily triumph.

Jung is in error, though a relatively minor one, writing of the early myths of Egypt when in *Aion*, a relatively late work subtitled *Researches into the Phenomenology of the Self* he describes Horus and Set as brothers and cites them as 'the ancient Egypt pair of hostile brothers, the sacrificer and the sacrificed'. His confusion of Set with Osiris is in itself interesting; in fact Horus is Set's nephew in all but the most obscure versions of the myths involving the two gods. But he is disposed to see the two contenders,

Horus and Set, as types of the twins, linking them with Gemini. In no early Egyptian myth can Horus be said to be Set's sacrificer; indeed the two are reconciled in the end at the instigation of the high gods.

In his letter to Frau Michaelis Jung makes reference to her views on the significance of red and white. These colours were of profound importance in Egypt. Red was the colour associated with the north, whilst white was the colour of the south. The two were always maintained in opposition and always paired: the red and white crowns, the red and white houses (for their respective centres of government), even the White Land and the Red Land. It is clear that Jung did not appreciate fully the potent symbolism that red and white would have conveyed to an Egyptian, but it is very much to be doubted if that symbolism would have encompassed light and blood. On another occasion Jung was to come nearer to the Egyptian idea of the two colours when he referred to the alchemical notion of red and white as 'the Royal Pair', opposites perpetually destined to unite.

The scepticism with which Jung has sometimes been regarded by some of the more harshly materialistic practitioners of the analytical disciplines, because of his preparedness to admit into his consideration some of the more arcane areas of human experience, speculation, or fantasy, has been noted. His interest in alchemy, for example, which, in a peculiarly penetrating way, illuminates certain bypaths of the human soul's search for identity, has brought some of his more creative speculations into something approaching disrepute, particularly amongst Freudians. None the less, such bypaths, though they may be lush and overgrown, can lead to some compelling insights. In particular Jung was inspired when he saw alchemy as the latest product of ancient Egypt, passing through the mediation of the Gnostics.

In one case at least, however, it must be acknowledged that many will see Jung as coming perilously close to unbridled fantasy when he describes the chaos and distress at the time of the collapse of the Old Kingdom in Egypt at the end of the third millennium as evidence of the transition from one house to another in the sequence of the Universal Zodiac. This was an idea which seems always to have had a special meaning and significance to him, as he returns to it on several occasions. In speaking of the uncertainties of his own day he often attributed them to the fact that the world was passing from the sign of Pisces to that of Aquarius, a transition bringing in its train changes which he considered as calamitous as those which heralded the transition from Taurus to Aries, around the year 2000 BC, when the Old Kingdom ended (*Letters*, vol. 2, p. 225).

He saw these periods, when the universe is conceived as moving from one sign in the great zodiac to another (just as the solar zodiac moves from one to the next through the twelve signs), at intervals somewhat in excess of 2,000-year periods, as times of particular distress and melancholy when cataclysmic events are likely to beset mankind. Jung described these periods as 'transitions between the aeons'. The order of the 'houses' in the Universal Zodiac is the reverse of those in the solar. The duration of the Universal Zodiac is said to be some 26,000 years.

So far as we know, knowledge of the Universal Zodiac, if indeed it may be presumed to exist at all outside the imaginations of astrologers and magi, does not extend back into the third millennium but seems to have been first defined in late antiquity. To give it validity it is necessary to understand the principle of the Precession of the Equinoxes, which was apparently only recognized in Hellenistic times. It was, however, inevitable that to Jung, as to anyone who follows his ideas with sympathy, the recurrence of symbols associated with certain of the signs in the several epochs, will be compelling, even irresistible. The twins, bulls, rams, and fish all feature in the catalogue of ancient symbolism and all were important to Jung as enduring evidence of the repetition of forms throughout human experience.

During most of Jung's lifetime a somewhat less formalistic approach to archaeology would have prevailed than would generally be the case today. The disposition towards the mystical in human experience, the preparedness to admit the significance of what people might commonly describe as the occult, would have led him, naturally, to a view of early Egypt determined by a belief in the profound levels of consciousness to which the individual psyche may have access but probably is unable to recognize. His view of the Egyptian Kingship would seem generally to lend weight to this view.

However, in one particular Jung's concept of analytical psychology would seem to be specially pertinent to the study of the emergence of a society as highly individual as Egypt in its first flowering. Though it can only be expressed through analogy it is none the less revealing; it must however be emphasized that nothing in his writings explicitly permits the extension of Jung's theories relating to the individual psyche to the emergence of a state organization, whether Egypt's or any other. None the less, the exceptional quality of the Egyptian experience, which he himself recognized, the rapid development of sophisticated institutions, rituals, hierarchies, and canons of belief, supported by the outflowing of a stream of what can only be recognized as classic Jungian archetypes make it possible to identify something very like an emerging 'self' in Archaic Egyptian society. In considering Jung's response to Egypt it is illuminating

275

to examine the nature of early Egyptian society in terms of some of the postulates of analytical psychology, which he defined.

Thus, it is possible in these terms to speculate about the drives which lie below Egypt's early flowering of art and the creation of the first fully realized artistic tradition allied to emergent nationhood, in the history of man. In doing so it will be well to acknowledge the problems attendant on any attempt to relate the findings of one discipline to the study of another, a procedure which often results in something like an attempt to count apples with pears. In this case, however, it is tempting (and, more, it is revealing) to draw a comparison between what appear to be the processes at work in the earliest appearance of the Egyptian state together with the arts which flourished there, and the condition known to the Jungian canon as *individuation*. Whilst it can only serve as a metaphor, it is surely permissible to draw some analogy between the experience of the individual growing to self-awareness and the emergence of the first fully articulated nation state, for the state may be considered to be the 'self' of the extended group.

It should be possible to do this, if only because, in the case of Egypt, so much of the actual procedures of development can be traced. It is also a witness to the truth that states, even those which manifest such extraordinary characteristics as Egypt in its early centuries, are man-made.

The concept of individuation, as expressed originally by Jung, describes the progress towards maturity experienced by the self, in the course of which the self acquires awareness of its own individuality, its own separate existence, distinct from its fellows. This procedure is comparable with the transition to self-awareness which the Nile Valley culture seems to have undergone, particularly in the period from the end of the fourth millennium to the last part of the third.

Individuation marks the transition from the collective experience and from the pervasive influence of the collective unconscious to the identification by the individual of specific and distinct responses to his environment, at all levels. The collective unconscious is, according to Jung, to be found at work in all societies and at all ages; its identification was amongst the most profound insights of the century. Jung saw the collective unconscious as constituting 'a common psychic substrate of a suprapersonal nature which is present in every one of us'. He was deeply interested both in myth and in the development of early societies. But he, like Freud, tended to consider only the evidence presented by the more accessible models of ancient society, which any reasonably well-educated individual of their generation might have been expected to know: the Jews of the Old Testament, and the Greeks for example. The earliest society for example that Freud reviewed at all in depth, was the Egypt of the New Kingdom, well on into the second millennium BC.

But the experience of such societies was, by the standards of Egypt in the Archaic period and the early Old Kingdom, vitiated by the influence of other peoples whose ideas and ideologies had been formed in circumstances at odds with those which persisted in Egypt at the beginning of the historic period. Given the cultural traditions in which Freud in particular and even Jung grew up, their idea of the historic Archaic experience of man would inevitably be limited and circumscribed. Even now, to many people the myths and legends contained in the Old Testament stand for the remotest history of man. Since the Old Testament books are largely the product of the second half of the first millennium BC they have in fact little value in tracing the early social origins of mankind.

Both Jung and Freud suffered from the relatively common error that proposes a special *historical* value for the Old Testament simply because the inexorable and incomprehensible workings of chance have given it a special importance in the cultural heritage of the society which has been dominant in Europe since the Reformation, and to a lesser degree of significance, in pre-Reformation times. It is this fact which has confused so many attempts to relate the books of the Bible to the events of history. The Hebrews of the Old Testament, for example, may be important to societies like those of the Christian west, but they were of relatively little importance in the world, the events of which the Old Testament purports to relate.

The Christian experience is generally irrelevant to any analysis either of the conditioning factors or of the responses which they provoked which were experienced by men living in societies formed in the period immediately after the invention of writing and the creation of sophisticated political structures. To make any attempt at such an analysis it is essential, with all the hazards involved, to try to establish some of the parameters of the consciousness of men living in this third millennium, to speculate on such evidence as may be thought to survive and on the less conscious factors which influenced them.

Jung demonstrated that the concept of the collective unconscious casts light on many of the less rational or otherwise inexplicable apprehensions and motivations of the human psyche at its most profound level. In a pristine society such as Egypt's it should be possible to see it at work in a way quite different from the experience of later cultures. The collective unconscious is the fountain from which the archetypes flow, that concept so close to the Platonic vision of the *eidos*. The collective unconscious in

Egypt would, in this view, be especially powerful and as pristine a phenomenon as the society itself.

To apply the idea of individuation to Egypt in the earliest centuries of its corporate existence is not, of course, to deny the role of the individual, nor the variety and diversity of the specific experiences undergone by all the individuals then living in the Valley. But in the collective phase of their experience may be found an explanation for the swift and apparently ready acceptance of forms, customs, beliefs, and social organization over extended distances and time-scales, which are evident at this time and which are otherwise difficult to explain. It is even possible that the Egyptians had some sense, in this early phase, of the psychological implications of the transition from the collective unconsciousness to the individual; this would account for their personification of the strange, indeterminate, bisexual divinity called Atum, who is sometimes spoken of as the 'Undifferentiated One'.

A telling parallel between the experience of individuation at the level of the individual self and what was happening collectively in Egypt at this time is demonstrated by the appearance of an almost obsessional pairing, the constant linking of apparent opposites in everything concerned with the emergent Egyptian state. As Jung observed,

> It is a psychological fact that as soon as we touch on these identifications we enter the realm of the syzygies, the paired opposites, where the One is never separated from the Other, its antithesis. It is a field of personal experience which leads directly to the experience of individuation, the attainment of the self.... In this matter words and ideas count for little. This realm is so entirely one of immediate experience that it cannot be captured by any formula but can only be hinted at, to one who already knows.
>
> (*Collected Works*, vol. 9, p. 106)

Jung also called individuation a 'mysterious conjunction, the self being experienced as a nuptial union of opposite halves'.

It is also to this phase of the experience that the widespread idea of the Twins belongs: the pair of something more than mortal beings, like Gilgamesh and Enkidu (the most potent example of the type), who encapsulate different, often opposing characteristics but yet are ineluctably bound together, two halves, almost, of some more total being. To the same idea belongs Plato's charming fairy tale of the Golden Age when the human race consisted of dual beings who, their felicity incurring the always spiteful jealousy of the gods, were divided by them and now roam the world, each looking for his (or her) pair.

1 Seen from space, as in this NASA photograph, the Nile Valley to the west and the Arabian peninsula to the east, bordered by the Red Sea and the Arabian Gulf, are clearly part of the same region. Contact between the Valley and people who at least knew the Arabian Gulf and the lands of Elam, in south western Persia and, possibly, Sumer in southern Iraq, seems less improbable when seen from this perspective. Given a moderately more benign climate in antiquity even the crossing of the Arabian peninsular is feasible, augmenting both the well-attested northern route, first into Palestine and then descending southwards to Egypt, and the sea-route, circumnavigating the peninsular.

II An eerie sense of menace is conveyed by this carving in bone (or schist) of a grotesquely elongated figure of a masked or hooded man from El Amra, from the Naqada I period. Men with the same enveloping hoods are occasionally depicted on early palettes. The high crown of the hood, with its rounded peak, may represent the origins of the tall white crown of the south; thus this figure may be an early southern prince, a chief perhaps, or divinely endowed shaman. (Musée Guimet D'Histoire Naturelle)

III The most splendid of all the icons to be recovered from Hierakonpolis must surely be this superb head of a hawk in beaten gold, with inset obsidian eyes. Hierakonpolis ('Hawk City') was consecrated to the royal cult of the hawk. Nothing could so perfectly encapsulate cult and city as this artefact, originally part of a large figure of the falcon god, made of wood and overlaid with gold, in the Sixth Dynasty. The identification of the divine Kingship with the falcon was a propaganda stroke of the most assured genius. (Photograph, Roger Wood)

IV Large quantities of carved ivories were found at Hierakonpolis, more than have ever been found at any other, comparable site. In some cases workmanship of the ivories, such as this plaque, does not at first sight look typically Egyptian. (From the main deposit at Hierakonpolis; University College Museum, London, UC14864)

V Some stone vessels are embellished with gold, presumably for the use of royal or noble owners. They can display a rather precious tendency to over-sophistication. (University College Museum, London UCL 15630, 15737)

VI In the First Dynasty the noble dead frequently took with them stone (or occasionally bone) discs on which hunting scenes are engraved, or as in this example, inset in coloured stones. They are pierced centrally, presumably so that they may be spun like a top, the hounds then appearing to chase the quarry for all eternity. (The Egyptian Museum, Cairo; photograph, Roger Wood)

VII A group of large mud brick tombs was built along the escarpment at Saqqara, looking down onto the Memphis plain. Virtually all the First Dynasty Kings are represented by sealings, though now it is thought that the tombs probably belonged to great nobles rather than to the sovereigns themselves. The architectural style, particularly the recessed panelling, is markedly foreign to Egypt and has its most obvious parallels in Sumerian temple façades. (Photograph, John Ross)

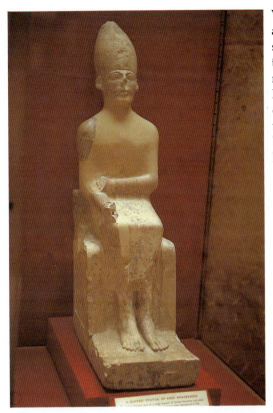

VIII In one of the first attempts — and surely a superbly successful one — in the history of art to produce a monumental portrait statue, King Khasekhem is shown ceremonially robed and wearing the White Crown of Upper Egypt. (Ashmolean Museum, Oxford)

IX In Nefer's tomb was found an intact and exceptionally well-preserved mummy, one of the oldest in Egypt and without doubt the most handsome. The head would be clearly recognizable to anyone who knew him in life, while the body seems to have preserved even its soft tissues. It is not clear by what process this remarkable result was achieved. (Deutsches Archaologisches Institut, Cairo, F. 5419; photograph, *Daily Telegraph*)

X The careful laying of the small stone blocks in the courses of the Step Pyramid, ultimately intended to be enclosed in a polished limestone skin, is impressive. It is a testimony to the industry which went into their quarrying and shaping.

XI (*opposite*) The most majestic artefact to survive from the early dynasties is this near lifesize painted limestone figure of King Djoser Neterikhet, of the Third Dynasty, lord of the Step Pyramid. It was found in its original setting, the *serdab*, a small chapel on the north face of the Pyramid. (Egyptian Museum, Cairo; photograph, Roger Wood)

XII The quality of the furniture and equipment buried with Queen Hetepheres is superlative. These probably represent the sort of accoutrements which would have accompanied her on a progress around the Kingdom and thus were appropriate for use on her last journey of all. The sheer elegance and restraint of the design of the whole suite is exceptional. (Egyptian Museum, Cairo; photograph, Roger Wood)

In this remarkable Egyptian preoccupation with dualism, the idea that everything has its counterpart or opposite, even the King himself was conceived as a twin. In the ancient world twins were always regarded as uncanny, the possessors of unusual powers and distinctly odd. The Egyptians believed that at the time of the fashioning of the King prior to his birth, a task discharged by the ram-headed god Khnum who had charge of such matters, his twin was created and translated at once to the Beyond, where he existed in a sort of parallel existence to the King's. It should be noted that the royal twin is not the same as the *Ka*, an etheric double possessed by everyone. The idea of the twin as the eternal counterpart of the living King is another African, probably originally Nilotic, concept.

Another striking demonstration of this idea of the dual identity of the King is provided by his invocation as the 'two-dwellers-in-the-palace; that is Horus and Set'. Here the King seems to be accepted as the personification of the two eternal opposites, the two perpetually warring ancient divinities who are only reconciled in his person. The queen was 'she who looks on Horus and Set'; only the great Khasekhemui ('the Two Powers are Reconciled') proclaimed the resolution of this duality of personality in his throne name. By proclaiming it in the *serekh*, surmounted by both the falcon of Horus and hound of Set, he proclaimed in a sense the twinship of the two gods, though not in terms of their notional kinship, for Horus was Set's nephew, at least in the explanation provided by Memphite theologians.

In Egypt this need to reconcile apparent opposites is one of the most explicit elements in the formulation of the early Pharaonic state. The Two Lands, the union of Upper and Lower Egypt, the Horus of the north and the Horus of the south, the two contenders, Horus and Set, the pairs of gods and goddesses at their creation, the Lions of Yesterday and Tomorrow, the shrines of Upper and Lower Egypt, the Two Ladies (one of the royal titles referring to the tutelary goddesses of the Kingdoms), the Two Crowns, even the remarkable repetition of red and white symbolism in the crowns, palaces, and the lands themselves, all conspire to emphasize the dual nature of the state which was evolving on the Nile's bank and the conscious expression of that duality by the people most intimately involved with it. Even at the King's coronation pairs of individuals representing the crafts which powered the economic life of Egypt appeared before the King: milkmaids, butchers, and cabinet makers, for example, two by two like characters in a nursery rhyme.

With the experience of individuation on a national scale came a streaming out of the archetypes, which is a phenomenon of the condition for, as Jung states, 'in this still very obscure field of psychological experience, where we are in direct contact, so to speak, with the archetype, its psychic power is felt in full force'. In early Egypt many of the archetypes are already apparent in the art of the time, particularly the art associated with the King and the state; they are already dominant and immensely powerful, having their origins in a past far removed from the time even of the unification. Jung defined the archetypes, in the context of the collective unconscious, as 'archaic or – I would say – primordial types, with universal images which have existed since the remotest times'.

The King was the centre of the universe; sometimes indeed he was simply titled 'Lord of All', an honorific otherwise held by the great and exalted god Ptah. In early times one of the royal titles was *ity* which seems to be associated with the idea of fatherhood; the King was father of his people, just as he was their shepherd and, occasionally, their herdsman. This last idea is obviously connected with the cattle cults of the peoples of the remoter reaches of the Nile Valley from whom the dynastic Egyptians were in large part descended. The people were sometimes called 'the cattle of god'.

The creation of the Egyptian state and the extraordinary psychic (in the analytical sense) forces which it released, produced a rich treasury of archetypal images. The gods themselves are archetypal, both as abstractions and, in their latest form, as humans writ large. But first of all the characteristic Egyptian archetype is the King himself, the Lord, not merely of the Two Lands but of all the gods, of the entire universe itself, if the Egyptians had been capable of conceiving of so vast a structure, beyond the central and sufficient fact of their own Valley. The Egyptians invented the idea of the Divine King, or at least elevated it to a supreme and audacious degree; no man before the Kings of unified Egypt remotely approached their splendid paramountcy. In creating the idea of the all-powerful King, isolated in majesty, the Egyptians were laying down for later ages the idea of the all-powerful god, enthroned and remote. The King is followed by the Magus, the High Priest, Master of the Mysteries, the Great Wise One, sometimes the King himself, sometimes his coadjutor, the healer who has the power to reverse time and unmake the world. The most typical example of this archetype is Ptah of Memphis, the supreme craftsman-god.

The relatively developed concepts of the King and the Magus are attended by the flock of Egyptian animal archetypes, each displaying not only his own potent nature, but also symbolic of some larger dimension. The tremendous bull, the majestic lion, both early symbols of the King, the swift hound, Horus the soaring falcon, the exemplar of Kingship itself, the alert and watchful dog, the baboon, an entire menagerie of zoomorphs surged out of the subconscious of the emerging Egyptian personality. As Jung again observed, 'The archetypes are the imperishable elements of the unconscious but they change their shape continuously.' The Egyptians were not, of course, the first to employ animal forms to express ideas so profound that they were beyond words, even beyond abstract symbols, but they fixed them so completely that no mythology could ever equal either their endurance or their penetration.

Amongst the most conforming and comforting of all archetypal shapes is the pyramid. It goes along with the circle, perhaps with the square. Its significance to the Egyptians can be gauged by the fact that, even in the Predynastic age, centuries before the pyramids themselves were built, paintings depicted lines of triangular hills on Naqada II pottery, suggesting the shape already lay somewhere deep in the Egyptian psyche. As noted earlier, three triangular hills in hieroglyphic form signified 'foreign country'. The actual construction of the pyramids is, in the sense that it represents the fulfilment of so profound an archetypal experience, the culmination of the first period of Egypt's existence as a nation.

In the world of the preconscious Egyptian experience there was not a great deal of room, it would seem, for the expression of the female principle. There is no great universal mother in Egypt, no chthonic earth goddess; when goddesses become important they are tricky, unpredictable, and one of the earliest of them known by name, Neith of Sais, is a warrior, distant and destructive. Male gods dominate the Egyptian world and it is only in Egypt's decline that the female principle becomes overt. Other than perhaps in the Badarian period, the Great Goddess archetype, so notable in many early societies, is not of particular force in Egypt. Later, Hathor and Isis, images of the Mother in bovine and human form, appear but both tend to be subservient to male divinities.

Egypt's decline, her gradual descent from the unimaginable heights of the third-millennium experience to the haunted shells of the temples of later times, parallels the individual's progress towards maturity and beyond. Once maturity was reached the period comparable with that of individuation was left behind. Egypt's coherence and the integrity of her pristine personality began to fragment, never to be wholly rejoined. In the time of the early Middle Kingdom Kings, whilst the earlier periods were still, as it were, in sight, some elements of immemorial Egypt were retained. But soon alien influences virtually swamped the Valley, corrupting for ever the unique experience that was Egypt in its first flowering.

To understand the aspirations of early Egyptian creative artists and administrators it would be rewarding to know of what an Egyptian of culture and substance, living in the time of the early dynasties, dreamed. The interest of such a question is not merely frivolous or prurient, though presumably the Egyptian dreamer went through the repertory of violence, sex, apprehension, and fantasy familiar from all succeeding generations. But the point, of course, is that the Egyptian would have dreamed only of what lay deep in his own unconscious (as indeed we all do) but that unconscious was both pristine and untrammelled. Moreover the impressions which he would have received from without would, in the early centuries, have been wholly integrated with him, the influences of his own natural and secure environment. Significantly, the Egyptians seem to have been well aware of the importance of dreaming and frequently return to it in their stories and folk-lore.

The Egyptians were the first nation to leave behind a coherent, highly developed, multifaceted art practised over an extended period. To appreciate their art it is necessary to recognize that they were highly responsive to the influences of the world around them but it was almost entirely a secure and tranquil world, ordered and safe. In this they were very different from their Sumerian contemporaries over to the east, involved in a world determined by the vagaries of two unpredictable rivers and the whims of a college of largely hostile divinities.

In contrast to the Sumerian experience, monsters rarely manifest themselves in Egyptian art; when they do they seem almost invariably to be Mesopotamian in inspiration, like the serpo-pards of the Archaic palettes. They are confined largely to the period of the unification, itself a time of turbulence and alien influence. Scenes of violence occur but they are somehow ritualized, like the representation of Horus presenting the King with his decapitated enemies on the Narmer Palette, or the defeated foes on the throne base on which Khasekhem sits, who seem to be tossed away in the winds of some violent storm (plate 51a). In this, incidentally, they are very like some of the characters in what appear to be battle scenes portrayed on Elamite and Susian seals of the same or a slightly earlier period.

Expressing a profound insight, Thomas Mann, a creative genius who himself consciously explored the process of creation throughout his artistic life, observed that 'the Ego of antiquity and its consciousness of itself was different from our own, less exclusive, less sharply defined'. Mann was writing in the context of the work of Sigmund Freud whose theories of psychoanalysis have only a limited relevance to the understanding of the psychology of high antiquity. But the truth which Mann expressed is fundamental to an understanding of the processes which were at work in the creative output of the men of the earliest high cultures. In particular the lack of exclusiveness of the Ego of which he writes is markedly true of the Archaic Egyptian personality. The Egyptian of the early periods is simply less individualized than has come to be expected from someone living in a highly cultured, well structured, and organizationally advanced society. The Egyptian experience of the time is still closer to the collective experience, the experience of the group, almost (though this is patently an overstatement) the experience of the species. Parallel with this collective experience, manifested also by an intense sense of 'belonging' and, perhaps paradoxically, of an identity as part of the group, was the developing awareness of the individual and the capability of the individual to express a separate identity. Initially perhaps this idea of individuality was yet another prerogative of the King and his closest companions, though doubtless it was not acknowledged in such specific terms. Throughout the later phases of the Old Kingdom, as demonstrated by the increasingly naturalistic art of the tomb reliefs for example, the emergence of the individual was evidently one of the factors which marked the most notable change in the society and which ultimately weakened the fabric of the state. At the end of the Sixth Dynasty this led to its sundering and to the distress and general misery of the years preceding the reassertion of royal authority by the founders of the Middle Kingdom. When that authority was restored it was notably different from what had gone before.

The essential and formative Egyptian experience had been that of the extended group, leavened with the occasional brilliant flash of individual genius. The images which are the common currency of Egyptian art and architectural decoration are the products, too, of the collective experience. The enduring quality, through the early reigns, of the falcon perched on the *serekh* for example, the everlasting symbol of the crowns, a poetic image like the two lions joined back to back signifying Yesterday and Tomorrow, even the falcon as the eponym of the royal clan, are all examples of this process. They are all the products of the early Egyptian collective unconscious; it is this which gives them their often mystical, faintly uncanny character.

Likewise the Egyptian gods, who are profoundly sophisticated beings, much more sharply (and, it must be said, individually) realized than, for example, their Sumerian counterparts, are the products of the Egyptian collective unconscious. This is particularly true of those who either were or were to become state divinities, of significance to the whole nation and not merely to a particular district or town. The relationship between the gods and the Egyptians of the early period was, essentially, a collective or communal relationship. There is little or no sense of a direct or personal connection between the individual, if he may be said to have existed, and the gods, other than through the person of the King. The actual process of identifying the divine in immanent form in Egypt, ranging as it appears to do through fetish, animal symbol, and finally human (or human-like) form mirrors the psyche's experience of individuation to a remarkable degree.

Innocence and a sense of collective election are fundamental elements in the ethos of the Egyptians who founded and sustained the Egyptian state in its early centuries. There is thus no sense of sin or guilt in early times, to be demonstrated by the individual. Such concepts, too, came later, again perhaps creeping in from the desert wastes, to blight the original innocence of the people of the Valley. The power of the original creation may be gauged by the consideration that the history of Egypt after the Pyramid Age is a history of decline. From its highest point, so quickly achieved and maintained with such assurance, Egypt gradually declined, though many of the outward forms remained.

The personality of the 'average' Egyptian, whilst his day-to-day concerns might seem to be remote from the ways of the gods as expressed in the obscurities of the Pyramid Texts, or, for that matter, from the ways of the Kings, supervising huge building projects designed to promote their own divinity, may yet be recognized as being substantially less differentiated from his fellows, than was the case in Egypt in later times or in other less pristine societies. The Egyptians were still close to the old collective ways of the hunting band and to the small communities which became stabilized and fixed in particular locations, as happened when the first settlers established themselves in the Valley, probably late in the sixth millennium BC. From that point onwards, culminating in the momentous events of the last quarter of the fourth millennium when the process towards unification really began, the Egyptians undertook the unprecedented course of creating a nation state, inventing in the process the paraphernalia of a complex political system and extending it over a large if relatively contained area, embracing apparently several local cultures with differing religious and social traditions. The Egyptian collective unconscious must have been dramatically activated by this process, releasing a variety of creative initiatives which, in a relatively small and closely knit community such as theirs still was, could be apprehended rapidly from, as it were, one end of the Valley to the other. It is a further tribute to the genius of the early Kings that they realized this to be the case and pursued the unification of Egypt relentlessly, ultimately to achieve it despite many setbacks and frequent disappointments.

It seems clear that many of the principles of analytical psychology can, by analogy at least, be applied to the first appearance and subsequent early development of the Egyptian state. Many of the factors which came to typify Egyptian culture and civilization can be defined and illuminated by recourse to Jungian concepts; the study of early Egyptian history can benefit to an exceptional and perhaps to a unique degree, by reason of its pristine character, from their application.

One especially provocative possibility presents itself, rising out of the more general considerations which have thus far been expressed. This is the suggestion that the phenomenon of the Divine Kingship itself, the most profound of all Egyptian inspirations, grew out of the same pristine and uncontaminated state which allowed the free flow of so many of those elements which have come to be associated with the process of individuation and which appear in such abundance in the late predynastic and Archaic periods, in the reaches of southern Egypt.

To apply the concept of individuation to the progress of a community, from its earliest expressions of self-awareness to the full engagement of all the complex elements of state politics and management, can provide a frame into which otherwise disparate and apparently inconsequential factors can be associated and made coherent. The concept works precisely because the individual in the society at this time does not yet really exist, in the sense of being a personality fully differentiated from his fellows. The beginnings of specific distinctions can however be traced: the emergence of trades and even the specializations of function within the state, though these will operate still to a very limited degree.

The Divine King is the supreme Egyptian political concept and the product of the unique Egyptian–African psyche. The idea of the Divine King emerged precisely at the point when the society over which he was to be raised was beginning its process towards the attainment of its own distinct and individual identity. But the King, once he is recognized as such, is fully individuated in name, in function, and in the numinous quality with which he and his office are already invested.

It is tempting to propose that the characteristics of the individuation process which the Egyptian state exhibits are actually designed to give expression to the King's own individuality; in this respect the King is, as Jung observed, Egypt's self and, quite properly as an extension of that idea, its paramount incarnate divinity. In the earliest periods the King's singular individuality is demonstrated most cogently by his unique experience of the survival after death; his survival ensures the continued existence and prosperity of Egypt but not of every Egyptian, the mass of whom are, as it were, subsumed in his individuality.

It is in this context, too, that the monumental public works which are so much a feature of the early centuries of the Egyptian state's existence must be considered. As the process of individuation advanced, and as the King assumed an ever more exalted position, the essential Egyptian spirit began to find expression in massive works which engaged the whole society and absorbed much of its resources. Such resources were not wasted, nor deployed extravagantly; their employment was the inescapable consequence of the burgeoning of the individuality of the Egyptian state. The monuments were, initially, the product of the need to protect and nourish the King's individuality. Later, as the individual Egyptian begins to take on a more precise outline, the role of the King diminishes, first to that of a god among gods, later still to something like the mediator between gods and men, with what amounts to little more than a sort of honorary divinity. The decline of Egypt from its pristine greatness can then be seen as part of the process of the state's realization of its own individuation.

The final seal of Egypt's progress to statehood and the full achievement of her historic personality was the creation of the Pyramids during the Third and Fourth Dynasties. The Pyramid is the supreme artefact linking earth and heaven, land and sky, the mortal and the divine, and the most powerful assimilation of light then possible to technology. The Pyramids came out of the deep levels of the unconscious of the Egyptian people and of the state in its first supreme manifestation. With their erupting into three-dimensional form Egypt was in effect, fully mature, its historic destiny achieved: all afterwards was, inevitably, decline.

The collective character of the society can also be seen in the customs attending the burial of the King. As a consequence of some extraordinary persuasion by the royal propagandists or by the evidently overwhelmingly charismatic figure of the King himself, the society was apparently prepared to accept the idea that only the King might, of right, avoid the dismal experience of death, and, as the supreme divinity, go on to an eternal existence beyond the stars, or in the easterly land of Paradise where the gods resided.

All other creatures were evidently fated only to continue to exist through him and through his survival; only by ensuring his continued existence could the future of the whole land of Egypt be preserved. The individual was nothing; Egypt, in the person of the King, subsuming all others to himself, was all. It is in this sense, particularly in the earliest years of the Kingship, that the King is Egypt's self.

This belief had in it the seeds of its own change. The idea that the people survived through the survival of the King led in time to the belief that the retainers sacrificed at the King's death (and perhaps also at the deaths of the very greatest nobles) would continue to serve, and then that proximity to the royal burial could ensure immortality for the King's family and his ministers.

Gradually the Great Ones (the nobles and high officers of the Two Kingdoms) began, particularly in the later centuries of the Old Kingdom, to adopt the forms of what had been the royal prerogatives of burial, though the example of the Helwan burials should be remembered: if indeed they do generally date to the First Dynasty, they suggest that even then it was quite possible for ordinary men to nurture hopes of immortality. Eventually, in the late period every man was his own Osiris, when that god, originally an alien in the Valley, became the symbol of regeneration and the focus of the hopes of eternal life by even the most humble servitor or tiller of the land.

The change which overcame the Egyptian view of the ceremonies appropriate after the death of the individual may also reveal an awareness of the transition from the collective to that of the individual consciousness. In the earliest times the death of the individual may not have been considered as especially significant to the community. The community, particularly in the person of its leader and personification, continued undying. As the process of individuation wore away the old communal and collective spirit of the society and the individual psyche began to flourish and to demand its own recognition, so the needs of the individual even after death began to be apprehended and all the complex industry associated with the care of the individual's immortality was brought into being.

The Egyptians have been described as a people inordinately preoccupied with death. Such an attitude misjudges them: the Egyptians were wholly preoccupied with life and with its prolongation. Death was an incident in man's experience of life; in the case of the King, death was attended by the most elaborate ritual. For all, death marked a transition from one state of being to another.

The considerable activity which was directed towards ensuring survival after death, first of the King, later of his closest assistants, and ultimately of all, had the effect no doubt of concentrating the Egyptians' minds on an acceptance of the inevitability of death. More than most people, therefore, their lives represented a preparation for the experience of dying. In thus preparing themselves they proceeded further along the path to a still more fully realized individuation.

Because they manifest a collective persona the Egyptians of this early period are, or at least seem to be, different from most people who have lived in the world after them; Jung, in the extracts quoted earlier, clearly apprehended this essential fact. Their genius is particularly expressed in the making of artefacts, from the relatively humble pottery vessel to the pyramid or the most majestic image of the Divine King; the most sublime artefact they made was Egypt itself, splendid, beautiful, and richly complex. Whilst the underlying, seemingly eternal principles of Egyptian art and design are the products of the peculiarly Egyptian collective unconscious, there is another specific manifestation of this collective stream, that body of spells, incantations, the mutterings of priests, and the first recorded inspired literary expression of the striving after the Divine, known as the Pyramid Texts.

The Pyramid Texts also enshrine collective memories. These memories are the products of the earliest aspirations of the Egyptians as a group, when they were first experiencing that sense of election which led to nationhood. Some of the texts are in the form of dialogues, demonstrating how ancient is the form of antiphonal exchange, sometimes between spirits, sometimes focusing on the King as the principal actor in the drama, sometimes in the form of exchanges between priests officiating in a complex ritual.

The Pyramid Texts are known from a series of 'editions' carved on the walls of royal tombs of the late Fifth Dynasty and the Sixth Dynasty. This was the high point of the Old Kingdom community's coherence and assurance; society then was in balance with nature and it must have seemed to be unthreatened, unchanging, and eternal. The texts do not display notable tensions such as, for example, those which the near-contemporary late Sumerian or Akkadian texts reveal; the Egyptians' characteristic state of tranquil complacency seems unimpaired until it is finally blown away with all the rest of the mooring posts of the Old Kingdom world.

The Pyramid Texts are still barely understood. The obscurity of their language and the strange images which they evoke are difficult, if not impossible, to comprehend. There is no evidence that Jung was conscious of their significance in any detail, though he probably knew of their existence. During his lifetime a version of the texts was translated by the great German Egyptologist Sethe who, though some of his interpretations have been questioned by more recent authorities, was the first to make them generally accessible to a modern audience. The exotic quality of the texts' imagery will already have been apparent in the pages of this book which describes the Egyptians' own version of the myths of origin, associated with an island far away to the east. What, one wonders, would Jung have made of these examples, taken almost at random from 'The Pyramid of Unas' (Piankoff, 1968)?

> Unas is the bull of the double brilliance in the midst of his eye. Safe is the mouth of Unas through the fiery breath, the head of Unas, through the horns of the Lord of the South. (Utterance 319)

Unas is this flower at the nose of the Great Mighty One. Unas has come out of the Isle of Fire after he has placed truth there in place of falsehood. (Utterance 249)

Unas is Babay, the Lord of Night, The Bull of Apes who lives without knowing it. (Utterance 320)

These are but three of the incantations carved in exquisite hieroglyphs on the subterranean walls of Unas' pyramid and originally infilled with a brilliant blue paste. The Unas texts, like the others which succeeded them, are a compendium of the most profound expressions of the ancient Egyptian spirit.

Jung's response to Egypt seems largely to have been stimulated by random factors of sudden insight rather than systematic study. However, in his attitude to his journey down the Nile in 1925 he seems to have come very close to penetrating the essential nature of Egypt's aboriginal and essentially African culture. It is the more surprising that he seems not to have written more extensively about his journey, though he always acknowledged the deep level of significance that he felt towards Africa. It was Egypt's African roots to which Jung most readily responded. It was precisely in those roots that the 'soul' of Egypt will be found and which provide the most productive sources of analysis. Africans seem always to have recognized the essential duality of man's nature.

Jung seems particularly to have been much taken with the complex Egyptian concepts of the psychic elements in man. The Egyptians recognized several distinct entities as different aspects of man's spiritual essence, or perhaps even as different essences. The *ba* was the soul, corresponding closely to the conventional idea of the immortal, enduring spirit possessed by everyone which would, in the later Osirian cults at least, be judged according to the individual's behaviour in life. The *ka* has been described as the 'etheric double' created at the time of the individual's conception and coexisting in a non-material order of existence. The *Kha* was the justified spirit, living in the realms of light, or in terms of a later eschatology, among the blest. The King, as described earlier, seems in addition to have had a double, a twin, who existed independently of the King's earthly life and who may have been identified with the royal placenta. The double kept, as it were, the King's place in the region beyond the Imperishable Stars, to which the King would be translated after death.

Jung thought long and deeply about that aspect of the psyche which reveals itself in dreams or in circumstances of profound trauma or near-death experience, and which seems to exist independently of space and time. In doing so he came close to that analysis, or probing of the self, which the Egyptian division of the psyche into the several parts or distinct 'selves' implies. His equation of the King with Egypt's 'self' was itself a profound insight; he clearly recognized that both the person of the King and the office of the Kingship were fundamental to the understanding of the origins of the Egyptian state and the ethos which underlay it.

Though Jung has been portrayed, as much by his admirers as by his critics, as a mystic, almost a magus (a persona which he clearly was not at all averse to assuming, for the occasion) he considered himself, first and foremost, to be a healer. In this, though he may not have been immediately aware of it himself, he comes very close indeed to one of the most singular aspects of the history of the earliest Kings of Egypt.

Most peoples, whether ancient or of more modern times, have tended always to celebrate their heroes as great warriors, preferably as conquerors. The Egyptians too, were not wholly without such pretensions, but they were outweighed by another, perhaps more ennobling trait. They admired amongst their earliest heroic figures especially Kings who were healers or who achieved their reputation by the reconciling of opposite or conflicting elements in the society over which they reigned so majestically.

Jung was aware of the power of the opposites in the structure of the Egyptian state, particularly in its formative phases. As a doctor and as a pioneer psychologist he, too, was a healer and a reconciler of opposites, expressed in the conflicting elements of his patients' personalities. He would, it is surely not too fanciful to suggest, have found much in common with the great if mysterious figures who occupied the throne of Egypt in the first brilliant centuries of its existence.

Appendix
The Egyptian hound

In memoriam
Nefer-Nefer Ru-Aten Tasheri,
a hound
born 24 August 1978, disappeared 12 November 1987,
that she might be honoured before the Great God,
Anubis.

No subsidiary burials of servants or attendants were found in Queen Her-Neith's great First Dynasty *mastaba* tomb at Saqqara, just to the south of Cairo, built during the reign of King Djer, which was excavated by Professor W. B. Emery in the 1950s. Instead the queen's sole companion on her dark journey was, in the excavator's description, a 'saluki-like' hound, buried at the threshold to the tomb (see plate 67). It is curious, to say the least, that one who in life must have been surrounded by clouds of handmaidens and attendants should have gone down into the darkness alone except for this one, eternally faithful companion.

The dog which was buried with the queen was not, in fact, a saluki nor was it very much like one. It was an example of the slender, prick-eared hound which is recorded on countless painted vases, wall reliefs, and still more monumental sculptures. Morphologically speaking, this dog is related probably only very distantly to the race of finely built hounds of which the saluki is one, which inhabits the deserts of the old world. The saluki, incidentally, probably originally inhabited the northern Arabian-Mesopotamian deserts; the early Mesopotamians often buried their dogs with them and one is known from the Ubaid period (*c.* 3800 BC) where a bone has been thoughtfully (and rather touchingly) placed near the head of the dead hound, who was buried with his master, a young boy.

Queen Her-Neith's dog is not a saluki, but rather a dog peculiar to Egypt and a part of its most ancient past. Physically the dogs are markedly different, for the saluki is generally of a lighter frame than the Egyptian hound, which is more powerfully built. The dog whose handsome profile has been recorded on Egyptian artefacts since Predynastic times appears still to exist today, though it is comparatively rare. Nowadays it is known as the Pharaoh Hound or Kelb al-Fenek. Anyone who has owned (or who has been owned by) one of these courteous, gentle, and charming dogs will recognize, for example, the 'Anubis position', that most frequent representation of canine Egyptian divinities which frequently they adopt, front paws extended, head laid along them or raised in an expression of aristocratic alertness, ears pricked or laid back: Anubis was clearly one of these, at least in some of his manifestations, though he differs from them in his glossy black coat, contrasting with the Pharaoh Hound's golden red.

Temperamentally, their character is gentle, affectionate, and, in the household, biddable; but set to the chase they revert to a more archaic wholly predatory *persona*, as, with ears pricked and tail high they hunt their prey. Then they become aloof from human contact until the urge to hunt burns itself out.

In many representations the Pharaoh Hound's tail is an important part of its equipment. The dog is shown with the tail slightly curled. This is probably the consequence of its having been docked; in its natural, untampered state the Pharaoh Hound's tail is one of its more handsome features, used to signal to its companions when it is closing on the quarry. In the best examples of the dog, the tip of the tail is flecked with white.

The Pharaoh Hound is essentially a hunting dog and a good deal is known about the methods adopted by Egyptian hunters in the management and control of their hounds and about their hunting techniques generally. These techniques were of very great antiquity, probably reaching back into late Palaeolithic times, at least, and the relationship with the immensely ancient hunting communities would still have been distinct.

Although there are many graphic references to hounds and hunting in the Predynastic and early dynastic records, the high point of the career of the Egyptian hunting dog was achieved in the Old Kingdom and early Middle Kingdom periods. The hunting techniques which are depicted on the walls of the regional governors' tombs at Beni Hasan in Middle Egypt, for example, would have been familiar at any time in the preceding ages, at least since the latter part of the third millennium.

The Egyptian hound is exceptionally fast; in this it reveals its relationship with the greyhound. The dogs were used to run down game (plate A1); they 'worried' gazelle, themselves creatures of no mean turn of speed, until the tired animal could be trapped or speared by the hunter. They would bring down quite large game by biting their hocks; even a large antelope like the oryx could be brought to bay by them with the dogs heading them into traps or corrals. Their intelligence was such that they could be trained to return to the hunter and then lead him to the injured or incapacitated animal. So exceptional was their speed that they were even trained to run down hares and to bring them back live to their masters.

The Pharaoh Hound is a sort of canine fossil, a living Egyptological survival. The breed apparently left Egypt long ago, probably coincidentally, though with a nice sense of the fitness of things, at the end of the Pharaonic period. It seems then to have disappeared until earlier this century when a small colony of the dogs was found living in isolation on the Maltese island of Gozo. Over the centuries which separated their disappearance from Egypt and their rediscovery they seem to have kept themselves wholly uncontaminated by less aristocratic animals, preferring to breed only amongst their own kind; a Pharaoh Hound bitch, even when she is on heat, seems inclined to put down with emphatic disdain the overtures of any male who is not of the breed.

The breed itself was probably developed by careful selection and cross-breeding, a practice which began in very early times; the ancient Egyptians were skilful stockmen. The dog which was the familiar companion of the Kings of Egypt was probably the product of well-matched stock from the gentle-eyed feral desert dogs (*canis familiaris*), which can still be found in Upper Egypt (plate A2), and the small Egyptian or golden jackal, producing a cross-breed called, by one Egyptological authority, *canis lupaster domesticus*. Of this type the very ancient god Wepwawet, a predecessor of Anubis, is the most familiar example.

The dog's probable descent from the jackal is suggested by several factors: its distinctive red-gold colour, its capacity as a scavenger, and its very curious practice of 'calling'. This consists of the articulation of a sort of keening moan, which the dog will sustain, varying it in pitch and tone and maintaining a dialogue with its interlocutor. This seems to be another jackal inheritance, for in the close family units of the animals in the wild, jackal parents will always recognize and respond to the call of one of their pups.

Few of the dogs survive today, but those that do are a singular and rather improbable link with the earliest days of Pharaonic Egypt, to the royal courts of which they added a touch of canine elegance. The distinctive golden-red of their coats, the colour of the god Set, whom perhaps they also symbolized, would have assured them a place in any of the major ceremonies attending the King. Their probable identification with Set is one of the most important roles displayed by an animal in the representation of the dogs of Egypt.

Set is frequently represented in Egyptian hieroglyphs and iconography by a strange, ambiguous quadruped which has variously been described as

A1

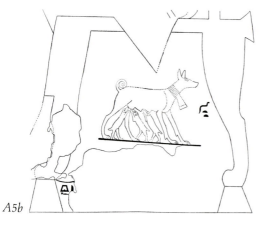

A2

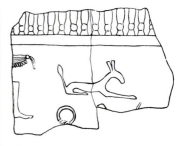

A3a

A3b

A4

A5a

A5b

A6

composite, imaginary, an okapi, a wolf, a jackal, an ass, sometimes even a dog (plate A3). There are many representations of the animal of Set: the earliest is thought to be a small ivory piece from a grave of the earliest Predynastic period, the Badarian *c.* 4000 BC. The Set animal is often shown standing up alertly, its head raised and ears pricked, its tail curving across its back. This stance is also typical of the Pharaoh Hound: the Set animal's two protuberances rising from the head, with which it is often depicted and which are frequently described as 'horns', are the large, triangular ears of the dog, which when its head is turned slightly, look remarkably like horns and not in the least like ears.

The Set animal's tail, which is often depicted held high with its extremity divided, or represented as an arrow, has greatly perplexed commentators. In fact, the method which the Egyptians adopted of showing the animal's tail is probably an example of their delight always to modify, even to obscure, reality. The best examples of the hound display a white fleck on the tip of the tail which serves as a sort of 'flag' to their companions when they have found a quarry, and this feathering of the tail may have suggested the idea of the feathers of an arrow.

Whilst those that love them will be loath to admit it, the Pharaoh Hound's least attractive physical feature is its prominent and pink fleshy nostrils which could easily be mistaken, in another beast, for a snout. This too is one of the features of the Set animal, whose muzzle, like the dog's, tends to curve somewhat, giving sometimes a rather lugubrious cast to the hound's expression. This slight arching of the dog's muzzle is one of its most distinctive characteristics, faithfully reproduced in representations of Set.

Egyptian craftsmen caught the character of the dog skilfully in their many representations of it. Though it is usually shown with its large, mobile ears raised, it often carries them flat against its head or drooping; it is sometimes depicted thus, as at Hierakonpolis where a fine carving of a hound was found amongst the many ivory carvings recovered from that early site. This portrays the long back of the animal – it is in fact slightly sway-backed – and in this case the dog's ears are down, rather than pricked up. Egyptian artists often show the dog in one of its typical stances, trotting purposefully, its long head set forward on its powerful neck.

The Pharaoh Hound's eyes are set high on its long, narrow head, giving it, particularly in full face, a curiously archaic, often rather doleful look. With its long slender muzzle and large, pointed ears pricked up, it is clearly the inspiration for other representations of Set; when represented full face or head-on, it has sometimes been mistaken for an ass.

Egyptian dogs were given elaborate names, often, like their human contemporaries, incorporating those of old interest. One owner of such a dog, Senbi the governor of Cusae in Upper Egypt, in the reign of Amenemhat I (*c.* 2000 BC) was so besotted by it that he named his hound 'Breath of Life of Senbi'. Another great prince, Serenput, the Keeper of the Southern Gate of Egypt, had himself portrayed for all eternity sitting on his chair beneath which sits, equally imperious, his hound (plate A4). Nefer, the director of the royal court at the end of the third millennium whose tomb at Saqqara was found virtually intact some twenty years ago, also has one of the dogs attending him when, with his wife, they inspected the management of their estate. Hounds are often shown at play with other domestic animals; one devours a goose beneath its master's chair (plate A5a), whilst another suckles her pups (plate A5b).

Not surprisingly for a people so wedded to the idea of the prolongation of life the Egyptians frequently ordered sumptuous obsequies in handsome tombs for their dogs, 'that', as one inscription said, the dog 'might be honoured before the great god Anubis'. In such a case, it might be presumed that Anubis would recognize one of his own.

The Egyptian hound is the first identifiable domesticated breed; the Egyptians probably called it *Tesem.* Its ancestry is obviously very ancient; apart from its probable relationship to the golden jackal its remotest ancestors were the feral dogs which attached themselves to the earliest human settlements, drawn to them by the irresistible combination of food source, companionship, and affection. They were – and indeed remain – enthusiastic and efficient scavengers, a role which they would have discharged with advantage in the courts of the Kings as much as in the hutted encampments of their earliest shared living places with man. When speaking of these remarkable animals the Egyptians said that the dog was 'one with the gods, more swift than the arrow'.

Bibliographical note

Since this book is written for the informed, intelligent, and hopefully responsive reader I thought that it would be pretentious to burden it (and him) with all the paraphernalia of notes and references. If a specialist in the field happens on it, he will know the references anyway; inserted here they are likely to do little more than bolster this otherwise quite diffident author's ego, with the semblance, if not in fact the reality, of scholarship. However, I have included a comprehensive bibliography, with all the works which I have consulted, listed in it.

The book explores an aspect of Egyptian history which seems to me to be profoundly interesting, very important, and, compared with other periods, relatively little known. In making the last observation however, I would not wish to be accused of an insensitivity to (or worse, an unawareness of) the work of professional Egyptologists who have worked in this strange and distant archaeological landscape. It is simply that for the past half-century or so, since in fact the discovery of the tomb of Tutankhamun and its treasures, attention has shifted away from the origins of Egypt to the later, perhaps more approachable periods, like the New Kingdom or the time of the Hellenized Ptolemies.

I cannot imagine anyone approaching the subject of Archaic and Pre-dynastic Egypt other than through the great gateway of that splendid series of publications launched and so tirelessly produced by Sir Flinders Petrie. Of course much of their detail has been superseded by subsequent discoveries but they are still non-pareil, without equal in their breadth, scholarship, immediacy, and presentation. The two volumes, *Royal Tombs of the First Dynasty*, set the pattern for such publications for years to come; when Emery came to write his volumes on his work at Saqqara, the best part of half a century later, Petrie's format is retained and is still valid. The stream of publications which he unleashed and which include the works of Quibell, Frith, Brunton, and many others is one of the triumphs of British scholarship.

Unfortunately the two volumes on Hierakonpolis are less thorough and, outside specialist libraries, virtually unobtainable today. Indeed they and some of the others cited have acquired an antiquarian value which is even more remarkable than their scholarly worth.

Emery's popular summary of his work at Saqqara is still in print and is invaluable though some of his ideas, on the dynastic race, for example, or the belief that the tombs he excavated at Saqqara were the burials of the Kings of the First as well as of the Second Dynasty, would not be so generally supported today as once might have been the case. The volumes that he published on his work at Saqqara are splendid and their value is greatly enhanced by the plans, perspectives, and detailed drawings which Emery, a most talented draughtsman, included in them.

Baumgartel wrote with perception and penetration about the Predynastic period, though some of her work has not gone uncriticized. I have used her extensively, though I hope with discretion; more than anyone since Petrie she wrote about the enigma of the connections between Predynastic Egypt and lands to the east – Sumer and Elam – but she perhaps over-stressed the physical similarities between the art and manufactures of the two regions. There *are* similarities but they must be viewed with caution.

The Cambridge Ancient History is curiously uneven in its treatment of Egypt before the pyramid age. This is partly the consequence of the policy of individual scholars writing each section and apparently being allowed a free rein; this results in some odd anomalies. Also the fact that the latest edition (1971) was more than twenty years in the writing means that much of the scholarship is already severely outdated. I have, in another place, drawn attention to the woeful lack of any reference, other than a single mention, to Arabia in the whole of the volume concerned with the early periods. In the context of Egypt this absence of reference to Arabia is even more deplorable.

For the art of the periods concerned, often so strange but, because it is generally not monumental, often touching and very immediate in its impact, Stevenson Smith is wholly admirable. From an earlier time Capart and De Morgan are remarkable in the comprehensive overviews they give to periods that are hardly better served today.

The catalogue of the exhibition at the Petit Palais, drawn from the museums of France and held in 1970, is incomparable, a document of the first importance, containing much material which is unfamiliar. Again, the fact that the objects included in the exhibition are generally small, adds greatly to their appeal.

The earliest periods of Egyptian history are gradually returning to the attention of scholars. The excavations at Hierakonpolis, perhaps the most important site of the Predynastic period yet to be identified, is being undertaken with daunting thoroughness by the Americans. The most active publicist amongst them, M. A. Hoffman, has published extensively, including a popular book which summarizes the work of many scholars working in all periods of Predynastic and Archaic Egypt. If it disappoints at all it is only because it is relatively reticent about current work, including that of himself and his colleagues at Hierakonpolis. This omission, however, is being repaired in the scholarly sphere with some admirable publications.

Trigger *et al.* have recently produced what is unquestionably the most comprehensive survey of current scholarship. It is perhaps most valuable to someone who already has some familiarity with the subject but it is an essential reference and is likely to remain so.

Because of my own particular interest, Arabia, and particularly the Arabian Gulf, feature more in the book than in most on the subject. I have published an extensive bibliography of current Arabian archaeological scholarship elsewhere (Rice, 1985).

I have invoked the powerfully magical name (to me at any rate) of C. G. Jung in these pages. I have relied extensively on the English-language version of his collected works, the letters, and other volumes listed in the bibliography.

Finally, a word about the illustrations. I have tried in general to demonstrate the extraordinary vitality of the art of the earliest centuries of Egyptian history, by using examples which may be less familiar to non-specialists. The quantity available is immense: I have not been able even to scratch the surface. I have however eschewed some of the more familiar, accessible objects which are reproduced in all good surveys of Egyptian art. I have a sense of great indebtedness to many of the institutions which have made prints or transparencies available to me. A list of acknowledgements appears separately but my gratitude is unbounded.

List of abbreviations

Afr. Hist. Stud.	*African Historical Studies,* Boston University African Studies Centre (later IJAHS)
Am. J. Archäeol.	*American Journal of Archaeology*
Austral. J. Bibl. Archaeol.	*Australian Journal of Biblical Archaeology*
Atlal	*Journal of Saudi Arabian Archaeology*
BBVO	*Berliner Beiträge zum Vorderen Orient*
Bull. Inst. fr. Archaeol. orient.	*Bulletin de l'Institut français d'Archaeologie orientale,* Cairo
EW	*East–West*
Geol. J.	*Geological Journal*
IEJ	*Israel Exploration Journal*
JAOS	*Journal of the American Oriental Society*
JEA	*Journal of Egyptian Archaeology*
JNES	*Journal of Near Eastern Studies*
JOS	*Journal of Oman Studies*
J. Afr. Hist.	*Journal of African History*
J. Am. Res. Cent. Egypt	*Journal of the American Research Centre, Egypt*
J. Econ. Social Hist. Orient	*Journal of the Economic and Social History of the Orient*
J. Soc. Stud. Egypt. Ant.	*Journal of the Society for the Study of Egyptian Antiquities of Toronto*
Khalifa and Rice	*Bahrain through the Ages: the Archaeology,* ed. Shaikha Haya Ali Al Khalifa and Michael Rice, London, 1986
MDAIK	*Mitteilungen des deutschen Instituts für aegyptische Altertumskunde in Kairo*

300

Mitt. dt. archaol. Inst. Abt.	*Mitteilungen des deutschen archäologischen Instituts*
Newsl. Soc. Study Egypt. Ant.	*Newsletter of the Society for the Study of Egyptian Antiquities, Ontario*
PPS	*Proceedings of the Prehistoric Society*
Proc. Linn. Soc.	*Proceedings of the Linnaean Society of London*
PSAS	*Proceedings of the Seminar for Arabian Studies*
Rev. d'Egyptologie	*Revue d'Egyptologie*
Z. ägypt. Sprache Altertumskunde	*Zeitschrift für ägyptische Sprache und Altertumskunde*, Leipzig

Bibliography

Adams, B. (1974) *Ancient Hierakonpolis*, with supplement, Warminster.

Adams, B. (1988) *The Fort Cemetery at Hierakonpolis (excavated by John Garstang)*, London.

Adams, R. McC. (1965) *Land Behind Baghdad: A History of Settlement on the Diyala Plains*, Chicago.

Adams, R. McC. (1972) 'Patterns of urbanization in early southern Mesopotamia', in P. J. Ucko, R. Tringham, and G. W. Dimbleby (eds) *Man, Settlement and Urbanism*, London.

Adams, R. McC., Parr, P. J., Ibrahim, M., and Al-Mughannum, A. S. (1977) *Saudi Arabian Archaeological Reconnaissance, 1976, Preliminary Report on the First Phase of the Comprehensive Survey Program – Eastern Province, Atlal*, vol. 1.

Adams, W. Y. (1968) 'Invasion, diffusion, evolution?', *Antiquity* 42: 194–215.

Adams, W. Y. (1970) 'A reappraisal of Nubian culture history', *Orientalia* 39: 269–77.

Adams, W. Y. (1977) *Nubia: Corridor to Africa*, London.

Alster, B. (1983) 'Dilmun, Bahrain, and the alleged Paradise in Sumerian myth and literature', in D. Potts (ed.) *Dilmun: New Studies in the Archaeology and Early History of Bahrain, BBVO* 2.

Amiet, P. (1966) *Elam*, Paris.

Amiet, P. (1986) 'Susa and the Dilmun culture', in Khalifa and Rice.

Amiran, R. (1962) 'The date of the end of the Old Kingdom of Egypt, *JNES* 21: 140–7.

Amiran, R. (1974) 'An Egyptian jar fragment with the name of Narmer from Arad', *IEJ* 24: 4–12.

Anderson, H. H. (1986) 'The Barbar Temple: stratigraphy, architecture and interpretation', in Khalifa and Rice.

Arkell, A. J. (1963) 'Was King Scorpion Menes?', *Antiquity* 37: 31–5.

Arkell, A. J. (1972) 'Dotted wavy-line pottery in African prehistory', *Antiquity* 46: 221–2.

Arkell, A. J., and Ucko, P. J. (1965) 'Review of Predynastic development in the Nile Valley', *Current Anthropology* 6: 145–66.

Arnett, W. S. (1982) *The Predynastic Origin of Egyptian Hieroglyphs*, New York.

Asselberghs, H. (1961) *Chaos en Behersing*, London.

Bains, J. (1962) 'The date of the end of the Old Kingdom of Egypt', *JNES* 21: 140–7.

Bains, J. (1973) 'The destruction of the pyramid temple of Sahure', Gottingen Misz. 4: 9–14.

Baumgartel, E. J. (1955) *The Cultures of Prehistoric Egypt*, 2nd edn, vol. 1, Oxford.

Baumgartel, E. J. (1960) *The Cultures of Prehistoric Egypt*, vol. 2, Oxford.

Baumgartel, E. J. (1966) 'Scorpion and rosette and the fragment of the large Hierakonpolis mace head', *Z. ägypt. Sprache Altertumskunde* 92: 9–14.

Baumgartel, E. J. (1970a) 'Predynastic Egypt', in *The Cambridge Ancient History*, 3rd edn, vol. 1, pt 1, Cambridge.

Baumgartel, E. J. (1970b) *Petrie's Naqada Excavation: A Supplement*, London.

Bent, J. T. (1880) 'The Bahrain Islands in the Persian Gulf', *Proceedings of the Royal Geographical Society* 12: 1–19.

Berry, A. C., and Berry, R. J. (1973) 'Origins and relations of the ancient Egyptians', in D. R. Brothwell and B. A. Chiarelli (eds) *Population Biology of the Ancient Egyptians*, New York.

Bibby, T. G (1973) *Preliminary Survey in East Arabia 1968*, Aarhus.

Bibby, T. G. (1986a) 'The land of Dilmun is holy', in Khalifa and Rice.

Bibby, T. G. (1986b) 'The origins of the Dilmun civilization', in Khalifa and Rice.

Borchardt, L., and Ricke, H. (1930) *Egypt: Architecture, Landscape, Life of the People*, London.

Bottero, J., Cassin, E., and Vercoutter, J. (1967) *The Near East: The Early Civilizations*, trans. R. F. Tannenbaum, London.

Boussian, J. (1981) *Pottery from the Nile Valley*, Cambridge.

Bowersock, G. W. (1986) 'Tylos and Tyre: Bahrain in the Graeco-Roman world', in Khalifa and Rice.

Breasted, J. H. (1905) *A History of Egypt from the Earliest Times to the Persian Conquest*, New York. (Published London 1906.)

Brice, W. C. (ed.) (1978) *The Environmental History of the Near and Middle East*, London and New York.

Brunton, G., and Caton Thomson, G. (1928) *The Badarian Civilisation*, London.

Burrows, E. (1928) 'Tilmun, Bahrain, Paradise', in *Scriptura Sacra et Monumenta orientis Antiqui*, Rome.

Burstein, S. M. (1978) *The Babyloniaca of Berossus*, Malibu.

Butzer, K. W. (1966) 'Archaeology and geology in ancient Egypt', in J. R. Caldwell (ed.) *New Roads to Yesterday*, New York.

Butzer, K. W. (1971) *Environment and Archeology: An Ecological Approach to Prehistory*, Chicago.

Butzer, K. W. (1975) 'Patterns of environmental change in the Near East during late Pleistocene and early Holocene times', in F. Wendorf and A. E. Marks (eds) *Problems in Prehistory: North Africa and the Levant*, Dallas.

Butzer, K. W. (1976) *Early Hydraulic Civilization in Egypt: A Study in Cultural Ecology*, Chicago.

Castillos, J. J. (1978) 'An analysis of the Predynastic cemeteries E and U and the First Dynasty cemetery S at Abydos', *J. Soc. Stud. Egypt. Antiq.* 8: 86–98.

Castillos, J. J. (1979) 'An analysis of the tombs in the Predynastic cemetery N7000 at Naga-ed-Der', *J. Soc. Stud. Egypt. Antiq.* 10: 21–38.

Castillos, J. J. (1981) 'An analysis of the tombs in the Predynastic cemeteries at Naqada', *J. Soc. Stud. Egypt. Antiq.* 11: 97–106.

Castillos, J. J. (1982) 'Analyses of Egyptian Predynastic and Early Dynastic cemeteries: final conclusions', *J. Soc. Stud. Egypt. Antiq.* 12: 29–53.

Caton Thomson, G., and Gardner, E. W. (1934) *The Desert Fayum*, 2 vols, London.

Childe, V. G. (1934) *New Light on the Most Ancient East*, London.

Chowdhury, K. A., and Buth, G. M. (1971) 'Cotton seeds from the Neolithic in Egyptian Nubia and the origin of Old World cotton', *Proc. Linn. Soc.* 3: 303–12.

Clark, J. D. (1971) 'A re-examination of the evidence for agricultural origins in the Nile Valley', *PPS* 37: 34–79.

Coldstream, J. N., and Huxley, G. L. (eds) (1972) *Kythera: Excavations and Studies Conducted by the University of Pennsylvania Museum and the British School at Athens*, London.

Cornwall, P. B. (1943) 'Dilmun: the history of the Bahrain Islands before Cyprus', unpublished PhD thesis, Harvard University.

Crowfoot Payne, J. (1968) 'Lapis lazuli in early Egypt', *Iraq* 30 (1).

David, A. R. (1982) *The Ancient Egyptians: Religious Beliefs and Practices,* London.

De Cardi, B. (1971) 'Archaeological survey in the northern Trucial States', *EW.*

De Cardi, B. (1975a) 'Survey and excavations in Oman', *JOS* 1.

De Cardi, B. (1975b) 'Archaeological survey in Northern Oman', *EW.*

De Cardi, B. (1978) *Qatar Archaeological Report, Excavations 1973,* Oxford.

De Cardi, B., Collier, S., and Doe, D. B. (1971) 'Archaeological survey in the northern Trucial States', *EW* n.s. 21 (3–4).

De Cardi, B., Collier, S., and Doe, D. B. (1976) 'Excavations and survey in Oman 1974–75, *JOS* 2.

De Cardi, B., Doe, D. B., and Roskams, S. P. (1977) 'Excavation and survey in the Sharqiyah, Oman 1976', *JOS* 3 pt (1).

Derricourt, R. M. (1971) 'Radiocarbon chronology for Egypt and North Africa', *JNES* 30: 271–92.

Derry, D. E. (1956) 'The dynastic race in Egypt', *JEA* 42: 80–5.

Doe, D. B. (1984) 'The Barbar Temple site in Bahrain: conservation and presentation', in Khalifa and Rice.

Doe, D. B. (1986) 'The Barbar Temple: the masonry', in Khalifa and Rice.

Dunbar, J. H. (1941) *The Rock Pictures of Lower Nubia,* Cairo.

Dunham, D. (1938) 'The biographical inscriptions of Nekhebu in Boston and Cairo', *JEA* 24: 1–8.

Dunham, D. (1978) *Zawiyet el-Aryan,* Boston.

Edens, C. (1982) 'Towards a definition of the western Ar-Rub al-Khali "Neolithic" ', *Atlal* 6.

Editions des musées nationaux (1973) 'L'Egypte avant les Pyramides', Paris.

Edwards, I. E. S. (1971) 'The early dynastic period in Egypt', *Cambridge Ancient History,* 3rd edn. vol. 1, pt 2, Cambridge.

Edwards, I. E. S., Gadd, C. J., and Hammond, N. G. L. (eds) *The Cambridge Ancient History,* 3rd edn, vol. 1, pt 2, 1971, *Early History of the Middle East,* Cambridge.

Ehret, C. (1979) 'On the antiquity of agriculture in Ethiopia', *J. Afr. Hist.* 20: 161–77.

Emery, W. B. (1949–58) *Great Tombs of the First Dynasty,* 3 vols, Cairo and London.

Emery, W. B. (1961) *Archaic Egypt,* Harmondsworth.

Englund, R. (1983) 'Dilmun in the Archaic Uruk Corpus', in Potts (ed.) *BBVO* 2.

Ertman, E. E. (1972) 'The earliest known three-dimensional representation of the god Ptah', *JNES* 31: 83–6.

Evers, H. G. (1929) *Staat aus dem Stein. Denkmaler, Geschichte und Bedeutung der agyptischen Plastik wahrend des Mittleren Reichs*, 2 vols, Munich.

Fairman, H. W. (1958) 'The Kingship rituals of Egypt', in S. H. Hooke (ed.) *Myth, Ritual and Kingship*, Oxford.

Fairservis, W. A. Jr, Weeks, K., and Hoffman, M. (1971–2) 'Preliminary report on the first two seasons at Hierakonpolis', *J. Am. Res. Cent. Egypt* 9: 7–68.

Fakhry, A. (1959) *The Monuments of Sneferu at Dahshur*, vol. 1: *The Bent Pyramid*, Cairo.

Fakhry, A. (1961) *The Monuments of Sneferu at Dahshur*, vol. 2: *The Valley Temple*, 2 pts, Cairo.

Fattorovich, R. (1976) 'Trends in the study of Predynastic social structure', in D. Wildung (ed.) *First International Congress of Egyptology: Abstracts of Papers*, Munich.

Faulkner, R. O. (1969) *The Ancient Egyptian Pyramid Texts*, Oxford.

Fouilles de El Kab (1954) Documents, Livraison III, Brussels.

Frankfort, H. (1948) *Kingship and the Gods*, Chicago.

Frankfort, H. (1956) *The Birth of Civilization in the Near East.* London.

Frankfort, H., Frankfort, H. A., Wilson, J. A., and Jacobsen, T. (1949) *Before Philosophy*, Harmondsworth.

Frifelt, K. (1975a) 'A possible link between the Jemdet Nasr and the Umm an-Nar graves of Oman', *JOS* 1: 57–80.

Frifelt, K. (1975b) 'On prehistoric settlement and chronology of the Oman Peninsula', *EW* n.s. 25 (3–4): 359–424.

Frifelt, K. (1976) 'Evidence of a third-millennium BC town in Oman', *JOS* 2: 57–74.

Gardiner, A. (1927) *Egyptian Grammar*, Oxford.

Gardiner, A. (1961) *Egypt of the Pharaohs: an Introduction*, Oxford.

Garstang, J. (1902) *Mahasna and Bet Khallaf*, London.

Garstang, J. (1904) *Tombs of the Third Egyptian Dynasty at Reqaqnah and Bet Khallaf*, London.

Gautier, H. (1907) *Le livre des rois d'Egypte*, vol 1: *Des origines à la fin de la XIIe dynastie*, Cairo.

Gleichen, Count Albert E. W. (ed.) (1905) *The Anglo-Egyptian Sudan: a Compendium Prepared by Officers of the Sudan Government*, vol. 1, London.

Goedlicke, H. (1969–70) 'An Egyptian claim to Asia', *J. Am. Res. Cent. Egypt* 8: 11–27.

Goettler, G. W., Firth, N., and Huston, C. C. (1976) 'A preliminary discussion of ancient mining in the Sultanate of Oman', *JOS* 2.

Goneim, M. Z. (1956) *The Buried Pyramid*, London.

Goneim, M. Z. (1957) *Horus Sekhem Khet*, vol. 1, Cairo.

Griffiths, J. G. (1960) *The Conflict of Horus and Seth*, Liverpool.

Griffiths, J. G. (1966) 'The origins of Osiris', *Munchner Agyptologische Studien* 9.

Grove, A. T., Alayne Street, F., and Goudie, A. S. (1975) 'Former lake levels and climatic change in the Rift Valley of southern Ethiopia', *Geol. J.* 141: 177–202.

Hallo, W. W., and Simpson, W. K. (1971) *The Ancient Near East: a History*, New York.

Hassan, F. A. (1980) 'Radiocarbon chronology of Archaic Egypt', *JNES* 39: 203–7.

Hastings, A., Humphries, J. H., and Meadow, R. H. (1975) 'Oman in the third millennium BC', *JOS* 1.

Hays, T. R. (1975) 'Neolithic settlement of the Sahara as it relates to the Nile Valley', in F. Wendorf and A. E. Marks (eds) *Problems in Prehistory: North Africa and the Levant*, Dallas.

Hayes, W. C. (1953) *The Scepter of Egypt*, vol. 1, Cambridge, Mass.

Hayes, W. C. (1965) *Most Ancient Egypt*, Chicago.

Hayes, W. C. (1970) 'Chronology I. Egypt to the end of the Twentieth Dynasty', *Cambridge Ancient History*, 3rd edn, vol. 1, pt 1, Cambridge.

Hayes, W. C. (1984) *Most Ancient Egypt*, Chicago.

Helck, H. W. (1962) *Die Beziehungen Agyptens zu Vorderasien im 3. und 2 Jahrtausend v. Chr*, Wiesbaden.

Helck, H. W. (1970) 'Zwei Einzelprobleme der thinitischen Chronologie', *Mitt. dt. archaol. Inst. Abt. Cairo* 26: 83–5.

Hennessy, J. B. (1967) *The Foreign Relations of Palestine During the Early Bronze Age*, London.

Hepper, N. (1969) 'Arabian and African frankincense trees', *JEA* 55: 66–72.

Herrman, G. (1968) 'Lapis lazuli: the early phases of its trade', *Iraq* 30 (1).

Heyerdahl, T. (1978) *Early Man and The Ocean*, London.

Heyerdahl, T. (1980) *The Tigris Expedition*, London.

Hoffman, M. A. (1979) *Egypt Before the Pharaohs: The Prehistoric Foundations of Egyptian Civilization*, New York.

Hoffman, M. A. (1980) 'A rectangular Amratian house from Hierakonpolis', *JNES* 39: 119–37.

Hoffman, M. A. (1982) *The Predynastic of Hierakonpolis – An Interim Report*. Cario.

Højgaard, K. (1986) 'Dental anthropological investigations on Bahrain', in Khalifa and Rice.

Hornung, E. (1971–83) *Conceptions of God in Ancient Egypt*, trans. J. Baines, London.

Humphries, J. H. (1974) 'Some later prehistoric sites in the Sultanate of Oman', *PSAS* 4.

Kanawati, N. (1977) *The Egyptian Administration in the Old Kingdom*, War- minster.

Kantor, H. J. (1944) 'The final phase of Predynastic culture: Gerzean or Semainean?' *JNES* 3: 110–36.

Kantor, H. J. (1952) 'Further evidence for early Mesopotamian relations with Egypt', *JNES* 11: 239–50.

Kantor, H. J. (1965) 'The relative chronology of Egypt and its foreign correlations before the Late Bronze Age', in R. W. Ehrich (ed.) *Chron- ologies in Old World Archaeology*, Chicago.

Kaplan, H. R. (1979) 'The problem of the dynastic position of Meryet-nit', *JNES* 38: 23–7.

Kappel, W. (1974) 'Irrigation development and population pressure', in T. E. Dowing and M. Gibson (eds) *Irrigation's Impact on Society*, Tucson, Ariz.

Kees, H. (1961) *Ancient Egypt: A Cultural Topography*, ed. T. G. H. James, trans. I. F. D. Morrow, London and Chicago.

Kelley, A. L. (1974) 'The evidence of Mesopotamian influence in Pre- dynastic Egypt', *Newsl. Soc. Study Egypt. Ant.* 4: 2–22.

Kemp, B. J. (1966) 'Abydos and the royal tombs of the First Dynasty', *J. Egypt. Archaeol.* 52: 13–22.

Kemp, B. J. (1967) 'The Egyptian First Dynasty royal cemetery', *Antiquity* 41: 22–32.

Kemp, B. J. (1968) 'Merimda and the theory of house burial in prehistoric Egypt', *Chronique d'Egypte* 43, 85: 22–33.

Kemp, B. J. (1973) 'Photographs of the Decorated Tomb at Hierakonpolis', *JEA* 59: 36–43.

Kemp, B. J. (1976a) 'A review of Hellstrom's *The Rock Drawings*', *JEA* 62: 926.

Kemp, B. J. (1976b) 'A note on stratigraphy at Memphis', *J. Am. Res. Cent. Egypt* 13: 25–9.

Kemp, B. J. (1982) 'Automatic analysis of Predynastic cemeteries: a new method for an old problem', *JEA* 68: 5–15.

Al Khalifa, H. A. and Rice, M. (eds) (1986) *Bahrain Through the Ages: The Archaeology* (Proceedings of the Bahrain Historical Conference 1983), London.

El Khouli, A. (1978) *Egyptian Stone Vessels*, 3 vols, Mainz-am-Rhein.

Kjaerum, P. (1983) *Failaka/Dilmun: The Second Millennium Settlements*, vol. 2: *The Stamp and Cylinder Seals*, Aarhus.

Kjaerum, P. (1986) 'The Dilmun seals as testimony of long-distance relations in the early second millennium', in Khalifa and Rice.

Kohl, P. L. (1978) 'The balance of trade in southwestern Asia in the mid-third millennium BC', *Current Anthropology* 19 (3).

Krzyzaniak, L. (1977) *Early Farming Cultures on the Lower Nile: The Predynastic Period in Egypt*, Warsaw.

Krzyzaniak, L. (1979) 'Trends in the socio-economic development of Egyptian Predynastic societies', *Acts of the First International Congress of Egyptologists*, Cairo.

Kuchman, L. (1977) 'The titles of Queenship: part I, the evidence from the Old Kingdom', *Newsl. Soc. Stud. Egypt. Ant.* 9–12.

Landstrom, B. (1970) *Ships of the Pharaohs*, London.

Larsen, C. E. (1983a) *Life and Land Use in the Bahrain Islands: The Geo-archaeology of an Ancient Society*, Chicago.

Larsen, C. E. (1983b) 'The early environment and hydrology of ancient Bahrain', in Potts (ed.) *Dilmun, BBVO* 2.

Lauer, J.-P. (1973) 'Remarques sur la plannification de la construction de la grande pyramide', *Bull. Inst. fr. Archaeol. orient.* 73: 127–42.

Lauer, J.-P. (1974) *Le mystère des pyramides*, Paris.

Lauer, J.-P. (1976) 'A propos du pretendu desastre de la pyramide de Meidoum', *Chronique d'Egypte* 51: 72–89.

Lawrence, B. (1967) 'Early domestic dogs', *Zeitschrift für Saugetierkunde* 32: 44–59.

Lucas, A., and Harris, J. R. (1962) *Ancient Materials and Industries*, 4th edn, London.

Lupton, C. (1981) 'The other Egypt. In search of the lost pharaohs', *Lore* 31 (3): 2–21.

MacDonald, J. (1972) 'Egyptian interests in western Asia to the end of the Middle Kingdom: an evaluation', *Austral. J. Bibl. Archaeol.* 2: 72–98.

Mackay, E., Harding, G. L., and Petrie, F. (1929) *Bahrein and Hemamieh, Publications of the British School of Archaeology in Egypt*, vol. 47, London.

Masry, A. H. (1974) *Prehistory in Northern Arabia: the Problem of Interregional Interaction*, Miami.

McClure, H. A. (1971) *The Arabian Peninsula and Prehistoric Populations*, Miami.

Mellaart, J. (1959) 'The royal treasure of Dorak', *Illustrated London News*, 28 November, 754.

Meltzer, E. S. (1970) 'An observation on the hieroglyph *mr*', *J. Egypt. Archaeol.* 56: 193–4.

Mendelssohn, K. (1974) *The Riddle of the Pyramids*, London.

Menu, B., and Harari, I. (1974) 'La notion de propriété privée dans l'Ancien Empire égyptien', *Cahiers de Recherches de l'Institut de Papyrologie et d'Egyptologie de Lille* 2: 125–54.

Mercer, S. (1959) *Earliest Intellectual Man's Idea of the Cosmos*, London.

Meshel, Z. (1974) *New Data on the Desert Kites*, Tel Aviv.

Michalowski, K. (1969) *The Art of Ancient Egypt*, London.

Mitchell, W. P. (1963) 'The hydraulic hypothesis: a reappraisal', *Current Anthropology* 14: 532–4.

Mond, Sir Robert, and Myres, O. H. (1937) *Cemeteries of Armant*, 2 vols, London.

Morenz, S. (1973) *Egyptian Religion*, trans. A. E. Keep, London.

Morgan, J. de (1895) *Fouilles à Dahchour, mars–juin 1894*, Vienna.

Morgan, J. de (1897) *Carte de la necropole memphite*, Cairo.

Morgan, J. de (1903) *Fouilles à Dahchour en 1894–1895*, Vienna.

Morgan, J. de (1925–7) *Prehistoric Oriental*, 3 vols, Paris.

Mortensen, P. (1971) 'On the date of the Barbar Temple in Bahrain', *Artibus Asiae* 33.

Mortensen, P. (1984) 'The Bahrain Temple: its chronology and foreign relations reconsidered', in Khalifa and Rice.

Moussa, A. M., and Altenmuller, H. (1971) *The Tomb of Nefer and Ka-Hay*, Mainz-am-Rhein.

Muhly, J. D. (1973) *Copper and Tin*, New Haven, Conn.

Munro, Peter (1972) 'Zu Einigen Agyptischen Terrakotta-Figuren', *Gottinger Misz.* 2.

Museum of Fine Arts (1940) *Ancient Egypt*, Boston.

Nagel, W. (1968) *Frühe Plastik aus Sumer and Westmakkan*, Berlin.

Nashef, K. (1986) 'The deities of Dilmun', in Khalifa and Rice.

Needler, W. (1981) 'Federn's revision of Petrie's Predynastic pottery classification', *J. Soc. Stud. Egypt. Ant.* 11: 69–74.

Newberry, P. E. (1922) *The Set Rebellion of the IInd Dynasty. Ancient Egypt*, 1922, pt 2.

Nibbi, A. (1969) *The Tyrrhenians*, Oxford.

Nibbi, A. (1975) *The Sea People and Egypt*, New Jersey.

Nibbi, A. (1981) *Ancient Egypt and some Eastern Neighbours*, New Jersey.

Nissen, H. J. (1986) 'The occurrence of Dilmun in the oldest texts of Mesopotamia', in Khalifa and Rice.

Nordstrom, H. A. (1972) *Neolithic and A-group Sites*, Uppsala.

Oates, J. (1986) 'The Gulf in prehistory', in Khalifa and Rice.

Oates, J., Davidson, T. E., Kamilli, D., and McKerrell, H. (1977) 'Seafaring merchants of Ur?', *Antiquity* 51: 221–34.

O'Connor, D. B. (1971) 'Ancient Egypt and Black Africa – early contacts', *Expedition* 14: 638–47.

O'Connor, D. B. (1974) 'Political systems and archaeological data in Egypt: 2600–1780 BC', *World Archaeology* 6: 15–38.

Oppenheim, A. L. (1954) 'The seafaring merchants of Ur', *JAOS* 74.

Petrie, W. M. F. (1896) *Naqada and Ballas*, London.

Petrie, W. M. F. (1900) *The Royal Tombs of the First Dynasty*, pt I: *Egypt Exploration Fund Memoir*, 18, London.

Petrie, W. M. F. (1901a) *The Royal Tombs of the Earliest Dynasties*, pt 2: *Egypt Exploration Fund Memoir*, 21, London.

Petrie, W. M. F. (1901b) *Diospolis Parva, Egypt Exploration Fund Memoir*, 20, London.

Petrie, W. M. F. (1902) *Abydos*, pt I: *Egypt Exploration Fund Memoir*, 22, London.

Petrie, W. M. F. (1903) *Abydos*, pt II: *Egypt Exploration Fund Memoir*, 24, London.

Petrie, W. M. F. (1909) *Qurneh*, London.

Petrie, W. M. F. (1920) *Prehistoric Egypt*, London.

Petrie, W. M. F. (1921) *Prehistoric Egypt*, Corpus, London.

Petrie, W. M. F. (1924) *A History of Egypt*, vol. 1: *From the Earliest Kings to the XVth Dynasty*, 11th edn, London.

Petrie, W. M. F. (1939) *The Making of Egypt*, London.

Petrie, W. M. F. (1940) *Wisdom of the Egyptians*, London.

Petrie, W. M. F. (1953) *Ceremonial Slate Palettes: Corpus of Proto-Dynastic Pottery*, London.

Petrie, W. M. F., and Quibell, J. E. (1895) *Naqada and Ballas*, London.

Piankoff, A. (1968) *The Pyramid of Unas*, Princeton.

Pope, M. (1966) 'The origins of writing in the Near East', *Antiquity* 40: 17–23.

Porada, E. (1980) 'A lapis lazuli figurine from Hierakonpolis in Egypt', *Iranica Antiqua* 15.

Porter, B., and Moss, R. L. B. (1927–51) *Topographical Bibliography of Ancient Egyptian Hieroglyphic Texts, Reliefs and Paintings*, 1st edn, 7 vols, Oxford.

Porter, B., and Moss, R. L. B. (1972) *Topographical Bibliography . . .*, 2nd edn, vol. 2.

Poscner, G. (1957) 'Les Asiatiques en Egypte sous la XIIe et XIIIe dynasties', *Syria* 34: 145–63.

Poscner, G. (1976) *Les archives du temple funeraire de Neferirkare-Kakai, les papyrus d'Abousir*; traduction et commentaire, Cairo and Paris.

Potts, D. (1978) 'Towards an integrated history of culture change in the Arabian Gulf area: notes on Dilmun, Makkan, and the economy of ancient Sumer', *JOS* 4: 29–51.

Potts, D. (1983a) 'Dilmun: new studies in the archaeology and early history of Bahrain', *BBVO* 2.

Potts, D. (1983b) 'Barbar miscellanies', in D. Potts (ed.) *Dilmun . . ., BBVO* 2.

Potts, D. (1984) 'The chronology of the archaeological assemblages from the head of the Arabian Gulf to the Arabian Sea (8000–1750 BC)', in R. W. Ehrich (ed.) *Chronologies in Old World Archaeology*, 3rd edn, Chicago.

Pritchard, J. B. (ed.) (1969) *Ancient Near Eastern Texts Relating to the Old Testament*, 3rd edn with supplement, Princeton.

Quibell, J. E. (1898) *El Kab*, London.

Quibell, J. E. (1900) *Hierakonpolis*, pt 1, London.

Quibell, J. E. (1907) *Excavations at Saqqara (1905–6)*, Cairo.

Quibell, J. E., and Green F. W. (1902) *Hierakonpolis*, pt 2, London.

Raphael, M. (1947) *Prehistoric Pottery in Egypt*, Washington.

Reed, C. A. (1966) 'Animal domestication in the prehistoric Near East', in J. R. Caldwell (ed.) *New Roads to Yesterday*, New York.

Reisner, G. A. (1918) 'The tomb of Hepzefa, nomarch of Siut', *JEA* 5: 79–98.

Reisner, G. A. (1923) *Excavations at Kerma*, pts 1–5, Cambridge, Mass.

Reisner, G. A. (1931) *Mycerinus: The Temples of the Third Pyramid at Giza*, Cambridge, Mass.

Reisner, G. A. (1932) *A Provincial Cemetery of the Pyramid Age, Naga-ed-Der*, vol. 2, Oxford.

Reisner, G. A., and Smith, W. S. (1955) *A History of the Giza Necropolis*, vol. 2: *The Tomb of Hetep-heres the Mother of Cheops*, Cambridge, Mass.

Renfrew, C. (1972) *The Emergence of Civilization*, London.

Reymond, E. A. E. (1969) *The Mythical Origin of the Egyptian Temple*, Manchester.

Rice, M. (1983) *The Barbar Temple Site, Bahrain*, Bahrain.

Rice, M. (1984a) *Dilmun Discovered*, London.

Rice, M. (1984b) 'The island on the edge of the world', in Khalifa and Rice.

Rice, M. (1985) *The Search for the Paradise Land*, London.

Ridley, R. T. (1973) *The Unification of Egypt*, Deception Bay.

Rundle Clark, R. T. (1969) *Myth and Symbol in Ancient Egypt*, Manchester.

Saad, Z. Y. (1947) *Royal Excavations at Saqqara and Helwan 1941–45*, Cairo.

Saad, Z. Y. (1969) The *Excavations at Helwan: Art and Civilization in the First and Second Egyptian Dynasties*, Oklahoma.

Safar, F., Mustafa, M. A., and Lloyd, S. (1981) *Eridu*, Baghdad.

Saleh, A. A. (1972) 'Some problems relating to the Pwenet reliefs at Deir el-Bahari', *JEA* 58: 140–58.

Saleh, A. A. (1974) 'Excavations around Mycerinus' pyramid complex', *Mitt. dt. archaol. Inst. Abt.* 30: 131–54.

Saleh, M. (1977) *Three Old Kingdom Tombs at Thebes*, Mainz.

Sanders, J. A. (ed.) (1970) *Near Eastern Archaeology in the Twentieth Century*, New York.

Sanlaville, P. J. (1986) 'Shoreline changes in Bahrain since the beginning of human occupation', in Khalifa and Rice.

Scamuzzi, E. (n.d.) *Egyptian Art in the Egyptian Museum of Turin*, New York.

Simpson, W. K. (ed.) (1973) *The Literature of Ancient Egypt; an Anthology of Stories, Instructions and Poetry*, with translations by R. O. Faulkener, E. F. Wente Jr, and W. K. Simpson, New Haven, Conn., and London.

Smith, C. H., (1890) 'The Bahrain Islands in the Persian Gulf', *Proceedings of the Royal Geographical Society* 12.

Smith, H. S. (1964) 'Egypt and C14 dating', *Antiquity* 38: 32–7.

Smith, H. S. (1966) 'The Nubian B-group', *Kush* 14: 69–124.

Smith, P. E. L. (1968) 'Problems and possibilities of the prehistoric rock art of northern Africa', *Afr. Hist. Stud.* 1: 1–39.

Smith, W. S. (1946) *A History of Egyptian Sculpture and Painting in the Old Kingdom*, Boston and London.

Smith, W. S. (1958) *The Art and Architecture of Ancient Egypt*, Harmondsworth.

Smith, W. S. (1962) 'Some recent accessions', *Bulletin of the Museum of Fine Arts, Boston* 60 (322): 132–6.

Smith, W. S. (1965) *Interconnections in the Ancient Near East: A Study of the Relationships between the Arts of Egypt, the Aegean, and Western Asia*, New Haven and London.

Swelim, A. (1983) 'Some problems on the history of the Third Dynasty', *Archaeological Society of Alexandria*.

Trigger, B. G. (1965) *History and Settlement in Lower Nubia*, New Haven, Conn.

Trigger, B. G. (1968) *Beyond History: The Methods of Prehistory*, New York.

Trigger, B. G. (1976) *Nubia under the Pharaohs*, London.

Trigger, B. G. (1978) 'Nubian, Negro, Black, Nilotic?', in S. Hochfield and E. Riefstahl (eds) *Africa in Antiquity: the Arts of Ancient Nubia and the Sudan*, vol. 1, *The Essays*, New York.

Trigger, B. G. (1982) 'The late Palaeolithic and Epi-Palaeolithic of northern Africa', in J. D. Clark (ed.) *Cambridge History of Africa*, vol. 1, *Social History*, Cambridge.

Trigger, B. G., Kemp, B. J., O'Connor, D., and Lloyd, A. B. (1983) *Ancient Egypt, A Social History*, Cambridge.

Tufnell, O., and Ward, W. A. (1966) 'Relations between Byblos, Egypt and Mesopotamia at the end of the third millennium BC. A study of the Montet jar', *Syria* 43: 165–241.

Ucko, P. J. (1968) 'Anthropomorphic figurines of Predynastic Egypt and Neolithic Crete', *Occasional Papers of the Royal Anthropological Institute*, 24.

Ucko, P. J. (1976) 'The Predynastic cemetery N 7000 at Naga-ed-Der', *Chronique d'Egypte* 42: 345–53.

Vandier, J. (1936) *La famine dans l'Egypte ancienne*, Cairo.

Vandier, J. (1952) *Manuel d'archéologie égyptienne*, vol. 1, Paris.

Vandier, J. (1958) *Manuel d'archéologie égyptienne*, vol. 3: *Les grandes epoques, la statuaire*, Paris.

Velde, H. te (1967) *Seth, God of Confusion: a Study of His Role in Egyptian Mythology and Religion*, Leiden.

Vercoutter, J. (1967) 'Review of Trigger, B. G., History and Settlement in Lower Nubia', *Rev. d'Egyptologie* 19: 203–12.

Vermeule, E., and Vermeule, C. (1970) 'An Aegean gold hoard and the court of Egypt', *Illustrated London News*, 21 March.

Waddell, W. G. (1940) *Manetho*, Cambridge, Mass., and London.

Ward, W. A. (1961) 'Egypt and the East Mediterranean in the early second millennium BC', *Orientalia* 30: 22–45 and 129–55.

Ward, W. A. (1964) 'Relations between Egypt and Mesopotamia from prehistoric times to the end of the Middle Kingdom', *J. Econ. Social Hist. Orient* 7: 1–45 and 121–35.

Ward, W. A. (1970) 'The origin of Egyptian design-amulets ("button seals")', *JEA* 56: 65–80.

Ward, W. A. (1971) *Egypt and the East Mediterranean World 2200–1900 BC*, Beirut.

Weeks, K. (1972) 'The Niched Gateway at Hierakonpolis', *Journal of the American Research Centre in Egypt* 9.

Weeks, K. (ed.) (1979) *Egyptology and the Social Sciences, Five Studies*, Cairo.

Weigall, A. E. P. (1907) *A Report on the Antiquities of Lower Nubia*, Cairo.

Weigall, A. E. P. (1909) *Travels in the Upper Egyptian Desert*, Edinburgh.

Weill, R. (1961) *Recherches sur la 1ère Dynastie et Les Temps Prepharaoniques*, 2 vols, Cairo.

Weisgerber, G. (1978) 'Evidence of ancient mining sites in Oman: a preliminary report', *JOS* 4.

Wendorf, F. (ed.) (1968) *The Prehistory of Nubia*, 2 vols, Dallas.

Wendorf, F., and Schild, R. (1980) *Prehistory of the Eastern Sahara*, New York.

Wendorf, F., Said, R., and Schild, R. (1970) 'Egyptian prehistory: some new concepts', *Science* 169: 1161–71.

Whittle, E. H. 'Thermoluminescent dating of Egyptian Predynastic pottery from Hemamieh and Qurna-Tarif', *Archaeometry* 17: 119–22.

Wilding, D. (1972) 'Two representations of gods from the early Old Kingdom', *Misc. Wilbourana* 1: 145–60.

Williams, B. (1980) 'The lost Pharaohs of Nubia', *Archaeology* 33: 12–21.

Williams, B. (1986) *Excavations between Abu Simbel and the Sudan Frontier*, Chicago.

Wilson, J. A. (1951) *The Burden of Egypt: An Interpretation of Ancient Egyptian Culture*, Chicago. (Reprinted as *The Culture of Ancient Egypt*.)

Wilson, J. A. (1955) 'Buto and Hierakonpolis in the geography of Egypt', *JNES* 14: 209–36.

Winkler, H. A. (1938–9) *Rock Drawings of Southern Upper Egypt*, 2 vols, London.

Witfogel, K. A. (1957) *Oriental Despotism: A Comparative Study of Total Power*, New Haven, Conn., and London.

Wood, W. (1987) 'The Archaic stone tombs at Helwan', *JEA* 73.

Yadin, Y. (1955) 'The earliest record of Egypt's military penetration into Asia?' *IEJ* 5: 1–16.

Zaba, Z. (1951) 'Dating of the social revolution in ancient Egypt', (Summary of a lecture) *Archiv Orientalni* 19: 615.

Zarins, J. (1978) 'Steatite vessels in the Riyadh Museum', *Atlal* 2.

Zarins, J., Whalen, N., Ibrahim, M., Morad, A., and Khan, M. (1980) 'Preliminary report on the Central and Southwestern Provinces Survey', *Atlal* 4.

Zeuner, F. E. (1963) *A History of Domesticated Animals*, London.

Index

Khasekhemui, King 109, 127, 179, 262; as conciliator 143–5, 191–2
Khaufre, King (Chephren) 169; temple at Giza 201–2
Khentiamentiu (god) 52, 117, 272
Khnum-Khufu, King (Cheops) 169, 199–200, 201, 206; pyramid of 182, 184
king; as archetype 280; as god 48–50, 83–4, 105, 189–9, 186–7; as link between two Egypts 25
kingship 96–7; achievement of early kings 3, 7; African influences on concept of 83–4; erosion of power 216; as reconciling of opposites 279; regalia of 4, 5; representing individuality of Egyptian people 271–2; Sumerian concept of 48; titles of 103–4; as ultimate Egyptian institution 3–4
kingship and magic 100–1, 217

lapis lazuli, use of 34–5, 89–90
Lauer, J.-P, 21
lighting techniques 202
literary achievement 210–11, 227
Lord of the Two Lands, as title of Egyptian king 127
Lower Egypt 25, 50–1, 135–6

Ma'adi, Predynastic settlement at 29
ma'at (Egyptian concept of harmony) 57, 83
Ma'at (Egyptian goddess) 50
maceheads 86, 102–3, 252
Magan (Oman) 64
magicians, kings as 100–1, 217
Manetho (historian) 19, 55, 115, 120, 127, 128, 141, 144
Manium 225
Mann, Thomas 282
mastaba 128, 130, 171, 172, 173, 175, 179, 180–1
medicine, practised by Egyptian kings 126–7, 290
J. Melaart 209

Menes-Narmer, King 38, 61, 62, 81, 103, 106, 218, 225; as first king of Two Lands 96, 134–6; foundation of Memphis 39, 190; tomb of 115
Menkaure, King (Mykerinos) 169, 201, 202, 203, 229
Merenre 218–19
Merimda, Predynastic settlement at 29
Meryt-Neith, Queen 122–3
metal, discovery of use of 40
Michaelis, Joanna 271, 274
mining 34
Morgan, J, de 116, 117
Mortenson, P. 90
mountain, significance of 174
Munro, P. 47
Mykerinos, King, see Menkaure
mystery, sense of in Egypt's achievement 3
Mystery Play of the Succession (religious drama) 97

Nun (Egyptian god) 124
Naqada 17, 33, 91–2
Naqada I (Amratian civilization) 20, 30–2
Nawada II (Gerzean civilization) 20, 32–4, 96
Narmer Palette 86, 103, 106–9, 130, 282
nation-state 284; Egypt as first 1, 134
Nefer 213–15, 296
Neferirkau, King 209, 210
Nekhbet (vulture goddess of Upper Egypt) 104–5
Neter Nefer (the Good God) 5
Nieth of Sais (Egyptian goddess) 50, 281
Nile, River 12–15, 38; flooding of 225–6
nobles, increasing power of 220, 222
nomes (districts) 26; standards belonging to 108–9
Nubia 136–7; level of civilization 10
Nynetjer, King 141

COMPARATIVE

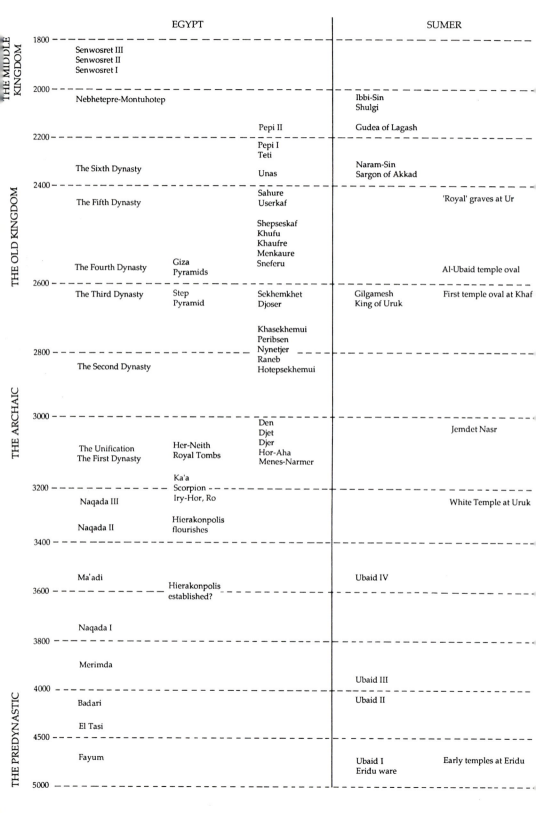

	Date	EGYPT			SUMER	
THE MIDDLE KINGDOM	1800			Senwosret III / Senwosret II / Senwosret I		
	2000			Nebhetepre-Montuhotep	Ibbi-Sin / Shulgi	
				Pepi II	Gudea of Lagash	
	2200			Pepi I / Teti		
		The Sixth Dynasty		Unas	Naram-Sin / Sargon of Akkad	
THE OLD KINGDOM	2400	The Fifth Dynasty		Sahure / Userkaf		'Royal' graves at Ur
				Shepseskaf / Khufu / Khaufre / Menkaure / Sneferu		
		The Fourth Dynasty	Giza Pyramids			Al-Ubaid temple oval
	2600	The Third Dynasty	Step Pyramid	Sekhemkhet / Djoser	Gilgamesh King of Uruk	First temple oval at Khaf
				Khasekhemui / Peribsen / Nynetjer / Raneb / Hotepsekhemui		
	2800	The Second Dynasty				
THE ARCHAIC	3000			Den / Djet / Djer / Hor-Aha / Menes-Narmer	Jemdet Nasr	
		The Unification / The First Dynasty	Her-Neith / Royal Tombs			
	3200	Naqada III	Ka'a / Scorpion / Iry-Hor, Ro		White Temple at Uruk	
		Naqada II	Hierakonpolis flourishes			
	3400					
	3600	Ma'adi	Hierakonpolis established?		Ubaid IV	
	3800	Naqada I				
	4000	Merimda			Ubaid III	
THE PREDYNASTIC		Badari			Ubaid II	
	4500	El Tasi				
		Fayum			Ubaid I / Eridu ware	Early temples at Eridu
	5000					